Screening the Stage

Screening the Stage:

Case Studies of Film Adaptations of Stage Plays and Musicals in the Classical Hollywood Era, 1914–1956

Steve Neale

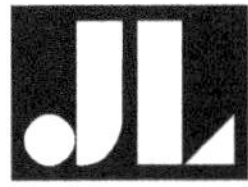

British Library Cataloguing in Publication Data

Screening the Stage:
Case Studies of Film Adaptations of Stage Plays and Musicals in the Classical Hollywood Era, 1914–1956

A catalogue entry for this book is available from the British Library

ISBN: 0 86196 726 1 (Paperback)

ISBN: 0 86196 929 6 (Electronic edition)

Published by
John Libbey Publishing Ltd, 205 Crescent Road, East Barnet, Herts EN4 8SB, United Kingdom e-mail: john.libbey@orange.fr; web site: www.johnlibbey.com

Distributed Worldwide by
Indiana University Press, Herman B Wells Library—350, 1320 E. 10th St., Bloomington, IN 47405, USA. www.iupress.indiana.edu

Printed and bound in the United States of America..

Contents

Acknowledgements
I would like to thank John Libbey for agreeing to publish this book and for taking such care over its presentation. And I would also like to thank all those whose work on the film adaptation of plays has taught me so much during the course of the last few years.

Introduction

Introduction

The proliferation of books and articles on film adaptations has been a feature of the last two decades. Preceded by the publication of *Novels into Films* by George Bluestone in 1957,[1] the study of film and other media adaptations has grown slowly, then at an ever-gathering pace as it has become institutionalised in colleges, schools and universities, and as the number of books, journals, conferences and websites devoted to the subject has expanded. In her blog, Imelda Whelehan states that 'adaptation studies is the analysis of a text and its adaptation, whether that "text" is a novel, film, dance, play, comic strip, musical score, sculpture, video, game, etc.'.[2] But while rightly seeking to be open, expansive and non-judgemental, a purely text-based approach such as this can all too easily ignore the institutions and practices that produce or mark or site them – hence the ever-expanding number of theoretical concepts that tend to dominate Adaptation Studies. This book does not eschew Adaptation Studies as such. But instead of inventing more terms and concepts, it focuses in detail on twelve Hollywood films produced between 1914 and 1956, their remakes where applicable, the twentieth-century plays or musical shows on which they were based, and the generic, stylistic, technological and institutional factors that either marked or governed them. Each chapter is preceded by a detailed summary of the play or show on which it was based and followed by an equally detailed account of the film or films.[3] The similarities and differences that mark them are noted, the key personnel are cited, and the stages in the process of adaptation are outlined where possible.[4]

Among the factors that governed the production of feature films in this period was the constant need for story material, and here the major and minor studios alike frequently drew on published and unpublished novels, short stories, and musicals and plays, including those, like *Sorry, Wrong Number*, that were written for radio.[5] Some of the novels were bestsellers, some of the short stories were well-known, and some of the plays and musicals were Broadway hits, and the rights to these properties usually cost more than the less well-known ones. But in all cases these rights would be purchased on the understanding that they would be adapted for the screen in ways that the studios saw fit: fidelity was a goal only insofar as particular characters, actions, songs, and lines of dialogue were regarded as essential to the commercial appeal of specific adaptations, and only insofar as they adhered to the prevailing norms and constraints of cinema censorship. As is detailed in chapter 7 on *Waterloo Bridge* and its film adaptations, these norms and constraints varied over time and were often out of synch with those that governed the theatre, and here the changes that mark the film versions exemplify the differences between the two institutions and their modes of representation as the classical Hollywood period wore on.[6]

Another factor here is that of a fundamental difference between films on the one hand, and stage plays and musical shows on the other. As was initially noticed and exploited by filmmakers during the first decade of the twentieth century, the viewpoint provided by film cameras differed fundamentally from the viewpoint of audience members in live performance venues. In the latter, each audience member viewed the stage and its performers from a unique and specific point, a fact that theatre directors catered for in their blockings and stagings. But in film-screening venues, audience members, wherever they sat, shared a viewpoint or series of viewpoints provided by the camera, as Ben Brewster and Lea Jacobs have pointed out.[7] This difference was grasped and consciously used from this point on, and in the 1910s it gave rise to specific 'pictorial' styles in Europe. But it marked the framing and staging of more highly-edited films in the USA as well, and remained a well-understood principle in the filming and editing of feature-length films, shorts and serials, and, in ersatz form, in animated shorts and features too. In this way shots became units in scenes and sequences, scenes being the structural bedrock of plays and stage musicals as well as of films, and sequences the sole province of the cinema prior to the advent of filmed television comedies and dramas. However, it should be noted that scenes in plays and stage musicals were usually longer than those in feature-length films, and that scenes in the theatre were often part of even longer acts, of which there is no marked equivalent in films.[8] Novels and short stories were used as the basis of feature-length films too. But while the story material in novels could provide the basis for feature-length narratives, and while chapters in novels could provide the basis of scenes, short stories always necessitated the provision of additional narrative material.

Early Adaptations

Like the production of original scripts, the production of adaptations was subject to the supervision of screenwriting protocols in all the principal Hollywood studios in or by the late 1910s. But before that there were two discernible periods followed by a third, which witnessed the emergence of feature-length films in parallel with the second.[9] The first period lasted from 1896 to 1904 and was marked by the heterogeneous production and exhibition of short films of all kinds and by occasional and much longer films such as Passion Plays and prize fights;[10] and the second period was marked by the emergence of nickelodeon theatres in or around 1905, and the production and exhibition of programmes of short films designed to ensure a rapid turnover of films and audiences in what were mostly small venues.[11] Both periods were marked by adaptations of all kinds. In addition to the early Passion Plays and prize-fight films, the former included *The May Irwin Kiss* (1896), a single-shot version of the kiss that marked the end of an 1895 musical play entitled *The Widow Jones*; two versions of *Uncle Tom's Cabin* (one produced by Edison, the other by Lubin), both of which were released in 1903 and both of which consisted of highlights from one or more "Tom shows"; and *The Great Train Robbery* (Edison 1903 and Lubin 1904) which were based on the 1896 play by Scott Marble.[13] The latter comprised split-reel, one-reel and occasionally two-reel films, and many of these were adapted, again in highlight form, from well-known novels, plays, and stage-play versions of famous works, and these included *Francesca di Rimini* (1907); *The Count of Monte Cristo*, *Dr Jekyll and Mr Hyde* and *East Lynne* (all 1908); *The Bride of Lammermoor*, *A Drunkard's Reformation* and *The Violin Maker of Cremona* (all 1909); *The Prince and the Pauper* and *Ramona* (both 1910); and *A Doll's House* and *Vanity Fair* (all 1911).[14]

By 1912 the distribution of films such as these was dominated by four cartels: The Motion Picture Distributing Sales Company, the Mutual Film Corporation, the General Film Company (the distribution wing of the Motion Picture Patents Company and the industry's dominant organisation),[15] and Universal. And by then some of the production companies began experimenting with longer films, and Vitagraph, which had already issued a four-reel version of *Les Misérables* and a five-reel version of *Life of Moses* over a number of weeks in 1909,[16] began to issue two-reel or three-reel films on a single day. However, even though most nickelodeons now possessed more than one projector and could therefore screen two or more reels on a continuous basis, 'by no means all did so', and in general 'they treated the multiple-reel films as they treated the programme of single-reel ones'.[17] There were occasions on which multi-reel Passion Plays and other Biblical films would be presented on Sundays and Christian holidays.[18] But for the most part the production and exhibition of films was still largely based on programmes of short films in the USA even as the production and exhibition of multi-reel films in Europe proceeded apace, giving rise to Italian films such as *L'Inferno* (*Dante's Inferno*) and *La Caduta di Troia* (*The Fall of Troy*) (both 1911), and French films such as *Le Courrier de Lyon* (also 1911), many of which were adapted from various sources, and all of which were exhibited in domestic cinema venues much larger than the nickelodeons in the USA. Thus while one-reel, two-reel and even three-reel films continued to sustain the nickelodeon market, alternative exhibition sites for longer imports and domestic films in the US began to be drawn on instead.

Feature-Length Adaptations, Roadshows and State Rights Markets, and Theatre Entrepreneurs

In 1913, George Kleine, a leading member of the General Film Company, decided to import *Quo Vadis?* from Italy, and arranged for this eight-reel epic to be premiered in New York and roadshown in large legitimate theatres throughout the country. *Quo Vadis?* was based on the novel by Henry Sienkiewicz and several stage-play adaptations (among them the 1901 version by Émile Moreau), and its success paved the way not only for other Italian epics, but for the roadshowing of large-scale films of other kinds as well.[19] Roadshowing was a well-established means of circulating plays and shows throughout the USA, usually on a percentage-of-the-gross basis, and its success prompted the roadshowing of domestic productions such as the six-reel version of *Cleopatra* (1912).[20] By the end of 1915, it had also been used to showcase *Cabiria* (1914), an Italian import based on *Fabiola; or the Catacombs* (an 1854 novel by Cardinal Wiseman) and *From Cross to Crown* (an 1897 play by Edmund Tearle), and *The Birth of a Nation* (1915), a domestic production based on the 1905 novel and stage-play by Thomas Dixon.[21]

An alternative mode of distribution for films like this was the state rights system, which was used to circulate shortened versions of *Dante's Inferno* and *The Fall of Troy*, a multi-reel double-bill of *Camille* (*La Dame aux Camélias*) and *Madame Sans-Gêne*, and a multi-reel version of *Queen Elizabeth* (*Les Amours de la reine Élisabeth*), these last three based either on plays or stage-play versions of novels.[22] This system involved purchasing the right to license a film's exhibition in a particular territory, allowing licensees 'to rent the film to exhibitors in a particular territory or subdivide and re-sell the territorial rights further'.[23] Amidst the growing number of multi-reel features, some imported, others domestically produced, the state rights system was a significant point of entry not only for play-based films, but for those who produced them. The latter included legitimate theatre entrepreneurs such as William A. Brady, Daniel Frohman, Marc Klaw and Abraham Erlanger, Oliver Morosco, the Shubert brothers (Lee and J.J.), and A. H. Woods, all of whom founded or managed new film companies dedicated to the production of stage-based feature-length films, giving rise to an influx of playwrights and theatrically-trained actors in the period between 1912 and 1915 as they did so.

One of the reasons for these developments was the growing audience for feature-length films, and another was the concomitant downturn in legitimate-theatre attendances. As Robert McLaughlin points out, at 'the turn of the century the American commercial theatre was a sprawling, nationwide business. Plays were produced in New York with an eye on the national market and were sent out to all corners of the country ... The average number of road companies operating in an average week in the first ten years of the century ranged from 250 and 350'.[24] This business differed from that of the nickelodeon and its short films and was able to flourish alongside it. But the advent of feature-length films had a considerable deleterious impact, and as Roberta Pearson has explained, the theatre 'entered a period of sustained economic downturn circa 1912', 'heralded by the disastrous New York theatrical season of 1911–12, in which legitimate houses closed for the entire season' as the theatre 'began to experience the full force of the cinema's rivalry', as theatres were converted to moving picture houses, and as 'theatrical moguls were converted into moving picture moguls'.[25]

New film companies dedicated to the production of stage-play adaptations emerged in the wake of these developments, and these included the Protective Amusement

Company, whose films included *The Fatal Wedding* (from the 1901 play by Theodore Kramer) and *The Road to Yesterday* (from the 1906 play by Beulah Marie Dix and Evelyn Greenleaf Sutherland) (both 1914); the All-Star Feature Company, whose films included *Arizona* (1913) and *In Mizzoura* (1914) (from the 1900 and 1893 plays by Augustus Thomas); the Morosco Company, whose films included *The Yankee Girl* (from the 1910 play by George V. Hobart) and *Tongues of Men* (from the 1913 play by Edward Childs Carpenter) (both 1915); and the World Film Corporation, whose films included *The Lure* (1914) (from the 1913 play by George Scarborough) and *The Pit* (1915) (from Channing Pollock's 1904 dramatisation of the novel by Frank Norris).[26] Toward the end of this period these companies were joined by the newly-formed Triangle Corporation, which produced adaptations such as *The Lamb* (1915), and which served as an early vehicle for Douglas Fairbanks, and *Macbeth* (1916), which served as a vehicle for the venerable Shakespeare actor Herbert Beerbohm-Tree. Adaptations such as these were charged at high ticket prices and were aimed largely at 'the classes' rather than 'the masses', and although original feature-length films such as *The Coward* (1915) and Mack Sennett's Keystone Comedy shorts possessed wider appeal, Triangle's policies failed and its operations ceased in 1919.[27] In contrast, the most significant companies in both the short and the long term were the Famous Players Film Company and the Jesse L. Lasky Feature Play Company, which along with Bosworth Inc. helped establish Paramount Pictures in 1914.[28]

Paramount Pictures and the Advent of the Studio Era

One of the founders of Famous Players was Daniel Frohman, who was reported in 1912 as saying that 'the amalgamation of the legitimate stage and the motion picture has come'.[29] Another was Adolph Zukor, who had invested in penny arcades, nickelodeons and vaudeville houses in turn in the years between the 1890s and the 1910s, who proposed and secured the importation and distribution of *Queen Elizabeth*, and who went on to produce a number of feature-length films based on the stage-play properties to which Frohman had access, among them *The Prisoner of Zenda* and *Tess of the D'Urbervilles* (both 1913, and both based on stage-play adaptations of novels).[30] Yet another company, the Jesse L. Lasky Feature Play Company, was formed in the summer of 1913 by Samuel Goldfish (later Goldwyn), Jesse L. Lasky and Cecil B. DeMille. Lasky was a theatrical promoter who 'foresaw that movies could improve upon certain aspects of the stage',[31] and on 3 January 1914 he announced that 'The World is Our Studio' and that 'we are sending the present company to South California and Wyoming for the atmosphere of the story'.[32] This company was charged with filming *The Squaw Man* (1914), an adaptation of the 1905 stage play by Milton Royle, and this and later adaptations are discussed in detail in Chapter 1. The 1914 version was great success and prompted the production of subsequent DeMille Westerns such as *The Virginian* (1914) (which was based on the 1904 adaptation by Owen Wister and Kirke La Shelle of Wister's novel) and *The Girl of the Golden West* (1915) (which was based on the 1905 play by David Belasco).[33]

The Squaw Man was distributed in the state-rights market. But although it made a profit, the state-rights system as a whole was unable to provide the regular cash flow necessary to sustain a continuous programme of expensive feature-length films. In response, an exhibitor named William Hodkinson realised 'that it was necessary to establish for features the equivalent of the distribution cartels dominating the short-film industry' and founded Paramount Pictures 'as a national distributor offering a full annual program of features to theaters that committed themselves to Paramount offerings'.[34] In September 1914, Paramount advertised 'a yearly program of features, consisting of 104 films of four to six reels each, released at the rate of two per week'; emphasised the importance of its stars in attracting new audiences to film theatres; and introduced percentage-based distribution fees, whereby producers and exhibitors 'each received a portion of the gross exhibitor rentals'.[35] Although Hodkinson was deposed by Adolph Zukor in 1916, these polices formed the basis of what we now know as the classical Hollywood studio system, and in this way the landscape of film production, distribution and exhibition in the USA was changed fundamentally.[36]

Paramount, First National, Fox, MGM, Universal, United Artists and Warner Bros., went on to dominate the feature-film industry in the USA from the late 1910s to the late 1920s, their corporate status underpinned by Wall Street investments, their studios equipped by the latest technology, and their personnel divided into specialised departments.[37] Among these departments were those dedicated to the reading and adaptation of novels, short stories and plays, and the production of new scenarios and scripts, all of which were crucial to the continual mix of story material that sustained the production of feature films.[38] One of the late 1910s Paramount films was *The Poor Little Rich Girl* (1917), which was adapted from the 1913 play by Eleanor Gates as a vehicle for Mary Pickford, which was scripted and directed by Frances Marion and Maurice Tourneur respectively, and which, along with its 1936 remake, constitutes the focus of chapter 2. Pickford was one in a number of stars who migrated to Hollywood from the stage, the former offering 'salaries and other inducements that the theatre could not begin to equal', and from this point on Hollywood began a talent raid on the theatre 'that in many respects has never ceased'.[39]

Overall, the period between 1910 and the 1920 was 'startling': In 1910 'the estimated number of theatrical companies on tour during the average week was 236 and by 1920 this average had fallen to thirty-four', and the 1920s saw little improvement as the 'film companies set up story departments in New York', tracked 'the progress of new productions', and competed for the screen rights, and in 1926 Brock Pemberton, a leading producer of the period, stated that aside from a handful of 'phenomenal successes, such as *Abie's Irish Rose* or *The Bat* ... the road no longer exists'.[40] However, the *Theatre Magazine* 'suggested that ... the sale of motion picture rights ... would in all likelihood earn more income than it lost',[41] and while the average rights for a successful Broadway play in the 1913–14 season cost approximately $2000, by 1919-20 the average cost was approximately $50,000, and by 1927 the rights for *Broadway* cost Universal $225,000, at which point a fifty-fifty split between the playwrights and film producers had became the norm.[42]

Scenarios, Scripts and Shots from the 1890s to the Late 1920s

The nature of the script for *The Squaw Man* is a clear indication of the extent to which scripts and scenarios were now necessary blueprints for much longer films. However, as Steven Price has pointed out, our knowledge of the history of scripts and scenarios is plagued by the extent to which terms such as 'screen play' and 'screenplay' meant different things.[43] Price has summarised Janet Staiger's work on early screenplay history in the USA as follows. Following the aide memoirs that marked the early period, 'outline' scripts became dominant. But 'the increasing size of companies and the need to increase supply' in the early 1910s gave rise to the 'scenario script' as the best way to plan the production of one-reel, two-reel and three-reel films;[44] and with the advent of feature-length films, detailed 'continuity' scripts became a necessity.[45] Price discusses a number of script formats in detail,[46] and endorses Staiger's view that 'higher-budget, prestige pictures created by established figures' allowed for a greater degree of 'authorial input'.[47] In this way the films scripted, co-scripted and/or directed by Frank Borzage, Cecil B. DeMille, D.W. Griffith, Rex Ingram and Erich von Stroheim in the late 1910s and 1920s were often distinctive,[48] and von Stroheim's 1925 adaptation of *The Merry Widow* and Borzage's 1927 adaptation of *Seventh Heaven* are discussed as examples in chapters 3 and 4 respectively.

By the mid 1920s the terminology adopted for scripts had proliferated further, and as Price explains, 'In 1912 the United States Copyright Office created two new classifications for feature films, of which the fictional films (as opposed to non-fiction or animation) were designated "photoplays"', and around this time the term 'synopsis' was used to designate 'prose narratives of anywhere between 300 and 8000 word in length' and to identify 'many different kinds of script, with varying functions'. For example, 'the synopsis' was often integrated into what was called a 'continuity': 'a separate item accompanied by other documents, including the script, or as a preface to the script itself'. But at the same time, a 'somewhat longer prose narrative, of perhaps five pages in length, was used as the "scenario" for many of the shorter films of the 1910s, and could in this form serve the function of a shooting script'.[49] Meanwhile, in 'its earliest citation' in 1911, a scenario could either be 'a rough sketch or a minutely detailed script', and by 1924, 'Frances Taylor Patterson was describing as a "scenario" the composite document (containing a list of characters, plot synopsis, breakdown of scenes and the "plot of action" or script itself) that is usually referred to as the "continuity"'.[50] Other terms and concepts in use in or by the 1920s were 'treatment' and 'screen play', the former described by screen-writer Frances Marion as 'an intermediate between the film story and the continuity', and the latter defined as documents that consisted of scenes 'without further segmentation into defined shots'.[51]

Given the now numerous instances of feature-film adaptation of stage plays and musicals, one of the tasks for those producing treatments, scripts or screen plays was to re-divide the action of three-act stage plays and their scenes into somewhere between 'nine and eighteen scenes and sequences'.[52] But these were not the only blocks of feature-length films. In 1915 and 1916 feature-length films consisted of between 240 and 1000 shots (with the commonest range being 'between 250 and 450 shots per film'), and in the period between 1917 and 1928 a 'typical film' would contain 'between 500 and 1000 shots, with never fewer than 400 and seldom more than 1300'.[53] The shots that comprised these films were by no means all unique in viewpoint (crosscutting and the repetition of framings were common, and the repetition of framings could often help establish a consistent style).[54] But in concert with the point made above about the viewpoint of camera, they provided a sequential array of views of the characters, actions and settings. The earliest films had no inter-titles. But during the course of the early 1900s expository titles that identified settings or summarised upcoming actions began to appear, and by 1910 'the text of summary inter-titles had expanded'.[55] Dialogue titles were much less common in this early period. But they began to emerge more frequently from the early 1910s on,[56] and given the increasing number of stage-play adaptations in the 1910s and the 1920s, it is likely that famous lines from at least some of these plays were reproduced in inter-titles as verbal highlights: 'When you call me that, smile' in the 1914 version of *The Virginian* and 'Chico-Diane-Heaven' in the 1927 version of *7th Heaven* would constitute memorable examples.[57]

Situations

In addition to these points and practices, it is important to note the publication of guidance books and manuals. Among these were *The Thirty-Six Dramatic Situations* by Georges Polti, which focuses on novels, operas and plays but was clearly applicable to feature-length films, and the *Photoplay Plot Encyclopedia* by Frederick Palmer, which focuses solely on films.[58] Both books include comic as well as tragic, dramatic and melodramatic examples, and both books underline the ways in which situations structure narratives and storylines as a whole. Examples include the ongoing dilemmas of love and duty in the 1914 version of *The Squaw Man* and its remakes and the 1925 and 1934 versions of *The Merry Widow*; the pretence that marks the relationship between Manuela and Serafin in *The Pirate* (1948); the planning that Tony Wendice undertakes in attempting to ensure the death of his wife in *Dial M for Murder* (1954); and the antagonism between a unit of US foot soldiers and the cowardly and indecisive Captain Cooney, who repeatedly puts them in lethal danger in *Attack* (1956).

But narratives and storylines are also designed to produce local situations, and these frequently give rise to what might be termed pictorial pauses: instances of deadlock that at their extremes are marked by formal tableaux.[59] These devices were a staple in the theatre in the 1800s and early 1900s. But in modified form they continue to mark plays and musicals in the twentieth and twenty-first centuries and can be found in most Classical and Post-Classical Hollywood films. Examples in this book include the quasi-frozen moment in which the protagonist in the 1914 version of *The Squaw Man* marks his response to the unexpected arrival of his brother's wife in the cow-town saloon; the pause as Diane hesitates to cross the rooftops outside Chico's apartment and the last-scene tableau in the 1927 version of *7th Heaven*; the pause that marks Serafin's pronouncement that he is the pirate in *The Pirate*, and the tableau that is later formed when Don Pedro, the real pirate, goes on stage and brandishes his pistols, and reveals his true identity. Other examples include the frozen moment in which Myra embraces Kitty as she too decides to engage in prostitution in the 1940 version of *Waterloo Bridge*; the frozen moment in which Tony realises that his watch has stopped prior to the would-be murder of his wife in *Dial M for Murder*; and the tableau that follows Lieutenant Costa's death and the killing of Cooney in *Attack*.

Sound Films and Adaptations from 1926 to 1932

Following the various instances of live and recorded music, spoken accompaniment, and live and recorded sound from the 1890s on, successful attempts to innovate synchronised pre-recorded music, sound and speech were a hallmark of the mid-to-late 1920s and early 1930s.[60] As is well known, the earliest feature-length sound films were *Don Juan* (1926) and *The Jazz Singer* (1927). The former was a silent film with recorded musical accompaniment on discs; and the latter consisted not of extensive dialogue scenes transported from the 1925 play by Samson Raphaelson, but of 'silent' scenes and sequences accompanied by recorded music on disc interspersed with inter-titles and two short instances of recorded speech and song.[61] Marked by much more dialogue than this, part-talkies were common during the course of the next few years, and many of these were based on plays and musicals. Examples include *The Barker* (from the 1917 play by Kenyon Nicholson) and *Glorious Betsy* (from the 1908 play by Rida Johnson Young) (both 1928), and *Show Boat* (1929) (from the 1927 musical play by Jerome Kern and Oscar Hammerstein II, itself adapted from Edna Ferber's 1926 novel).[62] However, although Broadway experienced 'a decline from which it has never recovered',[63] all-talkies became dominant, and all the major studios produced them. Examples include Paramount's *Interference* (from the 1927 play by Roland Pertwee and Harold Dearden); Fox's *The Ghost Talks* (from the 1924 play *Badges* by Max Marcin and Edward Hammond); MGM's *His Glorious Night* (from the 1928 play *Olympia* by Ferenc Molnár); United Artists' *Coquette* (from the 1927 play by George Abbott and Ann Preston Bridger); and Universal's *The Last Warning* (from the 1922 play by Thomas Fallon and the 1916 novel entitled *House of Fear* by Wadsworth Camp), all of which were released in 1929.

Alongside these films, the 1929-1930 season witnessed a cycle of 'claustrophobic dramas of trials, spies, police actions and racketeers set in courtrooms, night clubs and police stations', and a 'Superabundance' of revues and musicals.[64] The former included *Alibi* (from the 1927 John Griffith Wray, J.C. Nugent and Elaine S. Carrington play entitled *Nightstick*), *Broadway* (from the 1927 play by Philip Dunning and George Abbott), and *The Trial of Mary Dugan* (from the 1927 play by Bayard Veiller) (all 1929); and in addition to *The Cocoanuts* (1929) (from the 1925 musical comedy stage show by George S. Kaufman and Irving Berlin), which is discussed in detail in chapter 5, examples of the latter include *Rio Rita* (from the 1927 stage musical by Guy Bolton and Fred Thompson) (1929) and *Spring is Here* (from the 1929 stage musical by Owen Davis, Lorenz Hart and Richard Rodgers) (1930). According to McLaughlin, 'many theatre observers expressed concern that talkies might soon capture all the best houses [i.e. theatres] on Broadway', and 'many theatre owners ... converted to films permanently, completely dropping their legitimate activities ... By the fall of 1931 nearly twenty percent of all New York legitimate stages had been diverted to other uses',[65] but although movie attendances had risen from 50 to 90 million, attendances 'began to lag' as the Depression took hold.[66]

While many part-talking and all-talking sound films were financially successful, they were often adjudged by film-industry personnel to be stylistically deficient and technologically inflexible on account of oversensitive microphones, multiple cameras in sound-proof booths, and the general difficulties faced by sound editors. As Lea Jacobs points out, dialogue in sound films in or by 1930 was still 'direct-recorded in a single take' and 'efforts to render dialogue as clearly as possible led actors to articulate their lines very slowly and clearly', and these limitations helped account for the fact that 'dialogue is rife with pauses and can have a stilted quality', that actors found it difficult 'to pace their performances' and 'directors and editors to control the flow of the narrative', and that this gave rise to the adverse effects 'on tempo and pacing' that were frequently noted in the trade press, discussed at industry meetings and conferences, and published in journals devoted to technological issues.[67] William de Mille, an experienced playwright and filmmaker, identified some of these issues as follows:

> Probably the talking picture will develop its own form of writing, since stage-plays contain too many lines for the medium, and screen construction leaves room for too few lines. Less plot can be told in a given space when it has to carry the spoken word. The vocal photoplay must contain fewer words than the stage-play because the dramatic spacing of lines will be different, and intimate pantomime is bound to be a more essential element in the new form, since the close-up can do so much more work than the silent moment on the stage can do. Another conflict of inherited impulses occurs in the matter of tempo. The physical tempo of the screen, so much quicker than that of the stage, finds itself checked by the spoken word, which cannot be made consistent with such rapid movement.[68]

During the next few years it became the task of filmmakers and technicians to address and rectify these problems. Those involved in the 1931 film adaptation of *Street Scene* sought to provide as much flexibility as they could, and these and other aspects of the adaptation and its source are discussed in detail in chapter 6. But it was a series of operettas that demonstrated the possibilities of rhythmically flexible sound films. Hitherto, operettas tended to demonstrate these possibilities in occasional scenes only. But Ernst Lubitsch at Paramount began the production and direction of what became a mini cycle comprising four operettas – *The Love Parade* (1929), *Monte Carlo* (1930), *The Smiling Lieutenant* (1931) and *One Hour with You* (1932) — and this mini cycle was augmented by *Love Me Tonight* (1932), which was produced and directed, again at Paramount, by Rouben Mamoulian.[69] All five films were based on theatrical sources,[70] and all five films proved that 'the rhythmic integration of sound effects, speech, and figure and camera movement' was possible.[71] And this is also evident in the 1934 Lubitsch version of *The Merry Widow*, which is discussed in chapter 3 alongside the other Hollywood adaptations of Franz Lehár's operetta.

Following the catastrophic impact of the Great Depression and the more or less simultaneous attempts to introduce self-censorship regulations, the Hollywood studios began to recover, and as noted in chapter 7 on *Waterloo Bridge*, by the end of 1934 Will H. Hays was now in sole charge of the Production Code Administration and was responsible for the means by which these regulations would be handled from this point on. The period between 1928 and 1935 witnessed play-sales at rates that varied from $3,500 to $255,000, and for many playwrights sales such as this were a lifeline.[72] Cycles of gangster films, horror-thriller films, 'fallen woman' and 'forgotten man' films had largely played out by the end of 1933. And although Universal's horror-thrillers were produced throughout the 1930s, and although gangster films were revived in modified form in the mid-to-late 1930s, they were now accompanied by musicals, prestige adaptations and biopics, historical adventure films, and screwball comedies and woman's films,[73] all of which were accompanied by full musical scores from the mid 1930s on.[74] Among the screwball comedies and woman's films was *Stage Door* (1937), which was based on a 1936 stage-play by Edna Ferber and George S. Kaufman, but transformed by subsequent scripting and improvisation, as is detailed in chapter 8.

During the early 1930s, the US government supported Hollywood's oligopolistic practices as a means of ensuring its recovery and providing relatively cheap entertainment, and by the mid-to-late 1930s the industry comprised five major vertically-integrated companies (MGM, Paramount Pictures, RKO, 20th Century-Fox, and Warner Bros.), all of which possessed national and international distribution facilities and substantial movie-theatre chains; the so-called Little Three (Columbia Pictures, United Artists, and Universal Pictures), all of which were less well capitalised and all of which possessed fewer movie theatres; and a group of minor companies such as Monogram, Republic and PRC (Producers Releasing Corporation), which specialised in the production of B films and serials. However, although Depression was by no means over, the US Justice Department filed an anti-trust suit in 1940. The Department's decree demanded changes that did little to alter the plight of independent theatre-owners, and although the majors were forced to agree to 'blocks of no-more-than-five films', these practices dovetailed with the ongoing production of 'A and Super-A products' in an expanding domestic market in or by 1943.[75]

By then the USA had declared war on the Axis powers, leading to full employment, and the production of films set in combat zones in the air, land and sea; films depicting allies in occupied countries; dramas and comedies set on the home front in the USA or Britain; musical films of all sorts; and crime, spy and private-eye films.[76] With its ever-growing profits, the film industry was also able further to refine its use of sound, monochrome and colour, and experiment with long takes, cement its alliances with radio, and in some cases experiment with early television too.[77] And by the end of war, 'the effects of the 1940 consent decree, wartime film attendance trends, and tax laws promoted a movement away from mass production and toward independent production', and by 1946 'every major firm except MGM had some independent projects as part of their regular production schedule'.[78] Meanwhile the number of stage plays and musicals continued to decline 'from 135 new productions in 1935-36 to only 76 in 1945-46', but several 'hit shows set new gross receipts records during tours in the early forties', and although the total amount paid for screen rights rose, 'it could be said that Broadway and Hollywood for the first time were existing in relative economic harmony'.[79]

While a number of postwar films celebrate domesticity and women and their families, among them *I Remember Mama* (1948), which is discussed in detail in chapter 10, market uncertainty and the resurrection of the government's consent decree gave rise to difficulties for all the major studios.[80] MGM tended to rely on lavish Technicolor musicals such as *The Pirate* (1948), which is discussed in detail in chapter 9. But by 1950, 'additional factors led to domestic income losses: population shifts, changing recreational habits, regional unemployment, and particularly competition with television', and in or by 1953, the production of prestige adult adaptations from the plays of Tennessee Williams and others was accompanied by an influx of new and youthful stars and investments in new colour processes, 3-D, widescreen and large-screen technologies, and stereophonic sound.[81] Among the consequent films was *Dial M for Murder* (1954), which was adapted by Fredrick Knott from his highly successful play and directed by Alfred Hitchcock, which was available in Technicolor in both 'flat' and 3-D versions, and which is discussed in detail in chapter 11.[82]

By the mid 1950s even MGM made outside deals and nearly all the major companies financed independent productions, and it is at this point that the package-unit system finally replaced the studio-based one.[83] At the same time, the 'Writers Guild of America reported that between 1938 and 1952 nearly 65 percent of all hit movies had been original stories, but that from 1953 to 1956 this figure dropped to 28 percent', and that Hollywood interest in Broadway plays and shows had 'intensified'.[84] No longer a niche studio for a handful of independents, United Artists was now a major distribution company willing to finance and distribute adult-oriented films, and among them was an adaptation of a 1954 Broadway play entitled *Fragile Fox*. *Fragile Fox* was written by Norman Brooks and his play attracted the attention of Robert Aldrich. Eventually titled *Attack*, this film was one of a number that emerged in the mid-to-late 1950s, that sympathised with ordinary soldiers and that pinpointed the failings of officers, and these aspects are among those discussed in chapter 12. Similar films included the 1958 adaptation of *The Naked and the Dead*, and in the late 1960s, following the demise of the Production Code in 1966 and long after the demise of studio system, films such as *The Dirty Dozen* (1967) and *Kelly's Heroes* (1970) expressed similar views. Adaptations of stage plays and musicals of all kinds continued. But from this point on, their production, distribution and exhibition would be marked by practices that differed fundamentally from those that characterised the classical Hollywood cinema.[85]

Notes

1. George Bluestone, *Novels into Film* (Baltimore and London: The Johns Hopkins University Press, 1957). Bluestone discusses the 1935 adaptation of Liam O'Flaherty's *The Informer*, the 1939 adaptation of Emily

Bronte's *Wuthering Heights*, the 1940 adaptation of Jane Austen's *Pride and Prejudice*, the 1941 adaptation of John Steinbeck's *The Grapes of Wrath*, the 1943 adaptation of Walter Van Tilburg Clarke's *The Ox-Bow Incident*, and the 1949 adaptation of Gustave Flaubert's *Madame Bovary*. However, he fails to note that the adaptation of *Pride and Prejudice* was based on the 1935 play by Helen Jerome as well as on the novel.

2. Imelda Whelehan, 'What Is Adaptation Studies', https://blogs.utas.edu.au/adapt/2012/04/18/what-is-adaptation-studies/10/02/2016.

3. Detail is important. There are a number of books that either list film adaptations from novels, plays, stories and musicals or provide relatively succinct summaries of plays or musicals and their adaptations. These include Ellen Baskin and Mandy Hicken, *Enser's Filmed Books and Plays, 1928–1991* (Aldershot, Brookfield USA, Singapore, Sydney: Ashgate, 1993 ed.), on the one hand, and Thomas S. Hischak, *American Plays and Musicals on Screen: 650 Stage Productions and Their Film and Television Adaptations* (Jefferson, NC.: McFarland and Company, 2005) and John C. Tibbetts and James M. Walsh, *The Encyclopedia of Stage Plays into Film* (New York: Facts on File, Inc., 2001) on the other. Baskin and Hicken confine themselves to the sound era and are also unaware of Jerome's stage-play version of *Pride and Prejudice* and other stage-play adaptations of novels. But Hischak and Tibbetts and Walsh are aware of these issues and discuss silent as well as sound films (and in Hischak's case television adaptations too). They focus solely on feature-length films, and their summaries and comparisons are both knowledgeable and succinct. But in their pursuit of succinctness they tend to forego narrative and stylistic detail, and along with aspects of film-industry context, it is here that this book seeks to differ.

4. Alongside James Dark, who provided me with a brief description of the script for the 1914 version of *The Squaw Man*, I am indebted to the published accounts of the process of adaptation in Richard Koszarski, *Von: The Life and Times of Erich von Stroheim* (New York: Limelight Editions, 2001 edition) (on the 1925 version of *The Merry Widow*); James Curtis, *James Whale: A New World of Gods and Monsters* (Boston and London: Faber and Faber, 1998) (on the 1931 version of *Waterloo Bridge*); Elizabeth Kendall, *The Runaway Bride: Hollywood Romantic Comedy of the 1930s* (New York and London: Anchor Books, 1990 ed.) (on *Stage Door*), and Earl J. Hess and Pratibha A. Dabholkar, *The Cinematic Voyage of* The Pirate*: Kelly, Garland, and Minnelli at Work* (Columbia: University of Missouri Press, 2014). As far as I know there are no extant papers on *The Poor Little Rich Girl* and its 1936 remake, *7th Heaven* and its 1937 remake, and *The Cocoanuts, Street Scene, Dial M for Murder* and *Attack*, so I have been unable to trace the process of adaptation in detail in these instances. However, it is worth pointing out here that detailed accounts of adaptations from novels and short stories can be found in Michael F. Blake, *Code of Honor: The Making of Three Great American Westerns* (Lanham, New York, Oxford: Taylor Trade Publishing, 2003); Glenn Frankel, *The Searchers: The Making of an American Legend* (New York: Bloomsbury USA, 2013); William R. Meyer, *The Making of the Great Westerns* (New Rochelle, N.J.: Arlington House Publishers, 1979); Donald L. Rathgeb, *The Making of Rebel Without a Cause* (Jefferson, N.C.: McFarland & Company, 2004); and Sam Staggs, *Born to be Hurt: The Untold Story of Imitation of Life* (New York: St. Martin's Press, 2009). In addition, Leonard J. Leff, Joseph McBride, Elizabeth Kendall, Emanuel Levy, Todd McCarthy, Axel Madsen, Gabriel Miller, Marilyn Ann Moss, Ed Sikov, and Donald Spoto all take pains to detail the pertinent processes of stage-play, novel, and short-story adaptation in *Hitchcock and Selznick: The Rich and Strange Collaboration of Alfred Hitchcock and David O. Selznick in Hollywood* (Berkeley, Los Angeles, London: University of California Press, 1999 ed.); *Searching for John Ford: A Life* (New York: St. Martin's Press, 2001); *The Runaway Bride*; *George Cukor, Master of Elegance: Hollywood's Legendary Director and His Stars* (New York: William Morrow and Company, Inc. 1994); *Howard Hawks: The Grey Fox of Hollywood* (New York: Grove Press, 1997); *William Wyler: The Authorized Biography* (New York: Thomas Y. Crowell, 1973); *William Wyler: The Life and Films of Hollywood's Most Celebrated Director* (Lexington: University of Kentucky Press, 2013); *Raoul Walsh: The True Adventures of Hollywood's Legendary Director* (Lexington, Kentucky: University Press of Kentucky, 2011); *On Sunset Boulevard: The Life and Times of Billy Wilder* (New York: Hyperion Press, 1998); and *The Dark Side of Genius: The Life of Alfred Hitchcock* (New York: Da Capo Press, 1999 ed.), respectively. For novel and short-story adaptations only, see Lutz Bacher, *Max Ophuls in the Hollywood Studios* (New Brunswick, N.J.: Rutgers University Press, 1996). See also Staggs, *When Blanche Met Brando: The Scandalous Story of A Streetcar Named Desire* (New York: St. Martin's Press, 2006).

5. Unpublished novels, stories and plays form the basis of a number of Hollywood films. Among them were *Make Way for Tomorrow* (1937), which was based a 1934 book by Josephine Lawrence entitled *Years Are So Long* and an unproduced stage-play version by Helen and Nolan Leary; *The High Wall* (1947), which was based both on the novel by Alan R. Clarke and an unproduced play by Clarke and Bradbury Foote;

Act of Violence (1949), which were based on an unpublished story by Collier Young; *Border Incident* (1949), which was based on an unpublished story by John H. Higgins and George Zuckerman; and *Never Steal Anything Small* (1959), which was based on *The Devil's Hornpipe*, an unproduced stage musical by Maxwell Anderson and Rouben Mamoulian. Probably the best known example of an adaptation from an unpublished stage play is *Casablanca* (1942), which was based on *Everybody Comes to Rick's* by Murray Burnett and Joan Alison. For details, see Aljean Harmetz, *The Making of Casablanca: Bergman, Bogart, and World War II* (New York: Hyperion, 2002 ed.). *Sorry, Wrong Number* was adapted from the 1943 radio play by Lucille Fletcher, who went on write the screenplay for the 1948 film version, and to write and copyright a stage-play version, also in 1948, prior to the latter's publication in 1952. Radio plays and radio adaptations of films were legion in the 1930s, 1940s and 1950s, and Frank Krutnik details the latter in '"Barbed Wire and Forget-Me-Not": The Radio Adventures of *Laura* (1944)', *Journal of Adaptation in Film & Performance*, vol. 5 no. 3 (2012), pp. 297–314, and '"Be moviedome's guest in your own easy chair!" Hollywood, Radio and the Movie Adaptation Series', *Historical Journal of Film, Radio and Television*, vol. 33 no. 1 (2013), pp. 24–54. See also Rick Altman, 'Deep Focus Sound: *Citizen Kane* and the Radio Aesthetic', *Quarterly Review of Film & Video*, vol. 15 no. 3 (1994), pp. 1–33, Richard Jewell, 'Hollywood and Radio: Competition and Partnership in the 1930s', *Historical Journal of Film, Radio and Television*, vol. 4 no. 2. (1984), pp. 125–141, Jesse Schlotterbeck, 'Killing noir?: The Adaptation of Robert Siodmak's *The Killers* to Radio', *Journal of Adaptation in Film and Performance*, vol. 3 no. 1 (2010), pp. 59–70, Matthew Solomon, 'Adapting "Radio's Perfect Script": "Sorry, Wrong Number" and *Sorry, Wrong Number*', *Quarterly Review of Film & Video*', vol. 16 no. 1 (1995), pp. 23–40, and Neil Verma, 'Hollywood Shocker: Lucille Fletcher's "Psychological" Sound Effects and Wartime Radio Drama', *Journal of American Studies*, vol. 44 no. 1 (2010), pp. 137–153.

6. In addition to the articles and books cited in this chapter, see Richard Maltby, '"To Prevent the Prevalent Type of Book": Censorship and Adaptation in Hollywood, 1924–1934', *American Quarterly*, vol. 44 no. 4 (1992), pp. 554–583. See also John Wertheimer, 'Mutual Film Reviewed: The Movies, Censorship, and Free Speech in Progressive America', *The American Journal of Legal History*, vol. 37 no. 2 (1993), pp. 158–189, which notes that in 1952 the Supreme Court ruled that films warranted First Amendment protection, thus prompting further amendments to the Production Code in 1957 following those adopted in 1951. Another factor here was the price of tickets. According to Robert McLaughlin, *Broadway and Hollywood* (New York: Arno Press, 1974), p. 100, in 1930 'the price differential between the play and movie ticket was ... approximately five to one; people had to pay anywhere from two to six dollars for a play and very rarely over a dollar, and usually must less, for a movie'.

7. Ben Brewster and Lea Jacobs, *Theatre to Cinema: Stage Pictorialism and the Early Feature Film* (Oxford and New York: Oxford University Press, 1997), pp. 170–183; Ben Brewster, 'staging in depth', in Richard Abel (ed.), *Encyclopedia of Early Cinema* (Oxford and New York: Routledge, 2005), esp. pp. 606–607.

8. Intermissions in the presentation of long expensive roadshown films were a feature not only of silent films such as *Quo Vadis*, *The Birth of a Nation*, *The Big Parade* (1925) and *Wings* (1929), but of sound films in the 1950s and 1960s too. Examples of the latter include *Oklahoma!* (1954), *The Ten Commandments* (1956), *Ben-Hur* (1959), *The Alamo* and *Spartacus* (both 1960), *West Side Story* (1961), *Lawrence of Arabia* (1962), *The Fall of the Roman Empire* and *My Fair Lady* (both 1964), and *The Sound of Music* (1965). The number of intermissions in the presentation of the silent films varied, but the latter sound films were constructed so as to constitute two distinct parts, and although films like *The Alamo* were subsequently cut for conventional screenings, the marking of these parts added a new dimension to the ways in which the stories they told were segmented.

9. Ben Brewster, 'Periodization of Early Cinema', in Charlie Keil and Shelley Stamp (eds.), *American Cinema's Transitional Era: Audiences, Institutions, Practices* (Berkeley, Los Angeles, London: University of California Press, 2004), pp. 66–75.

10. For details on the period between 1894 to 1907, including the Passion Plays, prize-fight films and early nickelodeons, see Charles Musser, *The Emergence of Cinema: The American Screen to 1907* (New York: Scribner's 1990). For more on the prize-fight films, see Alan Gevinson, 'The Birth of the Feature', in Paolo Cherchi Usai and Lorenzo Codelli (eds.), *Sulla via di Hollywood, 1911–1929* (Pordenone: Le Giornato del Cinema Muto, 1988), p. 138. For more on the early period as a whole, see Robert C. Allen, *Vaudeville and Film: A Study in Media Interaction* (New York: Arno Press, 1980); John L. Fell (ed.), *Film Before Griffith* (Berkeley, Los Angeles and London: California University Press, 1983); Janet Staiger, 'The director system: management in the first years' and 'The "cameraman" system of production (1896-1907)', in David Bordwell, Janet Staiger and Kristin Thompson, *The Classical Hollywood Cinema: Film Style &*

Mode of Production to 1960 (London, Melbourne and Henley: Routledge & Kegan Paul, 1985), pp. 113–115 and 116–117, respectively.

11. See David Bowers, *Nickelodeon Theatres and Their Music* (New York: Vestal Press, 1986); Eileen Bowser, *The Transformation of Cinema, 1907–1915* (New York: Scribner's, 1990), pp. 1–20; Russell Merritt, 'Nickelodeon Theaters, 1905-1914: Building an Audience for the Movies', in Tino Balio (ed.), *The American Film Industry* (Madison: University of Wisconsin Press, 1985 ed.), pp. 83–102; Michael Quinn, 'Distribution, the Transient Audience and the Transition to the Feature Film', *Cinema Journal*, vol. 40 no. 2 (2001), pp. 25–56. Some of the venues in which the films discussed in this book are noted, but movie theatres and specific exhibition venues are not discussed as such. For a detailed bibliography on these topics, see Gregory A. Waller (ed.), *Moviegoing in America: A Sourcebook of Film Exhibition* (Oxford: Blackwell Publishers, 2002), pp. 324–345.

12. For details on the 1852 play and its 1903 film versions, see Musser, *Before the Nickelodeon: Edwin S. Porter and the Edison Manufacturing Company* (Berkeley, Los Angeles, Oxford: University of California Press, 1991), pp. 242–245, and *The Emergence of Cinema*, pp. 349, 351, 361, 393. For further details on the play, see Garff B. Wilson, *Three Hundred Years of American Drama and Theatre: From Ye Bare and Ye Cubb to Chorus Line* (Englewood Cliffs, N.J.: Prentice-Hall, Inc., 1982 ed.), pp. 123–127.

13. For details on the film version of *The Great Train Robbery* and Marble's play, see David Mayer, *Stagestruck Filmmaker: D.W. Griffith and the American Theatre* (Iowa City: Iowa University Press, 2009), pp. 32–34, 39–42; Musser, *The Emergence of Cinema*, 352–355, and *Before the Nickelodeon*, pp. 253–260.

14. Bearing in mind that these films were condensed or highlight versions and that some of their sources were multiple, the basis for these films was as follows: *Francesca di Rimini*, from the 1853 play by George Henry Boker; *The Count of Monte Cristo*, from the 1868 stage-play version by Charles Fechter; *Dr Jekyll and Mr Hyde*, from the 1906 stage-play version by Oscar Dane; *East Lynne*, from one of nine stage-play versions available in the USA from 1861 on; *The Bride of Lammermoor*, from the 1819 novel and the 1835 opera; *A Drunkard's Reformation*, from the 1897 play by Charles Reade entitled *Drink*, which was in turn based on aspects of Emile Zola's 1888 novel *L'Assommoir*; *The Violin Maker of Cremona*, from the 1876 French play by François Coppée. *The Prince and the Pauper*, from the novel by Mark Twain, which was first published in the USA in 1882; *Ramona*, from Helen Hunt Jackson's 1884 novel; *A Doll's House*, from the 1879 play by Henrik Ibsen, and *Vanity Fair*, from the Robert Hitchens-Cosmo Gordon Lennox 1911 stage-play adaptation of the 1848 novel by William Makepeace Thackeray.

15. For a comprehensive account of the Motion Picture Patents Company, see Robert Anderson, The Motion Picture Patents Company, Phd. Dissertation, University of Wisconsin-Madison, 1983.

16. For further details on Vitagraph's films, see William Uricchio and Roberta E. Pearson, *Reframing Culture: The Case of the Vitagraph Quality Films* (Princeton, N.J.: Princeton University Press, 1993).

17. Ben Brewster, 'multiple-reel/feature films: USA', in Abel (ed.), *Encyclopedia of Early Cinema*, p. 456. See also Bowser, *The Transformation of Cinema*, pp. 217–224.

18. See Roberta Pearson, 'biblical films', in Abel (ed.), *Encyclopedia of Early Cinema*, pp. 68–71. The Bible and Christian plays provided story material for biblical films of all kinds, and as Pearson points out, multi-reel films of this sort helped pioneer the production and exhibition of feature-length films in the 1900s as well as in the early 1910s, and the key film here was the three-reel *Passion Play* produced by Pathé in 1907. For more on the Passion Plays, see Caroline Vander Stichele, 'Silent Saviours: representation of Jesus' Passion in early cinema', in Pantelis Michelakis and Maria Wyke (eds.), *The Ancient World in Silent Cinema* (Cambridge and New York: Cambridge University Press, 2013), esp. pp. 169–180.

19. For more on the stage-play versions of *Quo Vadis*, see John Tibbetts, *The American Theatrical Film: Stages in Development* (Bowling Green, Ohio: Bowling Green University Popular Press), p. 25.

20. Bowser, *The Transformation of Cinema*, p. 193; Sheldon Hall and Steve Neale, *Epics, Spectacles, and Blockbusters: A Hollywood History* (Detriot: Wayne State University Press, 2010), pp. 28–34; Michael Quinn, 'USA: Distribution', in Abel (ed.), *Encyclopedia of Early Cinema*, pp. 660–661.

21. Hall and Neale, *Epics, Spectacles and Blockbusters*, pp. 34–36; Kim R. Holston, *Movie Roadshows: A History and Filmography of Reserved-Seat Limited Showings* (Jefferson, N.C. and London: McFarland & Company, Inc., 2013), pp. 15–18, 20–21. See also, David Mayer, 'A Select Filmography of Toga Films', in Mayer (ed.), *Playing Out the Empire: Ben-Hur and Other Toga Plays and Films, 1883–1908. A Critical Anthology* (Oxford: Clarendon Press, 1994); Mayer, 'Theatrical Sources', in the entry on *The Birth of a Nation* in

Paulo Cherchi Usai (ed.), *The Griffith Project*, vol. 8, *Films Produced in 1914–15* (London: BFI Publishing, 2004), pp. 81–87; and Mayer, *Stagestruck Filmmaker*, pp. 142–165.

22. For detailed accounts of *Camille* and *Queen Elizabeth* and their theatrical sources, see Victoria Duckett, *Seeing Sarah Bernhard: Performance and Silent Film* (Urbana, Chicago, and Springfield: University of Illinois Press, 2015), pp. 71–135. The US version of *Queen Elizabeth* previewed at Daniel Frohman's prestige Lyceum Theatre and subsequently played in opera houses and large legitimate theatres at a top rental cost of $50 per day. See Quinn, 'Distribution, the Transient Audience and the Transition to the Feature Film', p. 48. *Madame Sans-Gêne* starred Gabriele Réjane and was based on the 1893 play by Victorien Sardou and Émile Moreau, which in turn gave rise to the 1915 opera by Umberto Giordano.

23. Michael Quinn, 'USA: Distribution', in Abel (ed.), p. 661. See also Bowser, *The Transformation of Cinema*, pp. 192–194, and Brewster, 'multiple-reel/feature films', pp. 456–457. Although more lavish nickelodeons were built in the 1910s and could accommodate more patrons than the earlier or small-town ones, it should be noted that as yet the only bona fide picture palaces were the Regent in Harlem, which opened in 1913, and the Strand on Broadway, which opened in 1914 on the cusp of 'feature fever'. See Bowser, *The Transformation of Cinema*, pp. 125–135.

24. McLaughlin, *Broadway and Hollywood*, p. 1.

25. Roberta E. Pearson, 'The Menace of the Movies: Cinema's Challenge to the Theater in the Transitional Period', in Keil and Stamp (eds.), *American Cinema's Transitional Era*, p. 316.

26. Bowser, *The Transformation of Cinema*, p. 227; Tibbetts, *The American Theatrical Film*, pp. 71–77, 84–95.

27. Benjamin B. Hampton, *History of the American Film Industry from its Beginnings to 1931* (New York: Dover Publications Inc, 1970 ed.), pp. 140–145; Rob King, '"Made for the Masses with an Appeal to the Classes": The Triangle Film Corporation and the Failure of Highbrow Film Culture', *Cinema Journal*, vol. 44 no. 2 (2005), pp. 3–33, and *The Film Factory: The Keystone Film Company and the Emergence of Mass Culture* (Berkeley, Los Angeles, London: University of California Press, 2008); Kalton Lahue, *Dreams for Sale: The Rise and Fall of the Triangle Film Corporation* (Cranbury, N.J: Barnes, 1971); Tibbetts, *The American Theatrical Film*, pp. 95–106.

28. David Turconi, 'From Stage to Screen: Notes for a five-year history of Famous Players Film Company, Jesse L. Lasky Feature Film Company, and Triangle Film Corporation between 1912 and 1917', in Cherchi Usai and Codelli (eds), *Sulla via di Hollywood, 1911-1920*, pp. 16–131. See also, Gevinson, 'The Birth of the American Feature Film', pp. 146–152.

29. 'Theatrical Stars in Pictures', *New York Dramatic Mirror*', 10 July 1912, p. 34.

30. Bowser, *The Transformation of Cinema*, 225–226; Daniel Frohman, *Daniel Frohman Presents: An Autobiography* (New York: Claude Kendall and Willoughby Sharp, Inc.1935), pp. 275–290; Will Irwin, *The House That Shadows Built* (Garden City, New York: Doubleday, Doran & Company, Inc, 1928), pp. 3-194; Adolph Zukor, *The Public is Never Wrong: The Autobiography of Adolph Zukor* (New York: G.P. Putnam's Sons, 1953), pp. 3–74. Alexandre Dumas adapted *The Count of Monte Cristo* for the stage in 1850, but as is noted above, Charles Fechter's 1868 version appears to have been the preferred one. Edward E. Rice adapted Anthony Hope's *The Prisoner of Zenda* for the stage in 1895 and Lorimer Stoddard adapted Thomas Hardy's *Tess of the D'Urbervilles* for the stage in 1897.

31. Tibbetts, *The American Theatrical Film*, p. 78.

32. 'Jesse L. Lasky Pictures', *Moving Picture World*, 3 January 1914, p. 35.

33. For details on *The Virginian* and *The Girl of the Golden West*, see Tibbets, *The American Theatrical Film*, pp. 175–182 and 182–188, respectively.

34. Brewster, 'multiple-reel/feature films: USA', p. 457.

35. Quinn, 'USA: Distribution', p. 661. See also, Hampton, *History of the American Film Industry*, pp. 101–140; Richard Koszarski, *An Evening's Entertainment: The Age of the Silent Feature Picture, 1915–1928* (New York: Scribner's 1990), pp. 69–72; Michael J. Quinn, 'Paramount and Early Feature Distribution: 1914–1921', *Film History*, vol. 11 no. 1 (1999), pp. 98–133, and Quinn, 'Early Feature Distribution and the Development of the Motion Picture Industry: Famous Players and Paramount: 1912–1921', Phd. Dissertation, University of Madison-Wisconsin, 1998.

36. For a single detailed account of the US film industry from advent of the Motion Picture Patents Company

to the advent of Paramount Pictures, see Ralph Cassady Jr., 'Monopoly in Motion Picture Production and Distribution: 1908–1915', *Southern California Law Review*, vol. 32 no. 4, 1959, pp. 325–390.

37. Tino Balio, *United Artists: The Company Built by the Stars* (Madison, Wisconsin, and London: University of Wisconsin Press, 1976), pp. 3–74; Hampton, *History of the American Film Industry*, pp. 170–280, 304–361; Koszarski, *An Evening's Entertainment*, pp. 72–94; Staiger, 'The division and order of production: the subdivision of the work from the first years through the 1920s', in Bordwell, Staiger and Thompson, *The Classical Hollywood Cinema*, pp. 142–153. See also, 'First National Pictures', Wikipedia, 18 January 2011, for a brief history and a list of the films that it distributed as well as those it produced. It is important to note that the production of short films did not just disappear. The dominant companies began producing or contracting out the production short films as part of cinema programmes, and these included comedies, episodes of serials, and animated shorts as well as newsreels. In the 1930s and 1940s these programmes were extensive, and at this time Disney and Fleischer began to produce feature-length animations alongside their shorts ones and alongside the short cartoons produced or distributed by some the major and minor companies. It is worth noting that the feature-length animations produced by Fleischer and Disney were largely adapted from novels, plays and stories. These included the former's *Gulliver's Travels* (1939), which was based on Jonathan Swift's novel, and the latter's *Snow White and the Seven Dwarfs* (1937), which was based on Jessie Graham White's 1912 stage-play version of the Grimm Brothers' fairy-tale prose version. See Leslie Cabarga, *The Fleischer Story* (New York: Da Capo Press, 1988 ed.), pp. 149–171; Robin Allan, *Walt Disney and Europe: European Influences on the Animated Feature Films of Walt Disney* (London: John Libbey & Company Ltd., 1999), pp. 37–41; Neal Gabler, *Walt Disney: The Triumph of the American Imagination* (New York: Vintage Books, 2006), p. 217. Later feature-length Disney adaptations included *Pinocchio* (1940), which was based in part on Yasha Frank's 1937 stage-play version of Carlo Collodi's novel entitled *The Adventures of Pinocchio*; *Bambi* (1942), which was based on a story by Felix Salten, and which had been translated into English in 1928; *Cinderella* (1950), from Perrault's version; *Alice in Wonderland* (1951), from Lewis Carroll's novel; and *Peter Pan* (1953), from J.M. Barrie's 1904 play. See Allan, *Walt Disney and Europe*, pp. 181, 206–207, 211–212, and 218–220, respectively. For obvious reasons, cartoon shorts were unable to adapt extensive stories, plays and novels in full. But they could and did provide condensed comic pastiches, among them *The Rabbit of Seville* (1950) and *What's Opera Doc?*(1957), which were vehicles for Bugs Bunny, which were produced by Warner Bros., which in these instances were directed by Chuck (Charles M.) Jones, and which were based on Rossini's *The Barber of Seville* and the operas of Wagner, respectively. For more on Warner's pastiches, see, Donald Crafton, 'The View from Termite Terrace: Caricature and Parody in Warner Bros. Animation', *Film History*, vol. 5 no 2 (1993), pp. 204–230.

38. For discussion of specific cycles of stage-play adaptations in the 1910s and the 1920s, see Janet Greene, 'The Road to Reno: *The Awful Truth* and the Comedy of Remarriage', Lea Jacobs, 'The Seduction Plot: Comic and Dramatic Variants', and Billy Budd Vermilion, 'The Remarriage Plot in the 1910s', in *Film History*, vol. 13 no. 4 (2001), pp. 337–358, 424–442, 359–371, respectively. See also Charles Musser, 'Divorce, DeMille and the Comedy of Remarriage', in Kristina Brunovska Karnick and Henry Jenkins (eds.), *Classical Hollywood Comedy* (New York: Routledge, 1995), pp. 282–313.

39. McLaughlin, *Broadway and Hollywood*, p. 35. See also pp. 36–43.

40. McLaughlin, *Broadway and Hollywood*, p. 2 and p. 54. McLaughlin argues that by 'the early 1920s ... the road business' that had sustained the theatre in the early 1900s was 'diminished' as 'the theatre began to concentrate on playgoers from the sophisticated urban areas', citing a *New York Times* report to the effect 'that except for a handful of producers, all the theatres in America were owned and controlled by the movie industry'. See McLaughlin, *Broadway and Hollywood*, pp. 15, 18, who also notes, on p. 17, that several 'legitimate houses on Broadway, including the Astor, the old Criterion, and the New York Theatre, converted permanently to the movies during the mid-teens'.

41. McLaughlin, *Broadway and Hollywood*, unpaginated introduction.

42. McLaughlin, *Broadway and Hollywood*, pp. 55–56 and p. 61. In the 1925–26 season Fox made a serious attempt to capture the play market by entering into partnership with at least seven major play producers, among them Al Woods, Sam Harris, John Golden, Robert Milton and Arch Selwyn. However Fox's plans were eventually forestalled when it was realised that this attempt would damage the prospects for playwrights, leading to a rights agreement and a number of other provisions. See McLaughlin, *Broadway and Hollywood*, pp. 63–84.

43. Steven Price, *A History of the Screenplay* (London: Palgrave Macmillan, 2013), pp. 2 and 13.

44. Price, *A History of the Screenplay*, p. 7. See also, Edward Azlant, 'Screenwriting for Early Silent Film: Forgotten Pioneers, 1897–1911', Epes Winthrop Sargent, Jeanie Macpherson and Lloyd Lonergan, 'A Screenwriting Sampler from the *Moving Picture World*', and Patrick Loughney, 'Selected Examples of Early Scenario/Screenplays in the Library of Congress', in *Film History*, vol. 9 no. 3 (1997), pp. 228–256, 269–276, 290–299, respectively.

45. Price, *A History of the Screenplay*, p. 7. In addition to her afore-cited segments in *The Classical Hollywood Cinema*, see also Staiger, 'Mass-Produced Photoplays: Economic and Signifying Practices in the First Years in Hollywood', *Wide Angle*, vol. 4 no. 3 (1980), pp. 12–27, and 'Blueprints for Feature Films: Hollywood's Continuity Scripts', in Tino Balio (ed.), *The American Film Industry* (Madison: University of Wisconsin Press, 1985 ed.), pp. 173–192.

46. Price, *A History of the Screenplay*, pp. 23–98, which focuses largely on US examples but discusses a number of early European ones too. Later on Price draws attention to the *Ben-Hur* case, in which, in 1907, 'the publishers Harper and Row initiated legal proceeding against the Kalem film company' on the grounds that its one-reel version of *Ben-Hur* 'infringed Harper's copyright in the source novel'. Although the action focussed largely on the chariot race between its two principal antagonist, 'Gene Gauntier had written an adaptation of sorts' and the 'Supreme Court gave a decisive ruling on *Kalem v. Harper* on 13 November 1911', as follows: 'An exhibition of a series of photographs and things, arranged on film as a moving picture and so depicting the principal scenes of an author's work as to tell a story, and the person producing the film and offering them for sale for exhibition, infringes the copyright of the author. ' With 'this decision', notes Price, 'the Supreme Court arguably brought the category of the "adapted screenplay" into being'. See Price, *A History of the Screenplay*, pp. 52–53. See also Ted Hovet Jr., 'The Case of Kalem's *Ben-Hur* (1907) and the Transformation of Cinema', *Quarterly Review of Film & Video*, vol. 18 no. 3 (2001), pp. 283–294, and Jon Solomon, 'The Kalem *Ben-Hur* (1907)', in Michelakis and Wyke, *The Ancient World in Silent Cinema*, pp. 189–204.

47. Price, *A History of the Screenplay*, p. 7.

48. Staiger, 'The "central producer" system: centralized management after 1914', in Bordwell, Staiger and Thompson, *The Classical Hollywood Cinema*, cites Peter Milne's book, *Motion Picture Directing* (New York: Falk, 1922), p. 136, in reporting that Borzage was 'a champion for the continuity synopsis, a running account of the plot, undivided into scenes [i.e. shots]', and she herself draws attention to the fact that Griffith 'used the general outline script even in the multiple-reel era'. She also notes on the same page that in the 1920s Cecil B. DeMille favoured multi-camera shooting and filming in dramatic order. Extravagant costs and practices were a feature of the 1920s, as is evident in a number of well-known productions.

49. Price, *A History of the Screenplay*, p. 11.

50. Price, *A History of the Screenplay*, p. 13. It should noted here that Staiger uses the detailed scripts devised by Thomas Ince and C. Gardner Sullivan in the 1910s as early exemplars of classical Hollywood protocols and as pre-production blueprints for efficient production. However Ince and Sullivan were unusual, and do not represent typical practice in the early-mid 1910s. See Staiger, 'The "central producer" system of production', in Bordwell, Staiger and Thompson, *The Classical Hollywood Cinema*, pp. 136–137; Price, *A History of the Screenplay*, pp. 80–85; and Brian Taves, *Thomas Ince: Hollywood's Independent Pioneer* (Lexington: University Press of Kentucky, 2012), pp. 41–63.

51. Price, *A History of the Screenplay*, pp. 15-16. See also, Steven Maras, 'In Search of "Screenplay": Terminological Traces in the Library of Congress Catalog of Copyright Entries: Cumulative Series, 1912–20', *Film History*, vol. 21 no. 4 (2009), pp. 346-358.

52. David Bordwell, 'Shot and scene', in Bordwell, Staiger and Thompson, *The Classical Hollywood Cinema*, p. 62.

53. Bordwell, 'Shot and scene', pp. 60–61.

54. For more on crosscutting, see Bordwell, 'Time in the classical film', in Bordwell, Staiger and Thompson, *The Classical Hollywood Cinema*, pp. 48–49.

55. Kristin Thompson, 'The formulation of the classical narrative', in Bordwell, Staiger and Thompson, *The Classical Hollywood Cinema*, p. 183.See also, Charlie Keil, *Early American Cinema in Transition: Story, Style, and Filmmaking, 1907–1913* (Madison, Wisconsin: University of Wisconsin Press, 2001), pp. 60–65.

56. See Torey Liepa, 'Figures of Silent Speech: Silent Dialogue and the American Vernacular, 1909–1916', Phd. Dissertation, New York University, 2008.

57. As Staiger points out in 'The Eyes are Really the Focus: Photoplay Acting and Film Form and Style' , *Wide Angle*, vol. 6 no. 4, 1985, p. 20, the 'appearance of dialogue titles' was 'probably due in part to adapting classic works and wanting to keep the original's flavor and favorite lines'.

58. Georges Polti, *The Thirty-Six Dramatic Situations* (Ridgewood, N.J.: The Editor Company, 1917ed.); Frederick Palmer, *Photoplay Plot Encyclopedia: An Analysis of the Use in Photoplays of the Thirty-Six Dramatic Situations and Their Subdivisions* (Los Angeles: Palmer Photoplay Corp., 1922 ed.). For a succinct summary of 'The Thirty-Six Dramatic Situations', see http://en.wikipedia.org/wiki/The_Thirty-Six_Dramatic_Situations 23/03/2016.

59. Brewster and Jacobs, *From Theatre to Cinema*, pp. 18–78. See also, Brewster, '*Alias Jimmy Valentine* and Situational Dramaturgy', *Film History*, vol. 9 no. 4. (1997), p. 388, in which Brewster defines a situation 'as a moment of stasis in the ongoing movement of a plot in which the forces moving the action in one direction and another are momentarily in balance or abeyance – moments of deadlock and suspense, but also ones of surprise. Such interruptions of the narrative flow shift the attention from the actions themselves to their causes and potential effects, and, in general, to the action as such. Indeed, situational cause and effect is usually moral as much as or rather than physical, and moral contrast is one of the most typical features of situations', though they also 'help organise the narrative in time, providing alternations between movement and stasis, and ways of dividing a single causal chain into more convenient sub-units (on stage, the division into scenes and acts), these sub-units typically ending with a situation, whose resolution is delayed until the curtain rises again on a new act or scene. And they help to organise the action spatially, too, insofar as scene design and blocking are arranged to enable actors to reach the point of stasis in the action so that they form a composition which underscores the significance of the moment', which in nineteenth-century theatre, gave rise to 'the "tableau" or stage picture, the moment when all the actors on stage held a pose or attitude for a more or less long period'. For further accounts of situational dramaturgy in Hollywood films and serials, see Scott Higgins, 'Suspenseful Situations: Melodramatic Narrative and the Contemporary Action Film', *Cinema Journal*, vol. 47 no. 2 (2008), pp. 74–96, and *Matinee Melodrama: Playing with Formula in the Sound Serial* (New Brunswick, N.J. and London: Rutgers University Press, 2016), pp. 10–15.

60. For the 1890s to the early-mid 1920s, see Richard Abel and Rick Altman (eds.), *The Sounds of Early Cinema* (Bloomington: Indiana University Press, 2001); Altman, *Silent Film Sound* (New York: Columbia University Press, 2004); Gillian B. Anderson, *Music for Silent Films, 1894–1929: A Guide* (Washington, D.C.: Library of Congress, 1988); Charles Merrell Berg, *An Investigation of the Motives and Realization of Music to Accompany the American Silent Film, 1896–1927* (New York: Arno Press, 1976); James Buhler, David Nuemeyer, Rob Deemer, *Hearing the Movies: Music and Sound in Film History* (New York and Oxford: Oxford University Press, 2010), pp. 245–277; Mervyn Cooke, *A History of Film Music* (Cambridge: Cambridge University Press, 2008), pp. 1–30; Eyman, Scott, *The Speed of Sound: Hollywood and the Talkie Revolution, 1926–1930* (Baltimore and London: Johns Hopkins University Press, 1999); Julie Hubbert (ed.), *Celluloid Symphonies: Texts and Contexts in Film Music History* (Berkeley, Los Angeles, London: University of California Press, 2011), pp. 1–108; James Lastra, *Sound Technology and the American Cinema: Perception, Representation, Modernity* (New York: Columbia University Press, 2000), pp. 98–121; Martin M. Marks, *Music and the Silent Film: Contexts and Case Studies, 1895–1924* (New York: Oxford University Press, 1997); James Wierzbicki, *A History of Film Music* (New York and London: Routledge, 2009), pp. 13–85, and 'The Silent Screen' in Kathryn Kalinak, *Sound: Dialogue, Music and Effects* (London and New York: I.B. Tauris, 2015), pp. 15–36. For the mid-to-late 1920s and early 1930s, see Mary Lea Bandy (ed.), *The Dawn of Sound* (New York: Museum of Modern Art, 1989); David Bordwell, 'The introduction of sound', in Bordwell, Staiger and Thompson, *The Classical Hollywood Cinema*, pp. 298–308; Buhler, Neumeyer, Deemer, *Hearing the Movies*, pp. 278–307; Evan William Cameron (ed.), *Sound and the Cinema: The Coming of Sound to American Films* (New York: Redgrave Publishing Company, 1980), esp. pp. 2–97; Donald Crafton, *The Talkies: American Cinema's Transition to Sound, 1926–1931* (New York: Scribner's, 1997); Scott Eyman, *The Speed of Sound: Hollywood: Hollywood and the Talkie Revolution, 1926–1930* (Baltimore and London: Johns Hopkins University Press, 1999); Douglas Gomery, *The Coming of Sound: A History* (New York: Routledge, 2005 ed.); Hubbert (ed.), *Celluloid Symphonies*, pp. 109–167; Kalinak, 'Classical Hollywood, 1928-1946', in Kalinak (ed.), *Sound*, pp. 37–45; Lastra, *Sound Technology and the American Cinema*, pp. 157–215; Wierzbicki, *A History of Film Music*, pp. 85–130.

61. Robert L, Carringer (ed.), *The Jazz Singer* (Madison: University of Wisconsin Press, 1979); Charles Wolf,

'Vitaphone Shorts and *The Jazz Singer*', *Wide Angle*, vol. 12 no. 3 (1990), pp. 58–78. A discussion of the script format for the film version of *The Jazz Singer* and other early 1920s sound films can be found in Price, *A History of the Screenplay*, pp. 120–132.

62. Tibbetts, *The American Theatrical Film*, pp. 112–113. For more detail, see Crafton, *The Takies*, pp. 171–179.

63. McLaughlin, *Broadway and Hollywood*, p. 30.

64. Tibbetts, *The American Theatrical Film*, pp. 117–118; Crafton, *The Talkies*, pp. 313–344. For a comprehensive account of these and other early sound musicals, see Richard Barrios, *A Song in the Dark: The Birth of the Musical Film* (New York: Oxford University Press, 1995). For examples of script formats in the late 1920s and early 1930s musicals, see Price, *A History of the Screenplay*, pp. 132–139.

65. McLaughlin, *Broadway and Hollywood*, p. 97.

66. McLaughlin, *Broadway and Hollywood*, p. 91.

67. Lea Jacobs, *Film Rhythm after Sound: Technology, Music, and Performance* (Oakland: University of California Press, 2015), pp. 2–5.

68. William de Mille, 'The Screen Speaks', *Scribner's Magazine*, April 1929, pp. 371–372, cited in Jacobs, *Film Rhythm after Sound*, p. 5.

69. For details on these films, see Jacobs, *Film Rhythm After Sound*, pp. 109–165.

70. *The Love Parade*, *Monte Carlo*, *The Smiling Lieutenant* and *One Hour with You* were based respectively on a ca.1919 play entitled *Le Prince Consort* by Léon Xanrof (pseud. Léon Fourneu) and Jules Chancel; a 1914 play entitled *Die blaue Küste* (*The Blue Coast* or *The Love Coast*) by Hans Müller (pseud. Hans Lothar) and episodes from a 1901 operetta entitled *Monsieur Beaucaire* by Booth Tarkington and Evelyn Greenleaf Sutherland, which was itself based on Tarkington's 1900 novel; a 1907 operetta entitled *Ein Walzertraum* (*A Waltz Dream*) by Leopold Jacobson and Felix Doerman (pseud. Felix Biedermann), with music by Oscar Straus, from the 1905 novel, *Buch der Abenteuer* by Hans Müller (pseud. Hans Lothar) and a 1909 play entitled *Nur ein Traum* (*Only a Dream*) by Lothar Schmidt [Goldschmidt]. *Love Me Tonight* was based on a 1924 play entitled *Le Tailleur au Château* (*The Tailor in the Castle*) by Paul Armont and Léopold Marchant. Of all the directors in the classical era Lubitsch was the most prolific adapter of stage plays and musicals, and in addition to *The Merry Widow* these include: *Rosita* (1923), from the 1844 play entitled *Don César de Bazan* by Philippe François Pinel Dumanoir and Adolphe Philippe Dennery; *The Marriage Circle* (1924), from the 1909 play entitled *Nur ein Traum* (*A Waltz Dream*) by Lothar Schmidt, itself based on the 1907 operetta cited above; *Forbidden Paradise* (1924), from the 1913 play entitled *The Czarina* by Lajos Biró and Melchior Lengyel; *Kiss Me Again* (1925), from the 1880 play entitled *Divorçons* (*Let's Get a Divorce*) by Victorien Sardou and Émile de Najac; *Lady Windermere's Fan* (1925), from the 1892 play by Oscar Wilde; *So This is Paris* (1926), from the 1872 play entitled *Réveillon* by Henri Mailhac and Ludovic Halévy; *The Student Prince in Old Heidelberg* (1927), from the 1900 story entitled *Karl Heinrich* by Wilhelm Meyer-Förster, who went on write the 1901 stage-play adaptation, and the 1924 operetta by Dorothy Donnelly and Sigmund Romberg entitled *The Student Prince*; *The Patriot* (1928), from the 1927 play entitled *Der Patriot* by Alfred Nuemann; *The Man I Killed* (*Broken Lullaby*) (1932), from the c. 1925 play entitled *L'Homme que j'ai tué*; *Trouble in Paradise* (1932), from the 1931play entitled *Becsuletes Megtalalo* (*The Honest Finder*) by László Aladár; *Design for Living* (1933), from the 1933 play by Noel Coward; *Desire* (1936), from an unproduced play by Hans Székely and Robert Adolph Stemmle entitled *Die schönen Tage von Aranjuez*; *Angel* (1937), from the 1932 play entitled *Angyel* by Menhért Lengyel and its 1933 English adaptation by Guy Bolton and Russell Medcraft; *Bluebeard's Eighth Wife* (1938), from the 1921 play entitled *La Huitième Femme de Barbe-Bleue* by Alfred Savior and its English-language adaptation by Charlton Andrew that same year; *The Shop Around the Corner* (1940), from the 1936 play by Nikolaus László entitled *Illatszertár* (or *Parfumerie*); *That Uncertain Feeling* (1941), from the 1880 play entitled *Divorçons* (*Let's Get a Divorce*) by Victorien Sardou and Émile de Najac; *Heaven Can Wait* (1943), from the 1934 play entitled *Szuletesnap* (*Birthday*) by László Bus-Feketé; *Royal Scandal* (1945), from the 1913 play entitled *The Czarina* by Lajor Biró and Melchoir Lengyel (which was directed by Otto Preminger because Lubitsch fell ill); and *That Lady in Ermine* (1948), from the 1919 operetta entitled *Die Frau im Hermelin* by Rudloph Schanzer and Ernest Welisch and its various English-language versions, which was completed by Preminger when Lubitsch died on 30 November 1947. For a particularly interesting discussion of *Illatszertár* and its film versions, see Josh Cludary, 'Dear Friend: *The Shop Around the Corner* and *In the Good Old Summer Time*', *Movie* 5 (2014), pp. 15–25. See

also George Toles, 'Acting Ordinary in *The Shop Around the Corner*', *Movie* 1 (2010), pp. 1–15, and Ben Brewster, 'The Circle: Lubitsch and the Theatrical Farce Tradition', *Film History*, vol. 13 no. 4 (2001), pp. 372–389, which identifies and discusses a number of the European sources that Lubitsch drew on in his silent films.

71. Jacobs, *Film Rhythm after Sound*, p. 113. For an overview of sound technology in the 1930s and 1940s, see Helen Hanson, 'Sound Affects: Post-production Sound, Soundscapes and Sound Design in Hollywood's Studio Era', *Music, Sound, and the Moving Image*, vol. 1 no. 1 (2007), pp. 27–49, and Hanson and Steve Neale, 'Commanding the Sounds of the Universe: Classical Hollywood Sound in the 1930s and Early 1940s', in Steve Neale (ed.), *The Classical Hollywood Reader* (London and New York: Routledge, 2012), pp. 249–261; and Lea Jacobs, 'Innovation of Re-Recording in the Hollywood Studios', *Film History*, vol. 24 no. 3 (2012), pp. 5–34. For an overview of film sound and music from the early-mid 1930s to the end of the Classical era, see Kalinak, 'Classical Hollywood, 1928–1946', pp. 37–58, and Nathan Platte, 'Postwar Hollywood, 1947–1967', pp. 59-82, in Kalinak (ed.), *Sound*. The rhythms of sound and dialogue delivery that mark *Twentieth Century* (1934) and *His Girl Friday* (1940), both of which were directed by Howard Hawks, and both of which were adapted from stage plays by Ben Hecht and Charles MacArthur (the latter entitled *The Front Page*), are discussed by Jacobs in 'Keeping Up with Hawks', *Style*, vol. 32 no. 3 (1998), pp. 403-426, and *Film Rhythm after Sound*, pp. 166–216. See also, Katherine Spring, 'Pop Go the Warner Bros., et.al.: Marketing Film Songs during the Coming of Sound', *Cinema Journal*, vol. 48 no. 1 (2008), pp. 68–89.

72. McLaughlin, *Broadway and Hollywood*, p. 120. See also, p. 151, in which McLaughlin reports that by '1935–36 one out of every four new plays had Hollywood money behind it'. An attempt to negotiate a deal with Broadway was mooted, but although the deal was implemented by the Dramatists Guild, Hollywood objected, and as noted on p. 164, Broadway 'was largely void of film financing for almost five years' as a consequence.

73. Among the early 1930s horror-thrillers were *Dracula* (1930) (which was based on John Balderson's 1927 revision of Hamilton Deane's 1924 stage-play adaptation of Bram Stoker's 1897 novel) and *Dr Jeckyll and Mr Hyde* (1931) (which was based on Thomas Russell Sullivan's 1887 stage-play adaptation of Robert Louis Stephenson's 1886 novella, as were its earlier 1908 version, which focused largely on Jekyll's transformation, and its subsequent 1920 feature-length silent adaptation). For a detailed overview of the 1930s that includes B films, serials, non-fiction films and avant-garde films as well as cycles of feature films and issues of censorship, see Tino Balio (with chapters by David Bordwell, Jan-Christopher Horak, Richard Maltby, Brian Taves and Charles Wolfe), *Grand Design: Hollywood as a Modern Business Enterprise 1930–1939* (New York: Scribner's, 1993). See also David Bordwell, 'Deep-focus photography in the 1940s and 1950s' and Janet Staiger, 'The producer-unit system after 1931', in Bordwell, Staiger and Thompson, *The Classical Hollywood Cinema*, pp. 341–347 and 320–352 respectively, both of which encompass the 1940s as well as the 1930s. For an overview of woman's films in the studio era, see Jeanine Basinger, *A Woman's View: How Hollywood Spoke to Women, 1930 to 1960* (London: Chatto and Windus, 1993), and for the appeal to women in 1930s Hollywood, see Sarah Berry, *Screen Style: Fashion and Femininity in the 1930s* (Minneapolis and London: University of Minnesota Press, 1997). Examples of mid-to-late 1930s woman's-film adaptations from stage plays include *The Shining Hour* (1938), from the 1934 play by Keith Winter, and *The Women* and *Dark Victory* (both 1939), the former based on the 1936 play by Clare Booth Luce, the latter on the 1934 play by George Emerson Brewer Jr. and Bertram Bloch. Adaptations such as these continued to be produced throughout the 1940s and 1950s. Examples include *Susan and God* (1940) and *When Ladies Meet* (1941), from the 1937 and 1932 stage plays by Rachel Crothers; *Kiss the Boys Goodbye* and *The Little Foxes* (both 1941), from the 1939 play by Clare Booth Luce and the 1939 play by Lillian Hellman, respectively; *Claudia* (1943), from the 1941 play by Rose Franken; *The Heiress* (1948), from the 1947 Ruth and Augustus Goetz stage-play version of the 1881 Henry James novel entitled *Washington Square*; *Thunder on the Hill* (1951), from the 1950 play by Charlotte Hastings entitled *Bonaventure*; *The Member of the Wedding* (1952), from the Carson McCullers 1950 stage-play version of her 1946 novel; *The Actress* and *How to Marry a Millionaire* (both 1953), the former based on the 1946 Ruth Gordon play entitled *Years Ago*, the latter on a 1930 play by Zöe Atkins entitled *The Greeks Had a Word for It* and a 1946 play by Dale Eunson and Katherine Albert entitled *Loco*; *Teenage Rebel* (1956), from the 1955 play by Edith Sommer entitled *A Roomful of Roses*; *Bernardine* (1957), from the 1952 play by Mary Chase; and *The Restless Years* and *Stage Struck* (both1958), the former based on the 1955 play by Patricia Joudry entitled *Teach Me How to Cry*, the latter on a 1939 play by Zöe Atkins entitled *Morning Glory*. For a particularly interesting discussion of *The Heiress*, see George Toles, 'Eloquent

Objects, Mesmerizing Commodities in William Wyler's *The Heiress*', *Film International*, vol. 4 no. 5 (2006), pp. 48–67.

74. Webb scored over thirty films and is probably best known for the horror-thriller films produced by Val Lewton at RKO in the early-mid 1940s. For overviews and discussions of full-score music and its composers and arrangers, see Royal S. Brown, *Overtones and Undertones: Reading Film Music* (Berkeley, Los Angeles, London: University of California Press, 1994), pp. 38–174; Buhler, Neumeyer, Deemer, *Hearing the Movies*, pp. 146–150, 154–157, 177–179, 195–213, 216–224, 239–243, 308–335, 347–359; George Burt, *The Art of Film Music* (Boston: Northeastern University Press, 1994); Cooke, *A History of Film Music*, pp. 67–130, and Cooke (ed.), *The Hollywood Film Music Reader* (Oxford: Oxford University Press, 2010), pp. 55–188; William Darby and Jack Du Bois (eds.), *American Film Music: Major Composers, Techniques, Trends, 1915–1990* (Jefferson, NC. and London: McFarland & Company, Inc., Publishers, 1990), pp. 15–375; Hubbert (ed.), *Celluloid Symphonies*, pp. 169–322; Kathryn Kalinak, *Settling the Score: Music and the Classical Hollywood Film* (Madison, Wisconsin: University of Wisconsin Press, 1992) and *How the West Was Sung: Music in the Westerns of John Ford* (Berkeley, Los Angeles, London: University of California Press, 2007); Stephen Mayer, *Epic Sound: Music in Postwar Hollywood Biblical Films* (Bloomington and Indianapolis: Indiana University Press, 2015); Roy M. Prendergast, *Film Music: A Neglected Art* (New York and London: W. W. Norton, 1992), pp. 25–145; Mariana Whitmer, 'Reinventing the Western Score: Jerome Moross and *The Big Country*', in Kalinak (ed.), *Music in the Western: Notes on the Frontier* (New York and London: Routledge, 2012), pp. 51–76; Wierzbicki, *Film Music*, pp. 133–186.

75. Janet Staiger, 'The package-unit system: unit management after 1955', in Bordwell, Staiger, Thompson, *The Classical Hollywood Cinema*, p. 331.

76. Jeanine Basinger, *The World War II Combat Film: Anatomy of a Genre* (Middletown, Connecticut: Wesleyan University Press, 2003 ed.), pp. 1–108; Thomas Doherty, *Projections of War: Hollywood, American Culture, and World War II* (New York: Columbia University Press, 1993); Clayton R. Koppes and Gregory D. Black, *Hollywood Goes to War: How Politics, Profits, and Propaganda Shaped World War II Movies* (London: The Free Press, 1987); and Thomas Schatz, *Boom and Bust: American Cinema in the 1940s* (New York: Scribner's, 1997), esp. pp. 14–21, 131–262. It is worth noting that the theatre and war-related plays and shows were a major feature of 1940s home-front culture, as Albert Wertheim points out in *Staging the War: American Drama and World War II* (Bloomington and Indianapolis: Indiana University Press, 2004). In addition to the aforementioned *Casablanca*, play-based and show-based films in the wartime period and its immediate aftermath included *The Fleet's In*, from the 1933 Kenyon Nicholson-Charles Robinson play entitled *Sailor, Beware!* and *True to the Army*, from the 1933 play *She Loves Me Not* by Howard Lindsay (both 1942); *Cry Havoc*, from the 1943 play by Allan Kenwood, *This Is the Army*, from the 1943 stage musical by Irving Berlin, and *Watch on the Rhine*, from the 1941 play by Lillian Hellman (all 1943); *Winged Victory*, from the 1943 play by Moss Hart, *The Eve of St. Mark*, from the 1942 play by Maxwell Anderson, and *The Desert Song*, a contemporary wartime version of the 1926 musical by Sigmund Romberg, Oscar Hammerstein II, Otto Harbach and Frank Mandel (all 1944); and *Counter-Attack*, from the 1943 play by Janet and Phillip Stevenson (itself based on a play by Ilya Vershinin and Mikhail Ruderman), and *SNAFU*, from the 1944 play by Louis and Harold Solomon (both 1945).

77. Christopher Anderson, 'Television and Hollywood in the 1940s', in Schatz, *Boom and Bust*, pp. 422–444; Bordwell, 'Deep-Focus Cinematographyin the 1940s and 1950s' and 'Technicolor', in Bordwell, Staiger and Thompson, *The Classical Hollywood Cinema*, pp. 341–352, and pp. 353–357, respectively; Leo Enticknap, *Moving Image Technology: From Zoetrope to Digital* (London: Wallflower Press, 2005), pp. 121–122; Michele Hilmes, *Hollywood and Broadcasting: From Radio to Cable* (Urbana and Chicago: University of Illinois Press, 1990), pp. 26–120; Patrick Keating, *Hollywood Lighting from the Silent Era to Film Noir* (New York: Columbia University Press, 2010), esp. pp. 210–222, 227–264; Barry Salt, *Film Style & Technology: History and Technology* (London: Starword, 1992 ed.), pp. 212–215, 227–240; Janet Wasko, 'Hollywood and Television in the 1950s: The Roots of Diversification', in Peter Lev, *The Fifties: Transforming the Screen, 1950–1959* (New York: Scribner's, 2003), pp. 127–132. The first television transmission took place in 1928. But the authorisation of national networks did not take place until 1940 and the growth in television sets did not take off until 1945.

78. Staiger, 'The package-unit system', p. 332. For more on these developments, see Tino Balio, *United Artists: The Company That Changed the Film Industry* (Madison, Wisconsin: The University of Wisconsin Press, 1987), pp. 3–160; Schatz, *Boom and Bust*, pp. 285–394; Lev, *The Fifties*, pp. 7–63, 147–168, 197–255.

79. McLaughlin, *Broadway and Hollywood*, pp. 134, 135, 172. It is worth pointing out here that at least one

mid-1940s film, *Laura* (1944), was adapted from the 1943 novel by Vera Caspary, and that Caspary went on to co-script a stage-play version with George Sklar. The play opened on 26 June 1947 at the Cort Theatre in New York City and closed on 2 August later that year. It was produced by H. Clay Blaney, with Otto Kruger as Waldo Lydecker, Hugh Marlowe as Mark McPherson, and K.T. Stevens as Laura. The play was also presented in London in 1945 at the 'Q' Theatre and the St. Martin's Theatre respectively. See the English Theatre Guild Library edition, London, 1952.

80. Lea Jacobs, 'The Paramount Case: The Role of the Distributor', *Journal of the University Film and Video Association*, vol. 35 no. 1 (1983), pp. 44–49; Schatz, *Boom and Bust*, pp. 323–328; Simon N. Whitney, 'Antitrust Policies and the Motion Picture Industry', in Gorham Kindem (ed.), *The American Movie Industry* (Carbondale and Edwardsville: Southern Illinois University Press, 1982), esp. pp. 172–204.

81. Staiger, 'The package-unit system', p. 332. For more on the adult prestige productions, see Christine Geraghty, *Now A Major Motion Picture: Film Adaptations of Literature and Drama* (Lanham: Rowman & Littlefield Publishers, Inc., 2008), pp. 73–102, and Barbara Klinger, *Melodrama and Meaning: History, Culture, and the Films of Douglas Sirk* (Bloomington: Indiana University Press, 1994). For more on the technologies, see John Belton, *Widescreen Cinema* (Cambridge: MA.: Harvard University Press, 1992); David Bordwell, *Poetics of Cinema* (New York: Routledge, 2008), pp. 281–325; Buhler, Neumeyer, Deemer, *Hearing the Movies*, pp. 336–353; Harper Cossar, *Letterboxed: The Evolution of Widescreen Cinema* (Lexington, Kentucky: University Press of Kentucky, 2011), pp. 95–184; Richard W. Haines, *Technicolor Movies: The History of Dye Transfer Printing* (Jefferson, NC. and London: McFarland Company, Inc., 1993), esp. pp. 49–119; Hall and Neale, *Epics, Spectacles and Blockbusters*, pp. 110, 139–155; Lev, *The Fifties*, pp. 107–125; Platte, 'Postwar Hollywood', pp. 64–73; William Paul, 'The Aesthetics of Emergence', *Film History*, vol. 5 no. 3 (1993), pp. 321–355; Salt, *Film Style & Technology*, pp. 241–249; and the '3-D Cinema' edition of *Film History*, vol. 16 no. 3 (2004). Along with the large-gauge, widescreen, and stereophonic sound used for epic films, some of these technologies were also used for *Oklahoma!* (1955), *Carousel* and *The King and I* (both 1956), and *South Pacific* (1958), all of which were adapted from Broadway musicals by Rodgers and Hammerstein. See Geoffrey Block, *Richard Rodgers* (New Haven and London: Yale University Press, 2003), pp. 120–170; Hall and Neale, *Epics, Spectacles and Blockbusters*, pp. 150–153; Ethan Mordden, *Rodgers & Hammerstein* (New York: Harry N. Abrams, Inc., 1992), pp. 17–49, 69–85, 127–147, 106–125, respectively. For an overview of the various forms of impact of television in and on Hollywood, see Tino Balio (ed.), *Hollywood in the Age of Television* (Boston: Unwin Hyman, 1990), esp. pp. 3–256.

82. Film adaptations of live television plays were a feature of the 1950s and early 1960s. Examples include *Marty* (1955), from the 1952 teleplay by Paddy Chayevsky; *Crime in the Streets* (1956) and *12 Angry Men* (1957), from the 1955 and 1954 teleplays by Reginald Rose; and *Requiem for a Heavyweight* and *The Miracle Worker* (both 1962), the former from the 1956 teleplay by Rod Sterling and the latter from the 1957 teleplay by William Gibson.

83. Staiger, 'The package-unit system', p. 332. See also Staiger, 'Individualism versus Collectivism: The Shift to Independent Production', *Screen*, vol. 24 no. 4–5 (1983), pp. 68–79, and Denise Mann, *Hollywood Independents: The Postwar Talent Takeover* (Minneapolis and London: University of Minnesota Press, 2008).

84. McLaughlin, *Broadway and Hollywood*, p. 239.

85. One of the markers of this difference was the appearance in Fort Worth, Texas in 1961 of Charles K. Freeman's stage version of the 1953 film musical *Calamity Jane*, and the appearance on Broadway in 1968 of a stage musical entitled *Promises, Promises*, which was adapted by Neil Simon and Burt Bacharach from the1960 film entitled *The Apartment*. Musical adaptations of Hollywood films old and new are now common, but this was not the case in the 1960s.

Chapter 1

The Squaw Man

The 1914 film version of *The Squaw Man* was based on a four-act play by Edwin Milton Royle. Itself based on a one-act version written by Royle in 1904, the four-act version premiered at the Wallack's Theatre in New York on 23 October 1905 and ran for 222 performances with a cast that included William Faversham as Captain James Wynnegate (later known as Jim Carston), Selene Johnson as Lady Diana, Mabel Morrison as Nat-u-ritch, William S. Hart as Cash Hawkins, Theodore Roberts as Taby-wana, and a number of Ute Indians in minor roles employing 'their own speech and sign language'.[1] The play was roadshown throughout the USA and was performed in London and elsewhere abroad as *The White Man*, at which point it was novelised by Julie Opp Faversham and went on to form the basis of a 1906 burlesque version entitled *The Squawman's Girl of the Golden West.*[2] *The Squaw Man* was revived in the US in 1907, 1908, 1911 and 1921, and provided the basis for *The Kentuckian*, a single-reel film directed by Wallace McCutcheon in 1908,[3] as well as for the 1914 version and its subsequent remakes. Following the plethora of one-reel and two-reel Westerns produced by companies such as Essanay, Kalem, the New York Motion Picture Company, Pathé West Coast and Selig in the period between1909 to 1911, the 1914 version also helped inaugurate a trend toward feature-length Westerns.[4]

The Squaw Man was one of number frontier plays written in the nineteenth and early twentieth century. Among the former were *The Indian Princess, or La Belle Sauvage* (1808) by John Nelson Barker, *The Indian Prophesy* (1827) by George Washington Parke Curtis, *The Lion of the West* (1831) by James Kirke Paulding, *Across the Continent* (1870) by James J. McCloskey, *Davy Crockett* (1872) by Frank Murdock, *The Girl I Left Behind Me* (1893) by David Belasco and Franklyn Fyles, and *The Cowboy and the Lady* (1899) by Clyde Fitch; and among the latter were *The Virginian* (1904), a stage-play adaptation of Owen Wister's 1902 novel, *The Girl of the Golden West* (1905) by Belasco, which went on to form the basis of Puccini's 1910 opera,[5] and *Billy the Kid* (1906) by Walter Woods. While most of the nineteenth century plays came and went, later ones such as T*he Cowboy and the Lady* and *The Girl I Left Behind Me* formed the basis of one-reel film versions in 1903 and 1908 respectively, and feature-length versions in 1915.

The idea of producing a feature-length film version of *The Squaw Man* appears to have been mooted by Jesse L. Lasky and Cecil B. DeMille in 1913. Cecil was the youngest member of a famous theatrical family. His father (Henry C. de Mille) and his elder brother (William de Mille) were both successful playwrights ('de Mille' was the family spelling, but Cecil used 'DeMille' as his professional name), and Cecil also wrote plays and helped manage the family's theatrical agency. While doing so, Cecil cemented a lasting friendship with Lasky, who at this point produced vaudeville shows and stage plays exclusively. But as is noted in the introduction, the prospects for stage plays in 1913 were particularly bleak, and well aware of new film companies such as the Famous Players Motion Picture Company, Arthur Friend, Samuel Goldfish (later Goldwyn), and Lasky and DeMille decided to establish the Jesse L. Lasky Feature Play Company along similar lines. The company was capitalised at $20,000 and *The Squaw Man* was chosen as the basis for its first feature-length film, possibly because some of DeMille's earlier plays, among them *The Stampede* and *The Royal Mounted*, dealt sympathetically with Native American characters and themes.[6]

The Play

The storyline and settings of Royle's play can be summarised as follows. Act One takes place at Maudesly Towers, the English estate of the Earl of Kerhill, which Royle describes as a 'court' that looks out on 'a typical English park'. The house, which is on the left, 'is one of the timber edifices of the sixteenth and seventeenth centuries', and across the back and on the right lie 'the ruins of an abbey of a much older date'.[7] Amidst those present at the mansion there is much talk of noblesse oblige and the forthcoming donation of twenty thousand pounds to charity by the officers of the 16th Lancers. However, amidst the cant and double-dealing that marks the upper classes, it emerges that Henry, the Earl's son and Captain James Wynnegate's brother, has used the money to engage in a swindle on the stock exchange, and on learning that Henry has lost the money, James takes the blame in order to spare Henry's wife Diana, with whom he is in love. Forced to leave England in disgrace, James takes Diana's hand, 'looks lovingly into her eyes', then 'turns away and starts through the park' as the curtain falls.[8]

Act Two takes place two years later in the Long Horn Saloon in Maverick, a cow town on the Union Pacific Railroad in Wyoming. A train has just arrived outside and its observation car is in view through the saloon window.[9] Calling himself Jim Carston, Wynnegate is now a rancher, and some of his hands are in the saloon when he sends them a message advising them to avoid the villainous Cash Hawkins and his henchmen. Tourists from the train enter the saloon as Hawkins joins his men in a plan to swindle cattle from Taby-wana, chief of the Utes. Nat-u-rich, Taby-wana's daughter, appears in the doorway, and as Hawkins plies her father with alcohol she decides to intervene. But at this point Jim enters and prevents Hawkins from molesting Nat-u-ritch, and as Nat-u-ritch leaves with her father, Henry, Diana and Sir John Applegate enter the saloon from the train outside. In order to conceal his presence Jim steps back into the crowd. But as Hawkins makes more trouble, Jim intervenes and is recognised by Diana and the others. Diana and Jim begin to converse. But the train is ready to leave and their conversation is truncated. Jim buries his head in his hands and Nat-u-ritch looks on in sorrow. Then Hawkins re-enters and brandishes his guns, and unbeknown to all those present, he is shot and killed not by Jim, but by Nat-u-ritch, who walks over to Jim, kneels at his side, touches his hand, and simply says 'Me killum'.

For Richard Wattenberg, Act Two articulates 'Jim's descent into the world of western American savagery'.[10] But the limitations of English nobility have already been exposed in Act One, and the dichotomies of savagery and civilisation are further blurred by the presence and the actions of Nat-u-ritch and Taby-wana, who represent 'native savagery' but also occupy their own social space, and who, in the case of Nat-u-ritch, help dispense justice by killing Cash Hawkins, the most uncivilised character in the play.[11] These paradoxes also mark Acts Three and Four. Act Three is set in the dooryard at Jim's ranch, which is The ranch is 'flanked on one side by an adobe stable with a loft for the storage of hay. In front of the stable, and standing some feet back of it is the Carston ranch house'. It is now 'seven years after the killing of Cash Hawkins' and the ranch 'is in a state of partial dilapidation'.[12] A ranch hand called Big Bill is braiding strands of buckskin with young Hal, the son of Carston and Nat-u-ritch, and other hands drift in one by one, most of them worried about the falling price of cattle and the dismal prospects for work and wages. The ranch hands leave and Sheriff Hardy and his deputies arrive and are put up for the night. They are joined by Baco White, an Indian interpreter, then by Taby-wana. It appears that a stranger has been making enquiries as to Jim's whereabouts, and it emerges that Malcolm Petrie, a representative of the Kerhill family, has been searching for Jim, who is the holder to the family title now that Henry is dead. Aware of Diana's faith in him, and recalling the pleasures of England and the Kerhill estate, Jim is elated. But the strains of Native American music and the sounds of Hal calling for his father draw our attention to the entry of Nat-u-ritch, the woman who killed Cash Hawkins, the woman who nursed Jim through a fever following an accident in the snow, and the woman who gave birth to their son. Jim declares that 'I cannot go!' But his mind is changed by Petrie, who persuades him that Hal should have an education befitting his role as the future Earl of Kerhill. Nat-u-ritch is devastated and Hal is confused, and it is at this point that Diana arrives with Applegate and 'takes Hal to her heart'.

The final act takes place in the same setting. It is early morning and Sheriff Hardy is informed that Nat-u-ritch has disappeared. Observed by Taby-wana, Hardy enters the house then exits with a revolver that he is convinced belongs to Nat-u-ritch – and that he is equally convinced was used to kill Cash Hawkins. Jim is informed but insists that 'There are cases, Sheriff, where justice is superior to the law. And a white man's court is a bad place for justice to the Indian. Fortunately for all of us, Nat-u-ritch has disappeared. You couldn't arrest her, Sheriff – not while I live'. Diana enters a few moments later. She wants to know what is meant by the term 'Squaw Man', and on being told, she is sympathetic. But assuming the advantages of an aristocratic upbringing in England, she says that the boy must go 'home with us'. At this point Taby-wana enters and informs Jim that Nat-u-ritch has disappeared. Jim explains that Nat-u-ritch might be arrested for the murder of Hawkins, and as the cowboys arrive with leaving presents for Hal, we catch her watching the proceedings from the loft above. Hal leaves with Diana, and Jim is heartbroken. Nat-u-ritch looks down in sorrow, then re-enters the house and returns with the revolver used to kill Hawkins in her hand. As she does so, she spots Hal's moccasins, picks them up, presses them to her breast, and leaves. Jim enters the farmhouse to rest. But on discovering that the revolver in farmhouse has vanished, he rushes out again. Jim draws his own revolver. But as he does so, we hear the sound of a gunshot off stage. A dramatic pause ensues. Then Taby-wana enters with the body of Nat-u-ritch in his arms. The stage directions indicate that she is holding Hal's moccasins in her hand, and as Taby-wana brings her body to Jim, Diana ensures that Hal cannot see it. 'Poor little mother!' says Jim, and as he repeats these words, the curtain slowly falls.[13]

As John Tibbetts points out, the play tries 'to combine naturalistic concerns (the regional settings in Utah) with the more traditional form of the well made play'.[14] He also notes that 'Royle was determined to put the "real Indian" on the stage', hence the casting 'of at least one authentic Ute Indian to insure the proper dialogue and speech inflection', and hence Royle's sympathy for the native characters alongside his 'satiric jabs' at 'Englishmen and their titles'.[15] Tibbetts also notes the extent to which actions such as Jim's discovery that Hawkins is a cattle rustler, Nat-u-rich's rescue of Jim from a snowbound mountain ravine, and Nat-u-rich's suicide, take place off stage and are therefore reliant on expository dialogue. 'The one moment of real physical action', he writes, 'is the barroom confrontation in Act Two between Wynnegate and Hawkins'.[16]

The Squaw Man (1914)

DeMille was given a day's tuition in film production at the Edison studio in New York, and following the appointment of Oscar Apfel, an experienced director, and Alfred Gondolfini, an experienced cameraman, Dustin Farnum was cast as Jim and Winifred Kingston as Diana. The team set out for Flagstaff, and according to DeMille and subsequent scholars, Apfel and DeMille wrote a scenario for the film version of *The Squaw Man* on the train to Flagstaff in Arizona. The process of adaptation is not recorded. But it is clear that Apfel and DeMille understood that actions and settings were key and that dialogue had to be trimmed to a minimum, and this is reflected in the final thirty-five-page script.[17] On arriving at Flagstaff, the team was disappointed. DeMille was unimpressed by the light and thought that the terrain was insufficiently varied,[18] and Farnum suggested that they go on to Los Angeles, which was close to varied terrain and which was already becoming a major centre for film production. The team arrived there on 20 December1913,[19] and L. L. Burns and Harry Revier agreed to lease their studio at the corner of Selma Avenue and Vine Street for $250 dollars a month. They also agreed to enlarge its facilities, build a second stage, and develop and tint and tone a negative and positive print.[20] At this point 'DeMille and Apfel settled down to a preproduction schedule that lasted all of seven days'.[21] Red Wing, a Winnebago Indian whose native name was 'Ah-Hoo-Sooch-Winga' and who had already appeared in a number of Westerns, was assigned the role of Nat-u-Ritch. (The 'r' was capitalised in both the titles and the credits). Joseph Singleton was assigned the role of Tabywana (without the hyphen) and Billy Elmer the role of Cash Hawkins. And Monroe Salisbury, Dick La Reno, Monroe Salisbury, Fred Montagu and a girl called Carmen (who was billed as Baby DeRou) were assigned the roles of Henry, Bill, Petrie and Hal respectively.

As Richard S. Birchard points out, the 'extent of DeMille's involvement with the direction of the picture is unclear. A photograph taken on the first day of shooting clearly shows Oscar Apfel directing, while DeMille stands with the other members of the company offstage. Surviving prints give the credit "Produced by Oscar C. Apfel and Cecil B. DeMillle" (the word "producer" meant director in 1914), but the main titles are from an early reissue ... It would be another three months after the completion of *The Squaw Man* before DeMille had a solo outing as a director'.[22] Shooting began at a manor house in the West Adams district, which stood in for Maudesly Towers. The first title announces that 'Henry, Earl of Kerhill, and his cousin, Capt. James Wynnegate, are made trustees for the Orphan Fund of the 16th Lancers', and is followed by a medium long shot of upper-class men around a table and another standing at the back with a number of servants. The man at the back delivers the news about the fund and everyone applauds, and at this point the storyline deviates from the play by cutting to Diane, Henry and their friends at a racetrack. It transpires that Henry has bet on a loser, and markedly shaken, he writes out an IOU. The IOU is signed by James (henceforth Jim) as well, and from this point on Jim's immediate fate is sealed.

Back at Maudesly Towers, Henry is anxious about the IOU. He is also concerned about the friendship between Jim and Diana, and a shot encompassing all of three of them serves to lay out the narrative tensions. Henry's misdemeanours become apparent to Diana and her mother, and noblesse oblige (which here consists of deceit and lies) dictates that Jim assume Henry's guilt. Jim packs his suitcase and Diana invites Jim to kiss her goodbye. Gallantly refusing to do so, Jim leaves, and the final shots of this sequence begin with Henry at his desk surrounded by family members and members of the fund. Henry 'discovers' the cheque and exclaims that his signature his been forged by Jim. A servant is sent to Jim's room. But Jim is nowhere to be found, and at this point we cut to a title informing us that 'Jim Engages Passage to America'. In the play, Jim leaves in disgrace at the end of Act One and we next encounter him as a rancher in a saloon in Wyoming two years later. This is a startling juxtaposition, and is marked by contrasts of all sorts. But in the film we are presented with a number of intervening segments (most of them framed and edited in the style of alternation established in the film's initial scenes), and these segments serve to cement the bond between Jim and his mother (who draws money from a bank to help him pay his passage to the USA) and to establish Jim's love of children (he befriends a young girl and her mother as they set sail on a schooner). They also underline Jim's courage and physical prowess when he captures a detective who is trailing him for embezzling the fund, and when he subsequently helps the girl, her mother, the detective and the crew to abandon ship following an outbreak of fire. Some of these events appear to lack completion in the DVD version. But Jim and the others are 'Picked By An American Bound Vessel' and we cut to a series of shots (all of them taken at sea and most of them framed in long-shot) as they are all duly rescued.

Now 'Safe in New York', Jim is shown in a hotel room unpacking his suitcase. We cut to an exterior long shot of 42nd Street (probably a stock shot) then on to a rooftop restaurant where Jim (who knows a thing or two about thefts and swindles) 'Saves Big Bill From The Light Fingered Gentry' when a couple in the foreground try to steal Bill's money. The couple are asked to leave, and Bill joins Jim at the latter's table. 'Come Out West, Where Folks Keep Their Hands in Their Pockets', says Bill, and as they cement their friendship with another hand-shake, a title informs us that 'Jim Arrives At Maverick', and we cut to the interior of the saloon in Wyoming some time later. The layout of the saloon is clearly based on the set in Act Two of the play. The only real difference is that the locomotive in the film is not stationary, but instead draws up in rapid motion on the tracks outside. What follows though is by no means confined to the saloon interior, and from here we cut back and forth between a medium long-shot of Jim in his cabin and a group shot of Bill conversing with his friends in the saloon. A title introduces Tabywana and Nat-U-Ritch, and we cut to an exterior shot of on the plains some time later. Tabywana is seated on the right near a pair of horses, and as Jim and Bill and another cowboy approach on horseback, Nat-U-Ritch stands and gazes at Jim (figure 1). Gondolfini struggles to keep them all in frame. But it is clear that Nat-U-Ritch is interested in Jim, and this is further evident when the cowboys bed down for the night, when Nat-U-Ritch lights a match to get a clearer look at Jim's sleeping face (figure 2), and when she walks over to watch Jim and the others ride off the following morning.

Jim and his men are on their way to the Lone Butte ranch, which Jim is keen to buy. We witness the sale and cut to a shot of a number of cowboys. One of the cowboys takes a drink and is chastised by Jim for doing so, and this establishes a motif that is picked up later on. In the meantime, a title announces that 'Diana's Health Requires a Change of Scene', and we cut to Henry, Diana and Applegate at the Kerhill Mansion perusing a map of Wyoming, then on to Wyoming itself, where Nat-U-Ritch invites Jim to dance with her and others of her tribe. None of these events are present in the play, and as well as contrasting life at the Mansion with the outdoor life at the ranch and the equally outdoor life and customs of the Indians (however inauthentic they may be), this segment serves yet again to underline Nat-U-Ritch's feelings for Jim. Jim's cattle are rustled by Cash Hawkins and his henchmen. But Jim and his men intervene and the rustlers disperse, and from here we cut to Diana, who is now in the observation car at the back of a train. Diana gazes at the scenery and is joined by Applegate and Henry, and at this point we cut to Hawkins, who underlines that swindles are not confined to aristocrats as he plies Tabywana with alcohol in order to get him to sign away his cattle. Tabywana refuses. But Cash continues to tempt him, and leads him towards the saloon. Nat-u-Ritch tries to stop him, and is encouraged to do so by Bill, who arrives with a number of other cow hands. Cutting to an interior

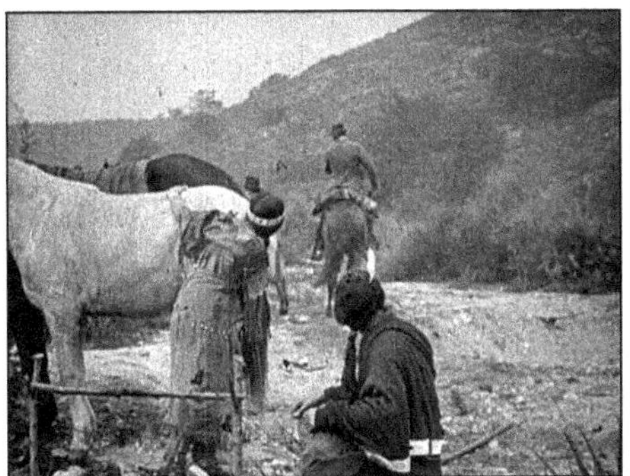

Figure 1

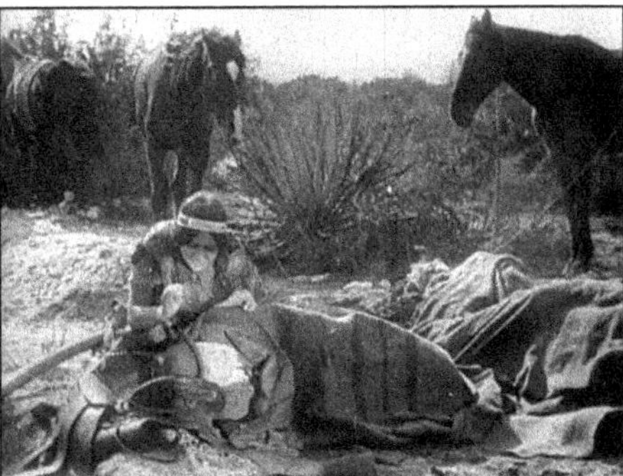

Figure 2

view of the saloon, Bill and his men group themselves on the right as Cash approaches the bar on the left. Cash draws his pistols and threatens Bill and his men. But Bill and his men refuse to be provoked, and we cut back to a drunken Tabywana, who stumbles into the saloon.

Suspense ensues as we cut away from the saloon and onto a shot of Jim in the stockyard completing the sale of his cattle. Then we cut back to the saloon. Cash and Tabywana are next to the bar and Nat-u-Ritch tries to intervene. In an echo of the earlier scene involving cowboys and alcohol, Jim throws Tabywana's drink away. Tabywana falls over in a drunken stupor, Nat-u-Ritch tries to help him, and Cash tries to grab her. Jim intervenes, Nat-u-Ritch leaves with Tabywana, and Cash leaves the barroom. From here we cut to Henry, Diana and Applegate gazing at the landscape from the train. A fire on the line not only seeks to provide spectacle (and to echo the fire on the boat en route to America), but to motivate a return to the saloon as we cut back and forth between the train, the saloon interior, and Cash outside with one of his henchmen. As Diana and the others enter the saloon, Jim tries to hide. But he is forced to reveal his presence when Cash returns, shoots bullets into the air, and tries to goad Henry and Applegate by demanding that they participate in an anti-English toast. Jim relieves Cash him of his guns. But he uses the presence of Henry to declare that 'I

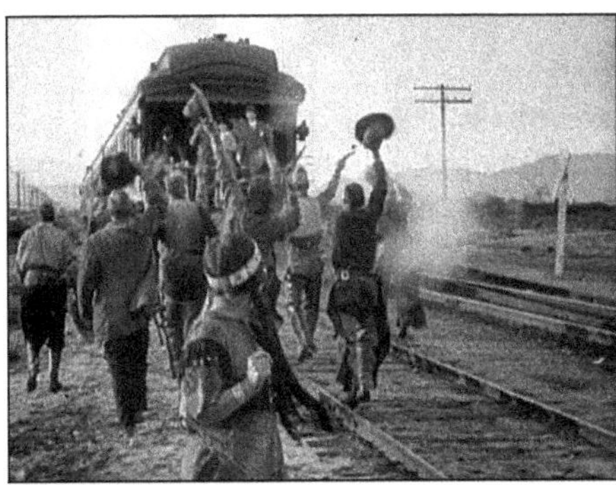

Figure 3

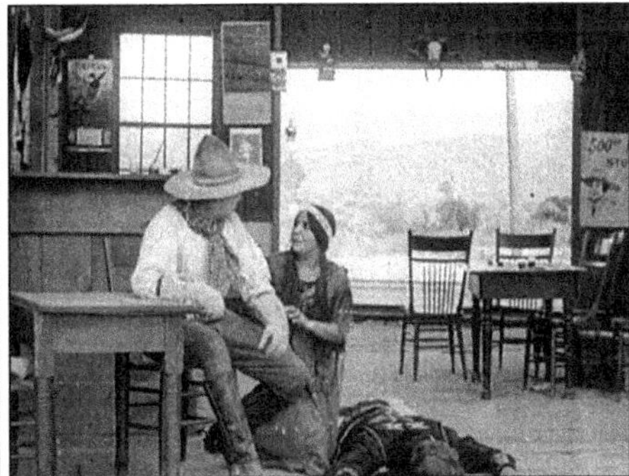

Figure 4

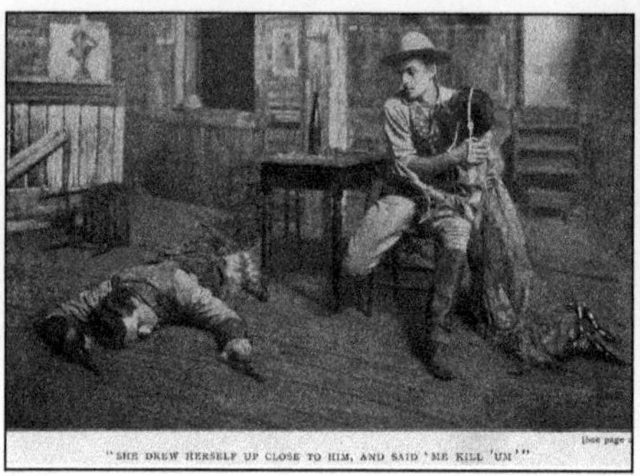
"SHE DREW HERSELF UP CLOSE TO HIM, AND SAID 'ME KILL 'UM'"

Figure 5

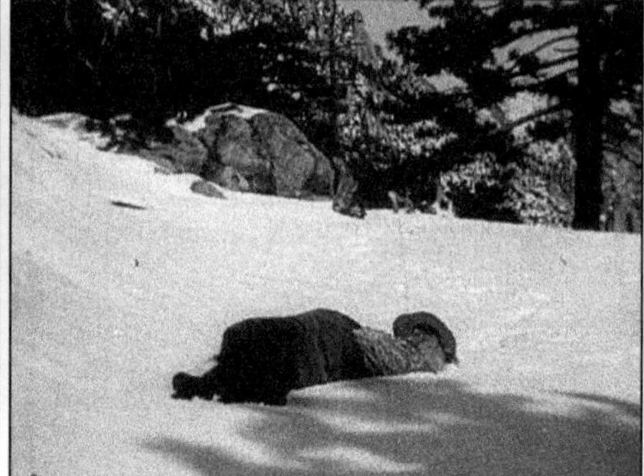

Figure 6

won't drink with a man who robbed the Orphans of the King's Soldiers', and as the passengers re-embark on the train, Jim kisses Diana's hand and bids her a reluctant farewell. And when we cut to Diana and the others in the observation car as they wave goodbye, Nat-u-Ritch takes the opportunity to take a look at the woman with whom Jim is clearly still in love (figure 3).

Cash takes a pair of pistols from one of his henchman as the mutual antipathy between Cash and Jim begins to reach its climax. In response to Jim's crestfallen demeanour, Nat-U-Ritch enters, shakes her head in sorrow, walks into an adjacent stockroom and pulls out a gun and inadvertently drops her purse. Cash fires his pistols into the air and Jim pulls his pistol from holster in response. But before Jim is able to fire, Cash is shot and killed. Men rush into the bar and the local sheriff tries to determine the source of the shot. Jim is the obvious culprit. But a close up of Jim's revolver reveals that none of his bullets have been fired, and it is at this point that we cut to Nat-U-Ritch, who tiptoes into the saloon and hides beneath a table as the bartender enters the stockroom and picks up her purse. The men in the saloon depart, leaving Nat-U-Ritch and Jim on their own. 'Me Kill Um' says Nat-U-Ritch, and Jim responds by putting his hand over her mouth in a bid to signal secrecy (figures 4 and 5. The former is a frame still and the latter is one of a number of illustrations of moments in the stage play that were published in the novel. Both underline the extent to which the action on stage and screen involves freezing the action and posing in tableau as the characters and spectators alike contemplate the significance of the situation).

Six months have passed since the death of Cash Hawkins. Jim is living at his ranch and is still in love with Diana, whom he pictures in superimposition as he looks at an illustration in a newspaper. With the exception of the night scene in the rooftop restaurant, the lighting and visual design in *The Squaw Man* has not been particularly striking, and while the outdoor sequences provide a variety of shot scales, framings and angles, the default framing, even in exteriors, tends to be the head-on medium long-shot, with one or more characters positioned in mid-ground or foreground strung across the frame. However the sequences that follow seek to rectify this, and largely succeed in doing so. Thus while Jim is pondering his feelings for Diana, light

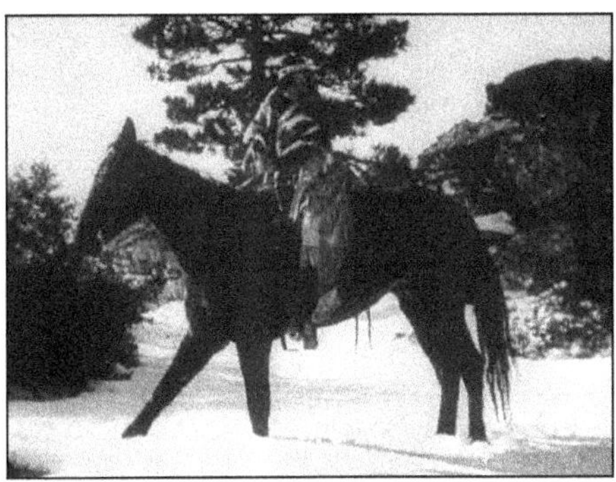

Figure 7

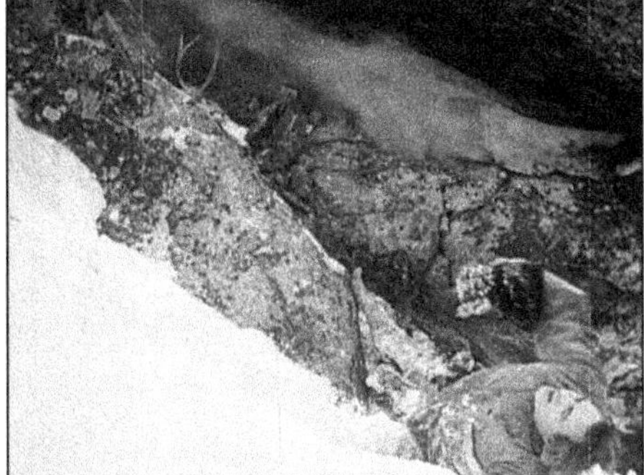

Figure 8

from a fire on the left provides a degree of chiaroscuro, a style of lighting that complements his melancholy feelings. And hence the sequence that follows, which takes place in a mountainous snow-bound landscape and which is only reported verbally in the play, and which makes full use not only of the terrain, but of the contrasts between dark human figures and horses and white snowy spaces; clumps of trees and a sulphurous mountaintop; shot-scales that range from close-up to long shot; and diagonal as well as head-on staging and framings as Jim becomes lost and snow blind, and as Nat-U-Ritch finds and rescues him (figures 6–9). There are over thirty shots in this sequence, in which Jim is not just rescued, but helped by Nat-U-Ritch and her people, and in which Nat-U-Ritch's love for Jim is further underlined as she alone manages not only to rescue him, but to bring him home safely. While in recovery, Jim hides Nat-U-Ritch's pistol, and although he tries to persuade her to leave, Nat-U-Ritch re-enters and kneels by his side as he embraces her in firelight (figure 10).

'Several Months Later' Jim and Nat-U-Rich are in the yard outside the ranch house. A tiny moccasin in Nat-U-Rich's hand signals that she is pregnant, and Jim rides off to find the Justice of the Peace in order to marry them. Initially reluctant to wed a white man and an Indian, the Justice of the Peace is unsure what to do. But Bill and the other ranch hands 'persuade' him to so, and we next see Hal, the couple's son, playing on horseback. Time has clearly passed, but a number of issues have yet to be resolved. Thus when we cut to the bartender with Nat-U-Ritch's purse, on to Bill and his men teaching Hal to use a lasso, and on to Henry dying in a mountain-climbing accident, the film continues along a path established by the play even as it adds new incidents and scenes.

We are now nearing the film's denouement. The sheriff pursues Cash Hawkins' killer, Tabywana rides off to warn Nat-U-Ritch, and Diana and her party enter the saloon, thereby mounting a threat to Nat-U-Ritch from two distinct directions: from Diana and England on the one hand, and from the sheriff and law on the other. Jim meanwhile is broke. Lacking the wherewithal to pay his men, he offers them his rifle and a much-prized medal, and at this point Tabywana enters and warns Jim that the

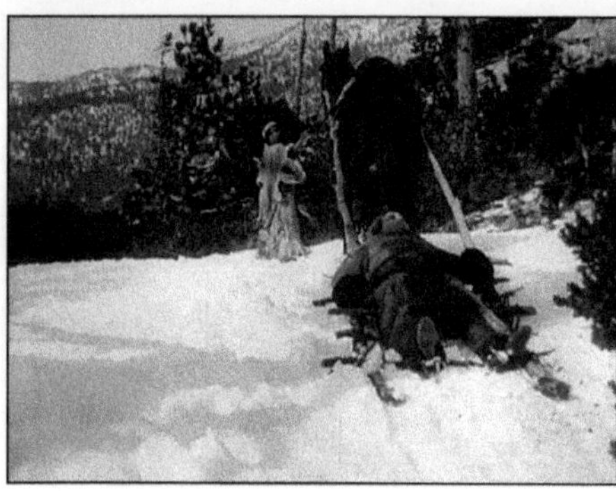

Figure 9

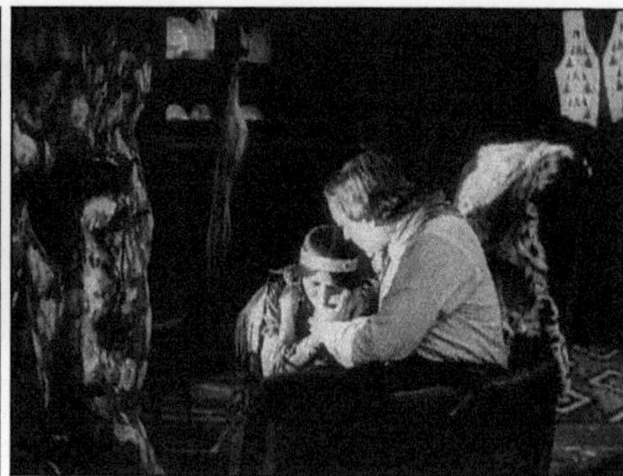

Figure 10

sheriff is after Nat-U-Ritch. As Tabyawana rides off, a spokesman for the Kerhill estate rides in and tells Jim to 'Come Home ... You Are Now the Earl of Kerhill'. Jim is torn between life with his wife and son in Wyoming and the pleasures of Maudesly Towers and England, and this is represented in a split-screen image showing Jim on the right hand side of the frame and images of an English regiment on horseback on the left. Nat-U-Ritch enters and Jim gestures to explain that Hal is 'The Future Earl Of Kerhill' and should go home to England, and we cut back and forth between Hal's Christian prayers in an otherwise Native American bedroom and the incantations of Nat-U-Ritch in the landscape at dusk (figures 11 and 12).

Diana arrives the following morning and takes Hal to her heart, and the sheriff discovers Nat-U-Ritch's pistol. Tabywana attacks the sheriff but is restrained by Bill, who steals the pistol and puts it back in hiding. The sheriff and his deputy depart. But the truth is out and Tabywana threatens to wage war on behalf his daughter. Diana discovers that Jim is the father of Hal and that Nat-U-Ritch is his mother. Diana is shocked but soon takes Hal to her heart. Jim and his men ride off to protect Nat-U-Ritch, and Nat-U-Rich comes out of hiding now that everyone has gone. We cut to Tabywana and his braves, then on to a room in the ranch house some time later as Diana, Bill, Jim and the others prepare for Hal's departure. Bill and his men give

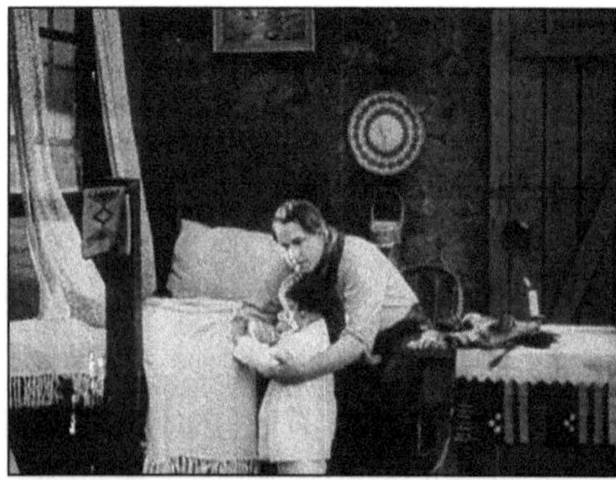

Figure 11

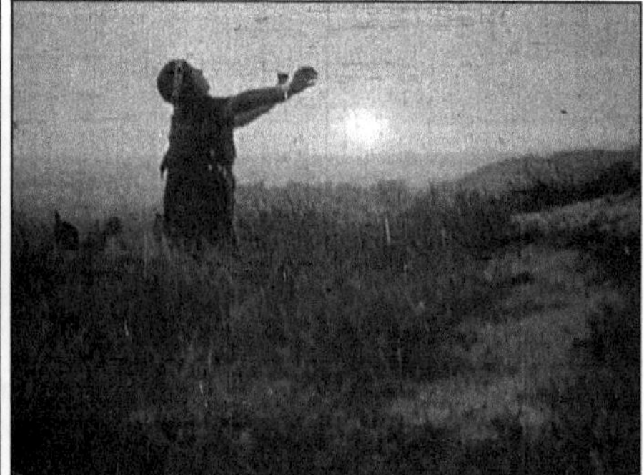

Figure 12

presents to Hal and we cut to Nat-U-Ritch, who is looking on in close-up. Diana and her entourage depart, and Nat-U-Ritch walks in tip-toe past Jim, who is now in tears in the foreground. Nat-U-Ritch enters the house in order to retrieve her pistol, takes her purse from the bench on which Jim is sitting head-in-hand, and leaves. Cutting back and forth between various groups of characters, the action culminates in two distinct settings: the yard outside the ranch house, and a space in the landscape near the stockyard in which Nat-U-Ritch is on her knees in prayer. Tabyana appears in the distance and rides toward his daughter as we cut to Jim in the ranch house interior. Jim discovers that the pistol is gone and takes out a gun from a holster nearby. We cut back to Nat-U-Rich kneeling in the foreground and Tabywana on his horse in the background, then onto to Jim, who is now in the yard brandishing his gun, and who threatens to shoot the sheriff and his men in order to defend his wife. But the next shot shows that Nat-U-Ritch has killed herself, and Tabywana rides in with his daughter's body, joining all those present at the yard. Jim cradles her body in his arms as he sits on the bench in the foreground. Diana puts her hand over Hal's eyes, and following the film's final title – 'Poor Little Mother' – we return to a final tableau, a tableau that lays out the racial logic of Jim's imminent return to England now that Nat-U-Ritch is dead.

Production was completed on or around the end of January 1914. One of the two sets of negatives was damaged and the perforations on the positive print had to be realigned. But the problems with the print were rectified and a copy of the film was trade shown in New York to potential state-rights buyers on February 17, 1914. As noted in the introduction to this book, the state-rights system was based on theatrical precedents. It involved franchising properties on an exclusive basis in specific states and territories and meant that franchisees could tour or rent copies to different towns and cities within them. In this way franchisees paid for a print of the film, publicised its availability, and made or lost money on ticket sales. This was a well-established system, and in the case of *The Squaw Man* it proved lucrative for franchisees and exhibitors and for Lasky and his colleagues alike: discounting the $20,000 spent on the rights to film the play, production and post-production costs amounted to $15,450.25, and the net producers' profits eventually totalled $244,700.[23]

The Squaw Man (1918 and 1931)

As is noted in the introduction, DeMille went on to direct film versions of *The Virginian* (1914) and *The Girl of the Golden West* (1915), both of which were based on plays or stage-play adaptations. He also directed two further versions of *The Squaw Man*, one in 1918 and the other in 1931. The final reel of six is all that survives of the 1918 version, but according to the AFI Catalog, there were few changes in the plot line. The 1931 version survives intact and was produced amidst a major cycle of early sound Westerns, among them *In Old Arizona* (1929), *The Big Trail* (1930) and *Cimarron* (1931). The 1931 version starred Warner Baxter as James Wyngate (later known as Jim Carsten), Eleanor Boardman as Lady Diana, Charles Bickford as Cash Hawkins, and Lupe Valez as Naturich (the spellings of Wyngate, Carsten and

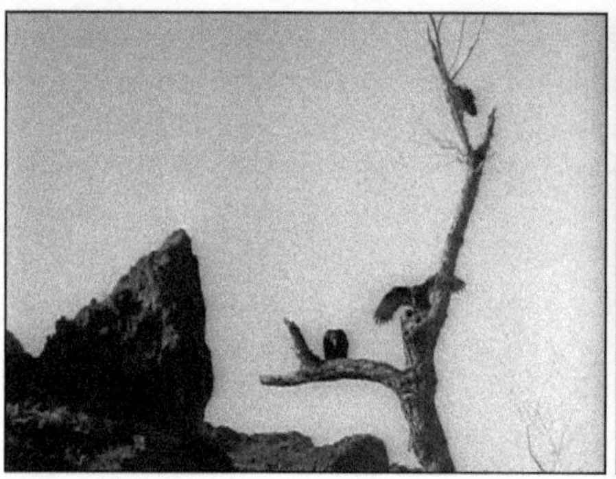
Figure 13

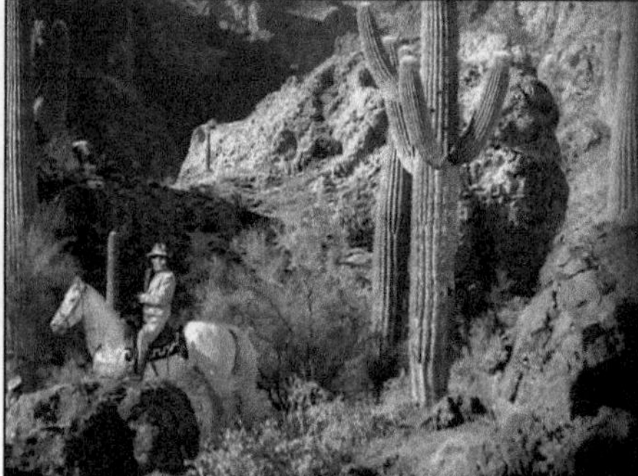
Figure 14

Naturich differ from those in the play and the 1914 version). The opening scene takes place in a railway carriage, in which it is revealed that Henry and an accomplice have been embezzling money from the Lancers fund, and this is followed by the scene at Maudesly Towers, which takes place at a party at night. During the course of the party Jim learns of Henry's swindle, and because he is in love with Diana, he takes the blame when she catches up with him in an open limousine later that night.

Omitting the journey to the US and the purchase of the ranch and cattle, we cut to the Arizona landscape, which is marked not only by bright light, but by buzzards and other markers of the primitive Western setting (the very obverse of Maudesley Towers and limousines) (figure 13). Cash and his men arrive at Jim's ranch, hoping to buy it, but Jim says that the ranch is not for sale, and it is this that exacerbates the tension between them. Shortly thereafter Tabywana and Naturich go to town in order to purchase goods from the trading post, and Cash heads for the saloon while Jim heads for the back room, where he tries to drown his sorrows with alcohol while poring over photographs of Diana and Henry in a magazine. In this condition Jim is vulnerable to the machinations of Cash Hawkins, who is still keen to purloin his property, but Naturich, who is already intrigued by Jim, kills Hawkins and follows Jim across a landscape that is now marked by the grandeur of Arizona's scenery (figures 14–15).

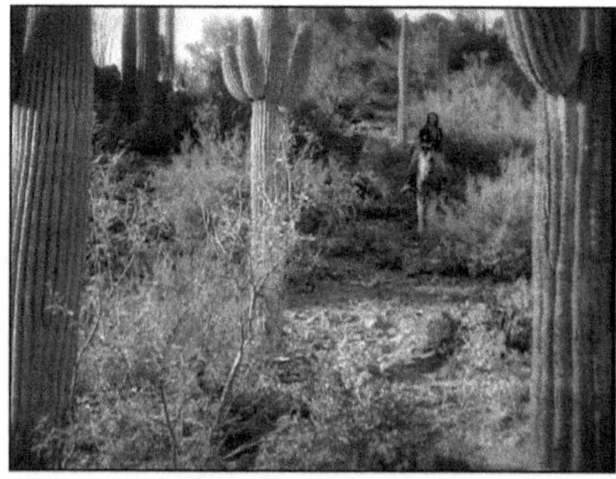
Figure 15

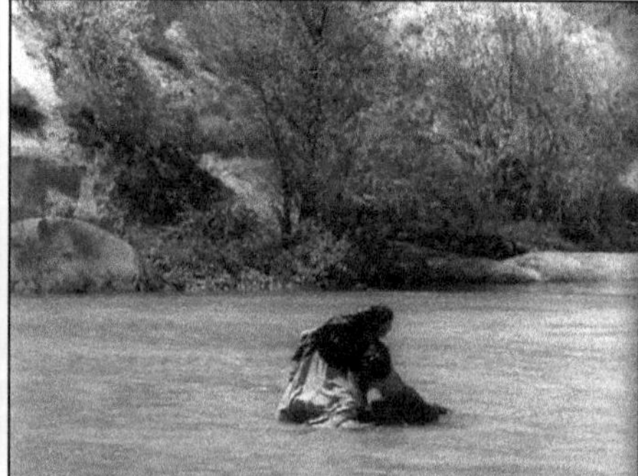
Figure 16

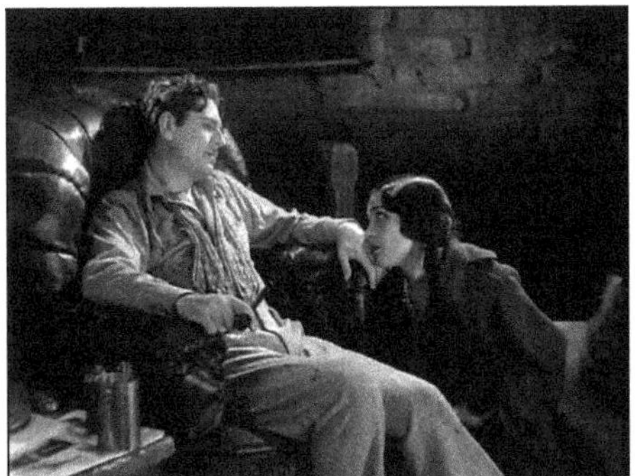

Figure 17

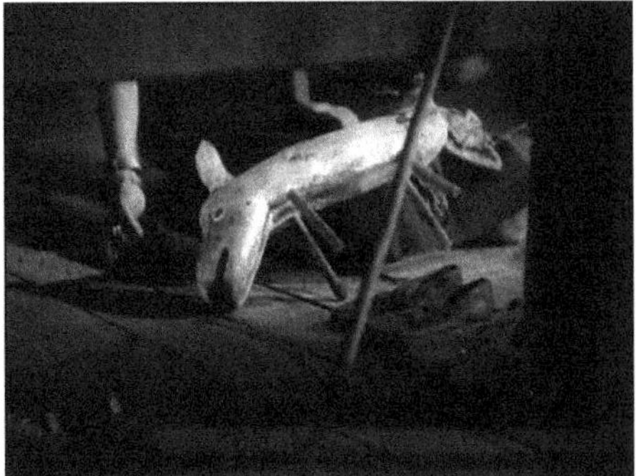

Figure 18

Naturich tells Jim that she killed Hawkins and Jim tells her to leave and not to tell anyone, and the remainder of the scene turns into a variant of the snow-bound sequence in the 1914 version as Jim is shot and wounded and as Naturich rescues him from a nearby river (figure 16). Jim is nursed by Naturich. But although he tells her leave, she returns in the rain one night, and their love for one another is palpable (figure 17). Back in England, Henry is killed in a fox hunt, and Diana and Sir John Applegate Kerhill go to America to find Jim. Sir John and Diana are driven to Jim's ranch and discover that Jim has married a squaw and that he has a child named Little Hal (Dickie Moore). Jim is told that he is now regarded a hero, but although he is invited to return to England, he refuses to leave Naturich, and reluctantly agrees to let Sir John (Roland Young) and Diana take Hal to boarding school in England. Naturich is heartbroken, and the sheriff and his men now have proof that it was her gun that killed Cash Hawkins. Naturich kills herself, and as her body is clasped by Jim, the camera moves down to focus on the wooden horse that she had made for Hal's birthday (figure 18) – and that contrasts with the modern train set given him by the white US cowhands earlier on.

Notes

1. Burns Mantle and Garrison P. Sherwood (eds.), *The Best Plays of 1899–1909 and the Year Book of Drama in America* (New York: Dodd, Mead and Company, 1944), p. 208, and Gerald Bordman, *American Theatre: A Chronicle of Comedy and Drama, 1869–1914* (Oxford and New York: Oxford University Press, 1994), p. 563, who wrote that 'Faversham's performance was a high-water mark in his career', 'displaying "fine emotional power and straight strokes of sincerity direct from the heart"'. As Mantle and Sherwood note, Royle regarded comedy as his forte, and the dramatic and melodramatic aspects of *The Squaw Man* were therefore something of a departure. According to the AFI Catalog of Feature Films (henceforth AFI Catalog), a version of *The Squaw Man* was released on 9 May 1906. But this version, which was presumably no more than a reel in length, is now lost.

2. Julie Opp Faversham, *The Squaw Man* (New York: Grosset & Dunlap, 1906); Richard Wattenberg, *Early Twentieth-Century Frontier Dramas on Broadway: Situating the Western Experience in Performing Arts* (New York: Palgrave Macmillan, 2011), p. 141.

3. David Mayer, *Stagestruck Filmmaker* (Iowa City: Iowa University Press, 2009), p. 278, Mantle and Sherwood (eds.), *The Best Plays of 1899–1909 and the Year Book of Drama in America*, p. 208.

4. Andrew Brodie Smith, *Shooting Cowboys and Indians: Silent Western Films, American Culture, and the Birth of Hollywood* (Boulder: University Press of Colorado, 2003), pp. 37–156. See also Richard Abel, *Americanizing the Movies and 'Movie-Mad' Audiences, 1910–1914* (Berkeley and Los Angeles: University of California Press, 2006), pp. 61–82 and 105–123, *The Red Rooster Scare: Making Cinema American, 1900–1919* (Berkeley and Los Angeles: University of California Press, 1999), pp. 151–175, and 'The "Imagined Community" of the Western', in Keil and Stamp (eds.), *American Cinema's Transitional Era: Audiences, Institutions, Practices*, pp. 131–137. And see also, Robert Anderson, 'The Role of the Western Film Genre in Industry Competition, 1907–1911', *Journal of the University Film Association*, vol. 31 no. 2, 1979, pp. 19–26; Bowser, *The Transformation of Cinema, 1907–1915*, pp. 169–177; Scott Simmon, *The Invention of the Western Film: A Cultural History of the Genre's First Half-Century* (Cambridge and New York: Cambridge University Press, 2003), pp. 3–97.

5. Rosemary Katherine Bank, 'Rhetorical, Dramatic, Theatrical, and Social Contexts of Selected American Frontier Plays, 1871 to 1906', Phd. dissertation, University of Iowa, 1972, and 'Staging the "Native": Making History in American Theatre Culture, 1828–1838', *Theatre Journal*, vol. 45 no. 4 (1993), pp. 461–486; Roger A. Hall, *Performing the American Frontier, 1870–1906* (Cambridge: Cambridge University Press, 2001); Stuart Wallace Hyde, 'The Representation of the West in American Drama from 1849 to 1917', Phd. dissertation, Stanford, 1954; Eugene H. Jones, *Native Americans as Shown on Stage, 1753–1916* (Lanham, MD.: Scarecrow Press, 1990); Wattenberg, *Early-Twentieth-Century Frontier Dramas on Broadway*.

6. Simon Louvish, *Cecil B. DeMille and the Golden Calf* (London: Faber and Faber, 2007) p. 61. For Zukor and Famous Players, see Quinn, 'Paramount and Early Feature Distribution', pp. 98–133; Tibbetts, *The American Theatrical Film*, pp. 57–58, 64–70. For the formation of the Jessie L. Lasky Feature Play Company, see Robert S. Birchard, *Cecil B. DeMille's Hollywood* (Lexington: University Press of Kentucky, 2004), pp. 1–4; William C. deMille, *Hollywood Saga* (New York: E.P. Dutton, 1939), pp. 35–43; Scott Eyman, *Empire of Dreams: The Epic Life of Cecil B. DeMille* (New York: Simon & Shuster, 2010), pp. 50–57; Tibbets, *The American Theatrical Film*, pp. 77–78. See also Gevinson, 'The Birth of the American Feature Film', pp. 132–155; Hampton, *History of the American Film Industry from its Beginnings to 1931*, pp. 101–145; David Turconi, 'From Stage to Screen: Notes for a five-year history of Famous Players Film Company, Jesse L. Lasky Feature Film Company and Triangle Film Corporation between 1912 and 1917', in Usai and Codelli, *Sulla via di Hollywood*, pp. 16–131.

7. Quoted from the 1906 edition of the play, and cited in Wattenberg, *Early-Twentieth-Century Frontier Dramas on Broadway*, p. 143. As Wattenberg goes on to note on page 154, Act One may well have undergone revision in order to 'smooth out some of the rough melodramatic edges and to make James Wynnegate even more clearly a heroic paragon of civilization'.

8. Mantle and Sherwood, *The Best Plays of 1899–1909*, p. 219.

9. Mantle and Sherwood, *The Best Plays of 1899–1909*, p. 220.

10. Wattenberg, *Early-Twentieth-Century Frontier Dramas on Broadway*, p. 147.

11. Wattenberg, *Early-Twentieth-Century Frontier Dramas on Broadway*, p. 147.

12. Mantle and Sherwood, *The Best Plays of 1899–1909*, pp. 229–230.

13. As Eyman notes in *Empire of Dreams*, p. 57, there is more than a hint of *Madame Butterfly* at the end of Royle's play.

14. Tibbetts, *The American Theatrical Film*, p. 156.

15. Tibbetts, *The American Theatrical Film*, p 156.

16. Tibbetts, *The American Theatrical Film*, p. 156.

17. Louvish, *Cecil B. DeMille and the Golden Calf*, p. 60. According to Tibbetts, *The American Theatrical Film*, pp. 156–157, Royle helped to prepare the script, and went on to note the extent to which the film's situations were 'told better by actions than words' and that its double-exposure juxtapositions, which were 'next to impossible' on the stage, 'were particularly effective in the film'. These comments were published in the *Moving Picture World*, 21 February 1914, p. 930, shortly after the trade show in New York. They appear to be the only ones to note that Royle contributed to the script. DeMille's scenario can be found in Box 1 of The Cecil B. DeMille Archives, L. Tom Perry Special Collections, Brigham Young University. It comprises a 35-page document that contains five-to-fifteen word descriptions of each of its 284 shots, and that renders its inter-titles in quotation marks. My thanks go to James Dark for his help.

18. Eyman, *Empire of Dreams*, p. 59. For DeMille's account of the formation of the Lasky Feature Play Company and the production of *The Squaw Man*, see *The Autobiography of Cecil B. DeMille* (Englewood Cliffs, New Jersey: Prentice-Hall, 1959), pp. 68–89.

19. According to Eyman, *Empire of Dreams*, p. 63, by '1913, there were over forty companies operating in Los Angeles county, most of them seasonally, and with one other crucial proviso – nearly all of them were making shorts [one or two-reel films] for the Motion Picture Patents Company'.

20. Birchard, *Cecil B. DeMille's Hollywood*, p. 6; Eyman , *Empire of Dreams*, pp. 61–62. It should be noted that the print used for the DVD is neither toned nor tinted.

21. Birchard, *Cecil B. DeMille's Hollywood*, pp. 6–7.

22. Birchard, *Cecil B. DeMille's Hollywood*, p. 8. The title credits on the print used for the DVD specify that the film was 'Picturized by Cecil B. DeMille and Oscar C. Apfel'. Apfel began his career as a producer and director of plays. He joined the Edison Manufacturing Company in 1911 and directed, among others, *The Heir Apparent* and *The Passer-By* (both1912). He left Edison for Reliance-Majestic later that year then moved on to Lasky in 1913, Fox in 1914, and Paralta and the World Film Corporation in the late 1910s. Following a lack of success with the films he directed in the 1920s he became a successful character actor. He died of a heart attack on 21 March 1938.

23. Birchard, *Cecil B. DeMille's Hollywood*, pp. 9–13; DeMille, *The Autobiography of Cecil B. DeMille*, pp. 87–94; Eyman, *Empire of Dreams*, pp. 71–76. According to Donald J. Stubblebine, *Cinema Sheet Music: A Comprehensive Listing of Published Film Music from The Squaw Man (1914) to Batman (1989)* (Jefferson, N.C.: McFarland & Company, 1991), pp. 336–337, a piece of music entitled 'Nat-u-ritch, An Indian Idyll' was written by Theadore Bendix and published by J. W. Stern & Co. in 1914. The extent to which this music was played during screenings of *The Squaw Man* is impossible to discern.

Chapter 2

The Poor Little Rich Girl

In 1912, Eleanor Gates published a novel entitled *The Poor Little Rich Girl* and went on to write a stage-play version. The play was produced by Arthur Hopkins and premiered on 21January 1913 at the Hudson Theatre in New York, with Viola Dana as Gwendolyn, Laura Nelson Hall and Boyd Nolan as Gwendolyn's parents, Howard Hall as the Doctor, Frank Currier as the Organ-Grinder, William S. Lyon as the Plumber, and Gladys Fairbanks as Miss Royle and Grace Griswold as Jane.[1] It eventually ran for 160 performances and was considered a success, and Gates became recognised as one of a number of female playwrights in the US in the early 1900s and 1910s,[2] as well as the author of the novel version of *The Poor Little Rich Girl* and *The Biography of a Prairie Girl* (1902) and *Good-night* (*Beunas Noches*) (1907). *Good-night* was illustrated by Arthur Rackham, whose work was marked by a combination of Art Nouveau devices and angular and sinuous lines, and some of these ingredients are evident in the costumes and settings in Act Two of *The Poor Little Rich Girl.* Also evident in *The Poor Little Rich Girl* were the devices associated with the plays of Maurice Maetterlink, especially *L'Oiseau Bleu* (*The Blue Bird*), which was first produced in 1908, and which exemplified aspects of nineteenth and early twentieth century Symbolism.[3] However, Gates used these devices for her own didactic purposes, notably to underline the power of adults and the powerlessness of children, and this is highlighted in Carole L. Cole's unpublished Phd. dissertation on women playwrights in the 1910s and 1920s.[4]

The Play

Act One of *The Poor Little Rich Girl* takes place in the reception hall of a lavish house owned by the parents of a young girl named Gwendolyn. The hall is decorated with fountains, flowers, arches and ornate patterns, with a view of woods outside and a lift on the inside alongside a coat-of-arms, a motto and a staircase. As the curtain rises, a group of teachers amuse themselves by trying out various dances and are interrupted by the entry of a female music teacher. The music teacher 'makes a warning gesture' as a butler named Potter enters and asks as to the whereabouts of Gwendolyn (The Poor Little Rich Girl). Although the teachers are employed to educate and care for Gwendolyn, and although it is Gwendolyn's birthday, they simply shrug their shoulders, and a governess named Miss Royle enters, invites them for tea, and describes them as 'a most competent and obliging staff of teachers'. A nurse named Jane enters, berates Miss Royle for having been cooped up with Gwendolyn all afternoon, and suggests taking Gwendolyn out for a car ride. Miss Royle bemoans the fact that a lady such as herself has become a mere employee, and goes on to say that although Gwendolyn can have 'everything her heart can desire ... she isn't even grateful'. Gwendolyn enters with Thomas the footman, who carries Gwendolyn's Teddy bear. Gwendolyn says that she intends to ask her parents to let her go to day-school, and her teachers respond with consternation, fearing that they will no longer be provided with guaranteed employment and the freedom they have been afforded hitherto. They also insist that Gwendolyn should go for a drive with her carers as usual, and when she expresses a wish to visit her father's office instead, Jane tries to put her off by declaring that her father's office is 'full of bears'.

Gwendolyn is driven away and Potter discovers a leak in the ceiling and calls a plumber. Gwendolyn's mother is planning a dinner to coincide with her daughter's birthday later that evening and Miss Royle assures Gwendolyn's mother that her daughter has had 'a pleasant birthday' thus far. At this point Gwendolyn's father arrives home from work. He is worried about his business affairs, but is pleased to hear that the Doctor who delivered Gwendolyn will be at Gwendolyn's birthday. Miss Royle and Jane vie for the chance to have the evening off and Gwendolyn is left alone with her Teddy bear. Gwendolyn hears the sound of a hand-organ outside and invites the Organ-Grinder in as Jane plans to administer 'sleepin' medicine' in order to ensure that Gwendolyn will be asleep and therefore off her hands 'till mornin''. Gwendolyn introduces her Teddy bear to the Organ-Grinder, and the plumber arrives and joins in the conversation and they all dance together, at which point Jane intervenes and orders Thomas and the Organ-Grinder to leave.

The Doctor arrives and Jane enters from the dining-room pulling Gwendolyn by the hand. Gwendolyn expresses her hatred of doctors, but the Doctor tells her that he advocates 'fresh air, exercise, plain food, good earth, and warm sun' and is thus no threat. Jane checks that Thomas has bought the sedative for Gwendolyn and leaves, and the party guests discuss the fact that Gwendolyn's father appears to be 'burning his candles at both ends' as a consequence of his financial dealings. Gwendolyn's mother enters, greets her guests, and calls for Gwendolyn's birthday cake to be brought in. Gwendolyn asks to sit with the grown-ups, but her mother insists that she must eat her cake elsewhere. Gwendolyn's father reiterates his financial concerns, and Gwendolyn tries to comfort him. But as she does so, Jane enters and forces Gwendolyn to take a teaspoon of the 'medicine', and as the medicine takes effect, thunder and wind drown Gwendolyn's voice. The hall has now 'melted away to a deep glade in the forest. The fireplace is a rocky cave; the staircase, a cascade; the couch, a mossy stone; the elevator, a large, gnarled tree; while the long velvet curtains are slender trees, through which the river is seen, shining under a great moon'. Gwendolyn looks in wonderment, then dips her hand into the stream and 'runs, leaping through the glade, swishing her hair in joyous abandon' as the curtain falls.

Act Two Scene One is entitled 'The Tell-Tale Forest'. 'The curtain rises on the open forest glade. Now it is seen that the great gnarled tree is the Face Shop. There are noses on display; eyes, too; also foreheads, cheeks, and chins. The rocky cave is the Bear's Den. And the cascade is a stream of Soda Water, which ends in a pool. Winding up beside the stream, goes a steep path. Gwendolyn is dancing, but somewhat wearily, to the fairy-like music which the Organ-Grinder plays on his hand-organ. The light in the glade is dim, and weirdly blue'. Gwendolyn is tired and unsure where she is, and the Organ-Grinder tells her that she is in the 'Tell-Tale Forest', 'a wonderful place' in which 'No matter what a person pretends to be, the moment he enters these woods, he changes', and they go together to 'the Face Shop'. The Organ-Grinder tells Gwendolyn that 'things will improve', that she must find her parents, and that she 'must get rid of those servants'. Jane tries but fails to wake her, a Policeman enters and Gwendolyn tells him that Jane is 'two-faced', and Miss Royle appears in the guise of a snake. The Policeman says that he takes 'little girls and boys ... to their fathers and mothers' and Gwendolyn is heartened. She embraces the Bear and begins to mend its stuffing as the Doctor enters and calls for fresh air.

Jane tries to hide the medicine, but the Doctor notices. Jane and Thomas claim that they 'don't know a thing' about the medicine and the Policeman investigates. Gwendolyn says that the Bear is in need of repair, and the Doctor calls for Gwendolyn's father, who enters and kneels in front her daughter. But Gwendolyn does not recognise her father and the Doctor is concerned. Gwendolyn's mother enters, but Gwendolyn does not recognise her either, and Jane and Thomas try to wrest Gwendolyn away. But Gwendolyn resists and asks the Doctor to get rid of the car in which she has so often been confined. The Doctor duly does so, feels the Bear's pulse, and declares that the Bear is now 'as good as new'. He encourages Gwendolyn to drink water and a change is soon apparent. Jane tries to intervene. But the Doctor intervenes in turn and puts his arm around Gwendolyn in order to protect her. He lifts her in his arms and they climb the steep path together. The Organ-Grinder follows, and behind him come 'the Bear, the Plummer, and the Policeman', all of them allies in the fight to overcome the effect of the drug foisted on Gwendolyn by her so-called carers.

Act Two Scene Two begins in 'rolling gray mist. The music of the Organ-Grinder now sounds far-away, and hauntingly mysterious. Then a faint glimmer appears at one side, lighting up the faces of' the Dinner Guests. Hushes and whispers are intoned as they wonder whether Gwendolyn will recover. The Organ-Grinder, the Policeman, the Plumber, and the Bear rally round and Gwendolyn's father arrives. Gwendolyn's father claims that he is too busy to help. But the Doctor urges her father to speak to her before it is too late, then the Doctor administers salt and Gwendolyn revives. All those who love her are overjoyed, and a Broker tells Gwendolyn's father that although he has neglected his daughter she is now beginning to recover.

Act Two Scene Three is entitled 'Robin Hood's Barn'. 'The strains of the hand-organ are full of tender longing' and behind them a semi-circle of trees 'suddenly show countless fruit-like globes of light'. Gwendolyn's enemies appear but are driven away by the Plumber, and Gwendolyn, the Doctor and Gwendolyn's father emerge from the woods at last. A Little Bird reveals that Jane was responsible for the overdose of medicine and is thrown into a rubbish-can. Gwendolyn's father announces that Jane will never trouble Gwendolyn again and Gwendolyn's mother enters. Miss Royle enters hissing like a snake and makes a final bid to block their plans. But the Bear, the Doctor, and Gwendolyn's parents thwart her, and Gwendolyn finally pulls through.

Act Three takes place in Gwendolyn's nursery. 'The curtain rises on what seems to be Robin Hood's Barn. For there, ranged in a semi-circle, are the trees with the fruit-like globes of light. But now the trees are very small' and among them is a single, larger light 'burning on a bed-side table'. The trees fade away then reappear as the dado on a wall. The contours of a bed appear, and between 'the bed and the door is a couch', which is scattered with toys, a dictionary, and the merry-go-round that Gwendolyn's father bought her. A doctor's bag, a hypodermic case, a glass of colourless liquid and a spoon are visible on a nearby dressing table. 'Three silent figures' are waiting by the bed, and on the bed is the figure of Gwendolyn. Light floods in as the Doctor draws the curtains, and 'the anxious faces' of Gwendolyn's parents can be seen as Gwendolyn shows signs of consciousness and begins to recover. Gwendolyn's parents are overjoyed, speak gently to their daughter, and express their gratitude to the Doctor as Gwendolyn opens her eyes at last. Gwendolyn asks why her mother is crying and the Doctor explains that she is happy. Gwendolyn says she is hungry and when Gwendolyn's father passes her two toy ducks and a snake, she throws them away. The Doctor returns her Teddy Bear, and Potter enters and is overjoyed when the Doctor says that Gwendolyn's temperature is now back to normal. Gwendolyn's father promises that her teachers will never bother her any more, and that she can go to day-school when she fully recovers.

'The music of a hand-organ is heard in the distance' and Gwendolyn waves to the Organ-Grinder. Then the Broker enters and Gwendolyn's father tells him that 'Some of us have to face death before we learn what is really precious in life'. The Broker understands and leaves, and the Doctor enters and writes a prescription specifying that Gwendolyn should gather flowers, ride a pony, chase butterflies with the help of a dog, make mud pies, climb hills and go barefoot. The Doctor leaves and Gwendolyn's mother plans a trip to the country with her daughter. Gwendolyn's father says that 'We're going to be happy, the three of us' and draws the curtain in order to allow Gwendolyn to sleep. Gwendolyn asks her mother to sing to her, and as 'the orchestra takes up the melody, the back of the nursery becomes transparent. Through it ... can be seen a grassy, wooden slope, and Father with a fishing pole; Mother in a simple out-door dress'; Potter carrying a hamper; Johnnie Blake wearing overalls; and Gwendolyn, with Rover the dog at her side.

The Poor Little Rich Girl (1917)

Although *The Poor Little Rich Girl* was a financial success, many other plays lost money that year on account of the gathering impact of feature-length films, and during the next few years many stage performers migrated to the screen and became film stars, among them Dustin Farnum, Helen Gardner, Lillian Gish, William S. Hart, Douglas Fairbanks, Norma Talmadge, Clara Kimball Young and Mary Pickford. Shortly thereafter, in 1917, Pickford demonstrated her fame and bargaining power by signing for Famous Players (soon to become Famous Players-Lasky), and by becoming a partner in the Mary Pickford Corporation. A distribution company called Artcraft Pictures was established to sell her films to movie theatres on an individual basis rather than in groups or blocks, and Pickford thus 'became the first star to become a producer of her own pictures and to win a considerable control over her work'.[5] Well aware of her image, Pickford chose *The Poor Little Rich Girl* as the basis for her second Artcraft production and assigned Maurice Tourneur to direct, following their collaboration on *The Pride of the Clan*, which was released on 7 January 1917.

It is not known whether Gates was consulted during the planning and shooting of *The Poor Little Rich Girl.* Like many other female stars and writers in the early 1910s, she was reported as organising a feature-film company as a vehicle 'for her books, plays, and stories'.[6] But although some of her novels were later adapted for the screen, among them *The Plow Woman* (1917) and *Cupid, the Cowpuncher* (1920), *The Poor Little Rich Girl* seems to be the only Gates play to have formed the basis of a film (and its much-altered 1935 remake).[7] In adapting the play, the 1917 version was influenced not only by Pickford but by Frances Marion, who wrote the scenario, dialogue and inter-titles, and who, in tandem with Pickford, made alterations during production and postproduction, the latter in response to a reportedly disastrous in-house preview screening. According to Cari Beauchamp these alterations were designed to re-establish Pickford's impish child-like tomboy persona, which had not figured in her recent films, and to lighten the tone in some of the reels prior to those that depict Gwen's illness, which Pickford and Marion considered too sombre.[8] But whatever the case may be, the final version was released on 5 March 1917, and Tourneur's direction and Pickford's performance were praised in *Variety*, *Moving Picture World* and *Exhibitor's Trade Review.*[9]

At this point in his career, Tourneur was both prolific and experienced. Born in France in 1876, he worked as a graphic designer and magazine illustrator, then as a performer in the theatre. In 1911, he began his career in the French film industry as an assistant director for Éclair, and in 1914 he began work at the Éclair studios in Fort Lee, New Jersey.[10] A major fire at the studio broke out shortly thereafter, but Éclair erected a new fireproof factory, built a larger studio, and assigned the role of producer-director to Tourneur.[11] When war broke out in Europe, Éclair transferred ownership of the

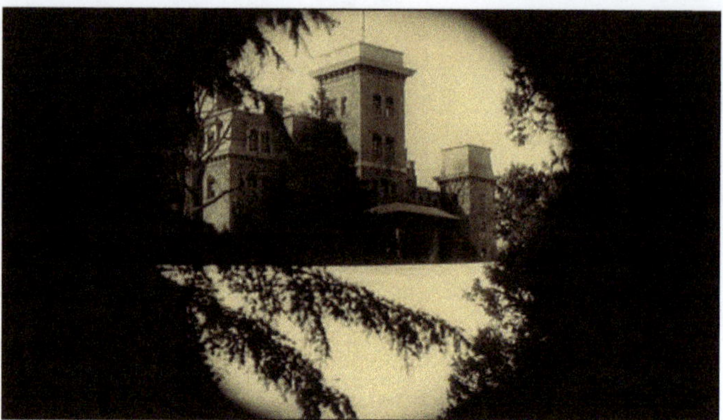
Figure 1

new facilities to World Pictures, and it was here, at Fort Lee, that Tourneur went on to direct feature-length films for Éclair-Brady World, then for the Equitable-World Film Corporation, Peerless, and Paragon-World and Paragon Films.[12] In 1917, Tourneur was hired to direct *The Undying Flame*, *The Exile* and *The Law and the Land* for Lasky-Paramount, and as noted above, Pickford assigned Tourneur to direct *The Pride of the Clan* and *The Poor Little Rich Girl.* By then Tourneur had honed a distinctive style that favoured deep staging, de-dramatised scenes, layered mises-en-scènes, contre-jour lighting, and proscenium arches, all of which are evident in *The Poor Little Rich Girl*, and all of which were enhanced by Ben Carré's production design and Lucien Andriot and John van den Broek's cinematography.[13]

Drawing on the Art Nouveau trappings that Gates details in her play script, an ornate credit shot follows and is followed in turn by the first of Marion's titles, which tells us that 'In the Home of Everything – except the Love she longed for, dwelt Gwendolyn, the Poor Little Rich Girl'. We cut to the film's first shot, which frames the family mansion in sunlight in the background and two large trees in the foreground, and which provides a naturally-lit version of Tourneur's contre-jour lighting patterns (figure 1). A title introduces 'Mary Pickford as Gwen, The Poor Little Rich Girl', and we cut to a deeply-staged shot of the mansion's hallway, which frames two

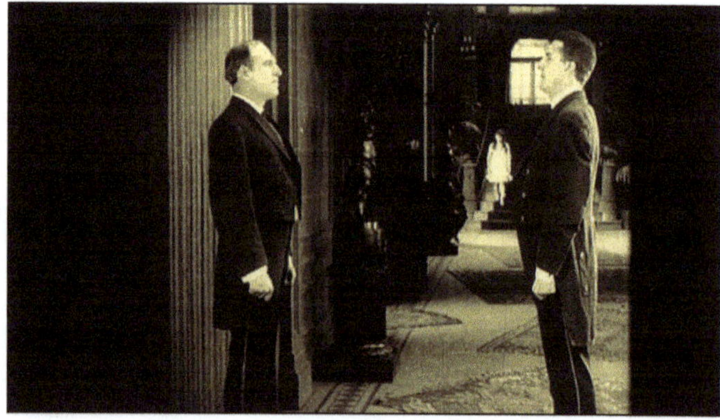
Figure 2

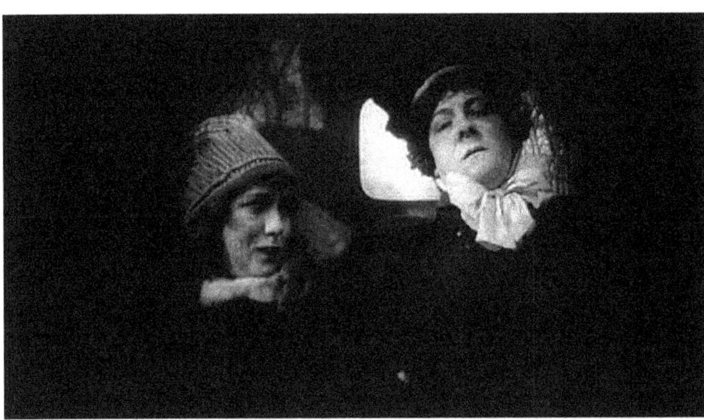

Figure 3

tall stationary male servants in the foreground right and left and the diminutive figure of Gwen on the distant staircase in the background (figure 2), thus stressing the former's power and the latter's powerlessness, and thus contrasting the static and rigid servants with the lively and playful Gwen. Gwen skips forward and addresses each of the servants in turn. But on getting no response she turns and exits, and we cut to a shot of Gwen looking through a window, then onto a point of view shot of children skating in whirling circles in the snow below. Gwen waves and calls out to the children, but another servant enters the frame and pulls the shade down, and we cut to a title that introduces 'The poor little rich girl's father, whose money making schemes left little time for tenderness'. Gwen enters her father's room, hoping to attract his attention, but her father (Charles Wellesley) is too preoccupied with his fellow businessmen to notice her and she slips out quietly on tip toe.

A title identifies servants as 'The Tyrants of Modern Civilization' and we cut to a shot of the servants snaking their way through one of the rooms. Then we cut to Gwen's mother (Madeline Traverse), 'whose social duties seem more important than the happiness of her child'. Gwen hopes to spend time with her mother. But her mother says that she is busy and that 'we'll have a little chat to-morrow', leaving Gwen with her in-house teachers, whose 'grim wisdom' is dispensed on a daily basis 'at the stroke of Ten'. Here a condensed and altered version of the opening portion of the play's first act is played out in a large school room, complete with homilies from Miss Royale (Marcia Harris) and old-fashioned dance steps provided by the music master. When Gwen decides that 'A school room of my own is too big and lonesome' and refers to her forthcoming birthday, it is clear that the film version has altered the narrative chronology, postponing the date of Gwen's birthday by a day. But as in the play, Jane (Gladys Fairbanks) insists that Gwen be taken for a car ride, and Gwen's unhappiness is marked by the restrictive nature of the car's interior space (figure 3).

Back at the mansion, a title summarises Gwen's unhappiness as she plays on her own in long shot, her lonesome condition and diminutive stature underlined by the size of her room, and her loneliness is further underlined by repeated shots of Gwen looking wistfully out of the window framed in tandem with a bird in a cage. However, the arrival of a Plumber to fix the faucet (Frank McGlynn Sr.) and the entry of a group of children and an Organ Grinder (Emile La Croix) in the street below leads on to a scene of music and dancing. This scene replicates events in the second half of the play's first act as Gwen persuades and pays the Organ Grinder to play a tune, as the Plumber joins in by using his hose as a musical instrument, and as Gwen dances with a young boy named Johnny Blake (George Gernon). However the servants hear the noise and the music, and they chase everyone away as Gwen's mother and her wealthy female companion enter.

At this point the film version deviates not only from the play, but from the initial script used by Tourneur, and the following sequences build on the musical scene just described, giving free range to the impish nature of Gwen's character and to Pickford's performance skills. The first sequence begins with Gwen confessing that she let the musicians in because she was lonely. Gwen's mother is sympathetic, and her female friend says that her daughter, Susie May (Maxine Elliott Hicks), would make a 'charming companion for Gwendolyn', and that she will bring her to Gwen's birthday party the following day. Gwen is delighted. But when the two girls meet they do not get on, and when Susie May boasts that her house is better than Gwen's and that Susie May's father is richer than Gwen's, Gwen retaliates by evoking scary bears (another of the play's animal motifs), and by getting Susie May to sit on a cake in the lavish gazebo in which the party takes place. On being chastised, Gwen rushes upstairs to her room and flings items of expensive clothing into the street, and having cut to the street children gathering up the clothes outside, the scene ends with Gwen dancing with joy and chasing Susie May round the now-wrecked room as the servants try to restore order (figure 4). The second sequence occurs shortly after. Gwen is forced to wear the suit that her father wore as a child, and while her mother and father are amused, Gwen is unhappy and tearful. But once her parents and the servants leave, Gwen takes another look at herself in the full-length mirror, decides that she cuts a dash, and puts on her hat and leaves. Inside the gazebo, the family's gardener is tidying up, and outside in the street a group of boys are playing baseball. One of the boys hits the ball through the gazebo window. But given that 'It's the poor little rich girl's house', the boys 'take a chance' and enter the gazebo to retrieve it, at which point Gwen enters in her suit and announces that 'My name is Gwendolyn and I'm a boy'. The boys laugh at her, prompting a mud fight, and the fight is only terminated when the gardener re-enters and hoses the boys and Gwen in turn, to which Gwen responds by saying that 'Now you've spoiled the best fight I ever had'.

It is at this point that we return to the storylines involving the plight of Gwen's father, Gwen's sedation, and the hallucinations to which the latter gives rise. A title informs us that Gwen's father 'is caught up in the collapse of the market and faces his life's crisis' and we cut to her father in despair. Gwen looks down at a photograph of her father and asks Miss Royale to take her to her father's office tomorrow. But Miss Royale responds by saying that 'I wouldn't go there, if I were you. It's full of bears', and leaves in tandem with Jane as we cut to a superimposed shot of Gwen's father, who is literally and figuratively overwhelmed by people in bear costumes (figure 5).

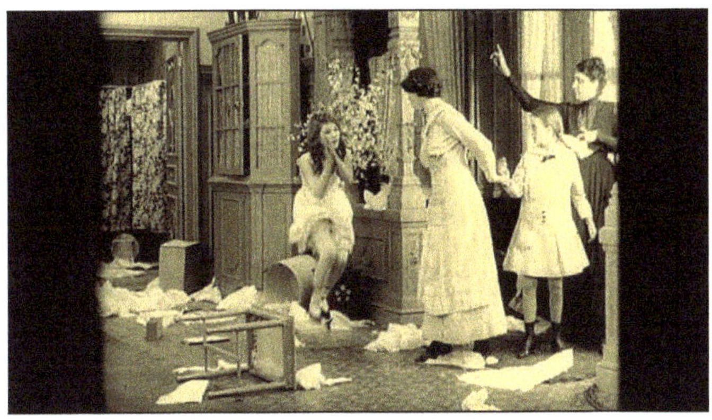

Figure 4

This is the first but by no means the last time that superimpositions and animal costumes feature in the film. But before moving on to the scenes depicting Gwen's fears and hallucinations, we return to the narrative thread concerning her father's financial crisis, and Gwen's plea for her father's love as Miss Royale takes Gwen to bed. The events the following morning are marked by another comic interpolation, this one involving the aforementioned faulty tap and the playful spraying of water in the bathroom. But in addition to an interpolated shot of a stylised snake (figure 6), which is prompted by Gwen's hearing Miss Royale's use of the phrase 'snake in the grass', the key events are those that involve the Doctor (Herbert Prior), who reminds Gwen that 'It was me who showed the stork where to bring you'; Thomas (Charles Craig), who purchases a drug in order to sedate Gwen and ensure a night off; and Jane, who here unwittingly rather than deliberately administers a double dose when Gwen is in bed while her parents and their guests are toasting her health on the occasion of her birthday.

The drug takes hold and Gwen wanders the corridor and the staircase, her delirious state conveyed by wavering hand-held camera shots as the Plumber, here to finalise the fixing of the broken tap, finds her lying at the foot of the stairs as a title informs

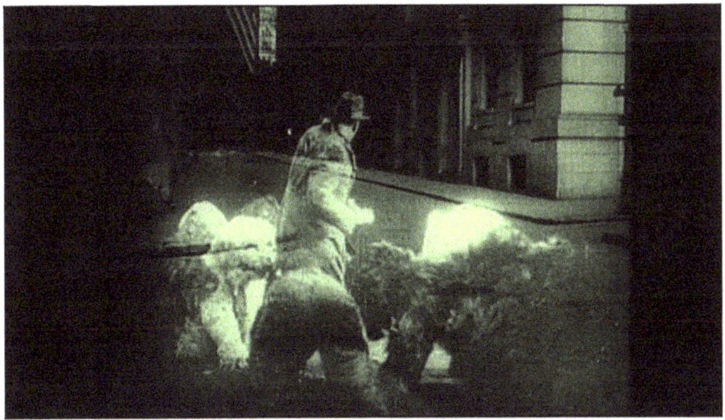

Figure 5

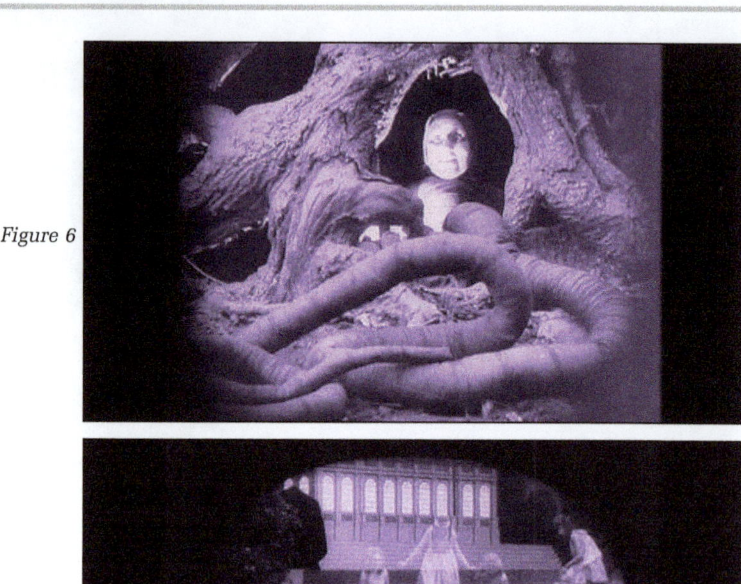

Figure 6

Figure 7

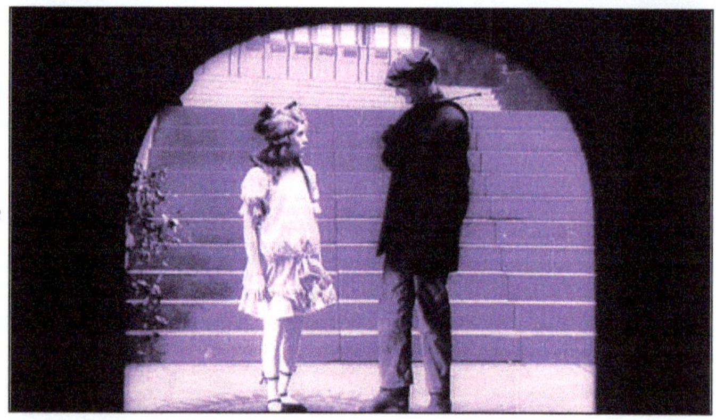

Figure 8

us that 'The Child's Mind Wanders. Real voices come and go whilst every character in her actual life is borne into her delirium'. This title inaugurates a lengthy sequence of alternation as the Plumber tries to revive Gwen and as Gwen's body is surrounded by superimposed female dancers (figure 7), then on to the Plumber, Organ-Grinder and Gwen in various fanciful settings, most of them framed by Tourneur's trademark arches (figures 8–9). We cut back and forth between these images and the real Gwen

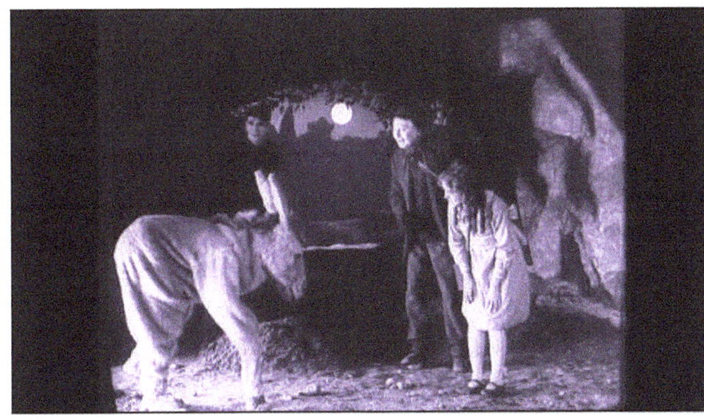

Figure 9

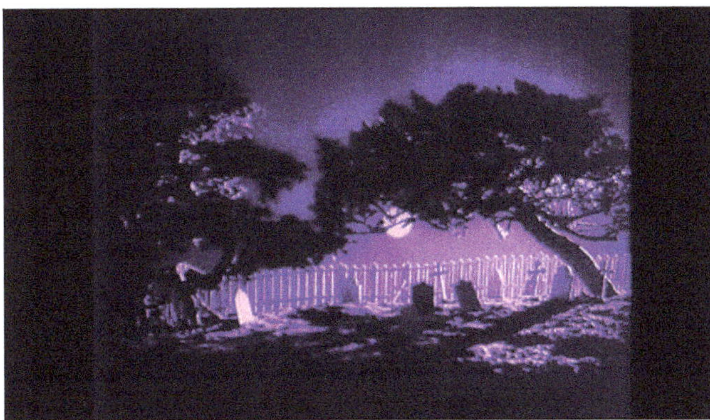

Figure 10

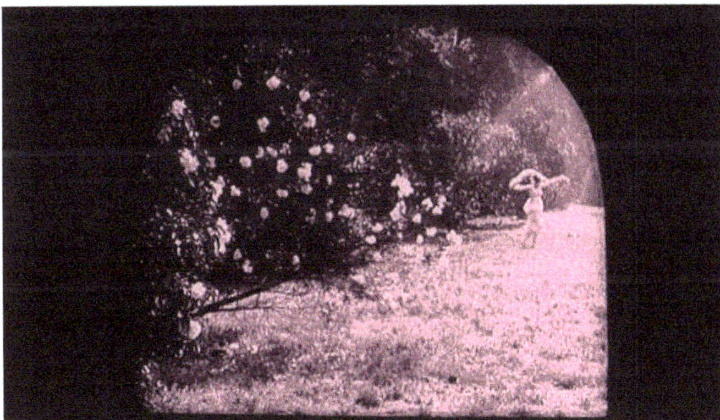

Figure 11

and her parents and her doctor, and the latter's anxieties are articulated in a sequence involving a graveyard at night (figure 10). But this sequence is finally displaced by a daylight shot of a female dancer in the open air (figure 11), and it is evident that the Doctor's medicine has finally taken hold and that Gwen begins to revive, and this is marked by images of Gwen and her parents outside 'The Old Home of Light and Life and Love'. Then Gwen finally wakes up ('Oh, Doctor!' she says. 'You brought me back') and her Father tells his broker that 'We have been fighting Death itself, and have learned what is truly precious. There is enough left for the life we are going to lead'. The Doctor writes a prescription that reads as follows: 'Start tomorrow for the country. Take some gingham dresses and a bottle of iodine for blackberry scratches, go barefoot, and make mud pies'. Then as Gwen falls asleep in her mother's arms next to her father, the Doctor pulls the curtain that acts as a final wipe and the 1917 version of *The Poor Little Rich Girl* comes to an end.[14]

Poor Little Rich Girl (1936)

According to the AFI Catalog, the Fox Film Corporation acquired the motion picture rights to Gates' play for $20,000 and paid an additional $20,000 to the Pickford Company prior to the merger between Fox and Twentieth Century Pictures. The merger took place on 31 May 1935, with Nicholas Schenck as Chairman and Chief Executive Officer, Sidney Kent as President, and Darryl F. Zanuck as Vice-President in Charge of Production, and by then Shirley Temple had forged an extraordinary career, first at Educational Pictures, then at Fox, where she featured in *Stand Up and Cheer! Little Miss Marker, Now I'll Tell, Baby Take a Bow, Now and Forever*, and *Bright Eyes* (all 1934), and in *The Little Colonel* and *Our Little Girl* (both 1935) prior to the production of a musical remake of *The Poor Little Rich Girl* as *Poor Little Rich Girl.* This version was produced by B.G. (Buddy) DeSylva; directed by Irving Cummings; scripted by Sam Hellman, Gladys Lehman and Harry Tugend; photographed by John Seitz, with art direction by William Darling, Rudolph Sternad and Thomas Little; music by Louis Silvers and Cyril Mockridge; dances staged by Jack Haskell and Ralph Cooper; and, with the exception of 'Ride a Cock Horse', the songs were written Mack Gordon and Harry Revel.[15] In a memo to DeSylva dated 6 August 1935, Zanuck noted that *Poor Little Rich Girl* 'is a great box-office title' and went on to state that 'I don't think anybody in the present generation remembers anything about the old play other than it had to do with a wealthy girl who was sad. Therefore, I think we could take any liberties we wanted and write an entirely new story – something that is a light, bubbling musical comedy with plenty of opportunity for Shirley to sing and dance and do clever pieces of business ... We should take a very funny story, a plot that has definite comedy situations, and probably adapt one of the adult parts to fit Shirley'. According to this and other correspondence, Ralph Spence, a prolific writer of film scenarios and scripts, books for musicals, and dialogue, lyrics and sketches for the *Ziegfeld Follies* and *Earl Carroll's Vanities*, wrote the scene in which Temple appears in the Warner Bros. film *Stand Up and Cheer!* (1934). Temple stole the picture, so Gertrud Livingston, Spence's secretary, wrote a twenty-page outline for a radio programme as vehicle for her. Spence developed and completed the story, which was now entitled 'Betsy Takes the Air', but did not submit it to Fox on account of personal differences with Winfield Sheehan, one of the company's production heads. However, with the subsequent merger between Fox and Twentieth Century Pictures now complete, Spence learned that the company was looking for a musical and sold the rights to 'Betsy Takes the Air' for $5000. (The film itself went on to earn $1.4 million in domestic rentals).[16]

Temple's persona and performance skills were in evidence throughout the 1935 version. (We do not know whether Temple ever viewed the 1917 version, so we do not know whether she drew on the upbeat and fearless aspects of Pickford's performance). This version is at its closest to the play and the 1917 film in two of its early scenes and sequences. In what is now an Art Deco rather than Art Nouveau mansion interior, the diminutive Barbara Barry (Shirley Temple) is cared for by three servants, Collins (Sarah Hayden), Stebbins (Charles Coleman), and Woodward (Jane Darwell). Although Collins (the closest to Jane in the play and the 1917 version) is a little pernickety, the other two are warm and caring (Woodward is the very obverse of Miss Royle and Miss Royal), and Barbara is clearly happy despite the absence of her father Richard (Michael Whalen), who works in the city, who finds the time to demonstrate his love for her in a number of ways (unlike Gwen's father in the play and the 1917 version), and who, as we soon find out, is busy inspecting chorus girls for an advertising exhibition. On discovering that Barbara has a chill, Richard rushes home, and Woodward convinces him to send her to school in the Adirondacks where she could meet and make friends with other children. But when Collins takes Barbara to the railway station, Collins' purse is stolen and Collins is knocked over by a car as she tries to find it, leaving Barbara to fend for herself. But despite the implausible and potentially traumatic nature of these events, Barbara is undaunted and upbeat (traits that mark Temple's persona throughout her 1930s films), and it is at this point that she encounters Tony (Henry Armetta), the 1936 version of the Organ Grinder, in the street. Barbara follows Tony to his apartment and Tony and his wife and children invite her in for the night, and it is here that we are introduced to the mysterious figure of a man who snoops and peers through her window.

From this point on any tangible traces of the play and the 1917 version (with the possible exception of the trope of a father's wish to see her daughter safe home) have been erased, and the remainder of the 1936 version is dominated not only by Richard's attempts to find Barbara, nor only by Richard's wooing of Margaret Allen (Gloria Stewart), but by the presence and dominance of radio in the narrative threads and performances that mark the invitation to Barbara from Jimmy and Jerry (Jack Halen and Alice Faye) to become a third member of their dance act, the initially reluctant but eventually enthusiastic involvement of advertising agent Simon Peck (Claude Gillingwater), and the radio broadcast that marks the success of this and other acts.[17] The film ends with the snooping man trying to hold Barbara for ransom, of which more in a moment. But Richard arrives with the police, the snooping man is arrested, and Richard is reunited with his daughter.

Coda

The presence of the snooping man has been linked by some to an overt sexualisation of female children and child stars and hence to paedophilia.[18] But it is made clear that the man is trying to kidnap Barbara for ransom (a much more prevalent criminal practice in the 1930s as John F. Kasson points out),[19] and as Kristen Hatch argues, 'Temple signals not a beginning but the end of a long period in which girls held a central place in American popular theater and film'; that 'the Victorian fascination with childhood appears perverse because we read innocence through a paradigm that was only beginning to emerge in the 1930s'; that her career 'marked the end of the child-era star'; and that 'her stardom was ... shaped by conventions that emerged out of the theater and were developed in Hollywood in the silent era'.[20] To that extent Pickford was shaped by the theatre and silent-era Hollywood too, and the comparisons and contrasts between her performance in *The Poor Little Rich Girl* and that of Temple in *Poor Little Rich Girl* are instructive. Where Temple is playful and upbeat throughout, Pickford's performance mixes the playful and sensitive, the serious and frivolous, and the ultimate powerless of a child. Yet she herself was a rich and powerful woman, thus playing out the tension between the 'old and new ideals of femininity' and 'the relationship between Pickford's on- and off-screen personae', suggesting that 'her appeal to men and women alike was related to her ability to be both child and woman, both old-fashioned and modern'.[21]

In conclusion it should also be noted that Temple starred as Mytyl in the 1940 version of *The Blue Bird*, which was filmed in Technicolor but marked by an opening monochrome war subplot, and which was based on the play but altered in a number of other ways. This was not the only version, for in 1918 Maurice Tourneur had directed a film adaptation for Artcraft, with set decoration by Carré, cinematography by van den Broek, a live music score by James R. Bradford, and Tula Belle as Mytyl and Robin Macdougall as Tyltyl. For an account of the 1918 version, see Kristin Thompson, 'The Limits of Experimentation of Hollywood', in Jan-Christopher Horak(ed.), *Lovers of Cinema: The First American Avant-Garde* (Madison, Wisconsin: University of Wisconsin Press, 1995), pp. 71–73. For a detailed account of its premiere at the Rivoli Theatre, see *The New York Times* report at http://www.nytimes.com/movie/review?res=9807E1DAE3FE433A25752C0A9629 C94996D6CF29/07/2016

Notes

1. These details can be found in Gerald Bordman, *American Theatre: A Chronicle of Comedy and Drama, 1869–1914* (New York and Oxford: Oxford University Press, 1994), p. 721. Harry Waldman, *Maurice Tourneur: The Life and Films* (Jefferson, N.C. and London: MacFarland & Company, Inc., 2001), p. 64, also notes that Viola Dana played the part of Gwendolyn but cites Madeline Traverse and Charles Wellesley as playing the parts of Gwendolyn's parents. This may be the result of a partial change of cast during the play's long run, but I have been unable to confirm whether this was the case or whether Waldman is mistaken.

2. These playwrights included Zöe Atkins, Rachel Crothers, Zona Gale, Alice Gerstenberg, Alice Susan Glaspell, Clare Kummer, Edna St. Vincent Millay, Martha Morton, and Josephine Preston Peabody. For details on these playwrights and their work, see Judith E. Barlow, 'Introduction' to *Plays by American Women, 1900–1930* (New York and London: Applause, 1981), esp. pp. xiii-xxiv. See also, Patricia R. Schroeder, 'Realism and feminism in the Progressive Era', Veronica Makowsky, 'Susan Glaspell and modernism', Jerry Dickey, 'The expressionist moment: Sophie Treadwell', and Brenda Murphy, 'Feminism and the marketplace: the career of Rachel Crothers', in Brenda Murphy (ed.), *The Cambridge Companion*

to American Women Playwrights (Cambridge and New York: Cambridge University Press, 1999), pp. 31–46, 49–65, 66–81, 82–97. See also Yvonne Shafer, *American Women Playwrights* (New York: Peter Lang Publishing Inc., 1995), esp. pp. 1–11, 15–78, and Shafer 'Whose Realism? Rachel Crothers's Power Struggle in the American Theatre', in William W. Demastes (ed.), *Realism in the American Dramatic Tradition* (Tuscaloosa and London: University of Alabama Press, 1996), pp. 37–52.

3. For Maeterlink and his plays, see Daniel Gerould, 'The Art of Symbolist Drama, A Re-Assessment' in Geroud (ed.), *Symbolist Drama* (New York: Performing Art Journal Publications, 1985), pp. 7–33; W.D. Halls, *Maurice Maeterlinck: A Study of His Life and Thought* (Oxford: Clarendon Press, 1960), esp. pp. 24–124; Bettina Knapp, *Maurice Maeterlinck* (Boston: Twayne Publishers, 1975); Linn Bratteteig Konrad, *Modern Drama as a Crisis: The Case of Maurice Maeterlinck* (New York: Peter Lang Publishing, Inc., 1986); Patrick McGuiness, *Maurice Maeterlinck and the Making of Modern Theatre* (Oxford and New York: Oxford University Press, 2000); and J.L. Styan, *Modern Drama in Theory and Practice: Symbolism, Surrealism and the Absurd* (Cambridge: Cambridge University Press, 1981), pp. 27–35. John Frick points out that during 'the first decades of the twentieth century, progressive American theatremakers like Maurice Brown, Arthur Hopkins, Robert Edmond Jones, and Samuel Hume "went to school" on the theories of Wagner, Appia, Craig, Georg Fuchs, the Symbolists, and other European artists who proposed alternatives to the Realism and Naturalism that had become popular in both European and American theatres' and that 'American experimental productions, like Hopkins's staging of Eleanor Gates's *The Poor Little Rich Girl* and Alice Gerstenberg's adaptation of *Alice in Wonderland*, followed, as directors and designers attempted to create a theatre that, like its European counterparts, was mythical, evocative, suggestive, atmospheric, and sensual', thus providing 'an alternative to the Belascoesque facsimile realism that was gaining favor on Broadway'. See Frick, 'A Changing Theatre: New York and Beyond', in Don B. Wilmeth and Christopher Bigsby (eds.), *The Cambridge History of American Theatre, Volume Two: 1870–1945* (Cambridge University Press: Cambridge and New York: 1999), pp. 222–223.

4. Carole L. Cole, 'The Search for Power: Drama by American Women, 1909–1929', Phd dissertation, University of Purdue, 1991, pp. 20–23. Gates went on to write and Hopkins to produce a play entitled *We Are Seven*. This play opened on 24 December 1913 at Maxine Elliott's Theatre and ran for 21 performances prior to its closure in January 1914.According to Bordman, *American Theatre: A Chronicle of Comedy and Drama, 1869–1914*, p. 735, *We Are Seven* focuses on 'a charity worker teaching eugenics to Lower East Side immigrants. Since the nice young man who accompanies her is deaf and dumb, she thinks nothing of talking out loud to herself about her dreams for a perfect mate and their seven children. Of course, the man isn't really deaf or dumb at all. The play ended quirkily with his pointing to their seven dream children silhouetted on a window shade, "step-ladder fashion'. This was the only other Gates play to be performed on Broadway. Indeed, as far as I know, this was her only other play.

5. Tino Balio, *United Artists: The Company Built by the Stars* (Madison: University of Wisconsin Press, 1976), p. 16. For further details on Pickford's dealings with Famous Players, see Benjamin Hampton, *History of the American Film Industry from its beginnings to 1931* (Toronto and London: Dover Edition, 1970), pp. 146–165, and Karen Ward Mahar, *Women Filmmakers in Early Hollywood* (Baltimore: The Johns Hopkins University Press, 2006), pp. 155–156.

6. Mahar, *Women Filmmakers in Early Hollywood*, p. 66. The source cited here is an article entitled 'Eleanor Gates in Photoplay Field', *Motion Picture News*, 30 May 1914, p. 1296, and in addition to Mahar's book, which encompasses the contributions made by women to the US film industry as a whole in the period between the 1890s and the 1920s, a detailed study of the roles and contributions of women filmmakers at Universal in the period between 1912 and 1919 can be found in Mark Garrett Cooper, *Universal Women: Filmmaking and Institutional Change in Early Hollywood* (Urbana: University of Illinois Press, 2010).

7. As far as I can determine, her only other contribution to a feature film was a short story entitled 'Search for the Spring', which was adapted for the screen by George Waggoner, re-titled *Once to Every Bachelor*, produced by Liberty Pictures and directed by William Nigh, premiered on 10 September 1934, then released more widely on 14 December 1934.

8. Cari Beauchamp, *Without Lying Down: Frances Marion and the Powerful Women of Early Hollywood* (New York: Scribner, 1997), p. 68. See also, Scott Eyman, *Mary Pickford* (London: Robson Books, 1992), pp. 91–94, and Eileen Whitfield, *Pickford: The Woman Who Made Hollywood* (Lexington: University Press of Kentucky, 2007), pp. 153–155. Although Eyman's account is more detailed, all three tell the same basic story, which derives for the most part from Pickford's autobiography, *Sunshine and Shadow* (London,

Melbourne, Toronto: William Heinemann Ltd., 1956), pp. 177–181, and which specifies that Pickford and Marion insisted that the film be leavened by comic scenes and moments, that Tourneur objected if these scenes and moments were not in the script, and that the unscripted comic scenes and moments included the one in which Pickford contrives to get a snooty young girl to sit on a pie. All three authors reiterate that Pickford was chastised by Adolph Zukor for altering the script, that this was largely because the film did not make a profit, and that Zukor calculated that he could curtail Pickford's power from this point on. Little did he know that Pickford would leave Paramount and become one of the founding members of United Artists two years later, on 5 February 1919. In addition to Beauchamp's book, the only other source for Marion is JoAnne Ruvoli's contribution to the Women Film Pioneers Project, which outlines Marion's career and lists her contributions to 121 feature-length films between 1915 and 1928. See https://wfpp.cdrs.columbia.edu/pioneer/ccp-frances-marion/15/02/2016

9. Harry Waldman, *Maurice Tourneur: The Life and Films* (Jefferson, N.C. and London: McFarland & Company Inc., 2001), p. 65.

10. Waldman, *Maurice Tourneur*, pp. 3–23.

11. Steven Higgins, 'American Éclair, 1911–1915', *Griffithiana*, 44/45, pp. 89–129.

12. Waldman, *Maurice Tourneur*, pp. 31–56. For further details on Fort Lee, Tourneur, and Tourneur's films, see Richard Koszarski, *Fort Lee: The Film Town* (Rome: John Libbey-CIC Publishing, 2004), passim.

13. These ingredients are discussed in Jan-Christopher Horak, 'Maurice Tourneur and the Rise of the Studio System', *Sulla via di Hollywood, 1911–1920*, esp. pp. 271–274, and Richard Koszarski, *An Evening's Entertainment: The Age of the Silent Feature Picture, 1915–1928* (New York: Scribner's, 1990), p. 225–226.

14. Tourneur continued to direct films in the US in the late 1910s through to 1926, when he left for Europe part way through directing *Mysterious Island*, which was completed by Benjamin Christensen and Lucien Hubbard. Tourneur went on to direct silent, part-talkie and sound films in Germany and France, then retired due to an accident in 1948. He died in France in 1961. For details, see Waldman, *Maurice Tourneur*, pp. 133–168.

15, These songs were 'But Definitely', 'When I'm with You', 'Oh, My Goodness', 'You've Gotta Eat Your Spinach', 'I Like a Military Man', Buy a Bar of Barry's' and 'Peck's Theme Song'.

16. Aubrey Solomon, *Twentieth Century-Fox: A Corporate and Financial History* (Lanham, Md. and London: The Scarecrow Press, 2002), p. 217.

17. Kristen Hatch, *Shirley Temple and the Performance of Girlhood* (New Brunswick, N.J. and London: Rutgers University Press, 2015), pp. 52–53.

18. See for instance, James R. Kincaid, *Erotic Innocence: The Culture of Child Molesting* (Durham, N.C.: Duke University Press, 1998), p. 114. See also, Valerie Walkerdine, *Daddy's Girl: Young Girls and Popular Culture* (Cambridge, M.A.: Harvard University Press, 1997), 'The Shirley Temple of My Familiar', *Transition*, no. 73, 1997, pp. 10–32, and Ara Osterwell, 'Reconstructing Shirley: Pedophilia and Interracial Romance in Hollywood's Age of Innocence', *Camera Obscura*, no. 73, 2009), pp. 1–39. Even though paedophilia was not publicly recognised as such in the late nineteenth and early twentieth century, it surely existed.

19. John F. Kasson, *The Little Girl Who Fought The Great Depression: Shirley Temple and 1930s America* (New York and London: W.W. Norton & Company, 2014), pp. 212–215.

20. Hatch, *Shirley Temple and the Performance of Girlhood*, p. 2.

21. Hatch, *Shirley Temple and the Performance of Childhood*, p. 38.

Chapter 3

The Merry Widow

The Merry Widow was and still is one of the most popular operettas ever written. Its storyline and songs have given rise not only to numerous theatrical versions, but to a number of novelisations and film adaptations too. In addition to a number of early Swedish and French film adaptations, at least three one-reel versions and spin offs were produced in the US between 1907 and 1910 (among them *The Merry Widow* in 1907 and *The Courting of the Merry Widow* and *The Merry Widow Takes Another Partner* in 1910) and subsequent feature-length versions were produced in Hollywood in 1925, 1934 and 1952. The one-reel US versions have been lost. But the three feature-length versions have all survived intact.

The Operetta

The Merry Widow was based on a comic play by Henri Meilhac entitled *L'attaché d'ambassade* (*The Embassy Attaché*), which was written and initially produced at the Théâtre du Vaudeville in Paris in 1861. The play centred on Baron Scharpf, the Parisian ambassador of an impoverished German duchy, who is charged with the arrangement of a marriage between Madame von Palmer, his country's richest widow, and embassy-attaché Count Prachs 'in order to prevent economic disaster back home'.[1] The play folded after fifteen performances. But when a German adaptation by Alexander Bergen was premiered at the Carltheater in Vienna the following year, it proved more successful and was revived on several occasions. One of these revivals was attended by Leo Stein (born Leo Rosenstein), an experienced and successful librettist who thought that the play could be made into a successful operetta, and who went on to discuss its prospects with Victor Léon (born Viktor Hirschfeld), a librettist and occasional collaborator. At this point 'the prestigious Theater An der Wein was reeling from a series of expensive failures' and its manager thought that an operetta set in Paris 'might be just what he needed', so Stein and Léon went to work on a libretto, updated the storyline, and 'came up with the provocative title *Die Lustige Witwe* (*The Merry Widow*)'.[2] Although Léon initially objected when Franz Lehár (born Ferenc Lehár) was considered for the score, but became more convinced when he heard the melody that Lehár wrote for 'Dummer, dummer Reitersmann' (subsequently known in English as 'Jogging On a One-Horse Gig'). However caution still prevailed and *Die Lustige Witwe* was produced in a hurry on a shoestring, using recycled scenery and costumes wherever possible.[3] Premiered at the Theater An der Wein on 30 December 1905, its cast included Mizzi Gunter as Hanna Glawari, Louis Truemann as Count Danilo, Annie Wunsch as Valencienne, Karel Meister as Camille de Rosillon, and Siegmund Natzler as Baron Mirko Zeta. Its storyline, songs and stagings were as follows.

Act One opens at the Grand Salon of the Pontevedrian Embassy in Paris, where the Grand Duke is hosting a ball to celebrate his birthday. The main double doors are at centre back, with arches leading off to the ballroom and buffet on the left and right respectively and portraits of the Duke and Duchess on the wall. It is the Duke's birthday and footmen serve champagne as 'Verehrteste Damen und Herren' is sung by Cascada. Cascada is joined by a chorus that includes Camille, Valencienne (the Duchess of Pontevedro), Bogdanovitsch, Pritschitsch and others, then by Baron Zeta (the Duke of Pontevedro), then by the chorus once again. The impression given is one of unalloyed celebration. But aside from an ongoing affair between Camille and Valencienne, which is reflected in a duet entitled 'So kommen Sie! 's ist niemand hier!' ('Look, Now's Our Chance. There's No One Here'), the principal narrative thread centres on the imminent arrival of Hanna Glawari, who has inherited twenty million francs from her late husband, and whom Zeta wishes to ensure will marry a Pontevedran and thereby save his country from bankruptcy. Hanna arrives singing 'Bitte, mein Herrn' ('Gentlemen, No More!'), underlining her change of fortune and its ironic consequences as she does so. 'When I longed for a beau, money was short', she sings. 'But now that my stocks are the high stocks, there's a boom in the marriage bureau ... Who's game for clinching the deal?' Valencienne welcomes Hanna and tries to get Camille to propose to her. But Camille is still smitten by Valencienne, and at this point Count Danilo enters with Negus, the embassy's secretary, who has fetched Danilo from Maxim's, a Parisian night spot renowned for its can-can dancers or 'grisettes'. Danilo sings 'O Vaterland', which segues into 'Da geh' ich Mazim' ('I'm Off To Chez Maxime'), and is surprised to hear that Hanna is in Paris. It emerges that Hanna and Danilo were once in love with one another prior Hanna's marriage, and that Danilo's uncle forbad Danilo from marrying Hanna on the grounds that she was penniless. Although they still love each other, Danilo refuses to court Hanna on account of her fortune, Hanna refuses to marry Danilo unless he tells her that he loves her, and the consequent deadlock becomes apparent in the Act One finale ('Damenwah!' or 'Ladies Choice' and 'Hilfe Komm! zur rechten Zelt!' or 'Rescued in The Nick of Time'). However this finale also hints at the true feelings of Hanna and Danilo as they head off to the ballroom and dance with one another, and thus paves the way for a happy ending.

Act Two is set at a garden party in the grounds of Hanna's mansion in order to celebrate Zeta's birthday. A small pavilion can be seen in the middle distance and there are garden tables to left and right. Most of the guests are wearing Pontevedrian costume, and following an introductory chorus ('Mi velimo dase haiaho!'), Hanna begins the entertainment by singing a love song entitled 'Vilja'('Vilia' in the English-language versions). Revealing that Hanna has invited the dancers from Maxime's as a surprise for Danilo, Zeta is convinced that his plan for Hanna and Danilo to marry one another is working, and this underlined by 'Dummer, dummer Reitersmann'. The men start a conversation about women as they begin to sing 'Wie die Weber' ('It's A Problem', otherwise known as 'You're Back Where You First Began'), and Hanna and Danilo try to provoke each other into admitting their love 'as the rhythms of the Pontevedrin *kolo* and the French *valse*' enhance their growing reconciliation.[4] Meanwhile the complexities of Valencienne's love life are prolonged not only by Camille's ardour (as in the duet entitled 'Mein Freund, Vernunft' or 'Friend, Be Calm' and the subsequent 'Vergib! Vergib, mein Liebe' or 'But Why, Why Must It End'), but by Zeta's discovery not of Valencienne and Camille, but of Camille and Hanna, who has swapped places with Valencienne, and who has yet to provide an explanation as she shields her female friend from scandal. When Hanna announces that she is engaged to Camille, she sings parts of 'Wie eine Rosenknopse' ('Red As The Rose Of Maytime') with Valencienne and Danilo in turn, and it is at this point that Danilo 'explodes in jealous fury' – thus confirming that he truly loves Hanna after all.[5]

Act 3 begins with an intermezzo. 'Inside Hanna's palais, a salon has been decorated so that the Pontevedrian half of her party can be followed by the Parisian half.' Njegus, the embassy secretary, 'has arranged for the interior of Maxim's to be reproduced, and has engaged some genuine grisettes – all for Danilo's sake'.[6] A dance scene follows, and is followed in turn by song entitled 'Ja, wir sind es, die Grisetten' ('The Grisettes of Paris Greet You'). Hanna explains her presence at the pavilion to Danilo and they waltz to 'Lippen schweigen' ('Love Unspoken'). But just as everything seems to be proceeding to a satisfactory conclusion, the arrival of a telegram confirms that Pontevedro is on the verge of bankruptcy and prompts Baron Zeta, who is now aware of his wife's affair with Camille, to divorce his wife and marry Hanna in order to avert financial catastrophe. A further twist reveals that a clause in her late husband's will specifies that Hanna will lose her fortune if she re-marries, and deadlock and crisis prevail. But only momentarily, for it is also revealed that a second clause in her late husband's will specifies that although Hanna will lose her fortune, it will and must go to her new husband. That new husband will of course be Danilo, and the members of cast join in the celebrations as they sing 'Ja, das Studium der Weiber ist schwer' ('What To Think, What To Say, What To Do') in conclusion.

After a hesitant start *The Merry Widow* was a huge success, and according to Bernard Grun this was due in part to 'the frankly erotic nature of its subject' and 'the ingenious boldness with which the vibrant sensuality of the story is musically interpreted',[7] and in part to the orchestral colouring adopted from contemporary composers such as Richard Strauss, Gustav Mahler and Claude Debussy.[8] Some of the songs in the 1907 Berlin version were among first to be recorded, and later that year an English adaptation by Basil Hood premiered at the Daly's Theatre in London and ran for 778 performances. Lehár himself made changes to the London version, adding two new numbers ('Butterflies' and 'Quite Parisien') and possibly prompting the setting of the

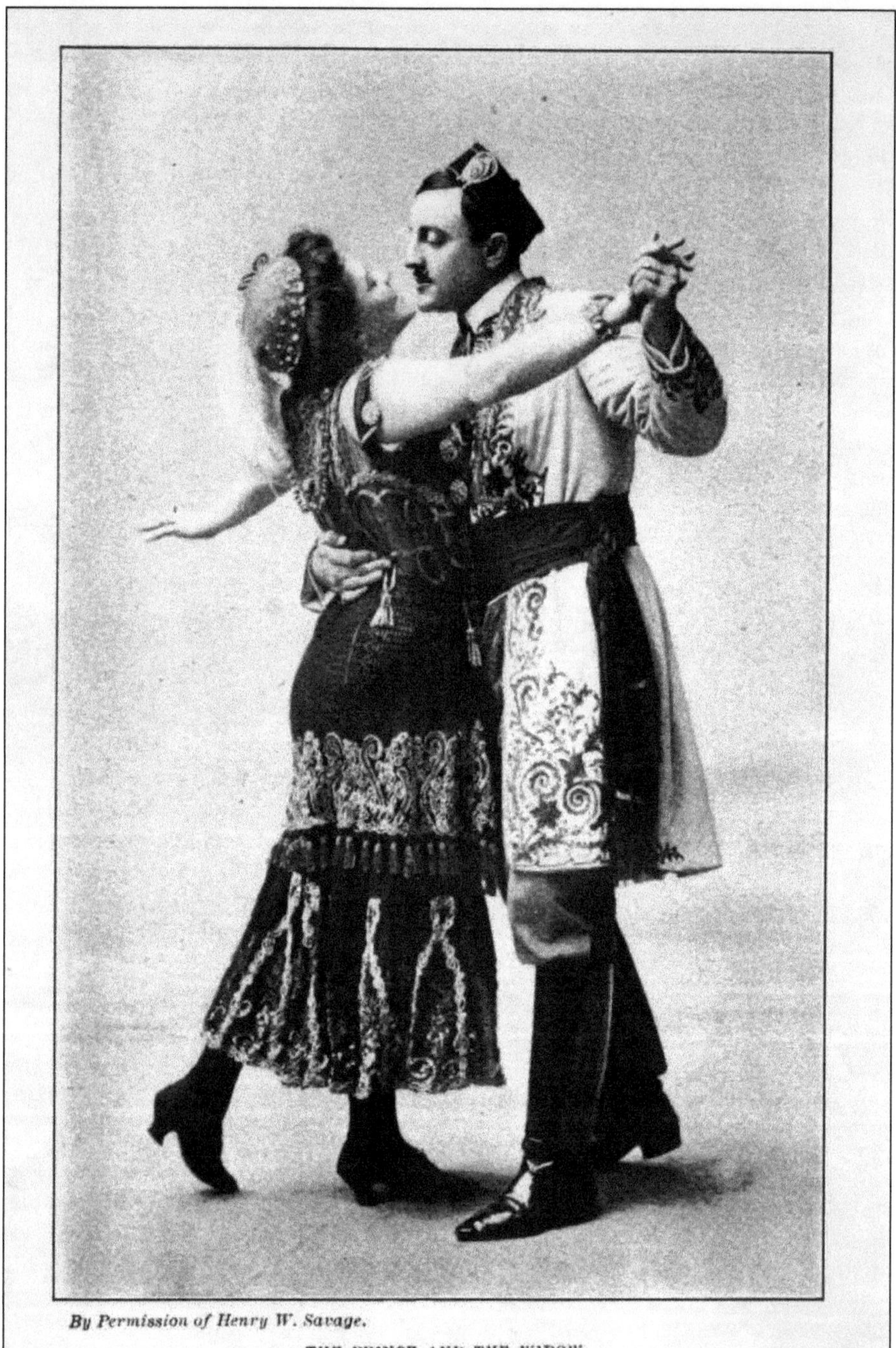

By Permission of Henry W. Savage.

THE PRINCE AND THE WIDOW.

Figure 1

final act in Maxime's rather than Hanna's palais. He also added numbers to a later German version, and in the interim, a Broadway adaptation was produced by Henry W. Savage and premiered at the New Amsterdam Theatre in New York on 21 October 1907. This version was a huge success as well, and was followed by numerous roadshows, prompting the production and sale of an English-language novelisation (figure 1 is a photograph of the Prince and the Widow), and numerous items of merchandise (among them hats, shoes and song books).[9] Other productions were premiered in Stockholm in 1907, Copenhagen, Milan and Moscow in 1908, Brussels in 1910, and subsequent revivals were produced in London in 1923, 1924 and 1932.[10] Aside from the settings in Paris, and largely because the identification of actual countries may have caused offence, many of these productions were set in fictional or unspecific locations, and this was at least partially true of the three feature-length Hollywood versions.

The Merry Widow (1925)

The 1925 version of *The Merry Widow* was adapted, scripted, produced and directed by Erich von Stroheim for MGM, which had just acquired Goldwyn Pictures, and which was now managed by Irving Thalberg.[11] Of all Hollywood directors, von Stroheim's temperament and talents would at first glance seem least suited to saccharine sentiment and most suited not only to irony, but to the laying bare of sexual motives and appetites, perverse behaviour, the pursuit and use of power and money, and the abandonment of conventional gender-based courtesies.[12] However, although irony is a mark of the operetta too, and although this particular adaptation departed from it in numerous ways (of the film's 477 scenes, '307 take place before the curtain even lifts on the action described in the stage play', and even those were added to or changed),[13] the rights were acquired as early as 1923. A score based on the operetta's music was written by David Mendoza and William Axt for upscale venues,[14] and the perverse romance between Danilo (John Gilbert) and Sally O'Hara (Mae Murray) (the film's distant equivalent to Hanna Glawari) finally concludes with a traditionally romantic happy ending as Sally and Danilo wed and take the place of old or rival ones, who are now all dead.

As Richard Koszarski has noted, Stroheim's adaptation of *The Merry Widow* is particularly marked by comparisons, contrasts and parallels as we cut back and forth between characters, actions and settings.[15] Thus the opening scene outside the cathedral in the Kingdom of Monteblanco focuses on the ageing King and Queen (George Fawcett and Josephine Crowell), and the equally ageing but much more wealthy Baron Sadoja (Tully Marshall). These three figures contrast with the two younger sons of the Duke and Duchess. But these younger sons, Prince Mirko (Roy D'Arcy) and Count Danilo (John Gilbert), are contrasted with one another in turn as we cut to their arrival at an inn, where the former is disgusted by and the latter delights in the presence of peasants, pigs and mud. When a troupe of American performers arrive, Mirko and Danilo become rivals over Sally O'Hara (Mae Murray), the troupe's female lead, and this rivalry is underlined when Danilo takes flowers to

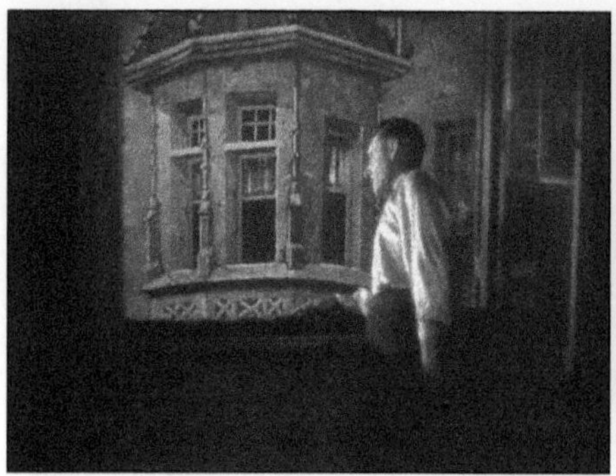

Figure 2

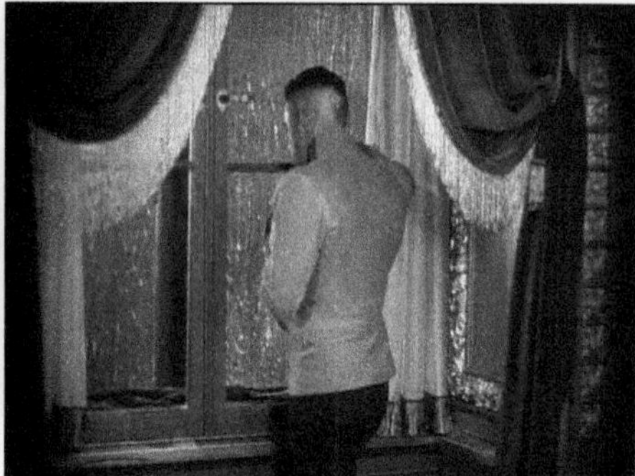

Figure 3

Sally's dressing room and is followed by Mirko, who is foiled by Danilo's presence. As Sally performs her dance in 'The Manhattan Follies' later that evening, the rivalries increase as we cut to Sadoja, Mirko and Danilo looking through lorgnettes, binoculars and opera glasses in turn, and as Sadoja gazes at her feet, Mirko at her crotch, and Danilo at her face. All three suitors invite Sally to supper. But Sally rejects Sadoja and Mirko, and Danilo takes her to a venue called 'François', a thinly-disguised high-class brothel whose gate-keeper (George Nichols) has lost an eye and a leg, and who represents yet another instance of the bodily grotesquery that peppers the film throughout.

Mirko and his friends are already in full swing when Danilo and Sally arrive, and while Mirko's group is entertained in boisterous fashion by a group of prostitutes, Danilo takes Sally to a quieter and much more exclusive room. Serenaded by a pair of masked musicians, Danilo woos Sally and they begin to fall in love. However, on discovering that Danilo is really a prince, Sally thinks she has been fooled, and this is underlined when Mirko and his party burst in to spoil their triste. A little while later Mirko and his friends gather outside, kicking the gate-keeper on their way out as they do so, and we cut back to Danilo, who thinks that Sally has left as we move on to the first in a series of window shots that pepper the film from this point on. Preceded by a shot of the gate-keeper locking the building's outer door, we cut to Danilo, who opens the window and looks out in vain for a glimpse of Sally (figure 2). But when Danilo finds Sally asleep in a separate room the following morning, he is overjoyed. He tells her that she is 'going to be mine. Always', and we cut again to the door being locked by the gate-keeper (a sign that she is his and only his) as the scene ends and the film's intermission begins.

The film's second half opens on a dismal day in the palace courtyard. The changing of the guard (a ritual that actually involves changing nothing) is followed by a scene in which the King, Queen and Mirko tell Danilo that he cannot marry a commoner, that marriage is a duty not an act of love, and that while he can always have affairs he must put aside his plans to marry Sally. And although the Queen is sympathetic to his plight, Danilo is forced to relent, and another window shot serves to underline his

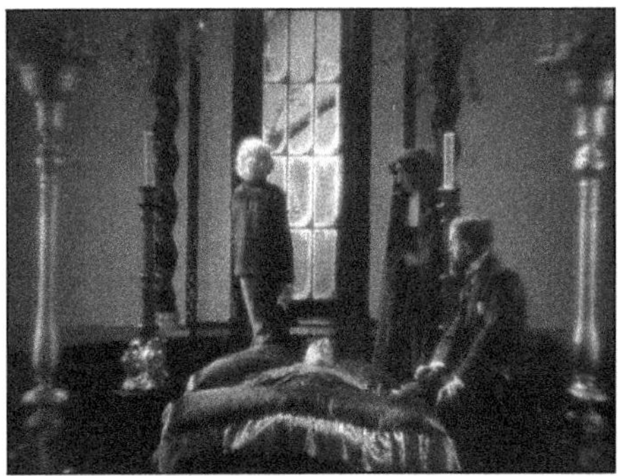

Figure 4

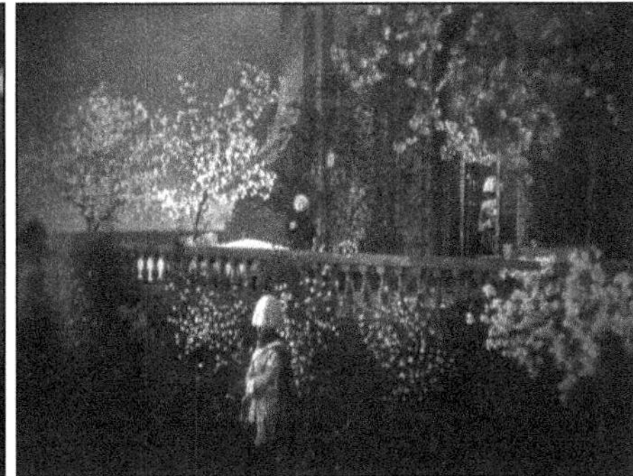

Figure 5

loss (figure 3). Sally is heartbroken and has no further prospects, so when Baron Sadoja offers her wealth and power, she agrees to marry him. But while Danilo is drunk and heartbroken in his hunting lodge, Sadoja has a heart attack as he indulges his fetish for Sally's feet, and we cut to Sally looking out of yet another window as her husband dies (figure 4), then on to a scene in which Mirko reports to his family that Sally is now worth millions, is now known as The Merry Widow, and is now living the high life in Paris.

At this point the settings and events begin to echo those in the operetta, though there are still a number of significant changes and additions. Thus we initially cut to Maxim's, where Danilo tells a sympathetic female companion of his plight as the grisettes dance the can-can, and only then do we cut to Monteblancan Embassy , the equivalent to the first location in the operetta. Here Mirko and Sally take centre stage, and when Danilo arrives and dances 'The Merry Widow Waltz' with Sally, she takes the opportunity to remind him of his behaviour: 'how could "Your Royal Highness" possibly judge what a man honourably in love would do'. The following day Mirko proposes to Sally while out riding in the Bois de Boulogne (a distant echo, perhaps, of the outdoor garden-party setting in the operetta's second act), and when Sally encounters a drunken Danilo asleep in the park, she tells him that she has just become engaged to Mirko and that Danilo is to be his best man. Danilo responds by challenging Mirko to a duel and from here we cut to Maxime's, where a distraught Danilo is struggling to come to terms with his feelings. When Sally enters she responds to Danilo's plight in silence. It is clear from her demeanour that she still loves Danilo and does not want him to die. But the distraught Danilo is unaware of this and thinks that she does not want him to kill Mirko, and when the duel finally takes place later on he allows Mirko to shoot him: 'I've saved him for you', says Danilo to Sally, who responds with genuine tears.[16] But Mirko, who is about to be crowned head of state now that the King and Queen are dead, is assassinated by the brothel keeper in revenge for Mirko's mistreatment, and thus clears the way for Danilo, who is wounded but nursed back to health on a sumptuous veranda by a repentant Sally (figure 5), and Danilo and Sally, a much younger couple than the former King and Queen, finally wed in Monteblanco's cathedral.

The Merry Widow (1934)

The introduction of sound led to a spate of musicals in the late 1920s and 1930s, and it is unsurprising that a sound version of *The Merry Widow* was among them. The 1934 version was produced by Irving Thalberg at MGM, directed by Ernst Lubitsch, and scripted by Lubitsch, Samson Raphaelson and Ernest Vajda. Its songs included 'Girls, Girls, Girls', 'Vilia', 'Maxim's', 'The Melody Of Laughter', 'The Merry Widow Waltz', 'If Widows Are Rich' (all adapted from Lehár's score, with lyrics by Richard Rodgers and Lorenz Hart), and 'Tonight Will Teach Me to Forget' (with music by Lehár and lyrics by Gus Kahn). The dances, a key aspect of the Lubitsch version, were choreographed by Albertina Rasch.

According to the entry on the 1934 version in the online AFI Catalog, the lyrics were updated and a copy of the music track was sent to Lehár for approval. MGM initially lost the screen rights to a sound version, but repurchased the story rights from Lehár and his partners and announced that Sidney Franklin would direct a version for release in 1930. However further complications led to a three-year delay, and it was not until the Fall of 1933 that pre-production began in earnest. Various performers were considered for the roles of Sonia and Danilo, and Jeannette McDonald and Maurice Chevalier, both of whom had starred in Lubitsch's earlier operettas and neither of whom were particularly keen to work with another again, were eventually cast. Production began on 9 April, 'with separate French and Belgian versions', and 'a version for English audiences that changed the ruler of Marshovia from a king to a general, so as not to antagonize the evidently hypersensitive royal family'.[17] Initially reluctant to intervene on account of its cost, which is normally cited at between \$1,600,000 and \$1,605,000,[18] Joseph Breen eventually wrote a memo on 29 October instructing MGM's executives to eliminate the following shots and lines: 'Marcelle takes garter off her leg, close up of garter', 'She jumped into a cold bath, and you'd be surprised, Captain, what cold water can do' (a line that is clearly audible on the soundtrack of the US DVD nevertheless), and what the AFI Catalog calls 'other lines and bits of action'. And various states and Canadian territories objected to the inscription on a garter which read 'Many happy returns' and the lines 'I know what to do but am too old to do it' and 'Have you ever had diplomatic relations with a woman?'

Set in the Kingdom of Marshovia in 1885, and evoking the peasant-village scene in the Stroheim version, the opening sequence in the 1934 version is suffused neither by martial ceremony nor by predatory male behaviour. Instead it is suffused by music and song as Danilo sings 'Girls, Girls, Girls', as numerous young women ogle and wave at him, and as the images and soundtrack segue to the wistfully romantic music played by a gypsy band in a nearby inn. Sonia approaches the inn then pauses and leaves. But although troubled by Sonia's apparent lack of the interest in him, the presence of her mourning clothes, the mask that hides her face and the intimations of mortality inherent in both of them, Danilo is intrigued, and finds a way to approach her on the terrace of her mansion. Claiming to know nothing about Danilo and his charms, Sonia rebuffs him. But once he has left the terrace she sings a particularly wistful version of 'Vilia', then joins her maids and discusses Danilo with them as they prepare her bed and put her black shoes, dress and hat alongside them. A little black dog completes these all-black items. But they are finally displaced by white ones when Sonia eventually decides to put aside her mourning clothes and head off to Paris.

William Paul argues that the editing in the first part of this sequence is fragmentary, and notes that the sequence as a whole is marked by song rather than dance.[19] But while Paul's point about song is important, the second part of the opening sequence is almost as fragmentary as the first, giving rise to the spatial incoherence evident in the Vilia sequence and the shots of the inn and terrace that comprise it, and underlining the dominance of wistful feelings as day turns to night. What is also true, though, is that Danilo is troubled by Sonia's apparent lack of interest in him. Thus although Danilo is sent to Paris to woo her, thereby curtailing his affair with King's wife and ensuring that Sonia's fortune will remain in Marshovia, the first thing he does is report to the Marshovian Embassy then head for Maxime's, where he knows that the grisettes all adore him.

On arriving in Paris 'there is a marked shift in the handling of space' and 'an increase in camera and in-frame movement', as Paul points out. What purports to be an elaborate crane shot (a shot that actually consists of three shots linked by dissolves) articulates motion and space as it moves down and across the exterior of a hotel facade, linking Danilo in one room and Sonia in another as each prepare to 'go out on the town', and pointing to the fact that in this respect 'they are closer to each other than they realize'. Danilo starts to sing an a capella version of 'Maxim's' then stands up and sings a full orchestral version, and by the time the song is over 'the camera has already dollied out his window and begun its descent to Sonia's room', and allowing expansive feelings 'to burst forth' as Danilo's song is echoed and transformed by 'The Melody of Laughter', which is sung by Sonia.[20] Paul concludes his discussion of this sequence as follows:

> If the point of the shot were simply to make the geographical connection between the two, the camera should logically stop when it reaches Sonia, but it does not. Instead, in a kind of unstoppable movement, it travels past Sonia's windows as if it were now being carried along by her vitality into the next bank of windows through which four suitors attending her may be seen ... For both characters, the new sense of space in Paris signifies a bursting forth, a breaking of barriers, an indulgent yielding to impulse that, by its very indulgence, is the greatest source of vitality. For both Danilo and Sonia the emotion must be purely egocentric since it sets the world in motion in conformity to their emotions. It is for this reason that the camera finally comes to rest only on Sonia's suitors because they present a multiplicity of partners that draw an unexpected parallel between her and Danilo. Sonia, the character who will soon come to stand for exclusive monogamous commitment, is here enjoying Danilo-like delights, [and as she] introduces a sense of constancy and mystery into Danilo's life, he introduces an indiscriminate exuberance into hers.[21]

This exuberance is further evident in the subsequent moving shots of Danilo and Sonia in their respective carriages, and the introductory shots of Maxime's, which are each full of whirling motion as the grisettes dance the can-can. Danilo is in his element,

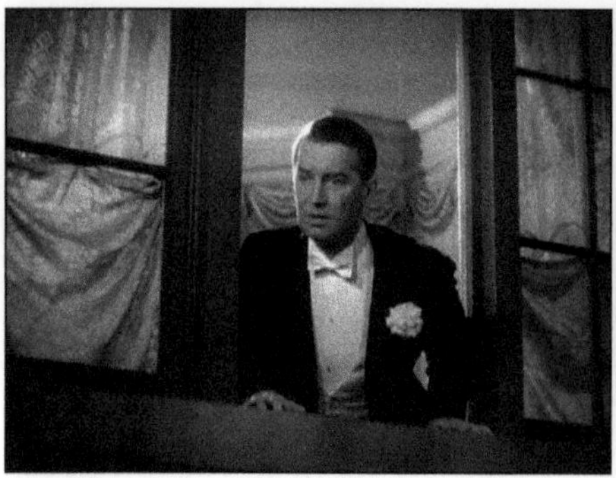

Figure 6

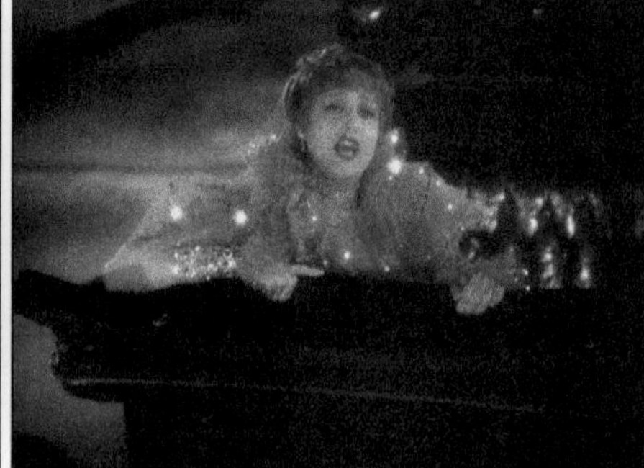

Figure 7

surrounded as he is by adoring grisettes, and when Sonia arrives and calls herself Fifi, it is clear that she has visited Maxime's and indulged in at least some of its activities before. Danilo is entranced. But he does not realise who she is, and as he invites her for supper upstairs, and as the conversation between them proceeds, she challenges his attitudes and routines, turns down his supper (and all it entails), and leaves. As she does so, the two final shots in this sequence show Danilo framed from outside the building, visually entrapped behind by the window in the dining room upstairs, then Sonia in her carriage as she drives away singing (figures 6 and 7), and in this way these shots evoke but reverse the feelings and framings evident in the earlier crane-shot sequence and the earlier shots of Danilo and Sonia in their carriages.

From this point on it becomes clear that Danilo has fallen in love with Sonia, that his subsequent pursuit of her is genuine, and thus that the marriage of convenience promulgated by the rulers of Marshovia could in fact be a marriage based on love. However, when Sonia discovers that Danilo's proposal is a Marshovian ploy, she calls off the wedding, and Danilo supports her decision to do so precisely because he is now in love with her. This particular plot twist is specific to the 1934 version, and the paradoxes involved here differ from the complications that mark the Stroheim version and the original operetta. In the Stroheim version, the complications arise largely from class difference and its perversities. And in the operetta, they centre on the feelings that arise from the widow's marriage, the fact that Danilo's love for Sonja had previously been thwarted by his uncle, and the extent to which Pontevedro's rulers are in need of her money and therefore require Danilo and Sonja to fall in love with one another all over again. All three versions entail or end in marriage. But the Lubitsch version focuses on one of the central paradoxes of monogamous love and marriage, a paradox that is founded on the uniqueness of each and every couple and its members, on the one hand, and the institutionalised similarities of coupledom on the other.

This paradox is underlined in particular in the scenes and tropes of dance, which displace the songs sung earlier on and which are best summarised by Paul as follows. Where 'the first half of the film has a more personal focus that is perhaps best seen in the fact that Sonia's first three songs are sung *to herself*,'[22] and where the can-can

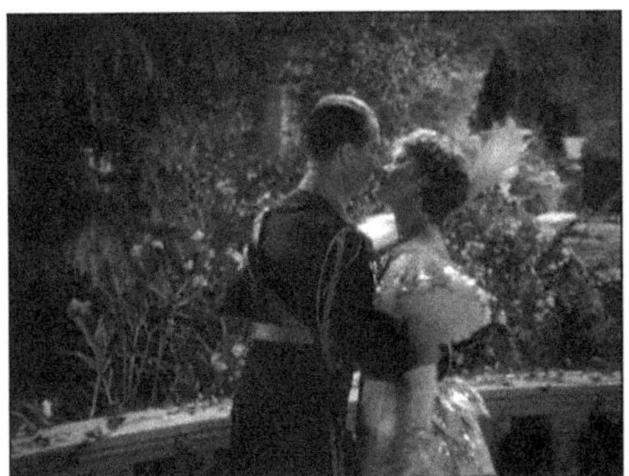

Figure 8

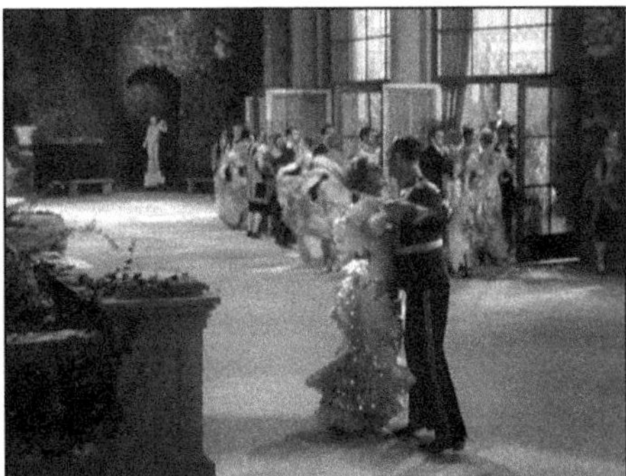

Figure 9

dancing at Maxime's is a form of vivid but impersonally-grouped female display, the dances at the Embassy are much more formal, and much more governed by upper-class status and etiquette. Here 'Sonia and Danilo are repeatedly placed in a larger social context of a chorus of dancing couples', and here they are thus deprived of freedom and uniqueness:

> Almost as a betrayal of the sense of free movement that dancing generally evokes, the two lovers dancing in an open space are over and over again surrounded by a large chorus as constriction becomes the dominant motif: Danilo and Sonia alone on the terrace at the beginning of the dance suddenly surrounded by other guests at the ball; a couple of rooms with the regular pattern of parquet floors setting up the swirling movements of Sonia and Danilo in the latter half of the dance, first in a shot a mirrored hallway filled with couples that are extended infinitely in two directions via the mirrors; and finally in a shot from the balcony that began the Embassy Ball sequence, now looking down at what appears to be hundreds of gracefully spinning people ... Subsequent shots show the dancing chorus flooding in on the lovers from all directions and encircling them, so that the chorus now seems to be directing the course of the lovers' movement rather than vice versa; that they can never be alone here is made emphatic by this constant repetition. [Moreover] Sonia and Danilo disappear from view entirely, apparently consumed by the faceless horde of dancing chorus. What began then as an expression of very personal emotion has transformed itself into a spectacle that obliterates the individuality of the two lovers ... [leading

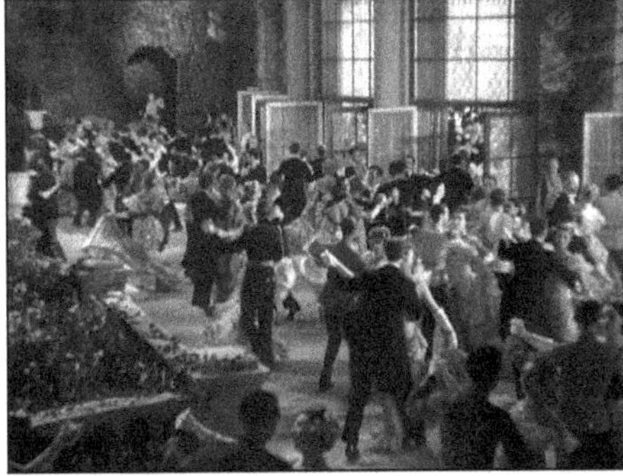

Figure 10

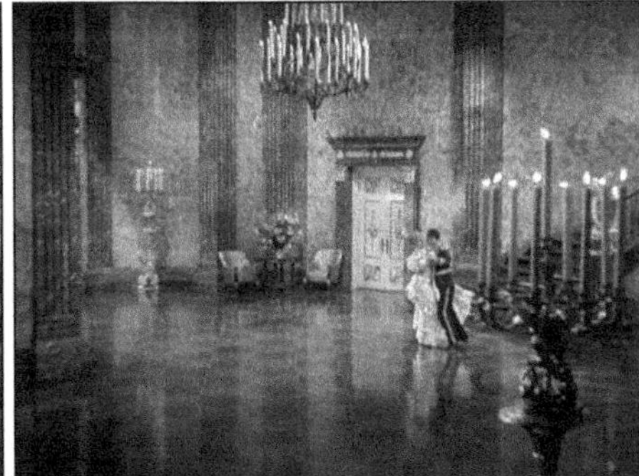

Figure 11

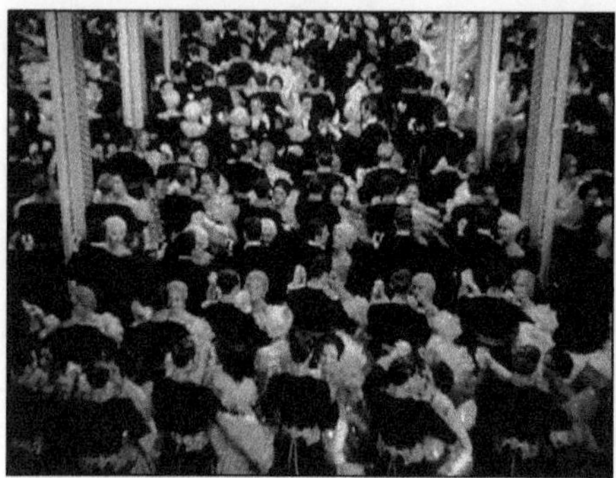
Figure 12

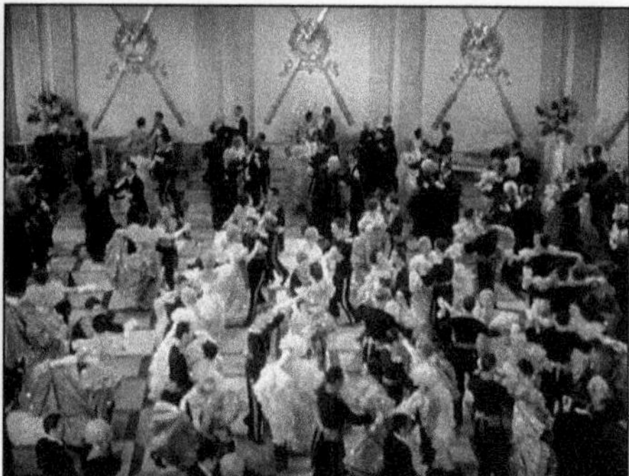
Figure 13

> on to a sense of] increasing constrictedness, a lack of free movement and a concomitant sense of inevitability attached to the movement that is made. Society is always flooding in on the couple, controlling their movement by rendering it part of a larger pattern ... [23] (figures 8–13), [though it should be noted that the couple dance together in the gazebo at the end of the sequence, suggesting that a degree of autonomy is possible. See figure 14].

Sonia's angry response to Marchovia's machinations, which entails her refusal to marry Danilo, is matched by Danilo himself, who refuses to marry Sonia because he really loves her. This particular plot twist and the paradoxes that mark them are unique to the 1934 version, and lead on to two equally unique final scenes. In the first, Danilo is put on trial and jailed for refusing to marry Sonia, and in the second, Sonia, who realises that his refusal means that really love her, visits Danilo in his cell and is locked in with him by Marshovia's rulers, who still need her money. In this way the trope of marriage as prison is literalised, and its implications are underlined in Paul's summary: 'While monogamous commitment is presented as the first step to growth for Danilo, it is also a last stop because marriage in the film is presented as a static experience: once reached, all further growth ceases'.[24] And as 'Danilo and Sonia move toward the social institution of marriage, they are moving toward an acceptance of themselves as social beings, a designation that must in part deny their individuality. If the marriage that generally ends a romantic comedy holds out the promise of a new social order, then the dialectical method of *The Merry Widow*, by cutting back and forth between controlling government officials outside the jail cell and the trapped lovers within, presents both an assured future for society at the same time that it makes clear the limited existence of the individuals'.[25]

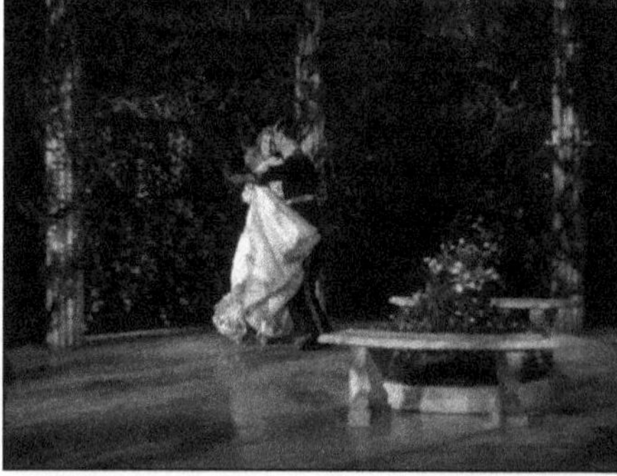
Figure 14

The Merry Widow (1952)

In 1952, MGM decided to produce a third version of *The Merry Widow*, which was produced by Joe Pasternak, directed by Curtis Bernhardt, and filmed in Technicolor by Robert Surtees, with Lana Turner as Crystal Radek (The Merry Widow) and Fernando Lamas as Danilo, and with 'Girls, Girls, Girls', 'Vilia', 'Nights', 'Maxim's', 'The Melody Of Laughter' and 'The Merry Widow Waltz' among the songs and numbers, with music by Franz Lehár and lyrics by Paul Frances Webster

This version opens in New York on New Years's Eve in 1899, where the fortune left to Crystal Radek by her late Marshovian husband is coveted by Marshovia's bankrupt rulers. The King (Thomas Gomez) invites Crystal to Marshovia in order to erect a statue in her husband's memory and engineer a marriage to the handsome Danilo, thus ensuring that her riches will remain in Marshovia and help pay off its debt. Surrounded by adoring women, Danilo initially appears singing 'Girls, Girls, Girls' as he leads his men to the railway station in order to greet Crystal (and her companion, Kitty, who is played by Una Merkel). But the train is delayed, and Danilo can next be found singing 'Vilia' in the square later that evening as he dances with a young gypsy woman accompanied by a band of local musicians. Crystal, who has now arrived, looks on unseen and is clearly entranced. Then she slips away and heads off to the palace to join Kitty. The layout of the square and other buildings, and the activities within them, strongly echo those in the 1934 version. But the fact that it is Danilo who sings 'Vilia', and the fact that he is later forced by the King to serenade the woman he eventually sees on the palace balcony (initially an unseen Crystal, but subsequently Kitty in her curlers), tends to deprive both scenes of the intimations of mortality that mark the equivalent scenes in the Lubitsch version. Moreover, when Crystal and Kitty decide to swap places with one another on the grounds that Crystal might attract fortune hunters, and when they maintain this ruse when they head off to Paris, this particular device means that Crystal can abandon her black clothing and adopt 'Fifi' as her name, but is otherwise an engine of complication that does little more than prolong the farce and allow her to wear white and other colours.

The private dining-room scene at Maxime's is largely derived from the comparable scene in the 1934 version. But here the nature of Crystal's identity remains a secret and Danilo remains charged with marrying a woman he thinks is the widow. Under orders from Marshovia, Danilo duly proposes, and Kitty, who is now aware of Crystal's feelings, postpones her response, and agrees to announce it at the Marshovian Embassy ball later that evening. Danilo tells the Marshovian ambassador to the United States that he is love with another woman and cannot marry the widow. But when Danilo, Crystal, Kitty and the ambassador all meet face to face, Danilo finally discovers Crystal's true identity. At this point Crystal and Danilo dance with another, recalling the dance sequence in the Lubitsch version. But although there are echoes of the mirror device, the sequence here has no real structure, and no purpose other than romantic spectacle. Moreover, when the dancing ends, Danilo criticises Crystal for the importance she attaches to money (of which there has been very little evidence), prompting her to leave in order to generate yet more farcical complication as the King arrives insisting that the American ambassador, Danilo and Nitki (King Donovan) all commit suicide. However, the King announces that Crystal has given up her fortune in order to pay Marshovia's debt, and Danilo rushes out so rapidly that he does not hear that the money donated by Crystal is only a tiny fraction of her wealth. In this way Danilo can pride himself on the fact that he will no longer be considered a fortune hunter – even though Crystal still has much more than he thinks, and even though the film ends on an unusual note, a note that leaves Crystal with plenty of money and Danilo in the dark with his pride intact.

Notes

1. John Kenrick, '*The Merry Widow* 101: History of a Hit', *Musicals 101.com: The Cyber Encyclopedia of Musical Theatre, Film & Television*: http://www.musicals101.com/widowhist.htm/30/12/201
2. Kenrick, '*The Merry Widow* 101'.
3. Karl Gänzl, '*Die Lustige Witwe, Operetta in 3 Acts*', http://operetta-research-center.org/die-lustige-witwe-operette-3-acts/30/12/2014
4. Karl Dietrich Gräwe, 'Synposis', trans. Mary Whittall, programme brochure for the 1994 Deutsche Grammaphon CD recording of *Die lustige Witwe*, p. 16.
5. Gräwe, 'Synopsis', p. 16.
6. Gräwe, 'Synopsis', p. 16.
7. Bernard Grun, *Gold and Silver: The Life and Times of Franz Lehar* (New York: David McKay Company, Inc., 1970), p. 119.
8. Grun, *Gold and Silver*, p. 120.
9. The first English-language novelisation was published by G.W. Dillingham in New York in 1909. A tie-in edition was published alongside the release of the 1925 film version, though I have been unable to locate one for the 1934 version. It should be noted that *The Merry Widow and the Devil*, a partly burlesque version, retained Lehár's score, but was newly scripted by George V. Hobart and premiered at Weber's Music Hall on 2 January 1908, where it ran for a total of 156 performances. See Orly Leah Krasner, 'Birth pangs, growing pains and sibling rivalry: musical theatre in New York, 1900–1920', in William A. Everett and Paul R. Laird (eds.), *The Cambridge Companion to the Musical* (Cambridge: Cambridge University Press, 2008 edition), p. 64. The original Broadway version was produced by Henry W. Savage, with English lyrics by Adrian Ross and musical direction by Louis Gottschalk, staging by George Marion, and costume design by Percy Anderson and settings by Walter Burridge. This version ran for total of 416 performances at the New Amsterdam Theatre, opening on 21 October 1907 and closing on 17 October 1908. Sonia was played by Ethel Jackson and Danilo by Donald Brian,
10. Kenrick, '*The Merry Widow* 101'. See also, Gänzl, '*Die Lustige Witwe*'. For later versions and alterations, see '*The Merry Widow*', http://en.wikipedia.org/wiki/The_Merry_Widow/01/01/2015. For an additional English-language biography of Lehár, see W. Macqueen-Pope and D. L. Murray, *Fortune's Favourite: The Life and Times of Franz Lehár* (London: Hutchinson, 1953).
11. Benjamin Glazer is credited as an assistant writer, but as he himself recalls, he contributed very little. See Richard Koszarski, *Von: The Life and Films of Erich von Stroheim* (New York: Limelight Editions, 2001), pp. 181–182.
12. In her book entitled *Ethics and Social Criticism in the Hollywood Films of Erich von Stroheim, Ernst Lubitsch, and Billy Wilder* (Westport, C.T.: Praeger Publications, 2001), p. 16, Nora Henry points out that von Stroheim's 1920s films can be divided into two consecutive groups. The first encompasses *The Devil's Passkey* (1920), *Blind Husbands* (1921) and *Foolish Wives* (1922), in all three of which the wife of an upper- or upper-middle class man 'finds herself in a moral conflict when a callous European officer tries to seduce her'; and alongside *The Merry Widow*, the second encompasses *Merry-Go-Round* (1923) and *The Wedding March* (1928), all three of which are marked by scenarios in which an officer of noble birth is attracted to a commoner and is initially bent on seduction. But the officer falls in love with the commoner, and this gives rise to various conflicts between duty, love and social status.

13. Koszarski, *Von*, p. 183.

14. Axt and Mendoza are credited for the music in the entry on the 1925 version in the online AFI Catalog of Silent Feature Films and their score is reproduced in the US DVD released by in 2002. Mendoza briefly discusses the score in Anthony Slide, *Silent Topics: Essays on Undocumented Areas of Silent Film* (Lanham MD.: Scarecrow Press, 2005) p. 71. Elsewhere in *Silent Topics*, p. 25, Slide claims that the 1925 version of *The Merry Widow* cost $622,500 (including an overhead of $70,000) but made a profit of $758,000. These figures differ slightly from those in Koszarski, *Von*, p. 199, who cites a total cost of $614, 961.90 and net receipts of $996,266. 24. It should be noted that Ray Rennahan photographed the coronation scene at the end the film in Technicolor, that other scenes (photographed largely by William Daniels) were tinted and toned, and that the roses left for Sally by Danilo were filmed in the Handschiegl Process. (See Koszarski, *Von*, pp. 192–93). The film opened at the Embassy Theatre in New York, a deluxe 609-seat venue that charged $2.20 per ticket and ran successfully for several months.

15. Koszarski, *Von*, p. 184.

16. According to Joel Finler, *Stroheim* (London: Studio Vista, 1967), p. 93, von Stroheim initially planned for Danilo to be killed in the duel, though how he planned to end the film is not made clear. The numerous changes to the storyline and script, both by von Stroheim and by MGM, are detailed in the chapter on *The Merry Widow* in Koszarski, *Von*, pp. 179–205. No mention is made of Danilo's death.

17. Scott Eyman, *Ernst Lubitsch: Laughter in Paradise, A Biography* (New York: Simon & Schuster, 1993), p. 219. See also, pp. 215–220, and Eyman, *Irving Thalberg: Boy Wonder to Producer Prince* (Berkeley: University of California Press, 2010), pp. 256–60. According to Edward Baron Turk, *Hollywood Diva: A Biography of Jeanette MacDonald* (Berkeley: University of California Press, 1998), p. 144, principal photography began on 13 April and ended on 13 July. For further background and details, see Turk, *Hollywood Diva*, pp. 140–146.

18. Eyman, *Ernst Lubitsch*, p. 222; Turk, *Hollywood Diva*, p. 149.

19. William Paul, *Ernst Lubitsch's American Comedy* (New York: University of Columbia Press, 1983), pp. 103–106.

20. Paul, *Ernst Lubitsch's American Comedy*, pp. 106–107.

21. Paul, *Ernst Lubitsch's American Comedy*, pp. 107–108.

22. Paul, *Ernst Lubitsch's American Comedy*, p. 108, emphasis in original.

23. Paul, *Ernst Lubitsch's American Comedy*, pp. 113–114.

24. Paul, *Ernst Lubitsch's American Comedy*, p. 110.

25. Paul, *Ernst Lubitsch's American Comedy*, pp. 110–111. Charles Afron makes similar points in *Cinema and Sentiment* (Chicago: University of Chicago Press, 1982), pp. 150–151: 'Widowhood, money, Don Juanism, and farce define the sexual politics of lovers who are forever being thrust together and driven apart by private and public waltzes. Can Danilo dance with one woman and then walk with her through life? He and Sonia find out only after the waltz has been examined through a spectacle of mirrors where the single couple is distinguished from and lost in an infinite series of couples ... and double meanings [as] champagne is served in jail; a priest performs the wedding ceremony through a slit in the cell door. All this leads to the voicing of those difficult words, "I love you"'. See also, Nancy Schwatz, 'Lubitsch's Widow: The Meaning of a Waltz', *Film Comment*, March-April, 1975, pp. 13–17.

Chapter 4

Seventh Heaven and 7th Heaven

In 1922 Austin Strong, a prolific but now largely forgotten playwright, wrote a highly successful play entitled *Seventh Heaven.*[1] Originally conceived by Strong as a one-act play, theatre impresario John Golden encouraged him to write a three-act version, which Golden went on to produce and direct.[2] The play opened at the Booth Theatre in New York on 30 October 1922, and ran for a total of 704 performances with George Paul as Chico, Helen Menken as Diane, Fred Holloway as Rat, Hubert Druce as Boul', Marion Kerby as Nana, William Post as Pere Chevillon, Beatrice Noyes as Arlette, and Frank Morgan as Brissac. Numerous roadshow versions followed. Then a film version was written by Benjamin Glazer and directed by Frank Borzage for the Fox Film Corporation. Now entitled *7th Heaven*, this version drew not only on the play, but on an emerging cycle of films set in and around World War One.[3] Along with a novelised version by Golden, the film was initially released on 6 May 1927 in Los Angeles and 25 May in New York City then re-released in New York on 10 September with a synchronised and pre-recorded sound effects and music track. One of three films to be nominated for an Academy Award for Outstanding Picture in 1929, Janet Gaynor, Benjamin Glazer, and Frank Borzage won awards for Best Actress in a Leading Role, Best Writing (Adapted Screenplay), and Best Directing respectively. However despite the film's success and its current status as a classic, the play has been largely been forgotten and is summarised in detail as follows.[4]

The Play

Act One takes place in a street in 'a "cul-de-sac" known as "The Hole in the Sock". An iron lamp post and a 'disreputable wine shop' are at the right and across the way on the left is a drab stone house with all its windows closed. Between them the 'Church of Heavenly Angels can be seen, and a sewer trap is visible in the gutter centre', and as the curtain rises 'a night-hawk' named Boul is cranking the engine of a dilapidated taxicab, watched by a Sergeant. After 'two futile efforts ... Boul stands back disgusted'

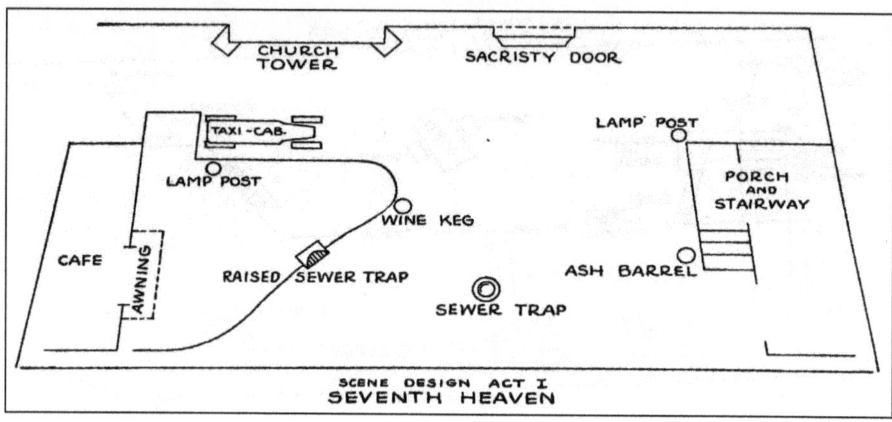

Figure 1

and the Sergeant exits (figure 1: scene design for Act One), and at this point 'The Sewer Rat' ('a small, long-nosed creature with the remnant of a beard and a quick, beady eye') enters and opens up a sewer trap. As he does so, a young woman called Arlette pulls him up by his collar and reprimands him for stealing a bottle of wine. Boul intervenes and Rat hands the bottle back to Arlette, who returns to the shop as Rat and Boul discuss the profitability of a stolen broach, arrangements for supper with Chico (whom we have yet to encounter), and the fact that Rat has stolen not one but two bottles of wine, which means that he and comrades will have wine to drink with their somewhat basic evening meal. At this point the grandly moustachioed Monsieur Gobin enters from the left, pulling the hose that he uses to clean the streets. He bumps into Nana, who lives with her sister Diane in the stone house opposite, and as Nana crosses the stage, she discusses the value of the stolen brooch, which she hopes to sell in order buy absinthe from the wine shop.

Gobin reacts to Nana's presence by exclaiming that if 'I had my way I'd turn my hose on all you street scum', then walks off dragging his hose as the Angelus bell booms out in the church behind him. Paul Recan, the private secretary to Colonel Brissac, enters and engages Boul in conversation. They discuss Boul's car (which he has named 'Louise'), then Recan leaves and waits for Brissac in the wine shop. At this point we encounter Diane, who 'is hurled backwards out of the house left and against the iron railing at head of the stairway'. Nana grasps Diane by the throat and attacks her with a whip, demanding that she sell it in order to buy more absinthe. Diane 'totters down the steps and sits, almost falling in a heap'. But Nana continues to threaten her and Arlettte tries to intervene. Recan attempts to get information on the sisters from Arlette. But Arlette refuses talk, and Recan leaves as Brissac and a lawyer named Blonde enter. Disgusted by the circumstances in which the sisters live, Brissac suggests that they hide the sisters from their Aunt and Uncle (Georges and Valentine), who are due to arrive a little later, and who expect the sisters to be living a proper Christian life. As Blonde and Brissac wait, we focus on The Sewer Rat, who passes by with a watch

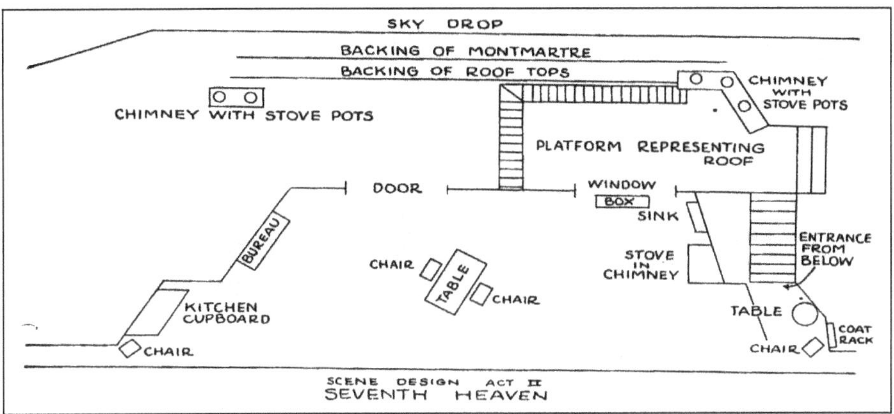

Figure 2

he has stolen from Pere Chevillon. A policeman attempts to retrieve the watch. But Chevillon intervenes and tells him that it's just a piece of tin: 'With a tin watch as my bait, I find out who the thieves are', he says, 'and when I find out who the thieves are, and when I've found them, I convert and baptise the rascals'. Chevillon is looking for Chico. But Rat informs him that Chico is a non-believer, and it is here that the issues of atheism and religion that mark the play throughout are first explicitly mooted.

In the meantime, 'the true nature of the sisters' lives' is exposed to Valentine and Georges. Reacting with shame and disgust, Georges flings money onto the ground and leaves with Valentine. Nana picks up the money and Diane reacts in terror as her sister attempts to strangle her, and at this point that 'the sewer trap is pushed open from below beside Diane's face' and that Chico, 'a handsome young giant, with curling hair and whipcord muscles in his neck', springs up from the sewer below. Chico parts the sisters, Boul lays Diane on the mudguard of his taxi, and Chico lowers Nana into the manhole, threatening to cut out her gizzard should she abuse Diane again. But as he chases Nana away, he begins to wonder whether Diane is worth saving. Chico philosophises: 'I am an atheist because I was religious', he says. 'I prayed for a good wife', but 'The only women I see are like that'. (He gestures to Diane). At this point 'Chevillon enters from the church and stands listening with a smile' as Chico continues: 'I want nothing in this world, Citizen. I am an atheist. I ask for nothing'. But Boul points out that Chico wants to be a street washer, and Chevillon grants Chico's wish in exchange for accepting two solid-silver medals. Chico is pleased, and he and his comrades end their meal in song as the church bells chime and an unseen church organ starts to play. Chico turns to Diane. He tells her that he is 'a very remarkable fellow' and that he is not afraid of anyone. He also says that he is Diane's friend and that he cannot let her feel such misery. A policeman enters with a group of women whom he intends to jail. Nana is among them and insists that Diane be arrested as well. But Chico intervenes. 'You can't arrest her because ... because she's my wife', he says, and Diane is stunned and the policeman suspicious. The policeman says that he will call on Chico in order to determine the truth, and as the policeman leads Nana away, Chico begins to wonder what he has done. 'How can we explain our marriage is not on the records', he says. But Diane replies that 'We can say we were married in Italy or Belgium' and Chico regains his élan: 'That's an idea', he says. 'You have a great head!' Diane replies that Chico has a great heart, and at this point Boul re-enters and Chico commands him to drive them home – 'me and my bride!' Chico turns to Diane: 'You're not going to take advantage of me?' 'No – oh, no!' she says, and Chico takes her hand as they drive off in Boul's taxi.

Act Two takes place in Chico's attic. 'Through a skylight we have an inspiring view of Heaven above and chimney pots ... below' and the white domes of Sacre Coeur can be seen 'rising into the distant clouds' (figure 2: scene design for act two). Arlette is quizzing Diane about her evening with Chico prior to their arrival at the attic that Diane calls 'Seventh Heaven'. And as they continue their conversation, we learn that Nana is now in prison — and that war may well be imminent. Gobin arrives and there are further discussions about the possible advent of war. Gobin and Arlette depart and Boul arrives looking for Chico. Chico has not yet arrived and Boul admires the view of 'heaven' through the skylight. 'So Chico didn't have to wait so long for a wife, eh, Madame Chico', he says, and Diane tells him that she is expecting the police and that she is staying here to prove that Chico has a wife. Boul assumes that Diane is married to Chico. But Diane tells him that they are not married and that Chico only comes to the attic for his meals, and at this point Chico enters with a box of wedding clothes, explains that he has been trying to track down the record of his birth, and that he and Diane can now be married. Boul is overjoyed. He gives them his gold watch and chain for a wedding present then exits, leaving Diane and Chico on their own. Diane attempts to kneel at Chico's feet. But Chico says that she must not do so: 'You and I did not exist until we met. Now we are one destiny'. He 'places a finger on his heart then gestures to her': 'Chico – Diane – Heaven', and continues to insist that 'there is no Bon Dieu'. He discovers the medals given him by Chevillon, but brushes this aside: 'Always these coincidences to frighten me! But I won't be fooled! ... I am myself – Chico – I march alone!'

Gobin re-enters and asks Diane for the soup she has been making for his wife. Diane is eager to show off the clothes that Chico has bought her, and 'holding the soup in one hand and the box of clothes in the other' she steps onto the roof. 'I'm not afraid', she says. 'I shall never be afraid again!' But the couple's happiness is threatened again, not only by rumours of war, but by the arrival of Valentine, who informs Chico that she and Brissac aim to bring Diane 'back to us'. Valentine is joined by Brissac and it looks as though Diane and Chico will have to part. But Chico stands firm and insists that Brissac and Valentine leave. 'Mon Dieu, I almost lost you', says Chico. 'Let us stay like this forever', says Diane. 'Never again will I be afraid ... I, too, am a very remarkable fellow'. But just as happiness beckons once more, Gobin arrives and announces that 'It's war'. Still unmarried to Diane, Chico says that 'We will marry ourselves'. He places the chain with one of the medals about her neck and continues: 'I take you, Diane, for my wife', he says, and in reply, Diane takes the other medal, kisses it, and hands it to Chico: 'I take you, Chico, for my husband, forever', she says. Martial music and church bells can now be heard in the distance as Chico picks up his bag and asks Diane to stand still: 'I want to see you last like this. Let me fill my eyes with you. I shall come to you each morning at this hour. Every day you will feel me here with you ... Au revoir –Heaven!' As Chico departs, and as Diane stands leaning against the door on her own, Nana enters and tries to steal her medal. But Diane is no longer afraid. She turns on Nana, grabs her whip, and throws it at her as she retreats down the stairs.

Act Three is set in Chico's attic on the morning of 11 November 1918. The attic 'is now a worn and shabby "Heaven"'. Arlette is putting the breakfast things away as Chevillon enters to look in on Arlette and Diane. Diane is out, and Arlette tells Chevillon that Brissac has been taking an interest in Diane, helping with the rent and arrangements for work at the munitions factory despite the fact she tries to avoid him. Chevillon asks whether there is any news of Chico, and Arlette says that Chico is reported missing. Arlette says that Diane thinks that Chico is still alive. But Arlette is not so sure, and at this point Gobin arrives with news that peace 'may be declared at any moment' then exits with Chevillon. Diane enters, tired and somewhat shabby. Arlette and Diane converse and Diane says that she thinks the war is over. Diane leaves as Brissac enters with two bottles of champagne. Brissac tells Arlette that the armistice is imminent and that 'nothing matters to me but Diane'. He also tells Arlette that Diane has been left a farm and an annuity by Valentine. At this point Recan enters and reveals that Chico is in hospital and is not expected to live. Recan leaves and Diane enters expecting good news. Brissac proposes to her. But Diane is adamant that Chico is alive, and they are both distracted by the entry of Gobin and Boul, who tells them how Eloise helped defeat the Germans. Diane asks Gobin whether he has news of Chico. But Gobin has no news, and Boul is optimistic but unconvincing. Diane recalls her initial meeting with Chico, rising from the ground to save her; she also recalls their vow to join each other in spirit at 11a.m. each day. But at this point Brissac returns with Chico's identification disc and the religious medal given him by Chevillon, and Diane assumes that Chico is dead. Doubting that she and Chico ever really communed with one another, Diane attempts to throw herself out of the open window. Brissac stops her, tries to comforts her, and stoops to kiss her. But as he does so, 'Chico enters, joyfully pushing his way' past Arlette, Boul, Gobin and Recan, 'who are clustered at the door'. Chico is blind. But he pushes his medical attendant away and searches for Diane. 'Cherie', he says, 'my eyes are still filled with you...But nothing can kill me! I'll never die! And I'll see. They can't keep me blind – because it's true, Cherie – those big thoughts were of the Bon Dieu after all. He is within us – now that I am blind, I see. I tell you, I'm a very remarkable fellow!'.

7th Heaven

Most of the characters and settings, many of the actions, and some of the dialogue in the play can be found in the 1927 film as well. But the dialogue is less prolific (as befits a silent film), and the opening scenes in particular are much more immediately

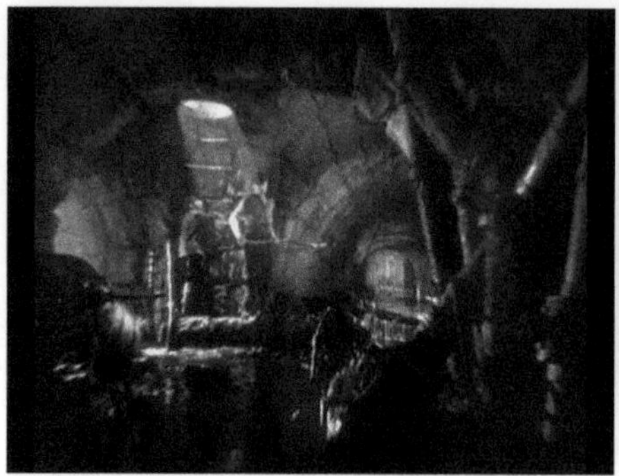

Figure 3

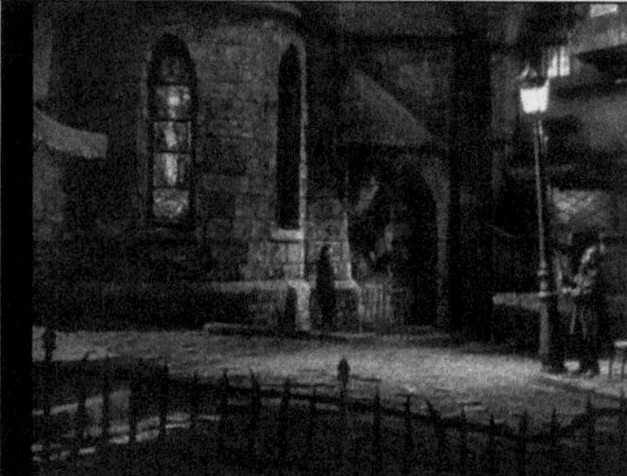

Figure 4

focussed on Chico and Rat (Charles Farrell and George E. Stone) and Diane and Nana (Janet Gaynor and Gladys Brockwell).[5] These scenes are designed to establish vertical patterns of camera movement, staging and framing, and these patterns pervade the remainder the film in later combination with horizontal ones.[6] Thus the opening title tells us that 'For those who those who climb it, there is a ladder leading from the depths to the heights – from the sewer to the stars', and thus a second title identifies the setting as 'the slums of Paris – under the street known as The Hole in the Sock'. The opening shot that follows focuses on Chico's feet in medium close-up just above the sewer's waters underground, and from here we cut to a long shot of Chico and Rat standing on a ledge, a ladder to the air above visible through an open manhole (figure 3). Water pours down from above as Gobin uses his hose to clean the street, and Chico turns to Rat: 'That's what I should be', he says, 'a street washer! Up there in the sunshine'. 'After all', he says, 'I'm a very remarkable fellow!'

Verticality is a hallmark of the ascent to 'heaven' later on, when Chico and Diane climb the stairs to Chico's attic apartment in what is now one of the famous camera shots in cinema history.[7] But verticality marks a number of previous shots and scenes as well, among them the low-angle close-up that introduces Nana, who looks down toward her sister, and the high-angle close-up that introduces Diane, who is cowering on the floor as her sister whips her. As in the play, Nana demands that Diane pawn a brooch in order to buy a bottle of absinthe. But in the film Diane leaves the apartment and sits in despair on the steps outside, the camera tilted downward in order to emphasise her diminutive frame. She looks up then down, then gathers her shawl as we cut to a medium long-shot showing her weary descent down the steps. From here we cut to a shot of Nana then onto the first of two reverse-angle travelling shots, this one framed slightly from above as Diane makes her way to the wine shop.[8] Dwarfed in long shot, Diane enters the wine shop and sells the brooch to one of two men in the corner, and from here we cut to Nana, who is visited by Chevillon (Emile Chautard), and who bears the news that their aunt and uncle 'have returned from the South Seas' and plan to visit the sisters soon. Diane begins to make her way home in forlorn long shot. But as she does so a man lights a streetlamp high-up on the right,

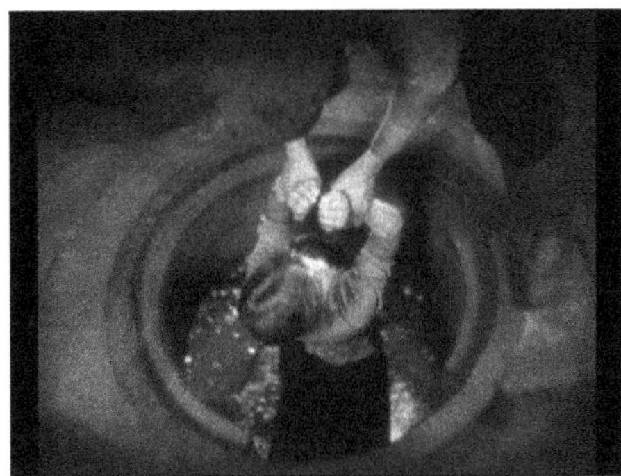

Figure 5

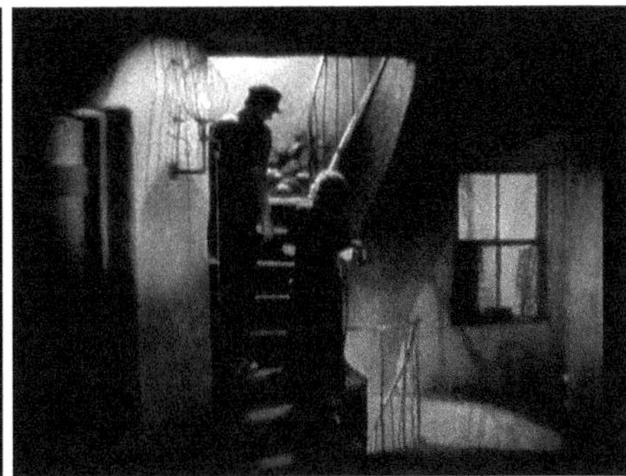

Figure 6

and in this way luminosity is added to verticality as one of the film's key stylistic motifs (figure 4).

The arrival of the sisters' aunt and uncle sets up another sequence involving high-angles. The visitors arrive and look up at the building then enter the sisters' apartment. Shocked by their mode of life, Uncle Georges scatters money on the floor, and he, his sister and Brissac leave. Nana picks up the money as we cut to another high-angle shot of the visitors leaving in the car outside, then approaches Diane with a whip, chases her round the room, onto the stairway outside, then down the steps and onto the pavement in a series of descents. Diane now lies helpless on the ground as Nana wields her whip, and from here we cut to Rat and Boul (Albert Gran), who can see what is happening from the kerb nearby. At this point Chico rises from sewer below, pulls Nana away from Diane, and suspends the former over the open sewer in yet another vertical framing (figure 5). But having frightened Nana away, Chico is dismissive of Diane, saying that a 'creature like that is better off dead'. Despite what he says, though, he cannot help turning to look at her, prone and unconscious on the ground near the sewer. He tries to revive her, begins to walk away, then turns back toward her, and these hesitant movements are subsequently echoed when Diane is finally revived, begins to walk away, then turns back to Chico. Chico's concern for Diane begins to mount, and from this point through to the ascent to heaven the dialogue and action replicate most of the dialogue and action in the play: Diane is in a state of hopelessness, Chico tries to spark her into life, and Chevillon gives Chico a pair of medals and tells him that he is now an official street washer, on a par with Gobin. Chico follows Diane across the street, and as they stand together under the street lamp, they are lit by its glow. As in the play, a policeman enters with Nana and a number of other women. Nana says that Diane should be arrested, but Chico pulls Diane away from the policeman and tells him that she is his wife. The policeman takes a note of Chico's address and leads Nana and the other women away. Then we cut to a two-shot of Chico and Diane. As in the play, Chico is distraught, thinking that he will lose his new job. But Diane suggests that she stay at Chico's apartment until the police come, at which point they exchange looks with one another as Chico rises from the pavement.

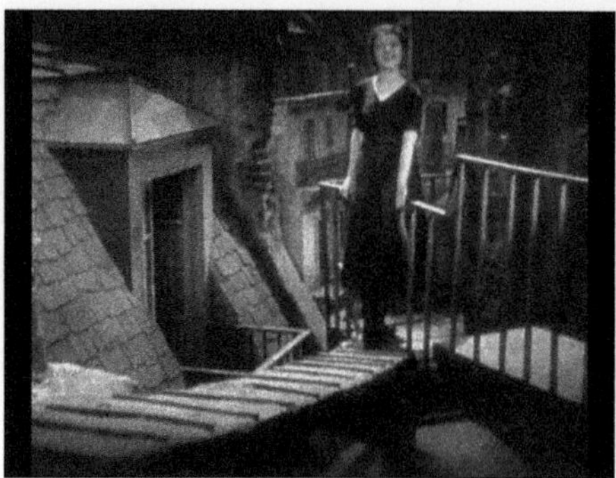

Figure 7

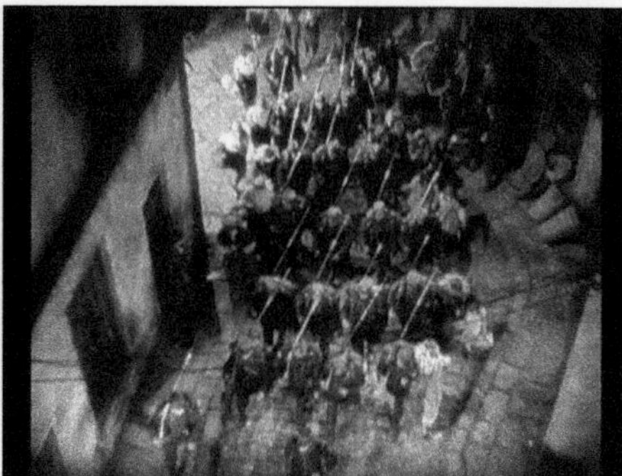

Figure 8

'You have a great head', he says, and Diana replies that 'You have a great heart', and from here Chico summons Boul and Eloise in order to tour of the boulevards before taking them on to Chico's home.

Having cut to Chico and Diane climbing the stairs to Chico's apartment, a justly famous vertical moving shot (figure 6), Chico and Diane enter and Chico tries to help Diane walk onto the boardwalk outside the open window. But Diane turns back after a few initial steps, and as she prepares for bed she is unsure as to where Chico will sleep. Bit by bit though her fears are assuaged as Chico invites her to look down on the streets below, and as they end up sleeping at a distance from one another. Chico and Diane share breakfast together, but Chico still insists that Diane must leave once the policeman checks on them. Gobin enters from the rooftop apartment opposite and walks off with Chico to hose the streets below. Diane watches them leave. Then she looks up, gets up, and crosses the rooftops with her new-found confidence (figure 7). Chico is confident too, and when a detective arrives, Chico says that he and Diane are married. When the detective leaves, Diane resumes cutting Chico's hair. Chico is pleased with his hair cut (and much more besides): 'If you want to stay', he says, 'you're not in my way'. Diane sheds tears of joy: 'Chico, I believe in the Bon Dieu – I believe He brought you to me', and as if to confirm her words we cut to Chevillon in the street outside.

Time passes and one day Chico arrives with a box and a flower pot. The box contains a wedding dress, and Diane is overwhelmed. 'But you never said you love me', she says. 'Couldn't you just say it just once'. 'Well this way then', says Chico as we cut to a two shot and a pair of close-up singles – 'Chico' and 'Diane' – then back to the two shot – 'Heaven'. Diane asks Chico whether they are going to marry in church. 'No – certainly not', he says. 'I am an atheist – I walk alone'. At this point Chico sits on the coat that Diane has been mending and finds the medals that Chevillon gave them earlier on. 'It's only a coincidence' he says, as Gobin arrives for the soup that Diane has made for Gobin's pregnant wife. Diane takes the soup to Madame Gobin across the rooftops, vowing that she will 'never be afraid again'. But as she does so, we cut to Chico and Gobin looking down on the streets below, which are filled with crowds and soldiers. 'Comrade, this is war', says Gobin. 'We leave within the hour'. Diane returns wearing her wedding dress – and Chico finally tells her that he loves her. It is now Chico who is fearful. But Diane lifts his chin up. 'Never look down – always look up', she says. 'I too am a very remarkable fellow'. They hug and kiss and sit on a chair together as we cut back and forth between the two of them and the crowds in the street below (figure 8). There is no time to get married, so they decide to exchange their vows 'now' and 'here' – and to exchange the medals given them by Chevillon. 'Stand still – don't move – I want to see you this way last', says Chico. 'Let me fill my eyes with you'. And as he fills his eyes – and as they exchange their wedding vows – we dissolve to clock on the wall: 'Every day at this hour – eleven o'clock – I shall come to you', says Chico as he leaves. At this point Nana enters. But Nana is a threat no longer, and Diane takes Nana's whip and chases her away.

Like nearly all the scenes so far, the scenes in the apartment – and the general array of characters and actions – are much more streamlined than their equivalents in the play, with fewer characters, a prolonged focus on Diane and Chico, and a subsidiary focus on Gobin and his wife. But at this point we cut away from the apartment and onto the 'relentless wave of death rolling relentlessly down upon Paris' as extensive shots and scenes of soldiers marching, generals planning, and concerned citizens preparing for battle are only briefly interspersed by shots of Diane and Gobin's wife. Some of the battle scenes that follow were filmed by John Ford, others by Borzage.[9] They culminate in model shots of Parisian taxis interspersed with regular live-action footage. Eloise is destroyed, but Paris is saved, and the news is conveyed its grateful inhabitants, and from here we turn to focus once again on Diane, and on Chico and his comrades. As in the play, Diane is working in a munitions factory with a number of other women and Brissac is pursuing her. But here we see them in the factory together and Diane is still steadfast: 'Chico fights at the Front', she says. 'I fight here'. Brissac leaves and we cut to the front. It is cold and wintry, and Rat and Chico and Gobin are searching for something to eat. They purloin a chicken from the chef who cooks the officers' meals then sit down to eat. Chico reaches into his coat pocket and pulls out his medal, and we cut back and forth between Chico and Diane, each of them standing vertically as the clock in the apartment strikes eleven, and as they each close their eyes and intone 'Chico – Diane – Heaven'.

From here we cut to a shot of Chico and his comrades marching 'Day after day year after year', then on to a shot of Chico and the others preparing for battle. Probably inspired by comparable scenes in *The Big Parade* (1925), the battle begins, flame throwers are deployed into the night, and on the following day we find Rat and Chico in a shell hole. Chico is badly injured and is now unable to see. But he and Diane (who is at the factory) both look up from seated positions at 11 a.m., clasp their respective medals, and incant their love in the usual way. However, their mutual communion is disturbed as a German soldier attacks Rat and Chico (a variant on another scene in *The Big Parade*), and we fade to black then cut back to Diane, who looks up with concern and puts her hand up to her eyes. Rat kills the German soldier and drags Chico back to the company's trench and Chevillon observes their arrival

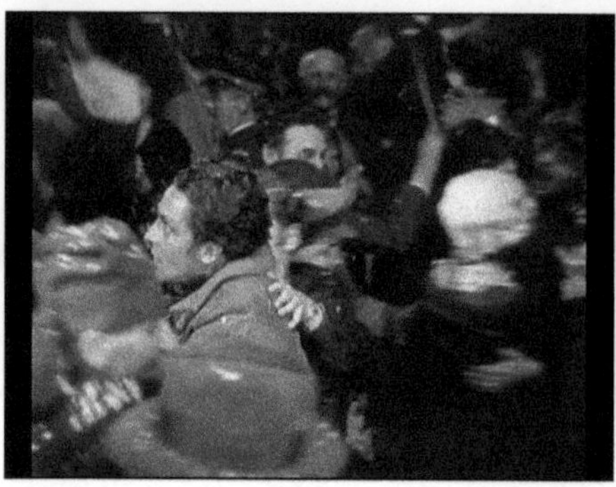
Figure 9

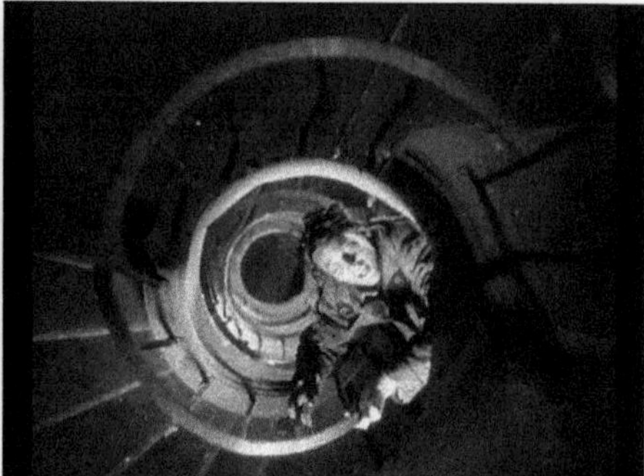
Figure 10

and helps lay Chico on the ground. Chico sits up but cannot see. He gives his medal to Chevillon and asks him to give it to Diane. 'Tell her I died looking up' he says as we fade then cut to Diane, who is now back in the apartment. At this precise point Brissac enters. 'I have very bad news' he says as he shows her a casualty list containing the words 'Chico Robas – corporal – killed'. Diane refuses to believe it. But Gobin arrives and tells her that the news is true – 'it's the Government that says so', he says – and in further confirmation Chevillon enters and tells her that Chico died 'looking up'.

Diane slumps down in a nearby chair, no longer buoyant, and no longer looking up. 'For four years I have called this Heaven – I prayed – I believed in God', she says. 'I believed He would bring Chico back to me ... And Chico is dead'. But as Diane ends her words, we cut to a view of the crowds and Chico, who is blind but very much alive. Driven by what John Belton calls 'an inner vision', Chico makes his way through the crowds as Palmer's camera tracks his determined lateral movements (figure 9).[10] We cut back and forth between Chico in the streets and Diane, Brissac and Chevillon in the apartment above. Chico finds the door to his apartment block and pushes it open, and from here we cut back and forth between Diane and the others in a lateral staging upstairs and a set of tight high-angle framings of Chico as he climbs the stairs on his way to heaven (figure 10). Chico bursts into the apartment and pauses, Diane crosses the room, and Diane and Chico embrace in medium close-up. 'They thought I was dead, but I'll never die', says Chico, 'those big thoughts I had were the Bon Dieu after all'. 'He is within me. Now that I am blind, I see that'. A vocal rather than orchestral version of 'Diane' begins to play on the soundtrack of the Movietone version as Chico continues.[11] 'My eyes are still filled with you', he says. Diane replies that 'I will be your eyes', and Chico continues: 'For a while, perhaps ... But nothing can keep Chico blind for long ... I tell you, I'm very remarkable fellow!'

Diane and Chico embrace once more and we cut to a medium long-shot of the apartment as a whole. Chico and Diane are on the right (the former kneeling, the latter standing) and Chevillon is standing on the left. Chico and Diane are lit by a diagonal beam of light and Chevillon is in shadow (figure 11), a configuration of light

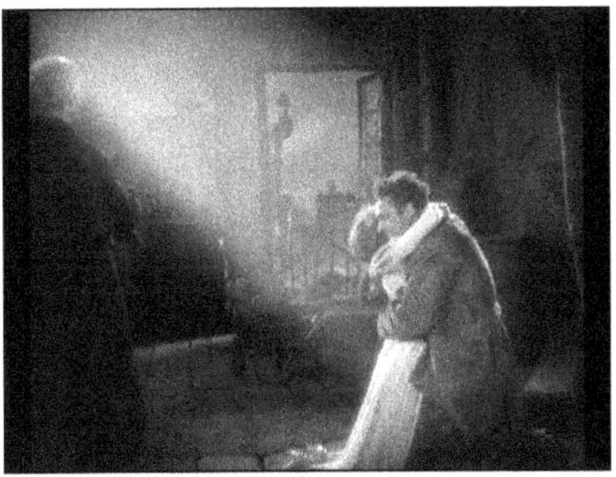

Figure 11

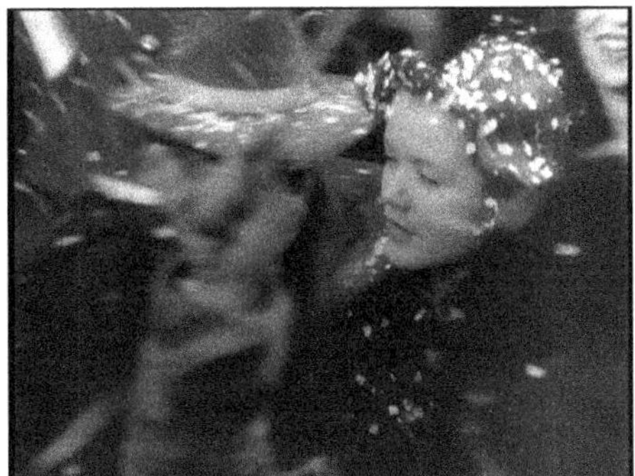

Figure 12

and shade that is neither specified in the play's instructions nor described in the pages of Golden's novel. Along with the improbabilities inherent in Chico's return, this shot and its significance have been discussed at length by John Belton, Frederick Lamster, and Philip Rosen. For Belton, 'Chico's miraculous return to life is no lapse in narrative continuity but an illustration of the transcendent nature of love in Borzage's work. Chico and Diane's love defies not only time and space but also mortality. The ending of *Seventh Heaven* [sic] destroys narrative logic and physical reality to reveal the strength of the spirit behind that reality and the existence of an eternal, abstract level of experience that mysteriously defies death itself'.[12] For Lamster, Chevillon's presence in the final shot is undercut by the lovers, 'who have transcended their immediate world as well as the set of beliefs imposed by a formal and often untested religion'.[13] And for Rosen, the logical contradictions inherent in the film's denouement mark an irrationally miraculous conflation religious and secular love.[14] These views are all germane. But what is crucial is that they pinpoint the extent to which *7th Heaven* defies conventional logic.

Seventh Heaven (1937)

A later film version, now spelt as *Seventh Heaven*, was produced by Darryl F. Zanuck and directed by Henry King for Twentieth-Century Fox in 1937. This version is less audacious than the 1927 version and tends to lack stylistic élan. But King and his screenwriters, Albert Hackett, Frances Goodrich and Charles Lederer, were not unintelligent, and were now working under the auspices of the Production Code administered by Joseph Breen, which may help explain the more dominant and less equivocal figure of Chevillon (Jean Hersholt) and the manner in which the ending is represented. In addition, this version streamlines the storyline involving Diane (Simone Simon) and Nana (Gale Sondergaard) by cutting out the sub-plot involving their aunt and uncle, and by suggesting that Nana is a madame and Diane a potential prostitute in the inn named 'The Hole in the Wall' in the play and the 1927 version. Diane was identified a prostitute in an early version of the play script,[15] and in the 1937 version Nana tries to coerce her sister into having sex with a client, but Diane

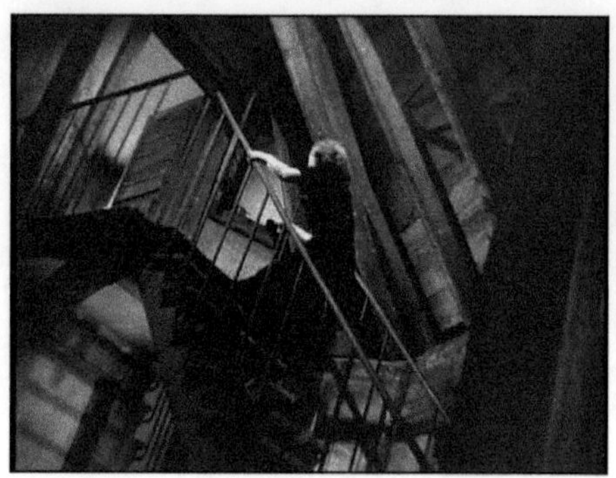

Figure 13

refuses. Later on and in despair, she tries to solicit a customer but is rescued by Chico. A new character named Aristide (J. Edward Blomberg) lives nearby on the rooftops of Paris. He is initially critical of Diane, thinking that she is taking advantage of Chico. But he is eventually won over, expressing his admiration for her steadfast nature while Chico is away.

King and his colleagues recycled some of the vertical framings and motifs. But they clearly decided to film the ascent to heaven in series of distinct and relatively complex shots rather than the single one that marks the 1927 version, and this is picked up in the denouement. Here Diane is working as a nurse in a hospital, and this is where she first encounters Brissac (Thomas Beck), who is portrayed as a much more decent, much less predatory figure than he is in the play and the 1927 version. Less emphasis is placed on combat and there are no taxis in battle near Paris, and the presence of Chevillon is more prominent and decisive despite (or because of) Chico's apparent death. But what is most striking are the reversals and alterations that follow, as Diane, not Chico, makes her away through the crowded streets (figure 12), and as Diane, not Chico, ascends the crowded stairway to heaven (figures 13). Once there Diane and Chico are reunited. But there is no sign of Chevillon or Brissac.

There have been no remakes since. But alongside the NBC radio version with Mary Pickford as Diane, four radio adaptations were aired on *Lux Radio Theatre* on 14 October 1934 (with Miriam Hopkins as Diane and John Boles as Chico), 17 October 1938 (with Jean Arthur as Diane and Don Ameche is Chico), 16 October 1944 (with Jennifer Jones as Diane and Van Johnson as Chico), and 26 March 1951, which reunited Janet Gaynor as Diane and Charles Farrell as Chico. A *Broadway Television Theatre* version was broadcast in the USA on 28 October 1953 and versions were broadcast on television in Brazil in 1956 and 1958. A stage musical version was produced by Grant Gaither and William Bacher, and following pre-Broadway dates in New Haven, Philadelphia and Boston, it ran from 26 May to 2 July at the ANTA Playhouse in New York in 1955, with a book by Victor Wolfson and Stella Unger, music by Victor Young, lyrics by Stella Unger, and Ricardo Montalban and Gloria De Haven as Chico and Diane. However, unlike the 1922 play and the 1927 film version, it was widely regarded as a failure.

Notes

1. Strong wrote eleven plays between 1906 and 1935 in addition to *Seventh Heaven*.
2. See John Golden and Viola Brothers Shore, *Stage-Struck John Golden* (New York: Samuel French, 1930), esp. pp. 179–183, 263–265, and http://wikipedia.org/wiki/ John_Golden. 15/10/2015, which cites some

of the numerous musical comedies and farces for he wrote the lyrics, some of the popular songs he wrote, and some of fifty-plus plays he produced for the theatre.

3. Sheldon Hall and Steve Neale, *Epics, Spectacles, and Blockbusters*, p. 60. See also Kim R. Holston, *Movie Roadshows*, pp. 43–44, 56–57.

4. It is worth noting that Borzage directed numerous adaptations of plays during the course of his long career. In addition to *7th Heaven*, they include *Get-Rich-Quick Wallington* (1922), from a play by George M. Cohan; *Secrets* (1924), from a play by Rudolph Besier and May Edington; *Lazybones*, from a play by Owen Davis, *Wages for Wives*, from a play by Guy Bolton and Winchell Smith, and *The Circle*, from a play by W. Somerset Maugham (all 1925); *The First Year*, from a play by Frank Craven, and *Marriage License?*, from a play by F. Tennyson Jesse and Harold Marsh Harwood entitled *The Pelican* (both 1926); *Street Angel* (1928), from a play by Monckton Hoffe; *Liliom* (1930), from a play by Ferenc Molnar; *As Young as You Feel*, from a play by George Ade and Viña Delmar, and *Bad Girl*, from a play by Brian Marlowe (both 1931); *After Tomorrow*, from a play by Hugh S. Stange and John Golden, and *Young America*, from a play by John F. Ballard (both 1932); *Secrets* (1933), a remake from a play by Rudolph Besier and May Edington; *Desire*, from a play by Hans Szekely and R.A. Stemmle, and *Hearts Divided*, from a play by Rida Johnson Young (both 1936); *The Shining Hour* (1938), from a play by Keith Winter; *Smilin' Through* (1941), from a play by Jane Cowl and Jane Murfin, and *Till We Meet Again* (1944), from a play by Alfred Mauray. All the adaptations directed thereafter were based on novels or short stories.

5. Farrell's acting and persona in Borzage's films are highly distinctive, a combination of proletarian strength, lyricism, sensitivity and expressivity that is explored in detail in Pat Kirkham, 'Loving Men: Frank Borzage, Charles Farrell and the Reconstruction of Masculinity in 1920s Hollywood Cinema', in Kirkham and Janet Thumim (eds.), *Me Jane: Masculinity, Movies and Women* (London: Lawrence & Wishart, 1995), pp. 94–112.

6. As Joe McElhaney points out in 'Frank Borzage: Architect of Ineffable Desires', *Senses of Cinema*, no. 25 2003, p. 12, the 'basic sense of movement in so much of Borzage is as vertical as it is horizontal, with spaces often conceived in terms of extreme levels and the characters ascending and descending'. See also, Hervé Dumont, *Frank Borzage*. Trans. Jonathan Kaplansky (Jefferson, N. C. and London: McFarland & Company, Inc., 2006), pp. 114–16, 121, 126, who links verticality to spiritual and redemptive ascension, and who links them in turn to the principles of Freemasonry, of which Borzage was an adherent.

7. According to Janet Bergstrom, the camera was on an elevator 'outfitted with ropes and pulleys so that Ernest Palmer and his camera could follow the couple in one shot, although a trick match hides the fact that three floors appear to be six, ending at the last stair-ladder to the top', which of course makes seven overall. See Bergstrom, '*7th Heaven*', p. 21, in the 2009 programme booklet for the BFI's double DVD of *7th Heaven* and *Street Angel*.

8. According to the notes on page 56 of the brochure written by Bergstrom for the 'Murnau, Borzage and Fox' DVD collection released in the US in 2008, this particular camera movement entailed the use of a platform as a crew of eight men carried Palmer and his camera, 'alternating their steps to try and keep the camera from bouncing'.

9. See Dumont, *Frank Borzage*, p. 119.

10. John Belton, *The Hollywood Professionals, Volume 3:Howard Hawks, Frank Borzage, Edgar G. Ulmer* (London: The Tantivy Press and New York: A.S. Barnes & Co., 1974), p. 79.

11. 'Diane' was written for *7th Heaven* by Erno Rapee and Lew Pollack. Theme songs such as this were relatively common in the 1920s and sales of sheet-music and disc recordings constituted a growing and lucrative source of income. As Ross Melnick points out, these songs could also be heard on the radio, generating further links 'between the film and music and publishing and recording industries' and acting as a further catalyst 'for the mid-to-late 1920s theme song craze'. See Melnick, *American Showman: Samuel 'Roxy' Rothafel and the Birth of the Entertainment Industry* (New York: Columbia University Press, 2012), p. 3, and Russell Sanjek, updated by David Sanjek, *Pennies from Heaven: The American Popular Music Business in the Twentieth Century* (New York: Da Capo, 1996 edition), pp. 52, 106. For further details on 'Diane' and *7th Heaven*, see Melnick, *American Showman*, pp. 293, 294, 321, 322.

12. Belton, *The Hollywood Professionals*, p. 79.

13. Frederick Lamster, *Souls Made Great Through Love and Adversity: The Film Work of Frank Borzage* (Metuchen, N.J.: Scarecrow Press, 1981), p. 49.

14. Philip Rosen, 'Difference and Displacement in *Seventh Heaven*', *Screen*, vol. 18 no. 2 (1977), pp. 96–101.
15. See Samuel L. Leiter, *The Encyclopedia of the New York Stage, 1920–1930,* vol. 2 (Westport, Conn.: Greenwood Press, 1985), p. 817.

Chapter 5

The Cocoanuts

Probably best known as the first Marx Brothers feature film, *The Cocoanuts* was produced by Monte Bell for the Paramount Famous-Lasky Corporation and directed by Robert Florey and Joseph Santley. With cinematography by George Folsey and a musical score was supervised by Frank Tours, it premiered in New York on 24 May 1929 and was released more widely on 3 August later that year.[1] The film was based on a musical comedy, also called *The Cocoanuts*, which was produced for the stage by Sam H. Harris, and which was written by Irving Berlin (who wrote the original songs) and George S. Kaufman (who wrote the original book).[2] Morrie Ryskind was a key additional figure, and although he did not receive a credit, he collaborated with Kaufman in the writing of the book, and fine-tuned some of the comic dialogue and business for Chico, Groucho, Harpo and Zeppo Marx as the stage-show and film versions evolved in turn.[3] Major factors in the film's production included the decision to remove most of the songs in the stage versions and insert new ones. They also included the ways in which the new sound technology, which was still in its inflexible infancy, affected the framing, staging and editing. As has also been well documented, the stage show retained its overall shape, but was subject to changes, additions and cuts. Some were a consequence of improvisations by Chico, Groucho and Harpo, some the result of changes in the cast, and some the product of decisions to insert new songs and discard others when the Broadway version closed and a newly-revised version went on tour.

The Stage Show

The Cocoanuts was one of a number of musical comedies on topical subjects on the stage in the latter half of the 1920s: *Oh, Kay* focussed on bootlegging, *Rosalie* on Lindberg's flight, and *The Cocoanuts* and *Tip-Toes* on real-estate speculation in Florida.[4] *The Cocoanuts* was given an initial tryout in Boston on 26 October 1925, then in Philadelphia. With direction by Oscar Eagle and musical staging by Sammy Lee, its Broadway run opened at the Lyric Theatre on 8 December 1925 and ended on 7 August 1926. It was briefly revived on Broadway at the Century Theatre from 16 May to 28 May 1927, following what was called the '1926 Summer Edition', which opened on 10 June 1926, and which featured the Bronx Sisters, who sang the songs originally assigned to a character called Penelope. A version of the script 'as it played on its opening night in New York in 1925' was published by Kaufman in 1979.[5] This version notes the titles of the songs and their placement, though it does not note the lyrics (or the music, to which Kaufman was famously averse). It also identified the original cast, and noted the extent to which 'business' ('stage action, either rehearsed or spontaneous') was crucial and a mark of the performances of Chico, Groucho and Harpo in particular.[6]

Act One Scene One begins in a hotel lobby. The curtain opens to disclose a number of hotel guests on stage, and along with a hotel clerk called Jamison (Zeppo Marx), the ensemble goes into an opening number entitled 'The Guests' and are joined by the Bellhops. Jamison tells one of the bellboys that the guests are unhappy about the lack of service and one of the other bellboys says that this is because they have not been paid. The latter bellboy demands to speak to Henry W. Schlemmer (Groucho Marx), the manager and owner, but is told that he is not up yet. 'The Guests' is reprised by the Bellhops, and Mrs Potter (Margaret Dumont) enters and asks Jamison whether he has seen her daughter Polly. Harvey Yates enters and tells Mrs. Potter that he has been looking for Polly but cannot find her. Mrs Potter says that she thinks that Polly is with Bob Adams, and at this point Penelope Martyn enters and Mrs Potter leaves. It soon becomes apparent that Harvey is after the money to which Polly is heir, and Penelope tells him that she has 'a plan that would take care of both of us'. Polly enters and makes it clear that she is only interested in Bob, an architecture student who is currently working as the hotel's chief clerk. But Mrs Potter forbids Polly from seeing him, and as the former exits, the latter laments her plight in a song entitled 'Family Reputation'.

The bellboys put their demands to Schlemmer, who distracts them with his double talk and goes up upstairs again. Schlemmer reappears and the bellboys press their demands. But Schlemmer fools them with his gobbledygook – 'Suppose George Washington's soldiers had asked for money? Where would this country be today? ... I want you to be free' – and the bellboys exit cheering. Mrs Potter enters; Schlemmer informs her that he is about to auction various plots of land; Mrs Potter and Schlemmer leave; and Bob takes his place behind the desk. Polly enters and talks to Bob. Then they exit together as the bellboys enter and sing 'Lucky Boy'. Schlemmer re-enters and Willie the Wop and Silent Sam (Chico and Harpo Marx) enter, wreaking havoc as they pursue two young women across the stage. Schlemmer tells Willie that 'you'll have to sign the book. If you don't register, you can't vote', and Willie replies that 'Last year I no register and I vote six times'. Following 'business with the register', Harvey and Penelope enter and the latter becomes engaged in 'umbrella business' with Silent Sam. 'Harpo, Chico and Groucho exit' (these names are used from this point on) and attention turns to Penelope and Harvey, who plan to steal Mrs Potter's necklace later that evening. 'Her room and mine are right next to each other', says Penelope, who plans to encourage Harpo and Chico to come up to her room in order to set them up as the necklace thieves. Harvey and Penelope leave and Groucho and a group of chorus girls enter. 'No girls, you're wrong', says Groucho. 'And besides, Valentino is much taller than I'. Then we move on to 'Why Am I Hit With the Ladies?', which ends as Detective Hennessy enters. Hennessy explains that he is looking for two wanted men, and that Chico and Harpo fit their descriptions. Hennessy leaves, Bob asks Polly whether she could live on a lot entitled Cocoanut Manor, and Bob and Polly sing a song entitled 'A Little Bungalow'.

Act One Scene Two takes place in front of a stage curtain depicting the palm trees outside the hotel, and the 'The "Bungalow" refrain is played softly through the entire scene'. Chico and Penelope enter and stroll across the stage. Penelope flatters Chico by telling him that he looks like the Prince of Wales (a running gag in the stage and film version alike), and invites him 'to room three hundred and twenty at eleven o'clock'. Chico replies that he'll be there at ten-thirty and they exit. Penelope re-enters with Harpo and goes through a similar routine. Then they exit too, and Groucho and Mrs Potter enter. Groucho tells Mrs Potter that she looks like the Prince of Wales and that he loves her. Mrs Potter says that 'I don't think you'd love me if I were poor' and Groucho replies that 'I might, but I'd keep my mouth shut'. 'I'll meet you tonight by the bungalow, under the moon' he says as we segue into a reprise of 'A Little Bungalow'.

Act One Scene Three is set in two adjacent hotel rooms. 'Room 320 at the left is Penelope's...and Room 318 is Mrs Potter's', and each has a door at the rear leading into the hall. As Penelope enters Mrs Potter's room, Harpo enters Penelope's room and hides under the bed. Penelope hears a noise, returns to her own room, and closes the door. Harvey enters with the key to Mrs Potter's jewellery box, and he and Penelope make plans to steal the necklace and other items of jewellery and hide them in a nearby tree trunk. Harvey draws a diagram of the tree and exits, and Penelope screws up the diagram and heads for Mrs Potter's room again. As she does so, Harpo crawls from under bed, retrieves the diagram from the waste basket, and exits through the window. Then Penelope opens the connecting door leading to Mrs Potter's room, and Groucho opens the door from the hallway. Chico enters Penelope's room and Groucho enters Mrs Potter's room. Chico reminds Penelope that he looks the Prince of Wales, and as 'Groucho throws open the connecting door and enters Penelope's room', Chico, 'escapes into the hall'. The scene continues in this vein, and Hennessy enters and declares that 'there's nobody putting anything over on me' then leaves. Then Penelope finally succeeds in stealing the necklace and re-enters her own room, proclaiming that she is 'Alone at last' even though Harpo is still under her bed.

Act One Scene Four opens with a song entitled 'Florida by the Sea'. Groucho and Chico enter and discuss the extent to which, as Chico puts it, 'we come here to make money...We hear you got big boom here, so we come too'. Groucho informs Chico that he will be holding an auction at Cocoanut Manor the following morning, and after further bouts of Marxian banter they exit.

Act One Scene Five opens with a performance of 'The Monkey-Doodle-Doo' at Cocoanut Manor. Harpo finds Mrs. Potter's necklace and exits, and Bob and Polly enter, hoping to find an affordable home. A chorus of 'Florida by the Sea' is sung, and the auction is prefaced by Groucho, who announces that Cocoanut Manor 'is one of the finest cities in Florida. Of course, we still need a few finishing touches, but who doesn't'. He opens the auction, which leads to Chico outbidding himself as the price rises from two hundred to eight hundred dollars. Another lot is bid for by a young boy, then by Bob and Harvey. Bob secures the purchase, but at this point Mrs Potter declares that her necklace has been stolen. Harpo intervenes, clears the path to the hollow stump, reaches down and pulls up a snake then 'triumphantly brings up the necklace'. Mrs Potter is delighted. But Hennessy tells Groucho that 'I saw you in that room last night' and accuses him of angling for the reward. He also suggests that Bob 'might know something', and at this point Penelope puts the blame Bob as well and Hennessy arrests him. Mrs Potter announces that Polly and Harvey will be engaged at a dinner the following night. The chorus reprises 'Lucky Boy', and following a reprise of 'Bungalow by the Sea', Harpo puts his arm around Polly to comfort her, and 'looks toward the audience and winks' as the curtain falls.

Act Two Scene One is set in the hotel lounge and begins with a number entitled 'Five O'Clock Tea'. Groucho enters and asks one of the bellboys to find him a place in a poker game upstairs. The bellboy exits and Polly and Chico enter. Chico and Groucho try to assure Polly that Bob will be alright. But Polly needs bail for Bob, and neither Chico nor Groucho have any money. Harpo enters and joins in their concern. Then Mrs Potter enters and tells Groucho that she is going to give him a thousand dollars for finding her necklace. Chico ups the ante to two thousand and Groucho to two million. Mrs Potter tries to stick to a thousand, but Groucho, Harpo and Chico steal her bag, and in the end she gives them a thousand dollars for finding her necklace and five hundred dollars for finding the bag. They exit and the chorus sings 'They're Blaming The Charleston'. Penelope summons Harvey and they discuss whether the discovery of the diagram could implicate them in the robbery. Harpo enters and they realise that he has the diagram and pursue him off stage. Groucho enters with Bob, who thanks Groucho and Harpo for bailing him out of jail. And following a routine involving paper and cutlery, Harpo shows the diagram to Bob, who realises that the diagram is evidence. Bob embraces Polly and joins her in a song entitled 'We Should Care'. Then Mrs Potter enters with Groucho to discuss arrangements for the impending engagement dinner. Groucho summons Jamison and the discussion continues. 'Do you want music, or would you prefer a jazz band?' says Groucho, and Mrs Potter suggests Spanish music as her guests will be wearing Spanish costume. Hennessy enters and asks everyone to be seated as he quizzes each of them in turn. Groucho distracts Hennessy with his word play and announces an ensemble number entitled 'Minstrel Days'. Hennessy tries to determine the whereabouts of the missing key, and Groucho distracts him with 'shirt business', which involves the disappearance of Hennessy's shirt, and which ends with a 'Tambourine Drill' performed by the entire company as Hennessy exits.

Act Two Scene Two takes place 'Before the Palms' and consists of a brief routine involving Groucho and a number of Spanish musicians, who are all called Manuel, and Act Two Scene Three takes place on 'The Patios'. Opening with 'A Tango Melody' by Penelope, Polly and Groucho enter, and Groucho converses briefly with Polly, and leaves when Bob enters. Polly and Bob plan to elope to Cocoanut Manor at midnight, and Bob draws a diagram for Polly then leaves. Polly feigns interest in Harvey, suggests that they elope and meet up at Cocoanut Manor, and asks him how to get there. Harvey draws a diagram then leaves when Mrs Potter and her guests enter. Chico flatters Mrs Potter and Harpo enters and engages in 'business'. Hennessy enters without his shirt, leading into a number entitled 'The Tale of a Shirt', which combines the Habañera and the Toreador song from Bizet's *Carmen*. Mrs Potter assigns the role of master of ceremonies to Groucho, and Harpo exits as Grouco tells a lengthy tale involving Irishmen, Swedes and Scotsmen. Harpo re-enters and Mrs Potter greets her guests. Harvey delivers a short speech, and is followed first by Chico's piano act then by Harpo's harp act. Bob and Polly enter and show the aforementioned diagram, and Bob points out the similarities between this and other diagrams drawn by Harvey. Hennessey suddenly notices that 'Yates and the girl have gone', Bob says that a millionaire named Berryman wants to buy the property from Bob and Polly, and Mrs Potter begs Bob to forgive her. Bob and Mrs Potter embrace, and Mrs Potter says that she wants to make announcement. Harpo enters and engages in further business involving a cape and pratfalls, then Mrs Potter finally announces the forthcoming wedding between Bob and Polly, and the show ends in a reprise of 'A Little Bungalow', which is sung by the whole company.

Although the storyline is important (it is what distinguishes a musical comedy from a revue), it is clear that it functions not only as a pleasant romance with a happy ending nor only as a piece of gentle satire, but as scaffolding for comic business and routines and (mostly upbeat) songs and their performers. As Jeffrey Magee points out, *The Cocoanuts* was Berlin's only 1920s book show, and although its songs are not well known now, they contributed to a trend toward what Magee calls 'legitimate vaudeville', a trend embracing 'minstrelsy, vaudeville, revue, and opera' within the framework of a narrative; and as he also points out, some of its improvisations, most notably the 'Viaduct/Why a Duck' routine involving Chico and Groucho, became entrenched only after its opening.[7] Although Groucho later considered the subsequent roadshow version as inferior, it proved as successful as the Broadway version, and it was these successes that helped prompt Paramount to produce a film version.

The Film

One of the obvious reasons for considering a film version was the availability of sound technology and hence the chance for audiences to hear some of its dialogue and songs, and to hear as well as see the Marx Brothers and some of the other stage-show's performers.[8] Its success on stage led to interest from United Artists. But United Artists withdrew and a successful bid from Paramount followed.[9] As has been extensively documented, the advent of sound brought with it almost as many problems as advantages, and these problems were manifest in a number of different ways. One was the sensitivity of microphones and the placement of sound recording equipment in large and often barely movable sound-proofed booths. Another was editing, which now entailed a sound track as well as an image track, and which was difficult to coordinate flexibly. And yet another was the consequent loss of tempo and rhythm, a topic discussed at length in *Film Rhythm after Sound* by Lea Jacobs,[10] and summarised briefly in the introduction to this book. Some of these problems were being tackled in or by 1929, a year in which the proliferation of sound terminology marked the extent to which and the ways in which sound was now deployed.[11] But a further problem for *The Cocoanuts* was the lack of filmmaking experience among the cast and the relative inexperience of Joseph Santley, one of the film's two directors. Santley was assigned on account of his expertise in directing musicals on stage. But Robert Florey, his co-director, had considerable filmmaking experience, having worked as an assistant director to Josef von Sternberg, made numerous avant-garde shorts, and directed silent feature films such as *One Hour of Love*, *The Romantic Age* and *Face Value* (all 1927) and his first sound feature, *The Hole in the Wall*, for Paramount in 1929.[12] Following a fire at Paramount's soundstages in Hollywood in January 1928, production of *The Hole in the Wall* and other films were relocated to the company's Astoria studios on Long Island, and *The Cocoanuts* was among them. This was convenient for the Marx Brothers, 'who could shoot the film by day while performing on Broadway in their play *Animal Crackers* by night',[13] and for other performers too.[14] Moreover, while Monta Bell described the production of *The Cocoanuts* as 'a six-month ordeal', and while Joe Adamson regards *The Cocoanuts* as little more than an antiquated disaster, others were and are enthusiastic, and much more aware of the ways in which aspects of the film were successful.[15]

The credits are printed over a negative image of the 'Dancing Bellhops' (The Gamby-Hale Girls) and accompanied by an instrumental version of 'The Monkey Doodle-Doo' as the camera pans from left to right, then right to left, then left to right again. This image is followed by a close up of the head of a young woman framed through the moving pattern of a spinning lace umbrella (figure 1).[16] Then as the 'The Monkey Doodle-Do' recommences, the camera moves back briefly and we cut to a long shot of the beach, which is clearly a studio set, and which is densely peopled by hotel guests and holiday makers, the Alan K. Foster Girls, and a roving waiter, as an instrumental version of 'Florida By The Sea' plays on the soundtrack. We dissolve to a close-up of the Foster Girls vaulting one-by-one on the beach, dissolve to a shot of a female guest on a chair in front of the hotel terrace, then dissolve to a head-on shot of two young woman and a lifeguard with other dancing guests on the terrace behind them. We cut back to the beach and the Foster Girls, who continue their exercises as others look on, then on to other female guests. We cut to a slightly angled view of the beach, back to the lifeguard and his companions as the lyrics of 'Florida By The Sea' are vocalised, then on to a shot of two more women on the beach. As 'Florida By The Sea' continues, we cut to an angled view of the terrace, which is now packed with dancing couples, with a group of female guests being served by a waiter in front of the terrace on the left.

In a sequence marked by a combination of holiday relaxation and playful physical

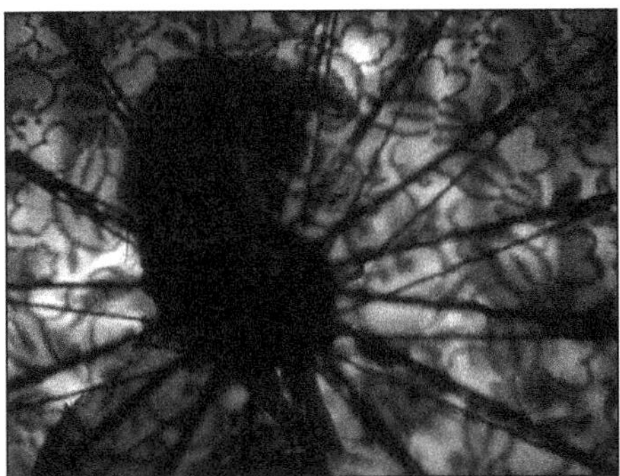
Figure 1

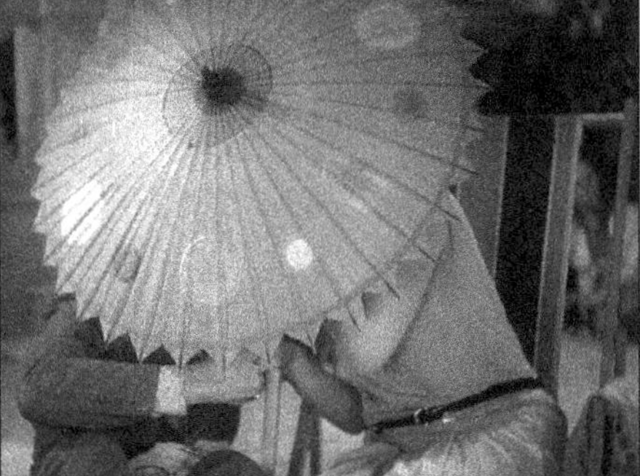
Figure 2

activity, none of these shots contain recorded dialogue, and this is evident in the fact that neither the dancers nor the female guests and their waiter can be heard even though we clearly see them speak, and means that *The Cocoanuts* is not quite the all-talking film it was claimed to be.[17] But most of the remaining scenes and sequences contain dialogue, and alongside the largely visual nature of the scene in the adjacent hotel bedrooms and Harpo's visual antics, it was the solo musical performances by Harpo and Chico, the sound of Harpo's bulbhorn, and the comic dialogue and banter delivered by Groucho and Chico that made the film popular.[18] In addition to the aforementioned use of angled framing, some of these ingredients are evident in the following scene in the lobby of 'The Hotel de Cocoanut', which begins with Groucho's entry as Hammer (the name was changed from Schlemmer) on one of the hotel's staircases.[19] Hammer is instantly surrounded by a bellboy and a group of female bellhops, who replace the all-male bellboys in the stage show and who, like the bellboy, demand to be paid for their work. But when Hammer tells the bellhops to 'forget about money', they shout 'hooray' and perform a dynamically staged, framed and edited routine to a musical number entitled 'The Bell-Hops', then dance off into the dining room.

Harmison (Zeppo Marx) and Groucho are now behind the hotel desk, and as Groucho walks off, we cut to two shot of Penelope (Kay Francis) and Harvey (Cyril Ring) sitting alone together on the patio. Penelope and Harvey discuss their money problems and plan to steal a diamond necklace that belongs to Mrs Potter (Margaret Dumont). Then the camera moves in and we cut to a two-shot of Bob and Polly sitting on the beach in front of the patio. The camera moves in closer as Bob and Polly sing 'When My Dreams Come True' (cutting to a close-up of Polly as they do so), then put up an umbrella – a variant on the ornate umbrella in the opening sequence – as they kiss behind it (figure 2). Penelope and Harvey join them. Polly exits as Bob reprises 'When My Dreams Come True'. Then Bob departs as well, leaving the villainous couple on their own in a closer two shot. Having compared and contrasted the two young couples, we cut to Polly, who walks across the hotel lobby in moving medium close-up then onto a wider two medium shot as Polly and her mother stop and talk. The ensuing

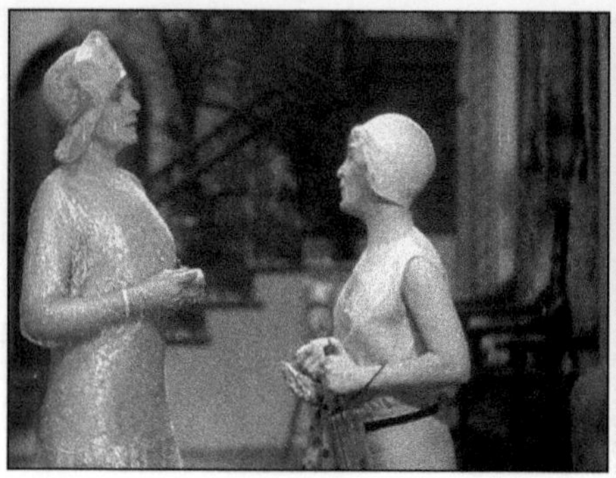

Figure 3

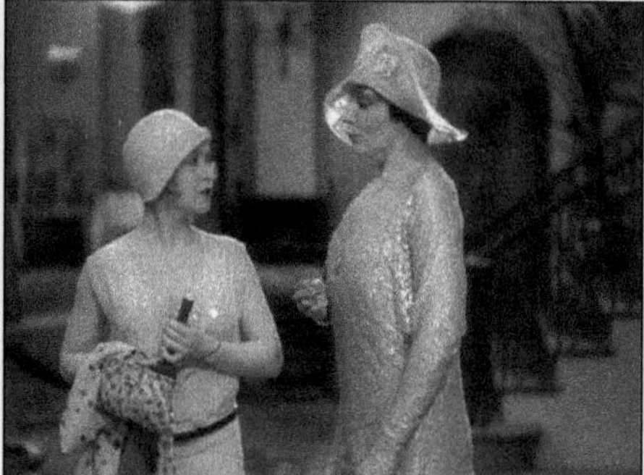

Figure 4

conversation, which focuses on Mrs Potter's view that Bob is unsuitable as a husband for Polly, is marked not so much by its content but by the manner in which it is shot, as a single lateral take is punctuated by four separate points at which the characters and camera stop before they head for the lift (figures 3–6).

As Polly and Mrs. Potter leave we cut to Groucho and a sleeping Zeppo behind the hotel desk. Zeppo leaves, Mrs Potter re-enters, and Groucho delivers an extensive speech extolling the virtues of Cocoanut Beach. Then Zeppo returns and Chico and Harpo enter, the latter in pursuit of a number of young women, and this leads on to an extensive scene in the hotel lobby. This scene contains numerous routines deriving either from the stage show or from the Marx Brothers' other stage performances. In addition to a hand-shake routine involving all four brothers, and in addition to their rendition of 'Monkey Doodle-Doo' and Chico's bit when stealing and donning a jacket from a hotel guest, most of these routines are performed by Harpo, who honks his bulbhorn repeatedly, tears up letters, drinks ink, eats buttons, flowers and a telephone, and consumes numerous other objects around him. Harpo also plays the clarinet, which serves, along with his mischievous antics, to underline his child-like, other-worldly persona. The clarinet number, a playful version of 'When My Dreams Come True', is interrupted by Penelope, who has encountered the Brothers with

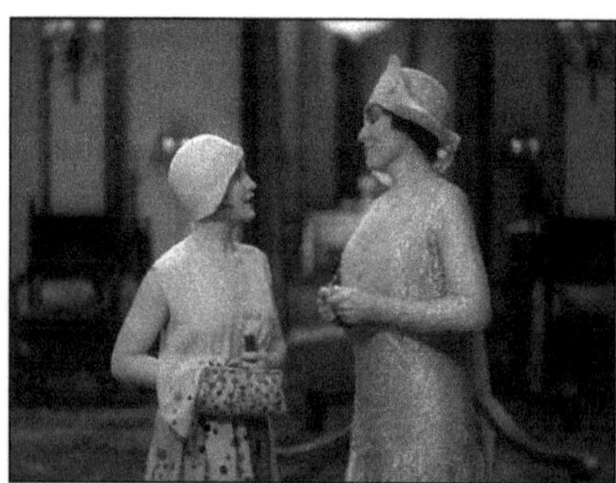

Figure 5

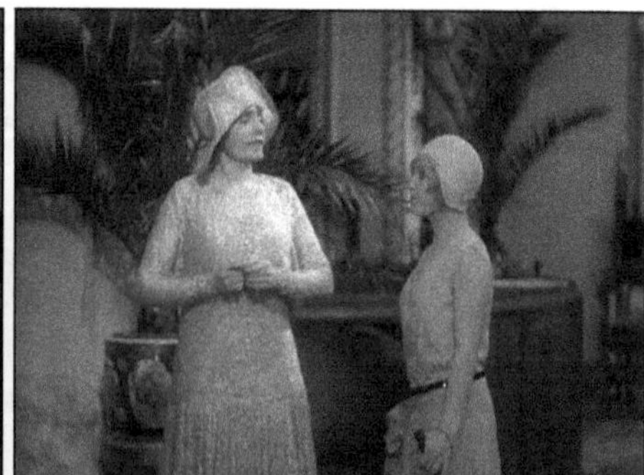

Figure 6

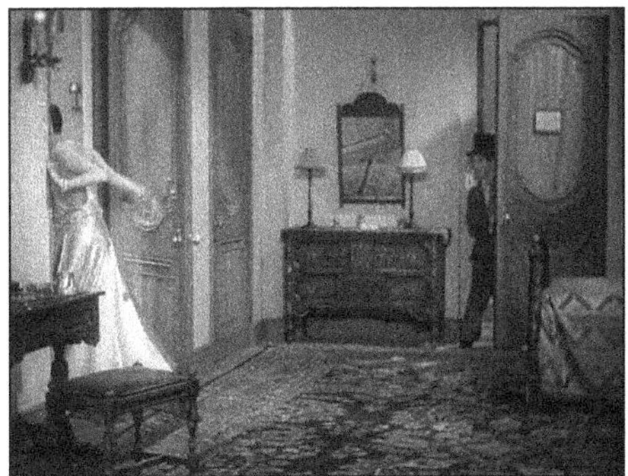

Figure 7

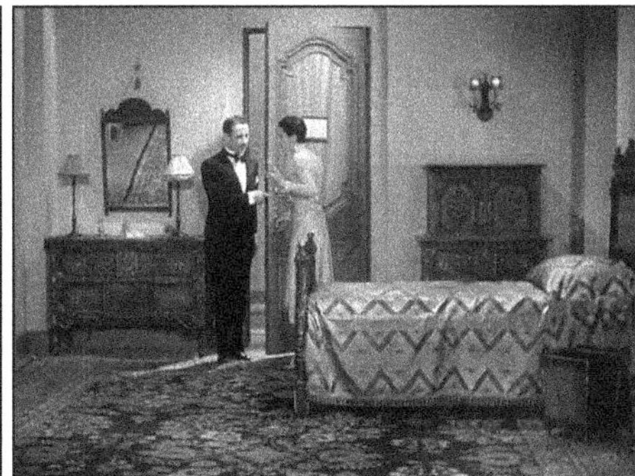

Figure 8

Harvey earlier on in the scene, who has already invited Chico up to her room, and who now invites Harpo too. Penelope leaves and Harpo enters the lift, playing a fetchingly soft and wistful clarinet reprise as the scene comes to an end with a pratfall.

The framing, staging and editing of this scene combines what David Bordwell calls 'clothesline' staging (in which the characters are strung across the frame) with attempts to create more varied and dynamic angled framings. Given the Marx Brothers' lack of filmmaking experience, and given the exigencies of sound recording, it is perhaps unsurprising that precisely-angled framings in particular proved hard to maintain, especially when large-scale physical actions and routines and more than two or three actors were involved. However, the subsequent scene involving Groucho and Mrs Potter opens and closes with precise head-on medium long-shot framings interspersed with relatively precise angled singles as we cut back and forth from one camera position to a second, and from here we cut to Harpo's harp scene, which consists of yet another version of 'When My Dreams Come True', and on to the adjacent-bedrooms scene.

The bedrooms scene is articulated in and through an edited array of framings rather than recorded in a single stationary take, and could be viewed as an attempt to showcase film techniques by deploying a marked array of angles and camera positions. But although this is indeed the case, one of the reasons why it works so well is that all

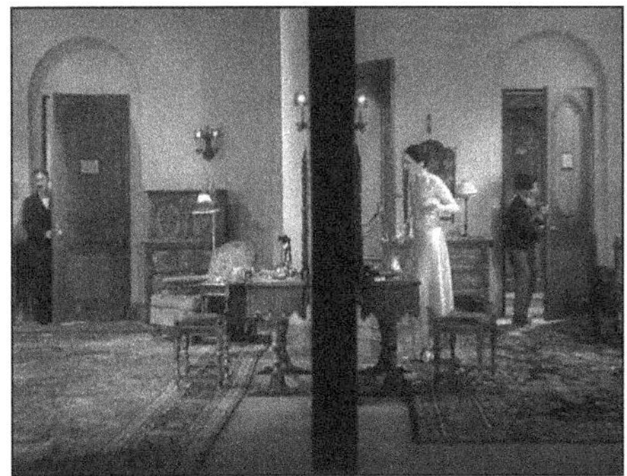

Figure 9

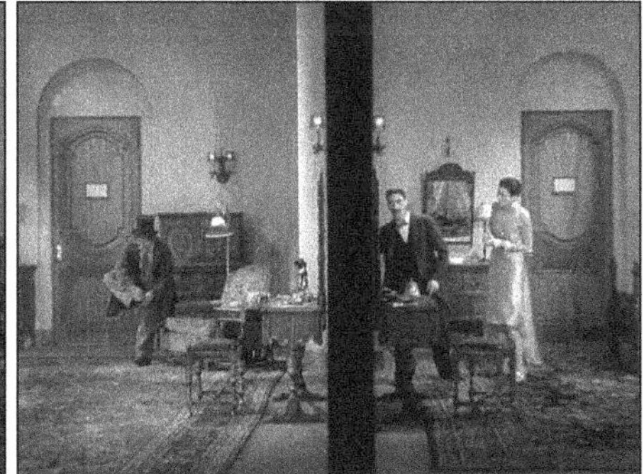

Figure 10

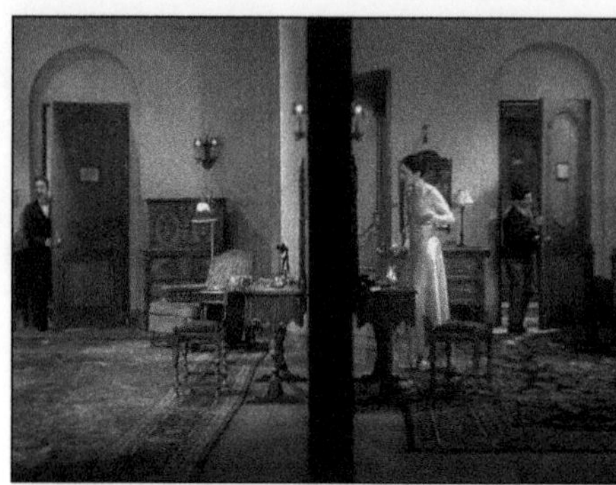
Figure 11

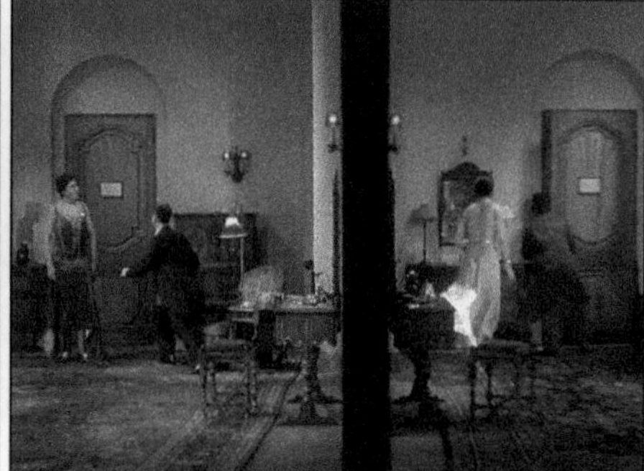
Figure 12

its shots, whether close or distant, are taken from within a single invisible semi-circle. This means that the camera does not 'cross the line'. But it also provides a sense of rhythm as characters enter and exit, move from one room to another and back again, and hide or look for places to hide (figures 7–12), and this rhythm is further articulated and underlined by sounds – notably those of doors being opened and shut – as Chico, Groucho and Harpo move in and out of the adjacent rooms, and in and out of the rooms' main doors to the corridor. Toward the end of the sequence, Mrs Potter enters and is joined by Hennessy (Basil Ruysdael), who is informed of the theft of Mrs Potter's stolen jewellery. We cut to Groucho and Chico on the terrace, and it is here that Chico voices the Viaduct/Why a Duck routine, and that Groucho explains the protocols involved in the forthcoming real-estate auction at Cocoanut Manor.

The auction scene begins with a lavish performance of 'The Monkey Doodle-Do'. Then we move on to the auction itself, which replicates the stage show more or less verbatim, and which is marked throughout by clothesline framings and stagings. The scene concludes with a two shot of Polly and Harpo, as the latter's wink in the stage-show version is replaced by the touching offer of a lollipop. Following a routine in front of the jailhouse involving the contents of Harpo's pocket and the key that Harpo steals as Hennessy departs, more comic business ensues. Harpo and Chico eventually manage to open the jailhouse door and leave with Bob, and from here we cut to Groucho at the hotel desk. Groucho plans to join a poker game in one of the rooms upstairs. But Harpo, Chico and Bob enter on the patio and Groucho joins them to form a four-shot clothesline framing as Harpo empties an array of items from his pocket. We cut in closer as Bob realises the significance of the diagram, then fade out and onto an overhead shot of the Gamby-Hale Dancers as another music-only version of 'When My Dreams Come True' begins to play on the soundtrack. We cut to various framings of the dancers and guests, one of which echoes the umbrella shot in the opening sequence as a man and woman are framed together behind strikingly ornate latticework (figure 13), and we return to the dancers performing a version of the can-can to the accompaniment of a piece of ballet music written for the film by an uncredited Frank Tours. The camera moves in to frame a medium close-up of

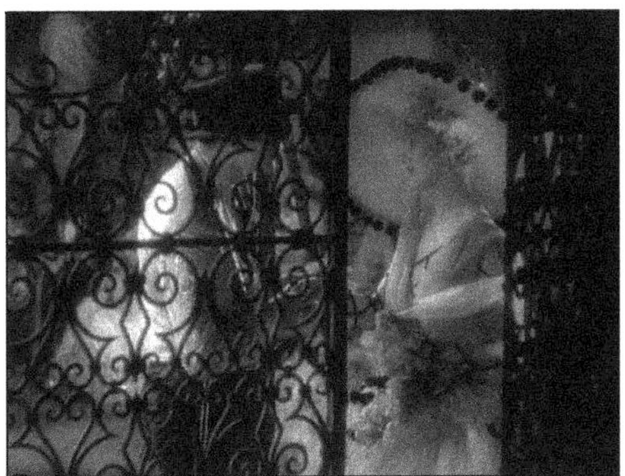
Figure 13

Polly, who sings a further version of 'When My Dreams Come True'. Then we cut to Mrs Potter and Harvey, who greet Penelope and Zeppo and the other three Marx Brothers (each of them wearing particularly outlandish Spanish outfits in line with the Spanish-party theme) on the occasion of Harvey's engagement to Polly. From this point on framings and stagings vary, some deploying singles, others two shots and groups shots taken from various positions in and around the table and the space adjacent to it. The latter forms the site for the entry of Hennessy, whose shirt is used for a game of noughts and crosses by Harpo and Chico prior to its sudden disappearance (a variant on the earlier jacket-theft routine) as Hennessy and a chorus of characters (Polly and Mrs Potter amongst them) break into 'The Tale Of The Shirt', a variant on the 'March Of The Toreadors' from *Carmen.*

Harpo gives Hennessey a spare shirt that he happens to be wearing, and from here we move back to the dinner table and guests as Groucho acts as Master of Ceremonies. Harvey delivers a particularly soporific speech, followed by an equally soporific speech from Mrs Potter, both of which lead Harpo to leave the table. As the festivities continue, and as the film moves on to its denouement, Harpo, who is now back at the table, and who has now woken up from the slumber induced by Harvey's speech, signals Polly to leave the table. At this point we move on to Chico's piano bit, an instrumental version of 'Gypsy Love Song' by Victor Herbert. Then when Polly returns, she confronts Harvey with the diagram indicating the whereabouts of Mrs Potter's necklace. Harvey leaves and Bob enters and announces that Berryman has agreed to buy Cocoanut Grove for a million dollars and tells the Marx Brothers that he wants to bring 400 guests to their hotel. The Brothers exit in a rush, paving the way for the arrest of Harvey and Penelope by Hennessy and an apology from Mrs Potter, who blesses Bob and Polly's forthcoming wedding. From here we cut to a final montage, which starts with a medium shot of Bob and Polly encircled by a small of group women as Polly begins to sing a final version of 'When My Dreams Come True', dissolves to Harvey and Penelope hand-cuffed together as Hennessy looks on, dissolves to the four Marx Brothers waving at the camera, then pulls back slowly as we dissolve back to the shot of Bob and Polly completing the song and as the camera moves in for the final time.

The film's rhythms are often uncertain, giving rise to awkward pauses and edits, and uncertain movements and blockings. But the film is also marked by clear attempts to give the film a style, and this is particularly evident in the lace-related shots, the Bell-Hops dance sequence, the adjacent-hotel-room scene, and the musical performances by Harpo and Chico. According to *Variety*, 21 June 1932, p. 62, *The Cocoanuts* earned $1,800,000 at the box-office and could thus be regarded as successful. By then Zeppo had abandoned performing. But the other three brothers had gone on to feature in *The Animal Crackers* (another stage show by Kaufman and Ryskind) and its subsequent 1930 film adaptation. *Animal Crackers* was the last show-based adaptation to feature the brothers for a number of years. But in 1938, a 1937 play entitled *Room Service*, which was written by John Murray and Allan Boretz, was made into a film starring Chico, Groucho and Harpo at RKO. All the while, and as is documented extensively in books by Simon Louvish, Glenn Mitchell and others, the three remaining brothers routinely honed the routines in their films by performing them live on stage throughout the 1930s.

Notes

1. The 24 May New York opening is specified in the entry on *The Cocoanuts* in the AFI Catalog. But in his entry on the film in *The Marx Brothers Encyclopedia* (London: B.T. Batsford, 1996), p. 63, Glenn Mitchell specifies the date and location of its New York opening as 3 May at the Rialto in Times Square.
2. As is well documented, none of Berlin's songs were major hits, with the exception of 'Always', which was cut prior to the opening of the stage version and which does appear in the film version either. For more on Berlin, see Philip Furia, *Irving Berlin: A Life in Song* (New York: Schirmer Books, 1998) and Jeffrey Magee, *Irving Berlin's American Musical Theater* (Oxford and New York: Oxford University Press, 2012). (Magee discusses the songs and music in *The Cocoanuts* in *Irving Berlin's American Musical Theater*, pp. 154-156). For more on Harris and on Kaufman, see Malcolm Goldstein, *George S. Kaufman: His Life, His Theater* (London and New York: Oxford University Press, 1979), Glenn Mitchell, *The Marx Brothers Encyclopedia* (London: B.T. Batsford, 1996), pp. 113 and 136–37, and Rhoda-Gale Pollack, *George S. Kaufman* (Boston: Twayne Publshers, 1988). As Goldstein and Magee both point out, Harris went on to produce numerous plays and shows by Kaufman and his associates, among them *Once in a Lifetime* (1930), *Of Thee I Sing* (1931), *Face the Music, Dinner at Eight* and *As Thousands Cheer* (all 1932), *You Can't Take It With You* and *Stage Door* (1936), and *The Man Who Came to Dinner* (1939). For further details on the production of the stage version of *The Cocoanuts*, see Goldstein, *George S. Kaufman*, pp. 125–130.
3. For more on Ryskind, see Morrie Ryskind with John H.M. Roberts, *I Shot an Elephant in My Pyjamas: The Morrie Ryskind Story* (Lafayette: Huntington House Publishers, 1994), and Mitchell, *The Marx Brothers Encyclopedia*, p. 234. Some of Ryskind's contributions to the stage version of *The Cocoanuts* are detailed in *I Shot an Elephant in My Pajamas*, pp. 63, 67–70, 73. Some of his contributions to the film version and to other Marx Brothers films can be found in *I Shot an Elephant in My Pyjamas*, pp. 106–115, 135–137.
4. Geoffrey Block, 'The melody (and the words) linger on: American musical comedies of the 1920s and 1930s', in Everett and Laird (eds.), *The Cambridge Companion to the Musical*, p. 104. Philip Furia, in *Irving Berlin*, p. 114, describes the Florida real-estate boom as follows: 'In that year in Miami alone there were 2,000 real estate offices and more than 25,000 agents ... Stories of fabulous profits abounded. Lots that cost $800 in 1920 were selling for $150,000 in 1924. People began to buy land solely with the notion of reselling it at such enormous profits, but by 1926 the bubble began to burst. By that summer, people who had put all their money into "binders" on lots found that they could not sell them and could not make the payments'.
5. George S. Kaufman, '*The Cocoanuts*', in Kaufman, *By George: A Kaufman Collection* (London: Angus and Robertson, 1980 edition), pp. 202–258.
6. Kaufman, '*The Cocoanuts*', p. 202; Mitchell, *The Marx Brothers Encyclopedia*, pp. 55–59.
7. Magee, *Irving Berlin's American Musical Theater*, p. 153.
8. In an advertisement in *Variety*, 24 July 1929, p. 34, Paramount stressed the extent to which movie audiences could see and hear the Marx Brothers and Oscar Shaw and Mary Eaton at prices well below the Broadway stage-show average.
9. According to Mitchell, *The Marx Brothers Encyclopedia*, p. 62, 'the stage show and its stars were offered

to Paramount by the William Morris Agency, who wanted $75,000. Walter Wanger, a New York representative of the studio, took the offer to Paramount chief Adolph Zukor, who considered the fee excessive. Wanger, clearly anxious to secure the property, arranged a meeting between Zukor, Chico and himself, during which Chico explained how Paramount would be getting the team's priceless backlog of material for the tiny sum of $100,000. The anguished Wanger looked on as Chico persuaded Zukor to buy the rights for $25,000 more than the original figure'. According to Matthew Coniam, *The Annotated Marx Brothers: A Filmgoer's Guide to In-Jokes, Obscure References and Sly Details* (Jefferson, N.C.: McFarland & Company, 2015), p. 7, a silent film version was mooted by First National as early as 1926, but discarded for obvious reasons.

10. Lea Jacobs, *Film Rhythm after Sound: Technology, Music, and Performance* (Oakland, Cal.: University of California Press, 2015), esp. pp. 1–24. See also Donald Crafton, *The Talkies: American Cinema's Transition to Sound, 1926–1931* (Berkeley and Los Angeles: University of California Press, 1999 edition), esp. pp. 225–354.

11. In her chapter on '1929' in her co-edited book on *American Cinema in the 1920s: Themes and Variations* (New Brunswick, New Jersey: Rutgers University Press, 2009), pp. 237–238, Lucy Fischer lists the following terms: 'dialog', 'sound', 'half dialog', 'all dialog', '10 percent dialog with song', '100 percent talking', 'dialog and songs', 'all dialog and songs', '10 percent dialog', 'songs only', 'no dialog', '25 percent dialog', '1/4 dialog', and 'Sound'. It is perhaps worth noting in addition that according to *Variety*, 16 January 1929, p. 7, 'the use of large groups' of extras had been 'cut down considerably'.

12. Joseph Santley went on to direct over twenty films, most of which were musicals (see the entry on Santley in https://en.wikipedia.org/wiki/Joseph_Santley 24/11/2015). For more on Florey in the 1920s, including his work on *The Cocoanuts*, see Brian Taves, *Robert Florey, The French Expressionist* (Duncan, OK.: BearManor Media, 2014), pp. 71–120.

13. Crafton, *The Talkies*, pp. 284 and 287.

14. As Richard Barrios points out in *A Song in the Dark: The Birth of the Musical Film* (New York and Oxford: Oxford University Press, 1985), pp. 93-94, 'Margaret Dumont and the Marx Brothers worked at the Paramount by day and at the 44th Street Theatre at night. On Wednesday's [sic], matinee day, shooting focussed on the remaining players, all drawn from Broadway. Romantic leads Mary Eaton and Oscar Shaw had recently starred in *The Five O'Clock Girl*, and the glamorous villainess was Kay Francis in her second film'. As he also points out, 'over forty minutes had been cut, mostly music, and retakes shifted the emphasis further away from Eaton and Shaw and the Gamby-Hale Dancers onto the Marxes'. And as he further points out, on p. 95, the film was received 'more as a comedy than musical'.

15. Herbert Cruikshank, 'Doing as He Doesn't Like', *Motion Picture Classic*, October 1929, p. 33, cited in Crafton, *The Talkies*, p. 287; Joe Adamson, *Groucho, Harpo, Chico and sometimes Zeppo* (London: W.H. Allen & Co. Ltd, 1973), pp. 77–99. For an eye-witness account of some of the activities involved the film's production, see *Variety*, 13 March 1929, p. 48 (not 15 March, as Coniam specifies on page 9 of *The Annotated Marx Brothers*), whose reporter, Ruth Morris, describes the filming of one of the dance numbers as follows: 'All the stages of the upper floor are in use, with one length of the studio given over to an enormous sweep of beach scene, complete with ocean effects. Besides the principals, show girls and chorus, there are four dancing troupes scattered around the studio. But the personnel to whip the picture into shape is the amazing thing. Firstly there's Joe Santley to direct dialog and rehearsals over and over again, until the scene is perfect for shooting...Then there's Morrie Ryskind to arrange the dialog should any changes be necessary, and Robert Florey to supervise photography and work out picture angles. George Foley, head photographer under Florey, commands the battery of cameras, four or five being used for each big scene. It is his job to watch the lighting and keep the scenes in original composition. Sound supervisor attends to the placing of microphones, his particular problem being to hang them where they'll get the best reception yet be outside the camera. He works in close association with the recorder in the sound booth who regulates the sound levels, intensifying or diminishing as the recording requires. Vocal sequences are "played back" after they have been taken, with corrections given to the cast. Then there is Frank Tours to supervise the 35-piece orchestra, and the four dancing directors to watch for lack of precision in the dance numbers; and Jimmy Cowan, head producer, to watch everything. It's amazing mechanical activity, taking hours of preparation for perhaps three minutes of actual shooting.' It should perhaps be noted that Sime Silverman, one of *Variety*'s reviewers, complained that the dancers 'worked very well but couldn't be placed in the focus. When the full 48 were at work only 40 and those behind first line could be scene but dimly. In one scene of six abreast on a close-up but four and one-half were

in sight. While to get a larger revealment long shots had to be utilized, ruining those scenes, leaving the physical illusion a total blank.' See *Variety*, 29 May 1929, p. 14. Finally, it should be pointed out that the DVD version derives from several sources and combines scenes and parts of scenes shot in 35mm with 16mm duplicates. Original US and UK prints were 8,613 feet long and 8,629 feet respectively. The film's original running time was 96 minutes. But the DVD version is only 92 minutes long and is therefore incomplete. Given that the discovery of missing footage is now unlikely, it will probably remain so. See Mitchell, *The Marx Brothers Encyclopedia*, p. 59.

16. As Taves points out in *Robert Florey*, p. 116, these images are redolent of Florey's avant-garde roots.

17. Crafton, *The Talkies*, p. 287.

18. Gerald Weales defines the personae of the Marx Brothers in *Canned Goods as Caviar American Film Comedy of the 1930s* (Chicago: Chicago University Press, 1985), pp. 62–64, underlining the extent to which dialect comedians 'were rampant in vaudeville' and suggesting that in the 1930s films the 'most fascinating thing about Chico's speech is not the dialect itself, but the way it fills space pointlessly. I am not thinking here of the non-sequitur content of the lines, but the way he uses sentences, fragments, phrases, single words, particularly in the scenes with Harpo, to build a kind of cradle around the purely visual business'. For an account that stresses the Jewish basis of the Brothers and their comedy, see Mark Winokur, *American Laughter: Immigration, Ethnicity, and 1930s Hollywood Film Comedy* (Houndmills: Macmillan Press, 1996), pp. 125–178.

19. Hammer was the name assigned to Groucho in 'The Mezzanine Floor', a stage routine that was re-titled 'On The Balcony', and that subsequently formed the basis of a now-lost publicity short for Paramount in 1931. For details, see Simon Louvish, *Monkey Business: The Life and Legends of the Marx Brothers* (London: Faber and Faber, 1999), pp. 123–128. According to Mitchell, *The Marx Brothers Encyclopedia*, p. 56, Hammer's entry in the film version initially included more dialogue and more evidence of Hammer's indolence, but was cut prior to release.

Chapter 6

Street Scene

In the Spring of 1931 Samuel Goldwyn invited King Vidor to direct a film version of a play entitled *Street Scene*, and having seen a production of the play at the Mayan Theatre in Los Angeles, Vidor eagerly agreed to do so.[1] Goldwyn was an independent producer whose films were released through United Artists, and Vidor was a well-established director who had had box-office success with *The Big Parade* (1925), Academy Award success with *The Crowd* (1928), and a number of critical plaudits for *Hallelujah* (1929), an all-black talkie. The play itself was written by Elmer Rice early on in 1928 and was based on earlier unproduced versions entitled *Landscape with Figures* and *The Sidewalks of New York*.[2] Sam H. Harris 'took an option of the play', but 'knowing that Harris habitually optioned more plays than he could conceivably produce', Rice 'limited Harris to three months with no right of renewal'. True to form, 'Harris became so involved in other productions that he had to let his option on *Street Scene* lapse', and William A. Brady agreed to produce it instead.[3] Brady gave Rice director approval and agreed to pay a thousand-dollar advance, and this was further augmented by a loan from Lee Shubert.[4] 'An early January opening was set, and since it was already November, great haste was made in selecting a cast and other necessary personnel'.[5] George Cukor was hired as the play's director. But Cukor abandoned the project and Rice convinced Brady to let him direct instead.[6] 'The show's costs ... prevented any out-of-town tryouts, and the show, despite great technical difficulties, had to open after only twenty-eight days of rehearsal' on account of Equity rules.[7] The rehearsals were conducted at the studios at Fort Lee, New Jersey, in which Brady still possessed a commercial interest, and the play was previewed on a Tuesday night prior to its premiere at the Playhouse Theatre in New York on 10 January 1929.[8] The play was huge success. It ran for a total of 601 performances at the Playhouse Theatre, won a Pulitzer Prize and an award for Best Play of the Year, and went on to play in numerous cities in the US and elsewhere abroad.[9]

The play's costs and technical difficulties were a consequence of its extensive cast and elaborate set, whose origins lay in 'a pantomime sketch showing, without words or plot, a tenement brownstone awakening to the day as its occupants began their daily routines'.[10] The set was designed by Jo Meilziner and based on a real house at 25 West

Sixty-fifth Street in New York. It was flanked by another brownstone undergoing demolition on one side and an apartment undergoing construction on the other,[11] and Rice conceived the set as a whole as 'a brooding presence, which not only dominated the scene, but which integrated and gave a kind of dramatic unity to the sprawling and unrelated lives of the multitudinous characters'.[12] Its origins and purposes were later detailed in *The Living Theatre*, the first of Rice's two autobiographies:

> The background and subject matter had been in my mind for many years: a multiple dwelling, housing numerous families of varying origins; and a melodramatic story arising from the interrelationships of the characters and partly from their environmental conditioning ... The house was conceived as the central fact of the play: a dominant structural element that unified the sprawling and diversified lives of the inhabitants. This concept was derived partly from the Greek drama, which is almost always set against the facade of a palace or a temple. But mainly I was influenced, I think, by the paintings of Claude Lorrain, a French artist of the seventeenth century. In his landscapes, which I had gazed at admiringly in the Louvre and other galleries, there is nearly always a group of figures in the foreground, which is composed and made significant by an impressive architectural pile of some sort in the background.[13]

The other novel aspect of the play was its striking use of sounds and noises and diverse ethnic accents, and this was underlined in the preamble to Act One as follows:

> Throughout the act, and indeed, throughout the play, there is constant noise. The noises of the city rise, fall, intermingle: the distant roar of the El trains, automobile sirens, and the whistle of boats on the river; the rattle of trucks, and the indeterminate clanking of metals; fire engines, ambulances, musical instruments, a radio, dogs barking, and human voices calling; quarrelling, and screaming with laughter. The noises are subdued and in the background, but they never wholly cease.

According to Anthony Palmieri, 'Rice had a recording instrument set up in an open window at Times Square. In this way, he managed to re-create for the play the hum of city traffic' and to augment these sounds with 'those created by two record players started a minute apart so as to provide an overlapping effect that was ever varied'. Not satisfied 'with the hollow sound given off by footsteps across the platform that substituted for the sidewalk, Rice prevailed upon Brady to put down a thin coating of cement'.[14] And to 'simulate the ethnic make-up of New York's lower middle class, Rice provided the play with characters of various national origins', their accents adding to the soundscape as it does so.[15]

The Play

Two photographs of the set were published in the 1929 stage-play version, and the first shows the dilapidated state of the brownstone and its air of foreboding (see figure 1). A Russian Jew named Abraham Kaplan is seated in a rocking-chair reading a Yiddish newspaper, and a middle-aged woman named Greta Fiorentino is leaning out of one of the other windows. Emma Jones, a 'tall and rather bony' middle-aged

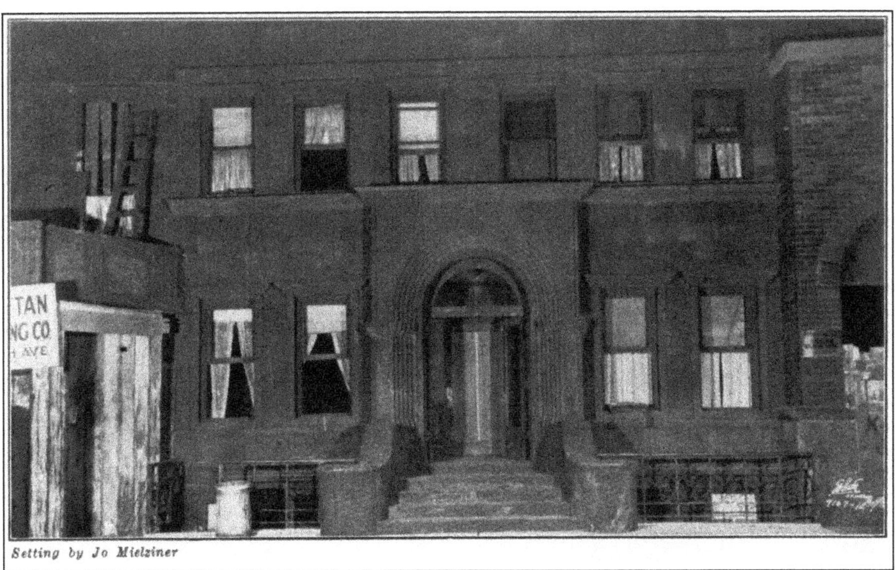

Setting by Jo Mielziner

Figure 1

woman, enters from the left carrying a parcel and is greeted by Greta in her 'faintly German accent'. They discuss the sweltering heat, a factor that dominates the play throughout, and Willie Maurrant asks Anna Maurrant, Willie's mother, for money to buy an ice cream. Anna gives Willie the money and leaves, Willie skates off left, and Emma tells Greta that Anna is having an affair with a man named Steve Sankey. Carl Olsen can be heard calling for his wife, and Emma says that 'What them foreigners don't know about bringin' up babies would fill a book'. Greta replies that 'Foreigners know joost as much as other people', and at this point Frank Maurrant, 'a powerfully-built man of forty-five', enters and is greeted by Greta. Frank works in the theatre, and when Anna asks him whether he will be at work tomorrow he responds with suspicion. He asks whether their daughter Rose has come home yet, and Anna tells him that she is working overtime because her boss's funeral is scheduled to take place tomorrow. A street cry can be heard off stage, and George Jones (Emma's son) comes out of the house. Anna says that 'it's a shame that people don't get along better', and at this point Sankey enters from the right. Emma and Greta exchange looks, and Emma reminds Sankey that he has a family. But Sankey 'strolls off' and a woman pushes a pram across the stage, underlining Sankey's status as a married man with children as she does so.

Agnes Cushing comes out of the house and says that her mother has heart trouble. Greta, Emma and Anna comment in turn on Agnes' ill health, and Anna walks off left, claiming to look for her son, but actually planning to meet up with Sankey. Greta and Emma comment on what is clearly a clandestine affair and Carl Olsen warns that 'Some day, her hoosban' is killing him'. Greta and Emma continue to gossip. Then a 'conspirators' silence falls upon them' as Frank comes out of the house looking for his wife. The voice of a young boy can be heard reiterating a street cry, and as Agnes enters the house, Shirley Kaplan, Abraham's daughter, appears at the ground-floor window with a glass of tea. Shirley gives the tea to Abraham, and Abraham laments the fact that his newspaper contains 'Notting but deevorce, skendal, and moiders'. Emma responds by complaining that Hebrew writing is hard to understand then notices that Filippo (Lippo) Fiorentino, Greta's husband, has arrived with a violin in one hand and five ice-cream cones in the other. Lippo hands out the ice-cream cones and at this point 'Alice Simpson, a tall, spare spinster, appears on the right' and is identified by Emma. Emma shouts out loudly that Alice is a charity worker, and Alice is outraged when she discovers that Laura Hildebrand, one of her charges, has wasted what little money she has on going to the movies with her two young children. Abraham questions Alice's concept of charity, and when Alice tells him to mind his own business, he suggests she 'read in your Bible de life of Christ'. Alice follows Laura and her children into their apartment, and as she does so, Lippo suggests that Alice has 'don' gotta nobody to sleepa wit' and Emma tells Frank that 'Here's your wife, now', thus underlining the topic of sex, both licit and illicit.

Frank asks where Anna has been and Anna tells him that she's been looking for their young son Willie. Frank threatens to give Willie 'a good fannin' and Anna and the others point out that boys like Willie are naturally wild. Alice leaves and the conversation turns to class and religion, 'women goin' around stealin' other women's husbands', and what Abraham calls 'de folt of our economic system'. Frank responds with 'we don't want no revolutions in this country' and 'we don't want no foreigners comin' in, tellin' us how to run things'. But Lippo points out that Christopher Columbus was a foreigner, and Carl points out that the first man to visit America was Lief Ericson. Frank returns to the topic of law and order and the problems associated with free love and birth control, and Abraham draws attention to the iniquities of private property. Frank threatens violence. But Anna intervenes, and Sam Kaplan, another neighbour, enters. The conversation turns to music, Greta plays the waltz from *La Boheme* on the piano, and Lippo takes Anna by the hand and dances with her, at which point Sankey re-appears and leaves as Frank asks why he's 'hangin' around here'. Frank also asks why Willie and Rose, the Maurrants' son and daughter, are not home yet. Willie enters and tells his parents that he has been in a fight, and Frank sends Willie to bed. The neighbours gossip about Anna and Sankey and the possibility of a confrontation with Frank. Then Rose and Harry Easter enter from the left and stop at the foot of the steps. Harry puts his arm around Rose, but Rose 'frees herself as the house-door opens' and as Mrs Olsen appears, Mrs Olsen 'darts a swift look at Easter' and Rose asks about the Olsen's baby. Easter tells Rose that he is crazy about her and tries to kiss her. But Rose reminds him that he is married, and when Easter suggests setting up a 'cozy little apartment', she eventually succeeds in saying goodnight to him.

Frank arrives and quizzes Rose about Easter, and Daniel Buchanan enters and tells Rose that he thinks his baby is due. Rose persuades her father to call the doctor and 'hurries off left', and Mae Jones and Dick McGann, both of them young and both of them drunk, appear and kiss each other. Rose tells Daniel that the doctor is on his way and Vincent Jones (Emma's son) makes a pass at her. Sam intervenes and Vincent enters his own apartment. Sam is angry. But Rose placates him, tells him that 'It's not always so easy, being a girl', and asks whether he thinks that the rumours about her mother are true. Their conversation is interrupted by a scream from Mrs Buchanan, who is now in labour, and Rose reminds Sam that there are flowers and other delights, and Sam recites one of his poems. Sam asks Rose for kiss. But Rose stands firm, and she leaves as Dr Wilson arrives. Hearing the sound of snores emanating from the Fiorentino apartment and the whistle of a distant steamboat, Sam 'raises his clenched hands to heaven', then drops his arms and head as the curtain falls.

Act Two begins at daybreak the following morning. Jones appears on his way home from the speakeasy and the street-light goes out. The Olsen baby starts to cry and these sounds are augmented by an alarm clock, barking dogs, and a singing canary. Voices can be heard in the distance, and as they die out they are replaced by others. Then the house door opens and Dr Wilson comes out and tells Sam to get some rest. Mae and Dick enter, and Mae goes into her apartment. Then Rose appears at the Maurrant window; Mrs Olsen climbs her cellar steps; Sam appears at his window; and Willie comes out of the house, followed a little later by Emma and her dog. Sam greets Rose, and various neighbours wake up. Shirley discusses Jews and food and Greta greets Daniel Buchanan, who encounters Sam in the vestibule, and who goes on to complain about the noise made by the new Buchanan baby. The Fiorentinos discuss the baby's arrival, and Lippo discusses the beauty of Italy and reiterates his view that Jews are only interested in money. Agnes Cushing tells Rose that Mrs Cushing is feeling unwell, two college girls pass by discussing the curvature of glass in spectacles, and Rose fixes the button on Willie's collar.

Thus far most of these events are either already established as everyday but important (as in the birth of a new baby and the reiteration of Lippo and Emma's anti-Semitic views) or a mix of the everyday and the relatively trivial (as in the fixing of Willie's shirt button). But events will shortly take a melodramatic turn as Frank leaves for work, and as Anna tells Rose that 'Sometimes I think I'd be better off if I was dead'. Rose heads off to the funeral with Easter, and Sankey 'appears at the right'. Anna invites Sankey up to her apartment and Sam 'looks up at the Maurrant windows, sees the drawn shades, and looks about, in perturbed perplexity, not knowing what to do'. A young female music pupil enters Lippo's apartment and starts to play the piano, and we hear her playing throughout the remainder of the scene. A city marshal and his assistant deliver a dispossession warrant to Laura and the neighbours get on with their daily chores. But at this point Frank arrives home unexpectedly and 'flings Sam violently aside'. Frank storms into the house, and 'Sam rushes down the steps' trying to warn Anna. A 'scream of terror' is followed by two gunshots and 'the sound of a heavy fall'. Sankey's voice can be heard as he tries to open the window. But 'Maurrant appears behind him', 'pulls him away from the window' and fires another shot. The neighbours gather and Maurrant re-appears. 'His coat is open and his shirt is torn'

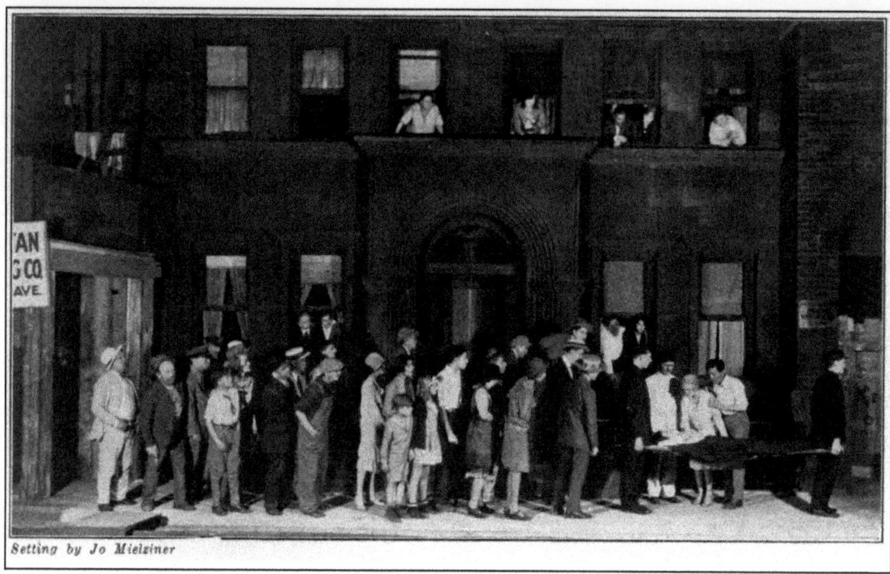

Figure 2

and his 'face, hands and clothing are covered in blood'. He tells everyone to stand back and pulls out his revolver. Then he runs down the cellar steps as a policeman runs in from the right and as Agnes Cushing calls for someone to get an ambulance. Another policeman and the City Marshal arrive, and an ambulance draws up outside the house, followed by a hospital intern. The intern announces that Anna is still alive and Rose rushes in, begging to know what has happened. And as the nearby neighbours gather by the Maurrant apartment window, Anna is carried out on a stretcher surrounded by neighbours and passers-by (see figure 2, another photograph published in the first edition in the play).

Act Three takes place later that day, and in keeping with the play's other sonic motifs, 'a woman can be heard singing scales faintly thereafter'. Two men appear at left to remove the furniture in Laura's apartment, and a policeman comes out of the house carrying Anna's blood-stained dress and Sankey's coat, cap, and bill-holder. Two young nurse maids enter, 'each wheeling a deluxe baby-carriage'. They stop under the Maurrant window, discuss the recent events, and read from an illustrated report in a tabloid newspaper. The baby in one of the carriages starts to cry, and a policeman prompts the nurse-maids to leave. Then Easter arrives and asks whether Rose is in the Maurrant apartment and whether Frank has been caught yet. The policeman leaves and Emma arrives with a handful of newspapers. Emma asks Carl whether Frank has been caught, Carl and Emma discuss the ethics of murder, and Rose comes in 'carrying four or five packages', asks whether her father has been caught yet, expresses the view that he cannot have been 'in his right mind', and confirms to Easter that Anna is dead. Rose tells Easter that the packages contain clothes for herself and her now-deceased mother and that she needs to find accommodation for her brother and herself. She enlists the help of Shirley Kaplan, and as Abraham starts to read his newspaper, various neighbours discuss the news and its significance.

At this point the sound of gunshots ring out and Lippo announces that Frank has been caught. Some of the neighbours run off and others lean out of their windows to see what has happened. Rose asks whether her father has been hurt, and Frank, who is covered with sweat, blood and grime, is led out from his hiding place by one of the policemen. Frank tells Rose that he 'must o' been out o' me head', confesses that 'It's the chair for me, I guess', and asks Rose to look after Willie. Rose 'throws her arms about his neck', and the gathering crowds swarm behind him as he is led off by the policeman. Shirley comforts Rose and Rose thanks her for her kindness. Sam asks Rose what she plans to do now, and Rose replies that the best thing to do is leave New York. Sam pleads to go with her. But Rose stands firm and tells him to believe in himself. They kiss goodbye and Sam walks off. Then Rose thanks Shirley for all her help and walks off with her suitcase. Abraham asks Shirley why his son is in tears, and Shirley tells Abraham to let him alone. An unnamed couple enter and ring for the janitor, hoping to rent the room vacated by Rose and Willie, as a group of off-stage children sing 'The Farmer in the Dell' throughout the remaining action. Greta seats herself at her window, and Emma and Agnes converse with her. The women enter the house, and as Olga climbs the cellar steps, a 'sailor appears at the left, with two girls, an arm about the waist of each', strolling slowly across the stage as the final curtain falls.

The Film

Despite recommending the play to Vidor, Goldwyn was not entirely convinced of its merits, partly because of its length, but largely because of its storyline and contents: adultery and murder were topics of increasing concern in the early 1930s; 'characters who were overtly Jewish had always been anathema to Hollywood producers; the play had but one exterior set, with no action other than people walking in and out of the building and stopping by the steps to talk; and Goldwyn himself had an aversion to stories that were in any way sordid'.[16] However, Arthur Hornblow, one of Goldwyn's associates, 'convinced him that producing *Street Scene* would add the luster he wanted' and 'suggested that the play was not Jewish so much as urban', and having paid $157,000 for the rights, Goldwyn initially signed Nancy Carroll as Rose, then turned to Sophia Kosow (Sylvia Sidney) when Carroll became unavailable.[17]

In the meantime, Vidor organised a run through of the play and began planning the handling of the camera and the filming of the set:

> The thought struck me that, to a camera lens, the variety of details of the front, sidewalk, and street of a tenement building can be unlimited. Through ever-changing camera set-ups, through carefully planned composition and design, the film could have a much more actual movement than with the conventional set-up of eye level in a western film with stage coaches, cowboys, and indians galloping by ad infinitum.

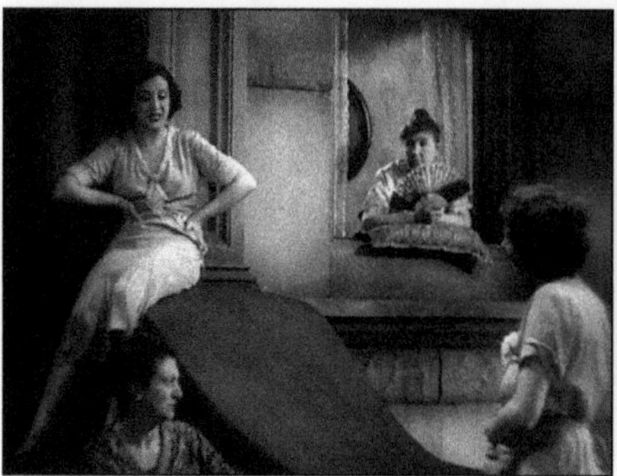
Figure 3

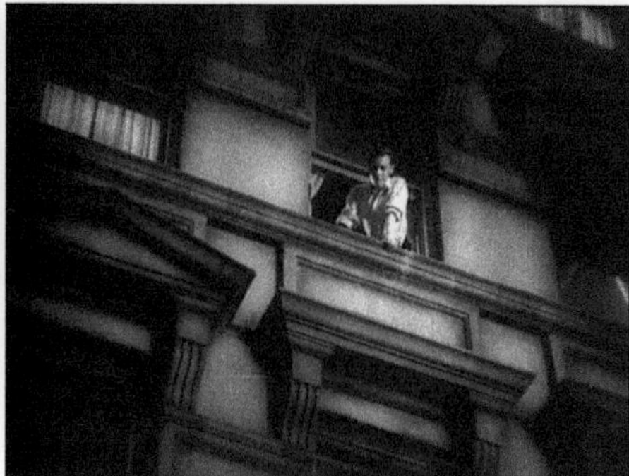
Figure 4

Working in close cooperation with the cinematographer [George Barnes] and the set designer [Richard Day], we indicated each camera set-up on a series of duplicate prints of the single set. I ... decided to avoid repeating the same camera set-up twice. Where the play had been confined to the facade of the building and the sidewalk before it, I could, without destroying the purity of the playwright's concept, pull back and also utilize the street in front of the building ... This treatment proved most effective in preserving the visual and dramatic impact of the play, without any artificial injection of movement.

Another interesting technical trick that was used in this film can be noted here. Most of the entrances and exits of the characters in the play showed them approaching or leaving along the sidewalk requiring us to shoot in both directions from the principal house. Had we put our house in the center of the street it would have meant constructing a full New York City block. By putting a duplicate main house at each end we could, by utililizing the proper house for shooting each direction, show a half block beyond. The duplicate house at the end of the half block was too far from the camera to be detected. Having two duplicate houses also enabled us to prepare difficult set-ups at one while shooting was progressing at the other ... .

The entire half-block-long structure and street with elevated railway station at one end was all covered with a network of wires so that light-colored diffusers could be used to eliminate direct sunlight when a diffused effect was needed. Above the white shade was

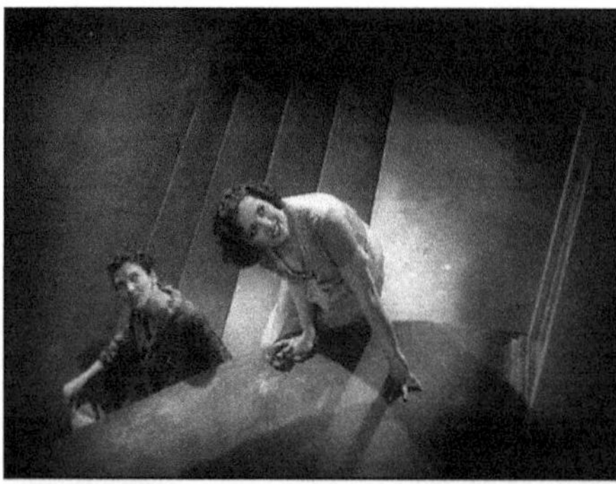
Figure 5

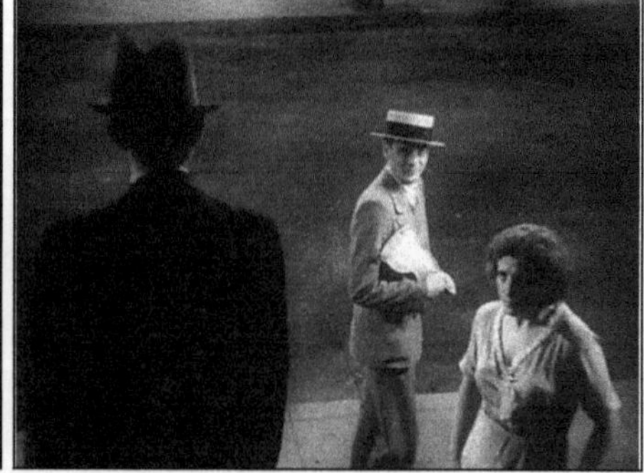
Figure 6

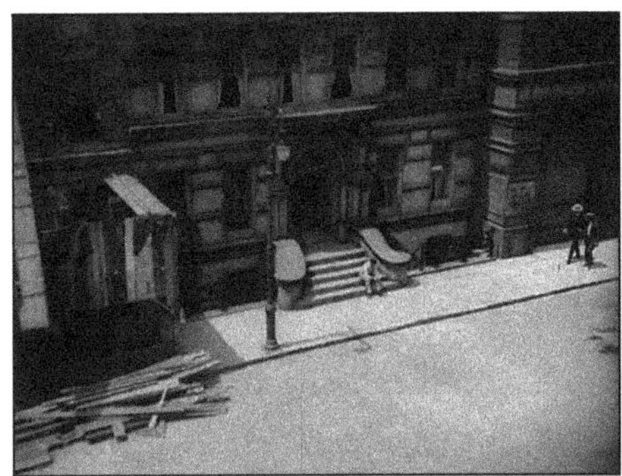

Figure 7

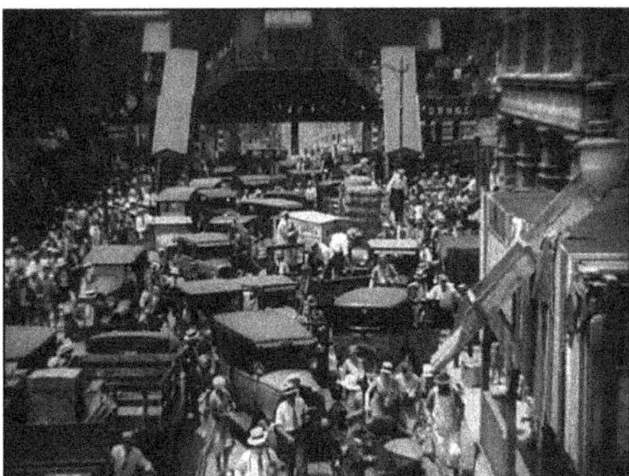

Figure 8

> arranged heavier black material which eliminated a large percentage of all daylight when the subject was to be lighted artificially.[18]

Although cross-cutting between characters is evident throughout the film, and thus although several framings are repeated, camera set ups are not, and the stylistic effects produced by these decisions are clearly evident in the film, which with one exception (a shot of Willie Maurant crossing the road from the other side of the street) confines the camera to one side of the street in the equivalent to Act One, albeit from different angles and positions (figures 3–6); which opens out to include views from the opposite side of the street in the equivalent to Act Two (figure 7); which opens out further to include shots of activities and crowds in and around the elevated railway station and the street below as Rose makes her way to the ambulance for Anna (figures 8–10); and which goes on to the capture of Frank (David Landau) and Rose's final departure in the equivalent to Act Three. Only on occasion are these scenes and activities accompanied by Alfred Newman's musical score. But along with the snatches of diegetic songs and music, Newman's score augments the sonic tapestry that marked Rice's play in a number of ways.

As Michael Slowik points out, Newman's score combined elements of jazz and

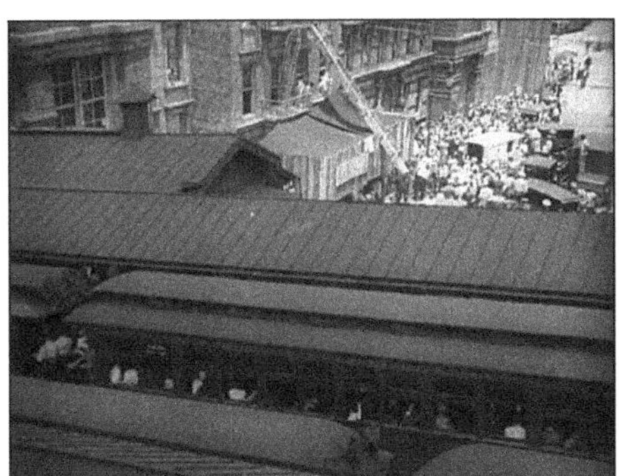

Figure 9

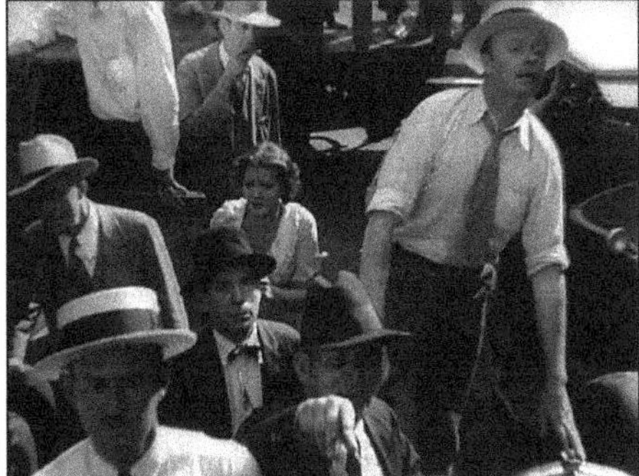

Figure 10

symphonic music, and was used initially to introduce the film and underline the nature of its urban setting, and to articulate 'the general routines of city dwellers rather than the actions of specific characters' as it does so.[19] Along with the images and evocations of sweltering heat, these introductory shots include 'cats, dogs, and humans, indicating a montage of types instead of individuals'.[20] And in addition to 'linking jazz to the rhythms of the city',[21] 'the music often adjusts to individual shots', as when hurdy-gurdy music accompanies a shot of children being hosed down by firemen in the street, as when pizzicatos accompany a worker chipping ice, and as when 'slow-paced music' accompanies 'a horse that is too hot to walk'.[22] Once the action proper begins though, Newman's music disappears, and only reappears when a drowsy and wistful version of 'I Can't Give You Anything But Love, Baby' plays out over the street at night, echoing Sam's feelings for Rose as it does so. This is followed at dawn by a brief, Wagnerian, *Tristan-and-Isolde*-esque piece of music that further underlines these feelings prior to reprising the jazz music that accompanies a second montage of early morning activities. Elsewhere, Newman's music is manifest when a 'drum roll matches Frank's upward glance, followed by heavy brass staccato notes that accompany his movement toward the apartment' prior to the murder of Sankey (Russell Hopton) and the mortal wounding of Anna (Estelle Taylor),[23] and when Rose finally heads off and leaves. It should also be noted that most of the diegetic music in the play is replicated in the film, though the piano music played by Lippo's pupil in the play is replaced by the music of a violin, and the 'The Farmer in the Dell', which can be heard at the end of the play only, bookends the film at the point at which the opening montage finishes as well as at the point at which Rose leaves in the film's last shot.

The script for the film was written by Rice, who sanctioned the change of location of Frank's work from the theatre to the movies and made numerous changes to the dialogue. These were largely minor, and included lines such as the open-hearted 'Here, catch it' as Anna throws a coin wrapped in paper to Willie (Lambert Rogers) when he asks her for money to buy an ice cream, rather than the parsimonious and uncharacteristic 'Remember this is the last one' that was written for the play. Others include a truncated discussion of socialism and the elimination of some of the anti-Semitic lines. They also include an extensively-revised version of Samuel Kaplan's poem. In the play Kaplan begins to recite a poem that begins with the following lines:

> When lilacs last in the dooryard bloom'd
> And the great star early droop'd in the western sky in the night,
> I mourn'd and yet shall mourn, with ever-returning Spring,
> I mourn'd and yet shall mourn, with ever-returning Spring? Yes!

Then at Rose's request, he reads out 'the part about the farmhouse':

> In the door-yard, fronting an old farm-house, near the white-washed palings,
> Stands the lilac-bush, tall-growing with heart-shaped leaves in rich green,
> With many a pointed blossom, rising delicate, with the perfume strong I love,
> With every leaf a miracle – and from this bush in the door-yard,
> With delicate-color'd blossoms and heart-shaped leaves of rich green,
> A sprig with its flower I break.

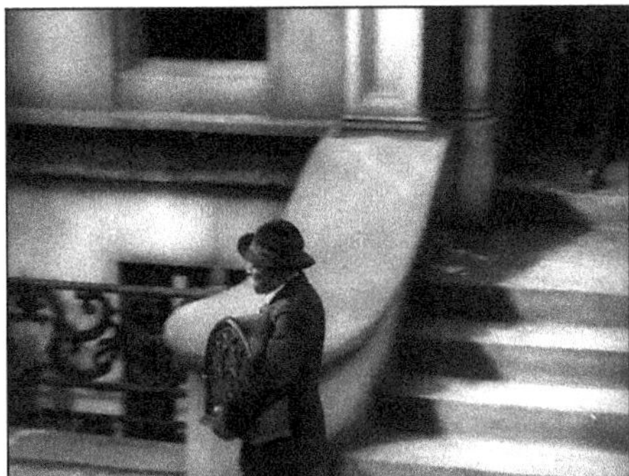

Figure 11

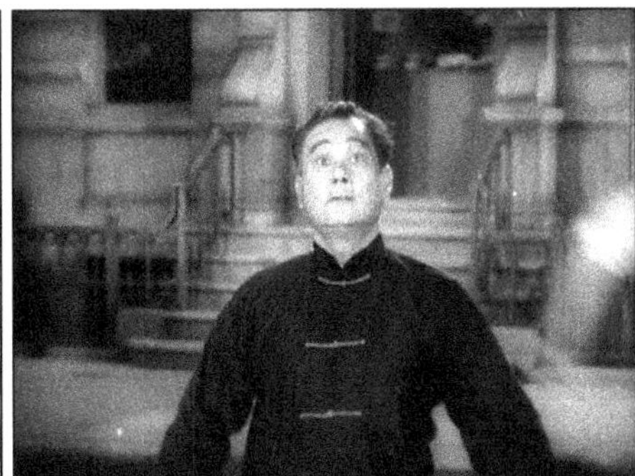

Figure 12

But in the film these lines are replaced by those of a shorter, stronger, and much more outgoing poem, which runs as follows:

> Sail forth, steer for the deep waters only,
> Reckless old soul exploring,
> I with thee and thou with me.
> That we may brave where man has yet to not yet dared to go,
> We will risk the ship ourselves and all.

At this point in the film, Rose says goodnight to Sam (William Collier Jr.), Sam goes and sits alone on the empty steps in front of brownstone, and the scene and the day come to an end with the aforementioned version of 'I Can't Give Anything But Love, Baby' (a hit song written by Jimmy McHugh and Dorothy Fields in 1928). The second early-morning montage ensues, and is followed by the arrival home of a tipsy Vincent Jones (Matt McHugh) and an equally tipsy Dick and Mae (Allan Fox and Greta Granstedt) as Dr Wilson (Howard Russell) exits the house, lights a cigarette and walks off right, and as the gradual build up to the killings begins.

As in the play, this build up encompasses the entry of a passing milkman, a passing policeman, Sam, who enters and looks up at Rose's window, Mrs Jones, who is walking her dogs, and a pair of young boys, one of whom tries to complete a cartwheel, the other of whom is Willie, who blows into a paper bag and pops it, and who thereby foreshadows the louder and more lethal sounds that will emanate from the Maurrant apartment. During the course of this build up, a black male walks across the screen from right to left (figure 11), and in response to the gun shots, we cut to an array of neighbours and passers-by, who rush in toward the brownstone one by one, and who include a Chinese man and another black male (figures 12–13).

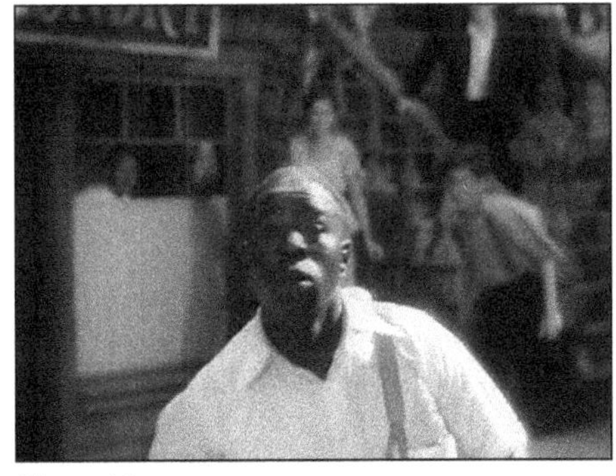

Figure 13

These are additions to the ethnic mix that marks the play, and this mix is further augmented by the inclusion of Hispanic as well as Anglo children on the two occasions in which 'The Farmer in the Dell' is chanted in the film. What is sobering, however, is the change of words from the first to the second occasion. On the first occasion, the children are outside in a circle in the evening as Mrs Jones makes her way in the sweltering heat toward the brownstone further down the street, and here the words are as follows:

The farmer in the dell
The farmer in the dell
Eye-o, the derry-o
The farmer in the dell

The farmer choose [sic] a wife
The farmer choose [sic] a wife
Eye-o, the derry-o
The farmer choose [sic] a wife

The wife choose [sic] a child
The wife choose [sic] a child
Eye-o, the derry-o
The wife choose [sic] a child

The child choose [sic] a nurse
The child choose [sic] a nurse
Eye-o, the derry-o
The child choose [sic] a nurse

But on the second occasion, the words the ring of children chant as Rose departs are not just different but shocking. They read as follows:

The farmer's in the dell
The farmer's in the dell
Eye-o, the derry-o
The farmer's in the dell

The farmer kills the wife
The farmer kills the wife
Eye-o, the derry-o
The farmer kills the wife

The wife kills the child
The wife kills the child
Eye-o, the derry-o
The wife kills the child

The child kills the nurse
The child kills the nurse
Eye-o, the derry-o
The child kills the nurse

The nurse kills the doll
The nurse kills the doll
Eye-o, the derry-o
The nurse kills the doll

Street Scene was filmed over 22 days in July 1931 and came in under budget, which was set at $584, 000 according to the AFI Catalog. The film opened for its premiere run at the Rivoli in New York on 26 August, and was released more widely on 5 September. During the course of its production, Goldwyn, Vidor and Rice had been obliged to submit the film's script to the Studio Relations Committee under Jason Joy, following the adoption of a 'Code to Govern the Making of Talking, Synchronised and Silent Pictures' on 31 March 1930. (For further details on the latter see chapter 7 on *Waterloo Bridge*). According to the Catalog, 'Rice's play was considered controversial because of the characterization of social worker "Alice Simpson." Rice received many complaints from social agencies' and Joy was warned about the controversy. In response, Joy cautioned Goldwyn as follows: 'we suggest that, unless some radical change be made in the characterization of Miss Simpson, it be definitely indicated that she is an agent for the party who is dispossessing the unfortunate family.' But Rice stood firm and no real changes were made, and '*Street Scene* was named one of the ten best pictures of 1931 by a poll in *The Film Daily*'. Later on, the play was dramatised on television on three occasions, and on 9 January 1947 an opera based on the play, with music by Kurt Weill and lyrics by Langston Hughes, opened at the Adelphi Theatre on Broadway, ran for 148 performances, and was subsequently revived on a number of occasions.[24]

Notes

1. King Vidor, *A Tree Is A Tree* (London, New York, Toronto: Longmans, Green and Co., 1954), p. 139. Vidor does not specify the theatre in which he saw the play, but the Mayan Theatre was the only venue playing *Street Scene* in Los Angeles in 1931. According to *Variety*, 20 May 1931, p. 133, the play ran for six weeks under the direction of Sid Grauman and earned $9,000 in its final week, but production costs were so high that the play did little more than break even. For further details on the Los Angeles production, see Elmer Rice, *Minority Report: An Autobiography* (London, Melbourne, Toronto: William Heinemann, 1963), pp. 272–274.
2. In *Minority Report*, pp. 236–237, Rice described *The Sidewalks of New York* as follows: 'It was another technical experiment: a play without words; not a pantomime, in which speech is indicated by gesture, but a series of situations in which there is no need of speech. It dealt with the struggles of a boy and a girl who come separately to New York to make their own way ... It contained a series of episodes illustrative of various phases of New York life. Some of the scenes were realistic, some symbolic, some expressionistic. The intended total effect was a panoramic impression of New York ... One of the settings ... was the exterior of typical Manhattan brownstone-front ... The scene depicted the awakening of a house, a few hours compressed into a few minutes of wordless action: homecoming roisters, the milkman, the patrolling policeman, alarm clocks, radios, bedclothes put to air, children off to school, an organ grinder playing "The Sidewalks of New York"'.
3. Anthony F.R. Palmieri, *Elmer Rice: A Playwright's Vision of America* (Rutherford, Madison, Teaneck: Fairleigh Dickinson University Press and London and Toronto: Associated University Presses, 1980), pp. 94–95.
4. Elmer Rice, *The Living Theatre* (London, Melbourne, Toronto: William Heinemann, 1960), p. 214.
5. Palmieri, *Elmer Rice*, p. 95.
6. Samuel L. Leiter, Editor-in-Chief, *The Encyclopedia of the New York Stage, 1920–1930, N-Z* (West-

port,Conn. and London: Greenwood Press, 1985), p. 871. For more details on these and other events prior to the play's opening, see Rice, *Minority Report*, pp. 242–254.

7. Leiter, *The Encyclopedia of the New York Stage, 1920–1930*, p.871.
8. The cast at this point included Mary Servoss as Anna Maurrant , Robert Kelly as Frank Maurrant, Erin O'Brien-Moore as Rose Maurrant, Joseph Baird as Steve Sankey, Leo Bulgakov as Abraham Kaplan, and Horace Braham as Samuel Kaplan.
9. According to Rice, *The Living Theatre*, p. 222, *Street Scene* was performed in Argentina, Austria, Belgium, Britain, Canada, Denmark, France, Germany, Greece, Holland, Hungary, Japan, Mexico, Norway, Palestine, Poland, South Africa, the Soviet Union, Spain and Sweden, among others. It is worth noting that *Street Scene* seems to have prompted the production of *Café*, a 1930 play by Marya Mannes which takes place in a single-set Parisian sidewalk, and *Dead End*, a 1935 play by Sidney Kingsley, which takes place in a single setting in New York as viewed from the East River. Both are noted in Gerald Bordman, *American Theatre: A Chronicle of Comedy and Drama, 1930–1969* (New York and Oxford: Oxford University Press, 1996), p. 4–5 and p. 124, respectively, and the set in the latter is described as comprising a 'new luxury high-rise' on one side and 'a dilapidated tenement' on the other ... The front of the stage was a pier, and the orchestra pit represented the river into which characters later jumped' and critics 'compared the play favourably to *Street Scene*' which ran for 687 performances'. A film version with a similar set was produced by Warner Bros. and directed by William Wyler in 1937 from a script by Lillian Hellman, giving unexpected rise to series of films that featured The Dead End Kids, The Dead End Kids and Little Tough Guys, East Side Kids, and Bowery Boys from 1937 to 1958.
10. Leiter, *The Encyclopedia of the New York Stage, 1920–1930*, p. 872.
11. Leiter, *The Encyclopedia of the New York Stage, 1920–1930*, p. 872.
12. Leiter, *The Encyclopedia of the New York Stage, 1920–1930*, p. 872.
13. Rice, *The Living Theatre*, pp. 208–209.
14. Palmieri, *Elmer Rice*, 96.
15. Palmieri, *Elmer Rice*, 96.
16. A. Scott Berg, *Goldwyn: A Biography* (London: Pan Books, 1999, initially published in London by Hamish Hamilton and in New York by Alfred A. Knopf in 1989), p. 209.
17. Berg, *Goldwyn*, pp. 209–210. Of the original Broadway cast those who replicated their roles in the film were Beulah Bondi as Emma Jones, George Humbert as Fillipo Fiorentino, Anna Konstant as Shirley Kaplan, T. H. Manning as George Jones, Matthew McHugh as Vincent Jones, John M. Qualen as Carl Olsen, Conway Washburne as Daniel Buchanan, and Eleanor Wesselhoeft as Greta Fiorentino.
18. King Vidor, *On Film Making* (London and New York: W.H. Allen, 1973), pp. 103–104. According to the AFI Catalog, Gregg Toland worked with Barnes on the cinematography too, and in a later interview conducted by Nancy Dowd in the early 1970s, Vidor recalls that he 'worked out a system with the camera following out of a door, then picking up the next actor and the next extra just entering through the same door. This gave a flow to it, and it was challenging to see how much movement we could put one static set in front of the building'. He also confirms that the long musical interlude in the middle of the film was used to adhere to the play's structure. See Nancy Dowd and David Shepard, *King Vidor,* (Metuchen, N.J. and London: Director's Guild of America and the Scarecrow Press, 1988), pp. 120, 122.
19. Michael Slowik, *After the Silents: Hollywood Film Music in the Early Sound Era, 1926–1934* (New York: Columbia University Press, p. 191.
20. Slowik, *After the Silents*, p. 191.
21. Slowik, *After the Silents*, p. 191.
22. Slowik, *After the Silents*, p. 192.
23. Slowik, *After the Silents*, p. 192.
24. See *Street Scene* (opera) at http://en.wikipedia.org/wiki/Street_Scene (opera) 31/12/2015. According to http://en.wikipedia,org/wiki/Street_Scene_(play) 23/11/2016, television versions of the play were presented by *The Philco Television Playhouse* on 31 October 1952, with Betty Field as Rose; by *Celanese Theatre* on 2 April 1952 (a 30-minute version starring Paul Kelly, Ann Dvorak and Michael Wagner); and by BBC-TV on 15 November 1959.

Chapter 7

Waterloo Bridge

Waterloo Bridge began life as a play by Robert E. Sherwood and eventually gave rise to three film versions and a number of radio versions too. The first film version was released in 1931 amid a number of films focussing on female prostitutes, chorus girls and 'fallen women' in the late 1920s and early 1930s, and these included *Sadie Thompson* (1928), *Anna Christie, The Kiss, Madame X* and *Our Modern Maidens* (all 1929), *The Easiest Way* and *Susan Lenox: Her Fall and Rise* (both 1931), *Blonde Venus, The Greeks Had a Word for Them, Rain* and *Red-Headed Woman* (all 1932), and *Baby Face, Gold Diggers of 1933*, and *She Done Him Wrong* (all 1933). Some of these films were based on original scripts. But others were based on what Katie N. Johnson calls 'brothel dramas', plays both highbrow and lowbrow that fed on anxieties about sexuality and eugenics and women's rights and urbanisation in the late 1800s and early 1920s, and that flourished alongside a fascination with the figure of the showgirl in burlesque shows, follies and revues.[1] Discussion of these and other films and adaptations was pioneered in a book by Lea Jacobs entitled *The Wages of Sin*, which was first published in 1991,[2] and which contextualises the films in terms of the trope of the fallen woman and the issues and practices of censorship in the period between the late 1920s and the early-mid 1930s.[3] Challenging the myth of what has become known as 'Pre-Code' Hollywood, and alongside research conducted by Ruth Vasey and Richard Maltby,[4] Jacobs provides conclusive evidence that these and other films were subject to regulation. The 1931 version of *Waterloo Bridge*, which is often called a Pre-Code film, is yet another example.

The Play

According to Sherwood, the stage-play version of *Waterloo Bridge* was prompted by an encounter with a woman in Trafalgar Square a few days after the war.[5] The woman was American and she told Sherwood that she had come to England as a member of the chorus in *The Pink Lady* and had 'stuck, through no choice of her own'.[6] The play was produced by Charles Dillingham, staged by Winchell Smith, and set in London in November 1917. It was previewed at the Tremont Theatre in Boston on 21

November 1929 and the Broad Street Theatre in Philadelphia on 23 December 1929 prior to its New York opening at the Fulton Theatre on 6 January 1930, where it played for a total 64 performances, with June Walker as Myra, Glenn Hunter as Roy Cronin, Florence Edney as Mrs Hobley, Cora Witherspoon as Kitty, and Eunice Hunt as Getrude. The play consisted of four scenes. The first and fourth take place on Waterloo Bridge; and the second and third take place in a room rented by Myra Deauville (the character based on the woman with the flat) in a lodging house run by Mrs. Hobley. The other principal characters are Roy Cronin, an American who has joined a Canadian regiment in order to fight the Germans and who has just been discharged from hospital, and Kitty, who is Myra's friend and fellow prostitute.

The play opens on a bay in the wall on the eastern side of Waterloo Bridge, an area well known as a site for the sex trade.[7] Kitty is seated on a bench eating an apple (an obvious allusion to the Biblical Eve) and 'watching for customers'. A military policeman enters from the right and converses with Kitty, and they are joined by Gertrude, another prostitute. The women complain about the lack of trade and Gertrude leaves to pick up customers at Waterloo Station. The policeman leaves and a Sergeant and Sergeant-Major enter from the left. The latter is polite, but the former calls Kitty a 'bloody tart' and complains that the bridge 'is infested with prostitutes'. The men leave as Myra enters from the left. Myra tells Kitty that she has been engaged in war work on a farm and that she is now in need of money, and Kitty responds by telling Myra about conditions in London: 'Nothing fit to eat or drink, no signs of life and no 'ope of any'. Kitty leaves and Myra bends down to pick up her suitcase. As she does so, she spots Roy, whom Sherwood describes 'as a palpable, forthright soldier, with a red, honest face'. Hoping to have found a much-needed customer, Myra gets Roy to stumble over her suitcase. Roy apologises and responds to Myra's American accent, and Myra explains that she is indeed American and that she came to London as a member of the chorus in *The Pink Lady*. Roy tells Myra that he has been recovering from his wounds and that he is flush with money, and at this point the sound of sirens, artillery and German airplanes prompts them to leave and head for Myra's apartment room nearby.

Act 1 Scene 2 is set in Myra's apartment in Mrs. Hobley's lodging house. 'The furniture is cheaply elegant but shabby'. At the right is Myra's battered trunk with 'The Pink Lady – Hotel' label and an antiquated gramophone.[8] Myra enters and Mrs. Hobley asks her for her rent. Myra tells Mrs. Hobley that she is waiting for Roy, that Roy is flush with money, and that she intends to 'get it out of him'. At this point Roy arrives with Myra's suitcase and a fish-and-chip supper. Mrs. Hobley leaves and Roy and Myra talk about money, Camel cigarettes, Roy's enlistment, and the failure of the show that Myra signed up for when *The Pink Lady* closed. They listen to the sound of planes and bombs then Roy asks Myra about her work in the theatre. Roy says that he would like to take a trip to Shakespeare's birthplace then changes his mind: 'I think I'd have a better time staying here in London', he says. 'Would you like to go out with me? I mean to shows and things like that?' Myra is surprised and tempted but not sure how to respond. She puts the dishes in the sink outside and Roy plays a gramophone recording of one of the songs from *The Pink Lady*. Myra returns and they reminisce about the show. Myra explains that she is an 'an ex-chorus girl', but Roy brushes this aside. Myra says that 'I don't think you've ever gone around much with girls' and Roy replies that 'in a strange country – how would I meet any decent girls? It took an air raid and a freak of luck to fix it up for me to meet you'. The raid subsides, and still in need of money, Myra says good-night to Roy. Roy says that he will be back tomorrow and Myra is still smiling as she picks up the bill for her rent, looks at her reflection in the mirror, prepares herself for work, and leaves.

Act 2 Scene 1 takes place in the boarding house the following morning. Roy arrives with flowers and waits for Myra. Kitty appears at the window looking for Myra and Roy invites her in. Kitty tells Roy that Myra leads 'a miserable life'. She also tells him that she has always hoped that a nice young man would come along and marry her. However it becomes evident when Myra returns and when Roy leaves to cash his money that Kitty has been setting him up: 'I give you my word', she says to Myra, 'that lad'll marry you today ... I've ... put you in the way of a good thing'. But Myra's response is not what Kitty expects: 'It isn't a good thing, Kitty. It's a stinking thing ... He don't even know me. And he never will know me, or about me, if I have to jump off Waterloo Bridge, into the river, to keep him from finding out'. At this point, Roy returns to reveal that all leave has been cancelled and that he has to take the last train out that night. Aware of Myra's straightened circumstances, Roy offers to help her. But Myra is adamant: 'Who gave you a right to question me about my affairs'. 'I gave myself the right', says Roy. 'And how'd you manage that?' says Myra. 'By loving you, that's how'. Myra is moved and bewildered. She insists that he is only kidding himself, that he is lonesome and far away from home. But Roy looks into her face and they embrace. Roy makes plans for an immediate wedding, but Myra says that she wants to change her dress, and as Roy leaves the room she writes him a note, takes 'two or three flowers from the pitcher', picks up her suitcase, and leaves. When Roy returns Mrs. Hobley tells him that Myra has left without paying her rent. Roy pays the rent and Mrs. Hobley tells him that Myra is likely to have gone to one of 'the regular places for prostitutes like 'er'. Then Roy finds a note from Myra which simply says 'I can't do it. Goodbye', and as he leaves, the sounds of sirens, artillery and gunfire can be heard once more.

Act 2 Scene 2 opens later that night. Myra is sitting on a bench as a special constable cycles across the bridge warning everyone to take cover as yet another air raid begins. A bomb explodes on the embankment nearby as Roy enters from the right and spots Myra. 'I've been looking for you', he says. 'I've been walking backward and forward on this bridge, and up and down the Strand and Leicester Square and Piccadilly for hours'. He gives Myra the receipt for the rent, tells her that he has arranged for her to be paid a regular sum of money from his wages, and says that has been ordered to take the eleven fourteen train from Waterloo. Myra bursts into tears then pleads with him to go: 'Its late Roy', she says. 'You've got to go to your train'. But Roy tells Myra that he intends stay with her. 'I've found you', he says. 'That makes everything different'. He leans over the wall on the bridge and voices his despair. But the only one who hears him is Myra, and the only other sounds are those of an airplane 'growing louder and louder'. A burst of machine-gun fire and the sound of a bomb drive the couple into each other's arms. Then the noise abates and Myra asks Roy for his address in France. Myra says goodbye and asks Roy to write to her. Roy replies that he will 'try to get back some time', kisses Myra goodbye, and exits. The sound of a German bomber 'can be heard directly overhead' as Myra looks upward and pauses. She opens her handbag, pulls out a wilted pack of Camel cigarettes, takes one and lights it, then holds up her lighted match. 'Here I am, Heinie ... I'm right down here', she says, and it is at this point that the final curtain falls.

Although receipts at the box office were initially respectable (Sherwood's play ran for 64 performances at the Fulton Theatre prior to touring), *Waterloo Bridge* was adjudged to be 'lacking in event and structure' by Brooks Atkinson and other critics and generally regarded as failure.[9] Sherwood's biographer argues that Roy 'neither condemns not laments Kitty's or Myra's status as prostitutes. He simply accepts it as part of their reality', and that Sherwood himself was neither prejudiced nor judgemental.[10] But although the ending is equivocal, Myra seems to invite her own demise as the only way out of the life she leads, and to that extent Myra is unlike the woman on whom she is based, and to that extent Sherwood's play invokes the trope of the fallen woman. Variants on this trope have been traced back to the Bible. But it was particularly prevalent in Europe and the US from the mid-nineteenth to the mid-twentieth century and can be found in paintings and illustrations as well as in novels, plays, operas and films: indeed, as Lea Jacobs points out, a relatively early example is a set of three paintings by Augustus Egg which depict in turn an accused woman lying prostrate before her husband as her children look on, the woman clutching one of her children while staring out of the window of a bare apartment, and the woman beneath the arches of a bridge, 'an icon traditionally connected to the moment of the fallen woman's isolation and suicide'.[11] Along with *Found Drowned*, an early 1850s painting by George Fredric Watts which depicts the dead body of a woman underneath the arch of Waterloo Bridge (figure 1), these images and tropes mark the play and the 1931 and 1940 film versions too, albeit in different ways, and albeit under different regimes of regulation.

Stage plays like *Waterloo Bridge* were not subject to nationwide censorship in the USA, but state and city officials could ban plays and shows that they considered (or were pressed to consider) immoral or offensive. However, despite its occasional use of words like 'whore', 'tart' and 'bloody', and despite the fact that its central female character is a prostitute, Sherwood's play was not one of them. This was probably because it was written by a respected playwright. But it was also probably

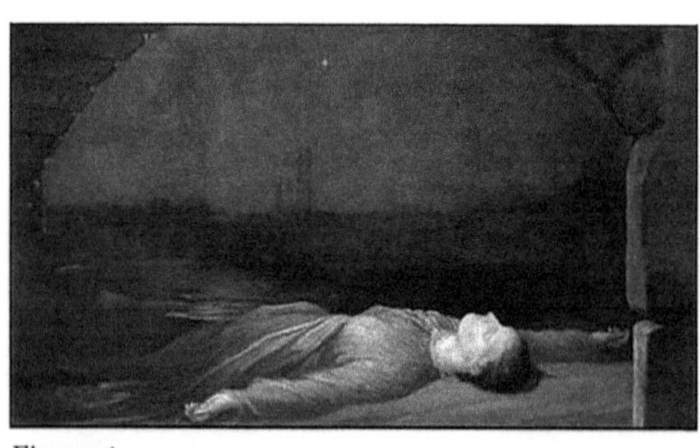

Figure 1

because it adhered to the traditional tropes of fallen womanhood and was thus unmarked by the controversial aspects of some of the plays and shows discussed by Johnson. However when Carl Laemmle Jr. acquired the rights to Sherwood's play on behalf of Universal Pictures, he found himself with a property that would have to be modified for two distinct reasons. One was the conversion of a play with only four scenes and two settings into a film with a greater number and variety of locations, scenes and sequences. The other was the adoption of The Motion Picture Production Code (a 'Code to Govern the Making of Talking, Synchronised and Silent Pictures') by the Board of Directors of the Motion Picture Producers and Distributors of America, Inc. (MPPDA) on 31 March 1930.

Waterloo Bridge (1931)

As noted above, the 1931 version of *Waterloo Bridge* is often cited as a 'pre-Code' film. However the Code, which was based on a list of 'Don'ts and Be Carefuls' drawn up in 1927, and which at this point was administered by Jason Joy on behalf of the newly-formed Studio Relations Committee (SRC), 'required that pictures be approved by the SRC before they were released'.[12]As a result most of the major companies (and many of the minor ones too) consulted Jason Joy, who administered the Code and its applications through to 1932, James Wingate ,who worked with Joy then administered the Code on his own through 1933, and Joseph Breen, who joined Wingate in 1933 before replacing him the following year.[13] Prior to the adoption of the Code, the functions of the SRC had been largely advisory, and the advice it dispensed based largely on decisions made by local boards of censorship. These decisions were legally underpinned by the 1915 Supreme Court ruling that the principles of free speech were inapplicable to motion pictures. But in an era of rapidly changing mores and diverse tastes, the decisions taken by different boards often resulted in cuts and bans of different kinds, thus resulting in expensive and time-consuming alterations for specific states and regions and thus hindering the efficient circulation of standardised prints in the home market (and, it should be noted, in foreign markets too).[14] Along with the 'Don'ts and Be Carefuls', the Code and its subsequent modifications were thus essentially designed to enable the efficient production and distribution of films. In adopting them, a series of representational devices and formulas were devised and tried out during the course of the early-mid 1930s and refined during the course of the late 1930s and early 1940s in order to handle potentially censorable words, acts, professions, character traits and modes of behaviour; the distribution of character's fates; and the ways in which these fates were justified. Their purpose throughout, as Jason Joy put it, was to develop a set of conventions 'from which conclusions might be drawn by the sophisticated mind, but which would mean nothing to the unsophisticated and inexperienced'.[15]

As already noted, Sherwood's play contained potentially censorable words such as 'whore', 'tart', 'prostitutes' and 'bloody', focussed on the relationship between a prostitute and a soldier, and represented other prostitutes plying and discussing their trade. The words were removable, but the film had somehow to suggest Myra's profession in order to motivate her actions. Carl Laemmle Jr., who was head of production at Universal Pictures and who acquired the rights to the play in 1930, initially assigned Tom Reed the task of adapting Sherwood's play. But Reed 'hardened the character of Myra, lessening her appeal, and completely eliminated the bridge as a setting' and James Whale, who had already been assigned as director, suggested that Reed be replaced by Benn Levy.[16] Levy's version, which is dated 21 March 1931, opened with the concluding moments of Myra's final performance on stage:

> In the communal dressing room, she gets a white fox fur from an admiring young officer and talks gaily about the various men in her life. As she leaves for a date in a cab, a poster on the wall behind her celebrates the first anniversary of *Chu Chin Chow*, an exotic revue ... Levy's device of using the show to date Myra's descent into hooking was at once both subtle and authentic. He dissolves to Myra posing nude for an artist, an empty whiskey bottle on the nightstand. Outside the window: a poster commemorating the show's second anniversary at His Majesty's Theatre. Dissolving once more, Myra and her friend Kitty are now seen working in the Strand, and on the wall behind them a poster proclaims the third anniversary of *Chu Chin Chow*.[17]

At this point the scene depicting Myra's last performance and the shot depicting Myra posing for the artist were cut from the script, probably for reasons of cost and censorship respectively: on the one hand Universal had just reported 'the biggest loss of its history' for the fiscal year ending 1 November 1930 and the filming of a sequence in a stage show in front of an audience in a theatre or studio set was considered too expensive; on the other hand the Code was now a factor, and nudity, however partial, was a risk.[18] In the meantime Levy made a number of other alterations. The word 'bloody' was retained at this stage, but the words 'whore', 'tart' and 'prostitutes' were not. In the script and in the film Roy and Myra meet in the midst of an air raid in one of the bays on Waterloo Bridge. But in the film there are no other prostitutes and there are no customers: Roy (Kent Douglass) and Myra (Mae Clarke) meet one another while helping a defiant old woman (Rita Carlisle) to shelter under the bridge as the bombs fall (figure 2).[19] Myra's death at the end of the film, however, is both

Figure 2

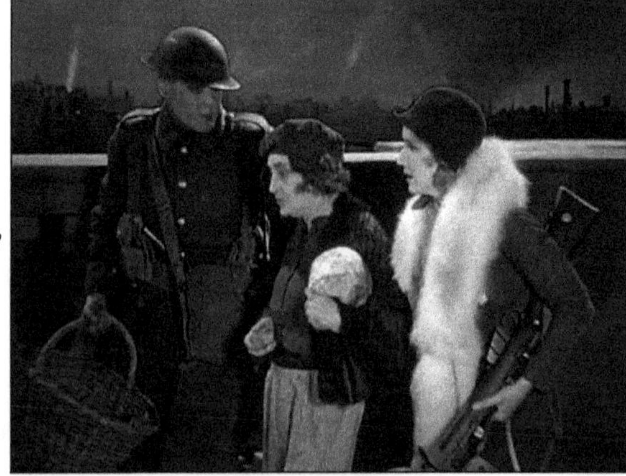

brutal and sudden. Roy finds Myra on the bridge and she agrees to marry him when he returns. But as she tries to escape from the bridge in an ensuing air raid she is killed by a bomb from a zeppelin. As well as depriving her of marriage to Roy, as in the play, this ending deprives Myra of her last defiant speech and the business with the match. In doing so it gives rise to a malevolent deus ex machina ending, an ending that obliterates Myra while at the same time erasing the clichés of fallen womanhood by avoiding any connotations of suicide. This is one of the most striking aspects of Levy's contribution both to the script and the final version of the film. But his most extensive contribution was the addition of two lengthy sequences set in a country estate owned by Roy's family.

Roy initially visits his family on his own then brings Myra with him later on. Roy's family welcome Myra with open arms. They take refreshments in the grounds and Myra is provided with a luxurious room to sleep in. But Myra is troubled. Aware that she has been welcomed as a potential wife for Roy – and hence a potential member of his upper upper-class family – she confesses her profession to Roy's mother (Enid Bennett). Roy's mother is sympathetic, but marriage to Roy is now out of the question, and Myra takes a train back to London on her own. Here she initially solicits a potential customer but leaves, but when she returns to her apartment in the morning she has earned money enough to pay rent. Possibly prompted by Roy's plan to visit Shakespeare's birthplace in the play, the sequences at the mansion were a means of mobilising the factors of respectability and class, representing their guardians, and articulating their moral values. For Roy's mother, Myra is a fallen woman and this must mean that love and happiness are out of reach. But while Myra's death ensures that Roy and Myra will never be happily married, it is marked by a prior refusal on both their parts to give up the chance of doing so and is therefore also marked as much by the sense of random and excessive punishment noted above as by the morally conventional consequences of her profession.

Following the completion of a reworked synopsis, Levy and Whale went to work on a shooting script. The two scenes in Myra's apartment are almost as long as those in the play.[20] But the overt verbal references to prostitution have been cut and the conversation between Roy and Kitty (Doris Lloyd) has been shorn of some its cynicism. Roy still brings fish and chips and flowers, but it is Myra not Roy who plays the record on the gramophone, and this is picked up later on in the final version of the film.[21] At this point, on 24 April 1931, a copy of the shooting script was sent for approval to Jason Joy. Joy had been the recipient of a letter from Lamar Trotti praising the Los Angeles production of Sherwood's play a year earlier. The letter was dated 16 January 1930, prior to Universal's interest in the rights and two months prior to the introduction of the Code. Trotti, a member of the SRC, described the play 'as the story of the redemption of a woman of the street through the love of boy' and wrote that: 'Since it is all a story of redemption, I don't think it has any great difficulties' as a motion picture. Indeed, he concluded, 'it might make a better motion picture than play because of the air raids, war, etc'.[22] On 9 September, however, six months after the introduction of the Code and in response to a request for advice from H.A. Fitelson at Tiffany Productions regarding a possible adaptation of the play, Trotti replied that although he believed 'that a suitable treatment can be found', 'the chief objection … lies in the fact that the girl, after falling in love and her character is shown to be changing, is forced back onto the streets to pay money for her lodgings'. 'This', he concluded, 'would be objectionable in the character and probably would be censorable', though he went on to suggest that Fitelson handle this 'in such a way as to make the girl so determined to give up the life she has been leading that she overawe the landlady and win her point to stay there that night rather than going back to her former life'.[23]

Meanwhile Joy discussed the shooting script with Whale on 30 April 1931 and 'agreed on treatment'. He sent a letter to Laemmle Jr. later that day, alerting him to the changes to which he and Whale had agreed, and advising him to use 'the utmost care' in the sequences of 'over-exposure and suggestive postures' in the reinstated finale to the show that now opened the film and that were particularly marked in the dressing-room and street scenes that followed. Joy also drew attention to the fact that 'from the standpoint of censorship in Great Britain the use of the word "bloody" is dangerous', suggested that a reference to George III be cut from British Empire prints, and that a 'reference to St. Louis' (Myra's birthplace in the play) be cut along with 'the slur on American prohibition' evident in the comments made by Roy's father while drinking alcohol at dinner prior to Roy and Myra's visit as a couple.[24] Three months later, on 29 July, Joy noted the earlier discussion with Whale and that he had now seen the film, which he summed up as follows: 'It is a story of regeneration. It deals with a prostitute who sacrifices her future material happiness because she feels that her past makes her unworthy of the boy who wants to marry her and whom she loves. There is increased sympathy for the girl because she is essentially fine, truthful and honest. No brief is held for her mode of existence. She knows it would be wrong and she forsakes it. But her previous profession has made her an outcast, a fact that she realizes and for which she ultimately pays with her life, rather than bring unhappiness to the boy whom she loves. Goodness and the happiness which comes as a result of following the correct standards of life are stressed from the beginning. It is amply shown that only grief and unhappiness can come as a result of immorality'.[25]

As we have seen, Myra 'ultimately' dies. But she does so in a manner that does not correspond to Joy's ideological summary and the fallen-woman trope that underlies it. This may be a piece of muddled or wishful thinking on Joy's part, or it may be that the ending was changed later on. Either way, Joy went on to record his persistent concerns about the word 'bloody' and the mocking of prohibition in the Cronin household in a letter to Laemmle Jr., also dated 29 July. In addition he advised that 'further consideration' be given to the 'portion of the scene in the dressing room of the theatre which shows Myra clothed only in a step-in and brassier' and went on to propose that it be cut. He also suggested cutting one of Kitty's lines.[26] Along with the reference to St. Louis, this line appears to have been removed, but the 'semi-nudity' in the dressing room remained. The film was previewed on 1 August, and two days later, in a response to Joy's letter of 29 July, Laemmle Jr. wrote that it had proved 'impossible' to eliminate the references to prohibition in the dining-room sequence involving Roy and his family prior to Myra's visit. However he went to say that 'we feel we have eliminated the objectionable features of this scene by retaking two close-ups'.[27] Although Wingate was worried, Joy himself stood by his view that the story was one of redemption and was therefore of no real concern.[28] He was thus presumably surprised when an array of censorship boards began requesting and instituting deletions both before and after the film's premiere release on 3 September.

On 24 August Massachusetts deleted all close-ups 'showing bare abdomens in dressing rooms', and on 31 August Maryland deleted three different lines and a suggestive fadeout and New York State deleted 'scenes of girl attempting to solicit man on street', 'views of girl preparing herself to go on street', and nine lines of dialogue from a silent print with sub-titles.[29] Other boards appear to have been more lenient: the Ohio board, for example, only deleted the scene in which Myra is shown looking into her mirror prior to going out on the streets.[30] But Pennsylvania and Chicago were much more censorious: Pennsylvania deleted sixteen shots, scenes and passages of dialogue, and Chicago deleted nineteen.[31] When augmented by censorship problems abroad, particularly in Australia, Japan and Singapore, the 1931 version of *Waterloo Bridge* proved itself to be a major headache.[32] It was by no means the only one – the list of problematic films at this time was legion. But it was no wonder that when Jack Warner mooted the possibility of a remake of *Waterloo Bridge* in 1936 he was instantly rebuffed by Joseph Breen.[33]

Waterloo Bridge (1940)

When he turned down Warner's proposal, and as noted above, Breen had been in official charge of the SCR for nearly two years. Once in office, and still in the midst of numerous censorship crises, he had helped create a new enforcement regime, the Production Code Administration (PCA), and added an amendment to the Code requiring that all prints of MPPDA films released after 1 July 1934 be marked with a seal of approval. In doing so, he forced all MPPDA proposals, scripts and films to be read, viewed and censored in advance. The result was a series of textual ambiguities and deniable activities, some of them the product of metaphors or ellipses in or in between scenes, some of them the product of ambiguous words or verbal slang, and some of them coded devices of other kinds – items of male or female dress, the nature of settings, times of day or night, and so on and so forth. In addition, as Jacobs in particular points out, the narrative arcs that permitted relatively explicit depictions of sinful activities providing that they resulted in redemption or punishment in films of the late 1920s and early 1930s were often modified in the mid-to-late 1930s and early 1940s so as to deprive these activities of explicit articulation while underlining their inevitable consequences.[34] However, the 1940 version of *Waterloo Bridge* contained explicit representations of prostitution, both verbal and visual, and in this film 'sinful activity' was treated in such a way as to underline its tragic consequences, to generate sympathy for its heroine by underlining her middle-class background and nobility of character, and by the fact she herself decides that death is better than the life she leads.

Interest in remaking *Waterloo Bridge* was prompted by the outbreak of World War II in Europe and, more specifically, by its setting in wartime Britain. (Britain was a key overseas market for Hollywood films in the late 1930s and early 1940s).[35] MGM acquired the rights from David O. Selznick on condition that Vivien Leigh (who was under contract to Selznick) would be assigned the role of Myra. Mervyn LeRoy was chosen as director and the script was written by S.N. Behrman, Hans Rameau and George Froeschel. Unlike the 1931 version, which like many early sound films was marked by 'sourced' or diegetic music only (as in the opening scene on stage or the point at which Myra plays her gramophone), the 1940 version was marked by a full orchestral score by Herbert Stothart. The other key differences between this and the 1931 version are as follows.

The MGM version begins and ends on Waterloo Bridge in 1940 and focuses on Roy (Robert Taylor), who is now a senior middle-aged officer and who remembers meeting Myra on the bridge in 1917. Myra is a member of a ballet troupe, not a chorus girl or working-class prostitute, and Roy is a junior officer, not a foot soldier. Roy is intrigued by Myra and decides to attend a performance of *Swan Lake* later that evening in order to meet her again. Against the wishes of her ballet mistress (Maria Ospenskaya), Myra accepts an invitation from Roy to dine at an officers' club later that evening. They fall deeply in love, and Roy proposes marriage the following morning. Myra accepts Roy's proposal. But she and Roy are unable to complete the necessary arrangements and events begin to conspire against them. Roy is ordered to the front and Myra returns to the ballet-troupe and is dismissed for disobedience. Her friend Kitty (Virginia Field) quits in solidarity, and she and Myra try to find jobs and lodgings. But jobs and lodgings are hard to find, and the only comfort for Myra lies in the letters sent by Roy. One these letters informs Myra that Roy's mother (Lucile Watson) has agreed to meet her in a restaurant. However, while waiting for her, Myra spots Roy's name in a casualty list in a newspaper. Thinking that Roy is dead, Myra is so stunned and bewildered that Roy's mother is unable to understand her behaviour and leaves. Myra and Kitty continue to live in penury. Kitty becomes a prostitute and Myra follows suit. However, while awaiting a trainload of soldiers at Waterloo Station, Myra is stunned to see Roy, who makes immediate plans for a wedding at the Cronin estate in Scotland. Accepted with open arms by Roy's family and friends, Myra almost allows herself to be carried away. But her conscience and her love for Roy will not permit her to marry him. She confesses her past to Mrs Cronin, who pleads with her not to make a hasty decision. Myra, however, is adamant. She returns to London and Roy pursues her. He begins to realise the truth, but he still strives to find her. Myra, however, cannot be found. Back on Waterloo Bridge, Myra comes across an ageing prostitute (Martha Wentworth). Horrified by the prospect of what she will otherwise become, she throws herself under a speeding ambulance. Crowds gather around to help her, but Myra is dead. We return to Roy on the bridge as a middle-aged man, still recalling Myra and still mourning Myra's death.

Aside from the extensive musical score and the 'pearly' lighting that marked the 1940 version,[36] the most obvious differences between the 1931 and 1940s versions are as

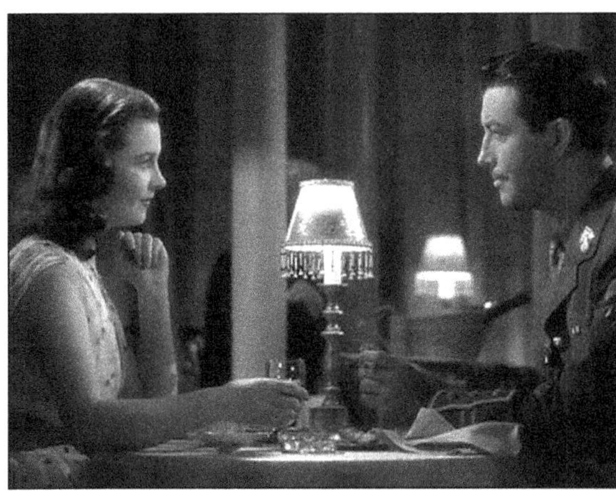

Figure 3

follows. Roy is Scottish rather than American, and he and his family are of even higher status than the family in the 1931 version. Like the character in the play and the 1931 version, Roy in the 1940 version is open-hearted and somewhat naive. However, in addition to his rank as a Colonel in the opening and closing scenes, Roy as a young man in the 1940 version is an officer (albeit a relatively junior one), not a private. He does not articulate a hatred of war as he does in the play; he does not share his memories of *The Pink Lady* or any such show with Myra; and he and Myra fall in love in a restaurant in a high-class club, not over fish and chips in Myra's room (figures 3 and 4). Myra and Kitty are members of a ballet troupe in the early scenes in World War One in the 1940 version, not prostitutes or members of a chorus line (though the repeated use of the word 'Madame' to identify the ballet mistress in the scene in the changing room after the ballet is clearly a deniable reference to the prostitution that pervades the play, the 1931 version and some of the later scenes in the 1940 version). And Myra and Kitty's descent into prostitution in the 1940 version occurs at a much later point than it does in the 1931 version. Following Myra's trauma, Kitty reveals

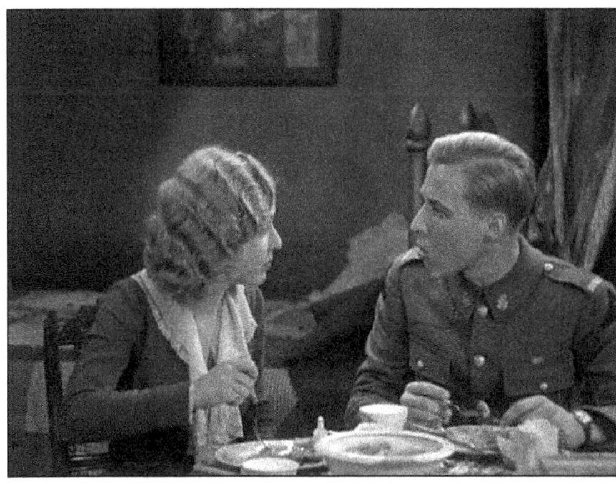

Figure 4

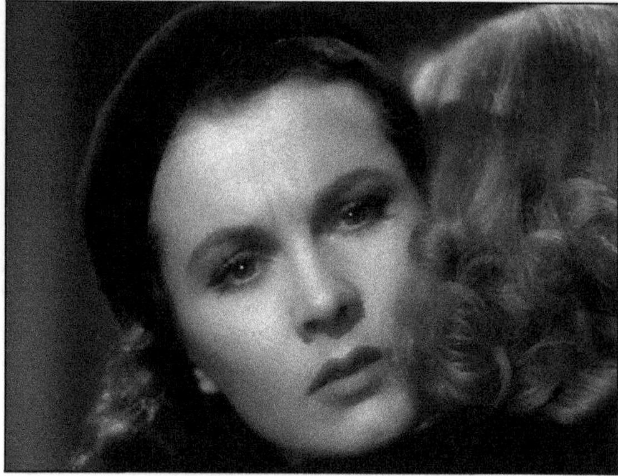
Figure 5

that she has been engaged in prostitution, partly to support Myra and partly to support herself. As they embrace one another a close-up of Myra not only alerts us to what might happen next, but recalls the shot of Myra looking into the mirror both in the 1931 version and in the play (figures 5 and 6). By the time Myra encounters Roy on Waterloo Station she has become resigned and hardened. Through no fault of her own, she thinks that Roy is dead; but Roy is still alive and she is now a fallen woman. Although Roy still loves her, she knows that she must leave him and she does. Significantly, it is Myra who tells Mrs Cronin that she cannot marry Roy, not the other way round as is the case in the 1931 version. This provides her with an impeccable sense of morality and agency. But it also means that her fate is sealed.[37]

Gaby (1956)

In addition to half-hour radio versions broadcast in the US in 1941 and in 1946, and in addition to a half-hour television version broadcast in the US in 1951, there was one more feature-film version. This version was called *Gaby*. It was produced in

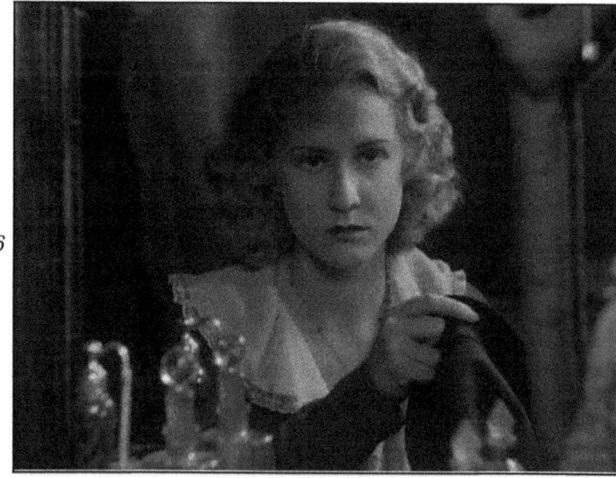
Figure 6

Technicolor by MGM and released on 11 May 1956, following a premiere opening in New York two days earlier. Directed by Curtis Bernhardt, its script was written by Albert Hackett, Frances Goodrich and Charles Lederer, its musical score was composed by Charles Wolcott and Conrad Salinger, and its cinematographer was Robert Planck. Myra was renamed Gaby and played by Lesley Caron and Roy was renamed Gregory Wendell and played by John Kerr, and the film was set on the eve of D-Day in 1944. They key difference between this and the earlier versions is not that Gaby sleeps with other men when she thinks that Gregory is dead, nor that she is not a prostitute, but that she does not die on Waterloo Bridge and that she and Gregory embrace one another on the bridge at the end.[38] Ironically, one of the principal reasons for this is that the Production Code had been amended in 1951 to specify that 'suicide should never be justified or glorified or used to defeat the due process of law'. But although Myra's death in the 1940 version is clearly represented as a suicidal act, her death in the 1931 version is portrayed as a sudden and accidental consequence of war, an arbitrary act that nevertheless happens to punish her for her sins. To that extent the 1956 version may be the only one that does not adopt or rely on the trope of the fallen woman.[39]

Notes

1. Katie N. Johnson, *Sisters in Sin: Brothel Drama in America, 1900–1920* (Cambridge: Cambridge University Press, 2006).

2. Lea Jacobs, *The Wages of Sin: Censorship and the Fallen Woman Film, 1928–1942* (Madison: University of Wisconsin, 1991). *The Easiest Way* is particularly interesting. The play is discussed at length by Johnson, and versions of the film script are discussed by Jacobs. (Although a DVD version is now available, Jacobs was unable to access a print when writing her book.) What is striking is that while the play stages the downfall of the central female character, ending with abandonment by her two lovers and the prospect of life in the brothels of the black quarter, the film reorders events in order to explain and justify her decisions, and to modify the ending by concluding with a scene in which her sister and his husband invite her into their home at Christmas. Unsurprisingly, the final version of the script was written by a woman, Edith Ellis.

3. Jacobs, *The Wages of Sin.*

4. Richard Maltby, 'The Production Code and the Hays Office' in Tino Balio, *Grand Design: Hollywood as a Modern Business Enterprise, 1930–1939* (New York: Scribner's, 1993), pp. 37–72, 'The Production Code and the Mythologies of "Pre-Code" Hollywood' in Steve Neale (ed.), *The Classical Hollywood Reader* (London and New York: Routledge, 2012), pp. 237–249, and Ruth Vasey, *The World According to Hollywood, 1918–1939* (Exeter: Exeter University Press, 1997).

5. Robert E. Sherwood, Preface to *Waterloo Bridge* (New York and London: Charles Scribner's Sons, 1930), p. xxiii.

6. *The Pink Lady* was a hugely successful musical comedy. For details, see Gerald Bordman, *American Musical Theatre: A Chronicle* (New York and Oxford: Oxford University Press, 1986 edition), pp. 264–265.

7. Jerry White, *Zeppelin Nights: London in the First World War* (London: The Bodley Head, 2014), pp. 180–186.

8. While allowing for a range of framings and for views and movements through windows and doorways, this set is reproduced with considerable accuracy in the 1931 version.

9. Harriet Hyman Alonso, *Robert E. Sherwood: The Playwright in Peace and War* (Amherst and Boston: University Press of Massachusetts Press, 2007), p. 14.

10. Alonso, *Robert E. Sherwood*, pp. 112. As Alonso puts it, 'Roy ... neither condemns nor laments Kitty's or Myra's status as prostitutes. He simply accepts it as part of their reality'.

11. Jacobs, *The Wages of Sin*, p. 6. As Jacobs points out, Egg's triptych was initially exhibited in 1858 without titles. She discusses the variants of fallen womanhood and its representation in novels, plays and operas in the nineteenth and early twentieth century in more detail in *The Wages of Sin*, pp. 5–9.

12. Maltby, 'The Production Code and the Mythologies of "Pre-Code" Hollywood', p. 240. For a list of the 'Don'ts and Be Carefuls', see 'Report of Meeting, MPPDA', 25 May 1927, Record 341, MPPDA Digital Archive, Flinders Institute for Research in the Humanities.

13. It should be noted that while all films produced by members of the MPPDA were subject to approval, this did not mean that they were all screened prior to release. It was not until 1933 that a refusal to exhibit 'any picture that does not come within the code' in any of the theatres affiliated to the MPPDA was introduced. See Robert H. Cochrane to Hays, 31 March 1933, Record 908, MPPDA Digital Archive.

14. For a detailed account of Hollywood's foreign markets and their impact on its films both before and after the adoption of the Production Code, see Vasey, *The World According to Hollywood.* Shows and stage plays were very rarely banned, and it was easier – and less expensive – to cut a line of dialogue or a gesture from one live performance to another than to cut or re-cut a film, especially now that most films contained a pre-recorded mix of dialogue, sound and at least some music, all of which had to be carefully synchronised with shots and edits at the point of production.

15. Joy to Wingate, 5 February 1931, PCA *Little Caesar* file, cited in Maltby, 'The Production Code and the Hays Office', p. 40.

16. James Curtis, *James Whale: A New World of Gods and Monsters* (Boston and London: Faber and Faber, 1998), p. 117. Levy was an experienced playwright and had already written seven successful plays. He also wrote the scripts for *Blackmail* (1929) and the 1929 version of *The Informer.*

17. Curtis, *James Whale*, p. 118.

18. Curtis, *James Whale*, p. 121.

19. As the outline of play makes clear, the sound of river boat whistles at the beginning of Act 1 Scene 1 is later joined by the sound of bombs, planes, gunfire and sirens at various points in this and other acts and scenes. The presence of these sounds in the Universal version is much more occasional and much less systematic and they are largely associated with the bridge at night on the two occasions that the bridge is featured. Sounds such these are only prominent in the MGM version at the beginning of the film, the beginning of the flashback, and the point at which Myra commits suicide, where the sound of lories and ambulance sirens are a marked and prominent substitute.

20. The apartment set was constructed later on. It was designed for a range of exterior and interior camera positions and framings, and for movements in and out of the apartment via a window on to the roof as well as via the door. In all other respects, though, it was clearly based on the apartment in the play.

21. All references to *The Pink Lady* have been cut and the song played on the gramophone is one of the songs from *The Bing Boys on Broadway.*

22. Trotti to McKenzie, Williken, Joy and Fisher, 16 January 1930, MPAA/PCA Collection, Margaret Herrick Library. Henceforth all cited documents are those in this collection.

23. Joy to Fitelson, 9 September 1930.

24. Joy to Laemmle, Jr., 30 April 1931. In the play, Myra tells Roy that she and her family lived East St Louis, a working-class area which was renowned as a site of prostitution.

25. Joy Memorandum, 29 July 1931. As is argued above, 'grief and unhappiness' are the actually result of a German bomb, not of 'immorality'.

26. Joy to Laemmle Jr, 29 July 1931.

27. Laemmle Jr. to Joy, 3 August 1931.

28. Telegram from Joy to Hays, 25, August 1931. See also Memos from Trotti to Joy, 26 August 1931.

29. These deletions were specified in reports signed by Joy on behalf of the MPPDA on 2 September, 8 September and 5 October.

30. Ohio's deletion was reported by Joy on 19 October.

31. Chicago's deletions were reported by Joy on 28 September and Pennsylvania's on 19 October.
32. The deletions in Australia, Japan and Singapore were reported by Joy on 8 December 1931 and 28 January 1932, 30 January 1932, and 5 March 1932, respectively.
33. Breen to Warner, 14 February 1936.
34. Jacobs, *The Wages of Sin.*
35. See Mark Glancy, *When Hollywood Loved Britain: The Hollywood 'British Film', 1939–45* (Manchester: Manchester University Press, 1999).
36. Barry Salt notes that MGM overexposed and underprocessed its negatives, resulting in 'pearly-grey' sheen, in *Film Style & Technology: History & Analysis* (London: Starword Press, 2009), p. 216, and this is also noted in Chris Cagle, 'Classical Hollywood 1928–1946' in Patrick Keating (ed.), *Cinematography* (New Brunswick, N.J.: Rutgers University Press, 2014), pp. 49–51. In the introduction to *Hollywood Cameramen* (Thames and Hudson: London, 1970), p. 13, Charles Higham argues that Ruttenberg's camerawork and lighting 'brought a strong visual flavour to *Dr Jekyll and Mr Hyde*, *Gaslight* and *Waterloo Bridge*: a lacquered, solidly contrasty surface, particularly effective in scenes of street lamps shining through fog [and] Thames bridges ghostly against the black flow of the river'. In his autobiography, *Mervyn LeRoy: Take One* (London and New York: W.H. Allen, 1974), pp. 146–147, Leroy notes the use of fog and recalls the extent to which the gradual snuffing of lights in the club-supper sequence served to underscore the extent to which Roy and Myra were now in love.
37. For a more detailed discussion of the 1940 version of *Waterloo Bridge*, see Steve Neale, 'Revisiting *Waterloo Bridge*: Censorship, Representation, Adaptation and the Persisting Myth of "Pre-Code" Hollywood', *Film Studies*, no. 12, Spring, 2015, pp. 71–81.
38. According to Jennifer Forrest, 'Sadie Thompson Redux: Postwar Reintegration of the Wartime Wayward Woman', in Jennifer Forrest and Leonard K. Koos, *Dead Ringers: The Remake in Theory and Practice* (New York: State University of New York Press, 2002), p. 182, Leslie Carron's persona – 'gamine making the transition to or being initiated into sexual adulthood – solicits our sympathy for her actions and encodes them as essentially innocent'.
39. This chapter is a modified version of Steve Neale, 'Revisiting *Waterloo Bridge*: Censorship, Representation, Adaptation and the Persisting Myth of "Pre-Code" Hollywood', *Film Studies*, no. 12, Spring 2015, pp. 62–81.

Chapter 8

Stage Door

Stage Door (1937) was based on the 1936 play by Edna Ferber and George S. Kaufman and initially conceived by Ferber, whose niece 'was an inspiring actress who lived at the Rehearsal Club, the obvious model of the residence in the play'.[1] Following rehearsals and out-of-town performances in Philadelphia in late September and extensive revisions on the road,[2] the play was produced by Sam H. Harris, designed by Donald Oenslager, and definitively staged by Kaufman at the Music Box Theatre on Broadway, where it ran for a total number of 169 performances between 22 October 1936 and March 1937 with Margaret Sullavan as Terry Randall, Phyllis Brooks as Jean Maitland, Richard Kendrick as Keith Burgess, Onslow Stevens as David Kingsley, Alex Courtney by Jimmy Devereux, Janet Fox as Bernice Niemayer, Frances Fuller as Kaye Hamilton, Sylvia Lupes as Olga Brandt, Lee Patrick as Judith Canfield, Leonora Roberts as Mrs Orcutt, Lili Zehner as Susan Page, Beatrice Binn as Little Mary, Mary Wickes as Big Mary, Dorothea Andrews as Mattie, and William Andrews as Frank. Ferber and Kaufman had worked together since the early 1920s, when they collaborated on a 1924 play entitled *Minick*. Ferber also wrote novels such as *Dawn O'Hara* and *The Girls* (in 1911 and 1924, respectively), and went on to write *Show Boat* (1926), *Cimarron* (1929), *Saratoga Trunk* (1941) and *Giant* (1952). *Show Boat* was adapted for the musical stage in 1928 and filmed in 1929, 1936 and 1951, and *Cimarron* was adapted for the screen in 1931 and 1960, *Saratoga Trunk* in 1946, and *Giant* in 1956. Kaufman's career was similarly long, prolific and successful. His earliest plays include *Dulcy* (1921) and *Beggar on Horseback* (1924). And is noted in the chapter on *The Cocoanuts*, he also specialised in writing sketches, revues and gags, some of which were specifically tailored for the Marx Brothers on film as well as on stage. Kaufman directed plays written by others too, among them *The Front Page* (1928–29), *Joseph* (1930), *Here Today* (1932) and *Of Mice and Men* (1937–38), and in addition to *Stage Door*, his collaborations with Ferber included *The Royal Family* (1927), *Dinner at Eight* (1932), *The Land is Bright* (1941) and *Bravo* (1949).[3]

The Play

Stage Door is 'a play in three acts', each of them subdivided into two scenes. Act One Scene One and Acts Two and Three are set in the communal living room in The Footlights Club in New York, a boarding house for actresses based on the real-life Rehearsal Club,[4] and Act One Scene Two is set one of the upstairs bedrooms. The first scene begins 'just before dinner hour', and most of the women are returning from matinee performances or job hunting. The exceptions are Olga Brandt, who is playing Chopin on the piano, and Bernice Niemeyer, who sits at the writing desk, both of them longstanding boarders. Susan Page enters and goes up stairs, and when the telephone rings (one of the play's aural motifs) a black maid named Mattie enters, picks up the phone, and tells the caller that 'Miss Devine is not back yet'. Voices are heard off (another aural motif) and Mary Harper and Mary McCune (Big and Little Mary) enter and tell those present that they have been 'in every manager's office on Broadway'. Madeleine Vauclain looks through a sheaf of letters and when Bobby Melrose asks whether Terry Randall is back yet, the women shake their heads. Madeleine asks whether any of the boarders would like to dine out on a double date. Olga and Ann Braddock decline, but Judith Canfield assents, and the person we hear next is Mrs Orcutt, the House Matron, who enters and says that Judith can room with Terry and Jean Maitland, thereby reducing Judith's rent. We focus momentarily on Linda Shaw, who is dressed to go out. Then the phone rings, and David Kingsley of the Globe Picture Company at the other end of the line asks to speak to Jean. Kingsley invites Jean to dinner and her fellow boarders join in a chorus of 'Here Comes the Bride', and from here we focus on Louise Mitchell, who is leaving to marry her fiancé and hoping to 'make a better wife than an actress', and in yet another instance of comparison and contrast, Terry Randall arrives and announces that she has secured a part in a play.

Most of the boarders head for the dining room, and as they do so the voice of a young man named Sam Hastings can be heard asking for Bobby Melrose. Bernice asks Sam whether he is David Kingsley and at this point the voice of Jimmy Devereaux can be heard asking for Susan Paige. Mattie invites Devereaux in, and Devereaux and Sam discuss their respective careers as actors. Devereaux boasts of his successes – 'Last month I played Emperor Jones and I'm cast now in Hamlet' – but Sam is in the early stages of his career and has yet to make an impact. Susan enters and leaves with Devereux, and Fred Powell and Lou Milhauser, two businessmen on holiday, ring the doorbell, call for Madeleine and Judith, and head off in pursuit 'a decent dinner'. The doorbell rings again, and Kingsley's voice can be heard calling for Jean. Kingsley enters and various members of the club display themselves and their acting talents in hopes of attracting his attention. Then Jean appears 'in her borrowed finery' and Terry arrives. Terry takes a verbal pot shot at the movies and Jean and Kingsley head off to eat. Then the doorbell rings again, and the voice of a young playwright man named Keith Burgess can be heard calling out for Jean Maitland. Terry tells Burgess that Jean has gone out on a date with Kingsley, and Burgess goes on to philosophise about plays, saying that he wants 'to tear the heart out of the rotten carcass we call life and hold it up, bleeding, for all to see', and Mattie reminds Terry that she has not yet eaten and fixes hamburgers prior to their exit.

Act One Scene Two opens at night in one of the bedrooms. Kaye comes in wearing a bathrobe and carefully counts the money in her purse, and when Judith enters, Kaye says that Terry is not yet back. Judith has been unable to secure work, and the voices of the Marys can be heard off stage. Big Mary and her sister have been to see 'the Breadline Players in "Tunnel of Death"', and when the Marys depart Judith remarks that Terry is late. Judith says that Terry is 'awfully good' in the play she in, but when Terry enters she reveals that the play has been closed down. Judith suggests a part in the movies, but Terry makes it clear that she considers the cinema inferior to the theatre. Bernice and Madeleine enter, and Bernice says that she is planning to see a revival of *Madame X*. Bernice and Madeleine depart and Terry and Kaye discuss their respective situations. Terry tells Kaye about her doctor father and her actress mother and the extent to which her mother missed her life on stage when she married. She also reveals that she has run away from her husband on two occasions, that he is still waiting for her, and that her life with him was marked by 'Nights of terror'. Terry opens the shade to reveal an electric sign outside and a cacophony of city sounds, and as she and Kaye wonder whether they will find acting jobs, Jean rushes in and tells them that Kingsley is planning to give seven-year contracts to all three of them. Terry is unsure, comparing films to soup cans, and arguing that the theatre has 'gone on for hundreds and hundreds of years' and is 'part of civilization'. But Jean says that she plans to go Hollywood come what may, and as the sights and sounds outside continue, the curtain falls.

Act Two Scene One takes place in the club the following morning. A black man called Frank is cleaning the carpet and Ann, Bobby and Judith enter in turn. Bobby reads a letter from Madeleine, and as Kendall rushes out late, Terry enters and Judith tries to assure her that there is plenty of time to find a part in another play. Terry picks up a lengthy letter from Louise and reads it out loud to the others. Bobby, Ann and Susan return to the dining room, and Judith and Terry discuss Terry's situation and whether Keith's apparent interest in her is genuine. Judith rushes off to read out recipes on the radio (the only work she can find), Bobby and Ann re-enter, and Ann tells Terry that Jean has a new contract and a large raise in salary. And in contrast, Mrs Orcutt, who is well aware of Kaye's impecunious situation, suggests that Kaye look for cheaper lodgings elsewhere. Then as the two Marys rehearse the dialogue in a play, the voice of Mrs Shaw, Linda's mother, can be heard off stage. Mattie greets Mrs Shaw and goes off to find Linda, and when Linda enters, her mother tells her to come home. But Linda stands firm and they agree to meet up later, and from here we focus on Olga, who is playing the piano as Bernice comes downstairs. Dr Randall, Terry's father, enters and is transfixed by Olga's playing. Then Terry rushes in and greets her father, Keith enters and is introduced, and Terry's father leaves for his hotel. Keith tells Terry that a well-known producer wants to stage his play, but to cast Natalie Blake, an established star, rather than the little-known Terry. Terry urges Keith to go ahead with play in any case, and Keith responds with gratitude and love. Then Linda comes down the stairs, asks Terry to tell Mrs Olcott that she is leaving, thrusts money into Terry's hand as payment for her board, and exits. Kaye enters and says that her part in a play has been given to someone else and Terry invites Kaye to dinner in response. But Kaye says that she will be alright, and Terry goes off in search of Mrs Olcott. Mattie 'hums a snatch of lively songs', adding to the tapestry of music and sound. But the humming is brutally interrupted by a 'piercing scream of terror' as Kaye hurtles down stairs, and as the boarders gather round they discover an empty pill bottle.

Act Two Scene Two takes place in the Club at 7pm two months later. Judith's hat and coat are on the piano and Sam is waiting for Bobby. Bobby 'floats downstairs, as Southern as ever' and they leave for dinner as the Two Marys argue as to whether they are prepared to stand in order to see the latest Burgess play. Then Burgess enters in full 'evening regalia', stopping Judith in her tracks. Judith is about to kick Burgess in retaliation for standing her up. But Terry enters and Judith exits, and Burgess chastises Terry for her lack of finery. He also reveals that he is going to Hollywood, and that he intends 'to write their garbage in the daytime', but to write his own plays at night. Kingsley arrives and asks whether Terry is in, and when Terry enters, Kingsley says that he's received a message inviting her to Hollywood and asks her whether she wants to go. But Terry confesses that she is still stagestruck and Kingsley, who is clearly more interested in Terry and her career than Burgess, says that she ought to tell Hollywood 'to go to hell'. He invites her to dinner, and she runs upstairs to fetch her hat as the curtain falls.

Act Three Scene One takes place on a Sunday the following October. Some of the women have departed and others have arrived. But many still live at the Club, and Olga is still playing the piano. The women discuss fashions and men, and Tony Gillette asks the Marys what Burgess is like. 'He's one of those fellows started out on a soapbox and ended up in a swimming pool' says Judith, and the others go on to discuss acting and plays. Then Bobby spots a newspaper photo of Jean stepping from an airplane and it transpires that Jean has flown to New York in order to play the female lead in a Broadway play. At this point a limousine draws up outside the Club, and Jean herself enters and is greeted by all those present. Her visit is somewhat fleeting and she is reminded that she is due to meet Adolph Gretzl, the film-company president. She says that she would like to meet up with the boarders at a more convenient time. But despite her tight schedule, she finds time to unveil her portrait, to have it photographed surrounded by the boarders on the ground floor, and to have it photographed upstairs too. Jean asks the women in the club for news. But Terry and Judith sense that Jean is only feigning interest, that Jean will waste the opportunity offered by the play, and go on to say that film people seem to think that 'the stage is something to advertise pictures with'. Burgess enters wearing a combination of expensive clothes but no necktie. He demands a cup of coffee, and says that the play he is writing is still not finished on account of his work in Hollywood and that he has signed up for another year there. Terry chides him about his screenplay for *Loads of Love*, Burgess replies that 'You spend years on Broadway and finish up in Macy's', and Terry replies that 'They speed up everything in Hollywood. In two years you're a star;

in four you're forgotten, and in six you're back in Sweden'. Mattie enters and is followed by Kingsley, who assumes that Burgess is back for good. Kingsley and Burgess express different views about films and the theatre, and Terry suggests they switch to a different topic. Burgess says that he intends to take Terry to Hollywood. But Terry says that she intends to remain a young woman with a career in the theatre, and at this point the curtain falls.

Act Three Scene Two takes place at midnight later that day. The Marys enter, complain about the play that they have seen then disappear upstairs. Milhauser enters with Judith and tries to arrange another date. But she too exits upstairs, and Kingsley rings the door bell, enters with Gretzl, asks Frank to wake Terry up, and persuades Gretzl that Terry, not Jean, would be perfect for the play that Gretzl plans to stage. Terry enters, somewhat tired and dishevelled, and Kingsley asks her whether she would able to star in the play. Terry begins her reading of the play and Gretzl is unimpressed, but Kingsley thinks otherwise, and offers to buy the rights to the play (thereby going back to his theatrical roots). Gretzl accepts and Kingsley and Terry embrace. Mrs Orcutt enters and Terry tells her that she is going to feature in Kingsley's play. Kingsley leaves and Mrs Orcutt says that Terry must be tired. But Terry is energised, and as she stands in the darkened room, a nearby street-lamp floods her face with light. 'Now that I am the Queen', she says, 'I wish in future to have a bed, and a room of my own'.

As Elizabeth Kendall points out, Kaufman and Ferber had helped invent the 'self-referential cleverness' of 1920s theatre. But after the Wall Street crash, they 'partook of Broadway's generalized grudge against Hollywood', and in *Stage Door* they idealised 'the small folk' of the theatre while taking 'potshots at a wide range of Hollywood types': 'On the "bad" side were Keith Burgess, a Clifford Odets-like playwright; Jean Maitland, an untalented stage actress turned movie star; and Adolph Gretzl, a gratuitously egregious version of Paramount's founder, Adolph Zukor'; and on 'the "good" side', were Terry Randall, an 'incorruptible actress heroine; David Kingsley, the young movie producer longing for Broadway; and assorted embittered residents of the Footlights Club, who, though hard pressed, remained true to their art'.[5]

The Film

As early as June 1936, Lillie Messenger, 'RKO's story watchdog in New York', drew attention to the play as a possible film vehicle for Kathryn Hepburn, who was proving hard to cast but who might suit the part of Terry Randall. RKO had been plagued by reorganisations and changes of ownership and senior management since the advent of the Great Depression. Although its Disney cartoons and Astaire-Rogers musicals were successful, and although some of its other more recent films performed well at the box-office now that some of the effects of the Depression had abated, the arrival of Sam Briskin from Columbia led to further changes in corporate policy.[6] However Briskin was well aware of the talents of producer Pandro Berman, and when Berman urged RKO to buy the rights to *Stage Door* in the face of stiff competition, the rights were duly acquired 'in November 1936 for $130,000'.[7]

Planning to co-star Ginger Rogers as Jean Maitland, Berman hired Anthony Veiller to write the script. But given the number of changes required or mooted, it was decided to hire an experienced director early on, and Gregory La Cava, who had worked for RKO before and who had just completed the highly-successful *My Man Godfrey* (1936) for Universal, was appointed.[8] La Cava was given 'at least six weeks of "story preparation"', 'retained the right to engage some members of his own production staff', and to 'okay ... the first "sneak preview"',[9] and working with Veiller, he initially sketched out 'a story about two girls from a small town in Vermont who come to New York to be actresses: one of them, the Hepburn character, an idealist; the other, the Rogers character, an opportunist. The Hepburn character falls in love with a left-wing playwright, acts in a play, realizes she's no good on stage, and goes back contentedly to the small town. The Rogers character meets a wealthy man-about-town, gets him to back her friend's play, then lands him as a husband'.[10] However, when Berman, La Cava and Veiller met up again in April, they realised that they had inadvertently recreated Hepburn's role as a Vermont-born actress in *Morning Glory* (1933), so they devised a new story 'in which Hepburn became a Long Island debutante, Rogers became a Missouri-born gold digger, the radical playwright virtually disappeared, and the man-about-town turned into a theatrical producer named Anthony Powell'.[11]

According to the entry on the film in the AFI Catalog, Burgess Meredith and Douglas Fairbanks Jr. were considered for the part of Powell. But Adolphe Menjou was hired instead, and Morrie Ryskind was hired to work on the script. According to Kendall, Veiller and Ryskind refused to talk to each other, and Ryskind 'picked up the rudiments of Veiller's story from La Cava'.[12] La Cava and Ryskind sat in the studio café for hours trying to identify voices in order to provide what Kendall calls 'a vocal symphony': 'the wistful, screwy tones of the young Lucille Ball; the ironic drawl of the even younger Eve Arden; and the Texas twang of the extremely young Ann Miller'.[13] The women were also encouraged to improvise and wear their own clothes, and following the procedures that La Cava and Ryskind had devised in making *My Man Godfrey*, 'they tried out the dialogue and spacing and made up new material if the old felt wrong', then 'La Cava, Ryskind and the script girl would write out readable versions of the morning's experiments' and in the afternoon 'they would shoot the finished scene'.[14] The extent to which these procedures were adopted is hard to determine. But it is clear that a mix of improvisation, rehearsal, and carefully staged and framed shots and edits all played a part, and this is particularly evident in the film's lengthy interior first scene, which is preceded by a mobile exterior crane shot of the Club's exterior showing a couple, members coming in and out, and passers-by.

The interior scene begins with a close-up of broken glass and trash being swept up in a dustpan, and as the camera dollies out we are introduced to Hattie (Phyllis Kennedy), the Club's maid and cook.[15] Hattie is humming a high-pitched tune, and as the camera dollies out further and follows her across the room, we are introduced to Judith Canfield (Lucille Ball), who complains about the noise in her mid-pitch accent. Hattie moves back across the room as the telephone rings, and as she responds to the ensuing call in her high-pitched voice again, she tells Judith that the call is for her and thus

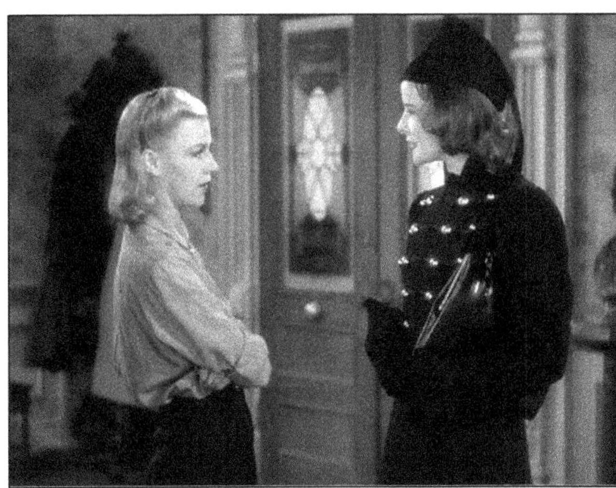

Figure 1

helps establish the paradigm of voices, accents and phone calls that mark the film throughout. As Judith crosses the room to take her call, Linda Shaw (Gail Patrick) crosses the room from the staircase. Linda is more expensively dressed than the other boarders, and the later appearance of Anthony Powell's chauffeur, who arrives to pick her up and take her out to wherever they eating, is a mark of her affair with Powell himself.

At this point Linda serves as the principal antagonist to Jean Maitland (Ginger Rogers), who enters in pursuit of the stockings that Linda has taken from her, and who seeks in general to maintain a line in terms of solidarity and permissible behaviour among the borders. Jean's athletic demeanour is in marked contrast to Linda's overly-poised and superior manner, and it is therefore unsurprising that Linda decides to vacate the room she currently shares with Jean. Linda's departure paves the way for Terry, whose awkward entry follows as she tries to find the Club's door, and whose relationship with Jean is yet to be determined, as is evident in the first two-shot framing in which they figure together (figure 1). Terry and Jean's relationship soon becomes more complex and three-dimensional, and in the meantime we are introduced Catherine Luther (Constance Collier), the only older boarder. Catherine tends to come across as snobbish in her reverence for the classics and the acting of Sarah Bernhard (whose chair sits near the stairs), prompting numerous jibes from the younger boarders. But while the old newspaper cuttings that she shares with Terry later on are a mark of her pride, they also mark a career that she knows is really over – hence the genuinely sympathetic nature of Terry's response, and hence Catherine's equally sympathetic response to the death of Kay Hamilton (Andrea Leeds) later on.

Meanwhile, Terry's looks and glances tell us that she is not entirely sure of herself as she tries to work out the Club's protocols, and this is also marked in the bedroom scenes that precede and follow the scene in which Jean and Judith meet up with Milbanks (Jack Carson) and Dukenfield (Fred Santley) (the equivalents of Milhauser and Powell in the play) prior to heading off for dinner and dancing. The first bedroom

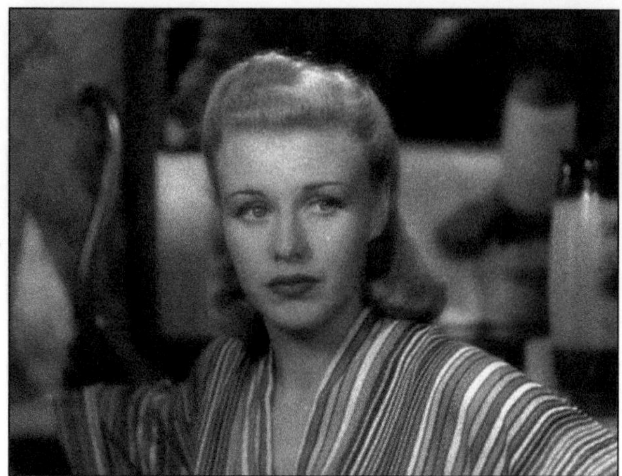
Figure 2

scene begins with the arrival of Terry's three luggage trunks, which leave little room for movement. Jean is wearing a dressing gown and when Terry arrives she is wearing an expensive formal hat and coat, thus accentuating their differences further (figures 2 and 3). Terry and Jean are wary of one another. But although Jean draws attention to the lack of space, they do not quarrel, and as Jean waits outside the bathroom we focus on Kay, who has entered alone, who tells Jean that she is desperate to play the lead in *Enchanted April*, and who now has very little money. We then move on to the second bedroom scene. Jean comes back from the dinner date, and Terry opens the shutters and lets in the electric light across the road (figure 4), and both women listen to the traffic and accommodate one another in a number of ways. In this way the scene echoes but also transforms the purpose of the equivalent scene in the play by making it more intimate, by focussing solely on Jean and Terry and their growing relationship, and by concluding with both women putting on eye shades as they settle down to sleep.[16]

At this point we are taken to a different location for the first time. It is daytime and two male choreographers are rehearsing a line of chorus girls. Jean and Annie (Ann Miller) are among them, and Olga (Norma Drury Boleslavsky), another member of the Club, plays the piano. Although the visible backers of the show include two older well-dressed women, it is men not women who are in charge here, and their proclivities and domination are further emphasised by the entry of Powell, who watches the proceedings, catches sight of Jean before she leaves, and quizzes Annie about her. Back at the Club, Jean says that Powell 'makes you feel like you ought to run home and put on a tin overcoat', and the connection to Powell is further underlined by the entry of Linda, who heads off for her date with him. Then the phone rings and Jean and Annie are told to report to Mr Burger at the Club Grotto, and as Jean and Annie depart, Terry and Kay philosophise about the hopes and fears of working in the theatre.

Echoing aspects of Act Two Scene One, Terry meets up with her father, Henry Sims

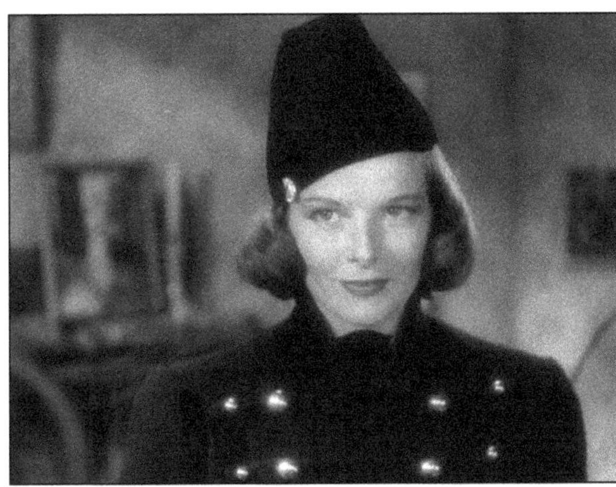

Figure 3

(Samuel S. Hinds), in a restaurant the following day. Henry tries to persuade Terry to give up hope of a stage career. But Terry stands firm, and from here we dissolve to the Club Grotto and its female dancers as Powell enters, gazes at the dancers, and joins Linda and Harcourt, Powell's butler (Franklin Pangborn). It is evident that Powell's focus of interest has shifted from Linda to Jean, and this is underlined not only by Powell's looks and glances, but by his subsequent entry into the dressing room backstage and his offer of a part for Jean. We move on to Powell's office-suite the following day. Judith and Eve (Eve Arden) are among those waiting for him, and Kay enters, says that she has an appointment with Powell, and faints when his secretary tells her that Powell has cancelled the appointment. Terry enters, hears about the cancellation, walks past the secretary and into Powell's office, and berates him. But Powell stands his ground, and when Terry leaves, he is visited by an agent whose client is interested in backing *Enchanted April*.

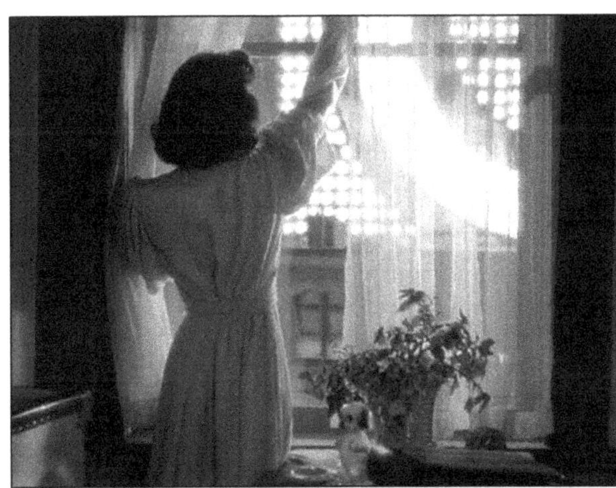

Figure 4

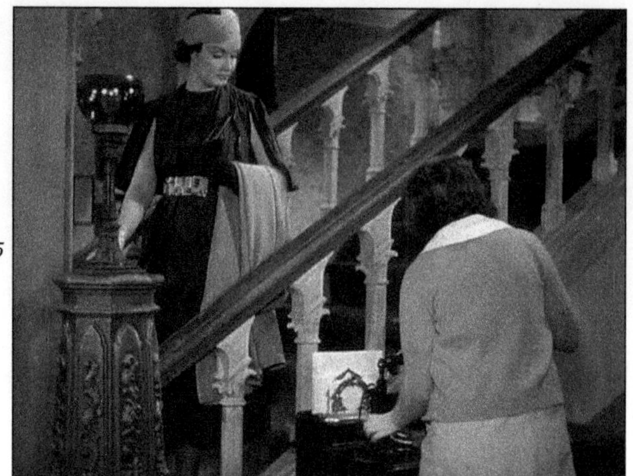

Figure 5

Back at the Club, Terry enters, and in the discrete conversation with Mrs Orcutt (Elizabeth Dunne) that follows, it is revealed that Terry has paid for medical help for Kay, thus underlining the extent to which our allegiance to Terry has been cemented. Upstairs in the room she shares with Terry, Jean prepares to perform with Annie at the Club Grotto and to visit Powell in his apartment later on that evening. Jean is wearing what turns out to be Terry's ermine jacket, and when Linda enters with a box of roses for Jean and a message from Powell, Linda alerts Jean to the fact that the roses and the message are part of Powell's routine, and that the same is true of Powell's penthouse suppers. Linda leaves and Terry enters. Jean is still wearing Terry's ermine jacket, and although Terry disapproves of Powell, she lets Jean wear it on her date with him. Jean hesitates for a moment then leaves, and the following shot frames her descending the stairs and echoes Linda's earlier entry on the stairs next to Jean as it does so (figures 5 and 6). Jean and Annie begin to leave for the Club and a reverse

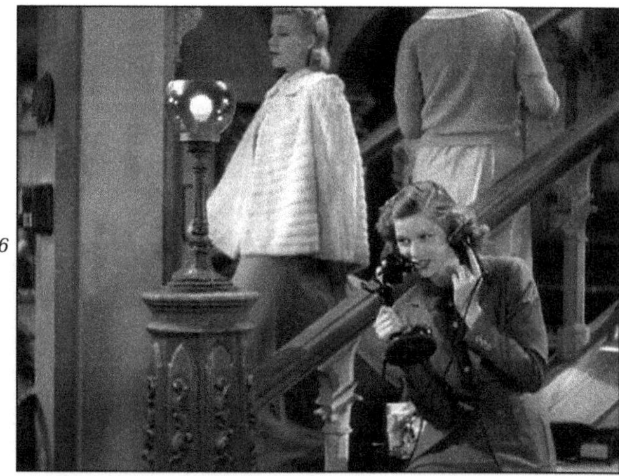

Figure 6

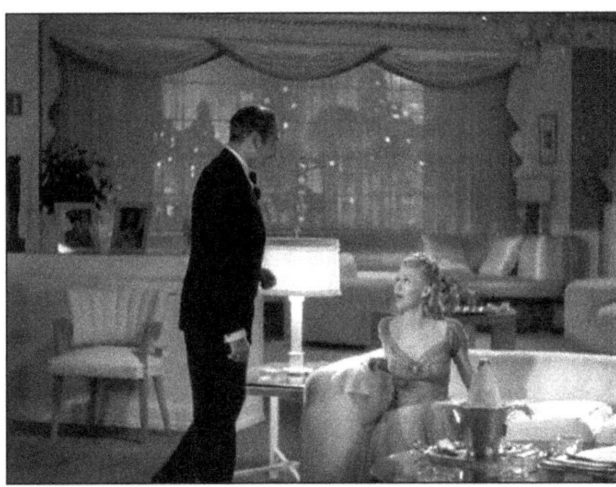

Figure 7

angle from the exterior frames their exit, at which point Jean is hailed by Bill (William Corson), who explains that he has been away promoting a play, who invites her to supper but is rejected, and who is clearly based on Sam in the stage-play version.

We cut to Powell's apartment, whose window affords a grander view and a version of the lights visible in Jean and Terry's room at night (figure 7). Jean is drunk, and Powell's routine eventually encompasses the story of Pygmalion and Galatea. Jean is now so drunk that Powell arranges a taxi to drive her to the Footlights Club, and when Jean departs, he takes out his address book and leaves through its pages in search of another date. Back at the Club, Jean gives Terry a drunken and incoherent account of Pygmalion and Galatea, and Terry helps Jean into bed. Downstairs later on, the boarders discuss the various forms of stage entertainment that drew them to their profession. Powell now calls Jean less frequently, and it is clear that he is no longer interested in her. Linda details the tell-tale signs of Powell's waning interest, and at

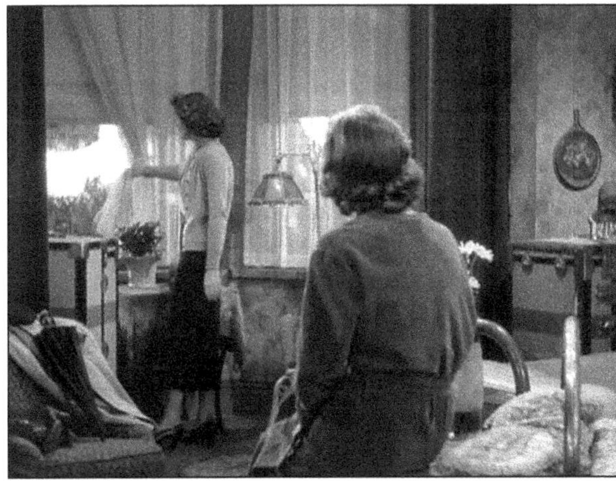

Figure 8

Figure 9

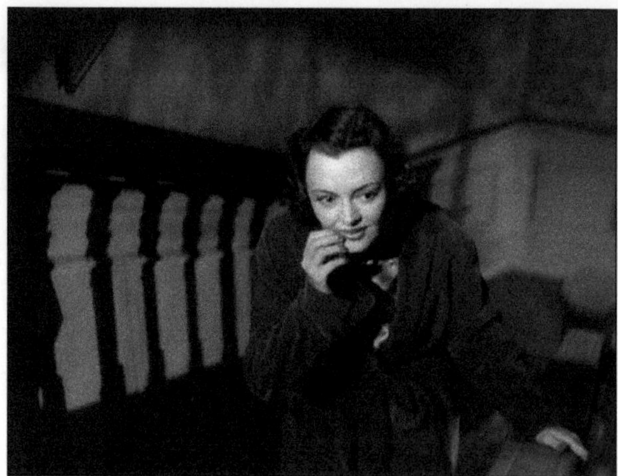

this point we dissolve to Powell in his apartment again, and this time he is entertaining Terry. Powell's routine is similar. But Terry exposes its ersatz basis, focuses on the play he is financing, and uses her presence to expose his routine to Jean, who enters then departs. Powell confesses that his routines are just routines, and impressed by Terry, he promises her the lead role in the aforementioned play. But unbeknown to Terry, Kay is desperate to play the lead role herself, and at her birthday party it is revealed that the play is *Enchanted April* and that Terry has been assigned the role. Although in despair, Kay voices her support for Terry, and the scene ends with Kay in tears supported by the boarders as we fade to black.

On cutting to a rehearsal of *Enchanted April*, it becomes clear that Terry is unused to stage-rehearsal practice and finds it difficult to deliver lines such as 'The calla lilies are in bloom again' amidst the stage hands and incomplete scenery. These difficulties are all too obvious to the play's director, who is played by Frank Reicher, and who is clearly made up to look like George S. Kaufman. They are also obvious to Powell, who enters in an agitated state, who now wonders whether Terry is suitable, and who also wonders whether the play should proceed. Powell decides to keep Terry in the show and braces himself for a failure, and we cut the Club some time later on as most of the boarders and Hattie and her butcher beau (Grady Sutton) get ready for the play's premiere performance. Eve plans to see the play the following day, and having already played the lead role in the part herself, Kay enters Jean and Terry's room as the neon lights flicker outside, this time in the rain (figure 8). Terry is still being coached by Catherine. But Kay proposes that a cradling of the lilies in tandem with the calla-lilies line would inevitably suggest the child that the parents in the play never had. Kay says that the events in the play 'really happened'. Then she leaves, walks upstairs in a trance hearing voices (figure 9), and flings herself downstairs off-screen in an act of suicide, somehow evoking the non-existent child in the play as she does so.

At the theatre we note the presence of Terry's father and Powell and his associates, all

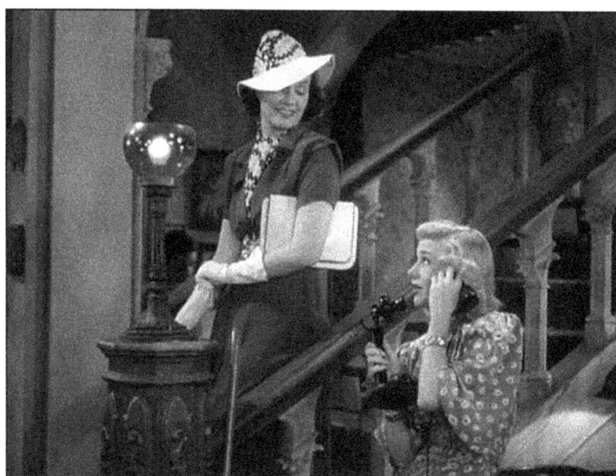

Figure 10

of whom are clearly sanguine. Then Jean enters Terry's dressing room, all but accuses Terry of killing Kay, and dares her 'to go on tonight'. As Kendall points out, 'Rogers's very concentratedness shapes the mood here, and Hepburn shows herself equal to its gravity. Without missing a beat, she takes the rising emotion Rogers has handed to her and brings it out in a wave of grief' then 'allows herself to be guided onstage ... and gives an affecting performance in the role she massacred in rehearsal'.[17] Terry's cradling bit is a huge success, prompting tears from nearly everyone, and enthusiastic applause greets Terry as she walks on stage in long shot and delivers a paean to Kay. Terry's father is moved and delighted by his daughter's performance, and shortly thereafter Powell ensures that he makes the acquaintance of Terry's father, orders the customary bunch of flowers for his leading lady, then leafs through his address book when it turns out that Terry has left.

Following a montage of alternating shots of Kay's headstone, various theatre mar-

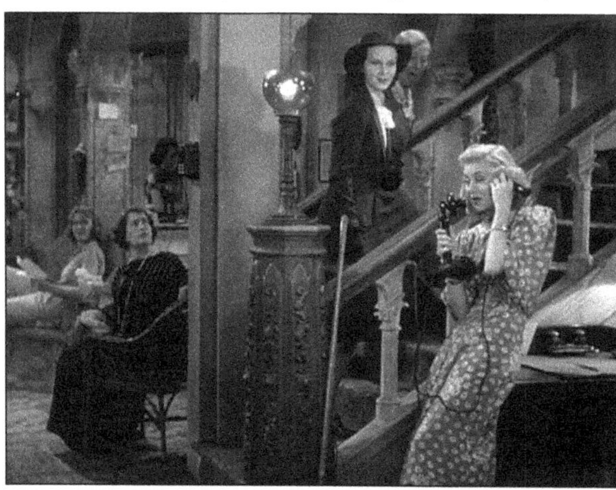

Figure 11

quees, and a rave newspaper review, we move on to the film's final scene, which takes place in the Club's ground-floor interior. Here we reprise the opening close-up of Hattie and her dustpan, and here the boarders gather together, circulate, and come and go as usual. Jean and Terry are now firm friends and are frequently framed together in two shot, and Eve is affronted by the fact that Henry her cat is female and has produced a litter of kittens. Mary Lou (Margaret Early) announces that she has a part in a play on account of her Southern accent, though her only line is 'Let's go up to Westchester', which the other boarders chant and dance to together. Judith enters and bids farewell to the boarders on her way out to marry Milbanks in Seattle. But as soon as she departs, a new boarder enters through the same door – the door through which Terry and others have entered before her. Jean is still in her shirt and slacks, and is now next to the staircase on the phone to Bill as Linda descends the stairs in her usual finery (figure 10), and as Mrs Orcutt greets her new boarder and shows her Sarah Bernhardt's chair, Jean in still on the phone as we catch a glimpse of Catherine in the background looking on (figure 11).

Coda

When the film was completed, RKO was extremely pleased. Pandro Berman called it 'the best picture in RKO history', and was particularly impressed by Hepburn's performance, which was rewarded with a renewal of her contract.[18] Ned Depinet, who worked in sales, 'predicted that the film would gross $1.5 million in the United States alone'; but sales in the Midwest and South were poor, and when 'final figures were tallied, the domestic gross was $1,250, 000, and the final profit only $81,000'.[19] The film was nominated for Best Picture, Best Director, Best Screenplay, and Best Supporting Actress (Andrea Leeds) at the Academy Awards that year, but lost out to *The Life of Emile Zola*; Leo McCarey; Geza Herczeg, Heinz Herald and Norman Riely Raine; and Alice Brady, respectively. A thirty-minute radio version was aired on the *Philip Morris Playhouse* on 5 December 1941, and a sixty-minute television version scripted by Gore Vidal was aired on CBS on 6 April 1955 as part of *The Best of Broadway* series, but as far as I know these were the only spin-offs.

Notes

1. http://georgeskaufman.com/play-catalog/15-play-catalog/library-of-america-collection, page 1.12/04/2016
2. Goldstein, *George S. Kaufman*, p. 267.
3. Julie Gilbert, *Ferber: Edna Ferber and Her Circle* (New York and London: Applause Books, 1999 edn.). It should be noted that Kaufman collaborated with others on a number of his plays and that these included *You Can't Take It With You* (1934) and *The Man Who Came Dinner* (1939), both of which were co-written with Moss Hart, and which were filmed in Hollywood in 1936 and 1942 respectively.
4. Founded by Jean 'Daisy' Greer and Jane Harris Hall, The Rehearsal Club opened in New York City in 1913 and was subsequently relocated to West 46th Street, West 45th Street, and West 53rd Street, where it remained for fifty years prior to its closure in 1979. Among its boarders was Margaret Sullavan, who played the part of Terry in the stage play.
5. Elizabeth Kendall, *The Runaway Bride: Hollywood Romantic Comedy of the 1930s* (New York: Anchor Books, 1990), pp. 162–163. The only sympathetic Hollywood character is Kingsley, who encourages Terry to pursue her career on stage, and who is generally considered to be based on MGM producer Irving

Thalberg. Ferber and Kaufman fill their script with references to the theatre in all its forms, but there are no allusions to the films that either or both of them worked on.

6. Richard B. Jewell, *RKO Radio Pictures: A Titan is Born* (Berkeley, Los Angeles, London: University of California Press, 2012), esp. pp. 40–127.
7. Kendall, *The Runaway Bride*, p. 162.
8. Kendall, *The Runaway Bride*, pp. 163–164.
9. Kendall, *The Runaway Bride*, p. 164.
10. Kendall, *The Runaway Bride*, p. 164.
11. Kendall, *The Runaway Bride*, pp. 164–165.
12. Kendall, *The Runaway Bride*, p. 165. For Ryskind's account, see *I Shot an Elephant in My Pajamas*, pp. 133–135.
13. Kendall, *The Runaway Bride*, p. 165.
14. Kendall, *The Runaway Bride*, p. 166.
15. It should be noted that in the play Hattie was black and was named Hattie as a tribute to Hattie McDaniel. It should also be noted that Frank, who was also black, does not figure in the film at all, though this may because La Cava, Ryskind and Veiller wanted the staff and members of the Club to be exclusively populated by women. The revelation that Eve's cat is female serves precisely to underline this point.
16. Kendall argues throughout her book that the touchstone for *Stage Door* and many other mid-to-late 1930s socio-romantic comedies is *It Happened One Night* (1934), and on p. 167, she notes not only that the original script for *Stage Door* 'opened with Hepburn landing on her family's Long Island estate in an autogyro – a direct steal from *It Happened One Night*', but that the scene in *It Happened One Night* in which Ellie and Peter (Claude Colbert and Clarke Gable) bed down for the night for the first time is echoed in this scene too. In these and other respects, she writes, 'La Cava's Footlights Club functions as an all-women version of Capra's Greyhound bus, a closed society that the Depression has radicalized'. Edward Gallafent, who discusses *Stage Door* briefly in his book *Astaire and Rogers* (New York: Columbia University Press, 2000), pp. 78–79, draws attention to 'the repartee between the Hepburn and Rogers characters, which proceeds from their perception of the other's class status'. This too is a mark of the couple in *It Happened One Night*, and Gallafent's final comments are also worth quoting. 'The closing sequence in the Footlights Club is notable for its suspension of judgment' he writes. 'We are offered a number of "roles": the wife (Judy, leaving for Seattle) ... , the unattached actress (Terry, who suggests that actors are a "different race of people")' and 'the attached actress (Jean, in the process of phoning her boyfriend)'. But in 'trading various sentiments and wisecracks, we see La Cava's refusal to imply that any of the different lives embodied here are superior or inferior to another'.
17. Kendall, *The Runaway Bride*, p. 176.
18. Jewell, *RKO Radio Pictures*, p. 145.
19. Jewell, *RKO Radio Pictures*, p. 145.

Chapter 9

The Pirate

With songs by Cole Porter, music by Lennie Hayton, Technicolor cinematography by Harry Stradling, Jr., and choreography by John Alton and Gene Kelly, *The Pirate* was directed by Vincente Minnelli for MGM's Freed Unit, which specialised in the production of musicals.[1] Having initially paid $225,000 for the rights to the play by S.N. (Samuel Nathan) Behrman, MGM initially assigned Joe Pasternak to produce and Henry Koster to direct a film version. However, the project was shelved in early 1944, and only resurrected in August 1945, when Behrman's play had finished its run and when MGM decided to produce a musical version as a vehicle for Judy Garland. *The Pirate* proved difficult to script. Between 1945 and 1948, versions were penned by Joseph Mankiewicz, Myles Connolly and Henry Koster; H.E. (Howard Emmett) Rogers and Frances Marion; Edwin Blum, Anita Loos and Joseph Than; and Francis Goodrich and Albert Hackett. Goodrich and Hackett were eventually credited as the authors of the screenplay. But modifications were made by Minnelli and Arthur Freed not only in production, but in postproduction too. Filming began on 17 February and ended on 20 December 1947, and further adjustments were made in response to previews and earlier correspondence from Joseph Breen. The film was eventually premiered at Radio City Musical Hall on 21 May 1948. But having cost $3,768,496, and having earned only $2,956,000 during the course of its initial release, it was the first and only Garland vehicle at MGM to make a loss. In addition to notes in the AFI Catalog, these aspects of the film's production are detailed in *The Cinematic Voyage of* The Pirate: *Kelly, Garland, and Minnelli at Work* by Earl J. Hess and Pratibha A. Dabholkar.[2] Amidst their findings, Hess and Dabholkar discuss the two stage-play versions on which the film was based, and it is here that an account of the film's origins begins.

The Plays

The initial version of *The Pirate* was written in Germany by Ludwig Fulda, who was born Ludwig Anton Salmon in Frankfurt in 1862, and who wrote and translated numerous plays during the course of his long career.[3] Fulda visited the USA in 1906 and returned in 1913, having completed a German-language version in 1911. An

English-language version was translated by Louis N. Parker and premiered in Milwaukee on 20 August 1917, where it ran for a single week only. This version was set in Andalusia in the seventeenth century, where a retired pirate named Estornudo (who was played by Alfred Lunt) has changed his name to Pedro and married Manuela (Cathleen Nesbitt), who is bored and frustrated, and who finds solace in the fantasies of love and passion in the novels she reads. A wandering minstrel named Serafin visits the town with his troupe of players and a local beggar recognises Pedro as Estornudo. Pedro hires the beggar in order to keep him quiet, and Serafin claims that he is Estornudo in order to boost the ticket sales for his troupe's forthcoming performance. When Serafin learns of Manuela's wealth and when Manuela hears that Serafin is the pirate they plan to run away together. But when Serafin tries to escape from Pedro by walking across the clothesline between Pedro's home and the house next door, he becomes stuck, and when Manuela tells Pedro that Serafin is the pirate Pedro insists that Serafin is lying. Serafin and Manuela are captured by the cavalry on orders from the local Magistrate. Manuela refuses to allow Serafin to be charged with abduction and Pedro is furious, revealing that he is the real pirate. Serafin admits that Pedro is the pirate and Manuela is stunned. The Magistrate pronounces Pedro and Manuela's marriage void, and Manuela's father insists that Serafin marry Manuela. Serafin is delighted. But as the play comes to an end Manuela warns him that she will find someone else if he gets lazy and fat like Pedro.

The second version of *The Pirate* was written by Behrman and staged by Alfred Lunt and John C. Wilson, with music by Herbert Kingsley and choreography by Felicia Sorel.[4] It premiered at the University Theatre in Madison, Wisconsin on 13 September 1942, and subsequently toured in Milwaukee, Cleveland, Indianapolis, Cincinnati, Pittsburgh, Philadelphia, Washington DC and Boston prior to its opening at the Martin Beck Theatre in New York City on 23 November 1942. Here it ran for 177 performances, with Serafin played by Lunt, Manuela played by Lynn Fontanne (Lunt's wife), James O'Neill as Capucho, Estelle Winwood as Ines, and Clarence Derwent as the Viceroy. The Behrman version is set in the racially-mixed town of Santo Domingo and consists of three acts. Act One Scene One takes place on the patio of Pedro and Manuela's house in Santo Domingo in the early nineteenth century. Pedro is asleep in a hammock snoring loudly, and Manuela sits beside him with 'her back to the audience ... deeply absorbed in a black-covered book'. The book appears to be a Bible but turns out to be a novel that details the escapades of a pirate called Estramudo (the spelling here is slightly different from the earlier play), and while Pedro's slumber is regularly punctuated by indications of his obsession with money, Manuela is joined by Isabella Galvez, a 'plump and amiable' widow, who discusses Estramudo's exploits with relish. Although seeking to defend her husband, Manuela repeatedly contrasts Pedro with the dangerous but dazzling Estramudo, thus underlining the extent to which she 'may be technically faithful' but is prone to mental 'excursions'.

Pedro wakes up, spots the book that Manuela is reading, and throws it out of the window. Manuela's parents enter and Ines, her mother, tries to persuade Manuela to count her blessings as Pedro falls asleep again. Manuela retrieves her book. Then she too falls asleep as she begins to voice her innermost fantasies: 'Estramudo, where are you now? What horizon compasses you? What glow kindles in what horizon? Where are you, is it sunset or is it daybreak? Oh, return from afar, and save me – save Manuela'. As 'she contemplates this impossible vision' music can be heard in the distance as Serafin's racially mixed troupe works its way down the mountainside to the village square. Manuela looks up, 'surely she must be dreaming this sound, and yet, there it is – louder, more insistent. Has she crossed too often the boundary of reality?' Manuela turns back to her novel, but the music is insistent, and her maid tells her that the music comes from the mountainside and confirms that it is coming 'Right down into the square' and 'Right down into this house'. Manuela is 'powerfully moved' and stands beside Pedro's hammock, fanning herself 'to the rhythm of the invading sound' as the curtain falls.

Act One Scene Two takes place on a mountain road outside the town. Serafin's troupe, 'white and coloured, incredibly weary and bedraggled but nevertheless making music', winds down the narrow road. The troupe halts and its members complain about the lack of food. But dragging their paraphernalia on a donkey cart, they nevertheless propel themselves forward as the scene shifts to the public square in town. As Act One Scene Three begins, the 'music of Serafin's Band begins to fill the square' as Serafin and his troupe make their entrance. Serafin vows that the 'power of art shall transform the paralytic into a dervish-dance' and seeks to energise his men by handing out what he claims to be his last cigar. He asks where he can obtain a license for his troop's performance but is told that Pedro, the most powerful man in the town, does not like actors. However it soon becomes clear that Pedro is Estramudo the pirate and that Serafin is aware of his identity, having been on board ship when Pedro bribed its captain in order to escape. Thus when Pedro refuses to sanction the performance, Serafin recalls these events, and Pedro reluctantly changes his mind. Serafin makes arrangements for the performance and encounters Manuela. He expresses his admiration and begins to encircle her, but Manuela tells Serafin that she is married to Pedro and begins to leave. Serafin persists, and on discovering that Manuela is reading a book about Estramudo, Serafin claims that he is Estramudo in disguise. Manuela claims that there is 'the practical world and the world of the imagination. I know which is which', then leaves and closes the door behind her. Serafin, however, is not to be denied, and with the help of Trillo he strings a rope to the railing facing Manuel's house. Declaring that his journey 'from the profane to the sacred' will now begin, he is tossed an umbrella by Trillo and begins to walk toward Manuela's balcony on the rope as the curtain falls.

Act Two takes place in Manuela's bedroom. 'We hear the singing and the shouting that, at the end of the first act, accompany Serafin's manouever', and we see Ines and Capucho shooting craps. Ines hears a serenade outside the window and reports that a handsome stranger is talking to Manuela on the balcony. The noise increases as Manuela comes inside and puts on a negligee. Serafin enters, carrying Manuela's parasol in one hand and his shoes on the other. Manuela claims that she cannot recall

Serafin's name as she introduces him to her parents, who invite him to lunch. Serafin claims that he is Estramudo and Capucho runs out to fetch Pedro. But Ines encourages Manuela to have 'a little fling', and leaves Serafin and Manuela together on their own. The banter between them continues, and Serafin finally grabs Manuela's hands and holds her close. When Pedro enters, Serafin and Manuela continue 'as if they were alone' then Manuela asks Pedro to eject Serafin from the room. Given what he knows (or thinks he knows) Pedro is unwilling to do so. But when Serafin tells Manuela that Pedro once held him captive, Serafin's plans misfire and Manuela begins to turn her attention to husband. Serafin seems to be defeated. But when he heads for the window Manuela follows him, betraying her feelings for Serafin even as Pedro tries to win her over by revealing that he has a horde of treasure. Pedro heads for the balcony in order to sever Serafin's rope. But Serafin re-enters, and Pedro leaves to inform the Viceroy that Serafin is the pirate. Manuela now confesses to Serafin that she is attracted to him, and Serafin heads for the balcony once more. But Manuela tells him to leave by the stairs, and as he does so, she tells her maid that 'I'll try to save him. But if I fail – I'll never forgive him!'

Act Three is set in the early evening. 'Serafin's show tent is now up', and Trillo is arranging Serafin's props and costume. Trillo and Bolo are aware of Serafin's plight, and this is underlined by the entry of half-a-dozen uniformed black soldiers, and their commander's pronouncement that 'No member of the troupe is to leave the premises'. Lizarda, one of Manuela's maids, arrives with a note warning that the Viceroy is on his way to apprehend Serafin, and Pedro enters and the Viceroy and his men arrive. Serafin ensures that the props include a revolving mirror and seems confident that he will 'cope with the Viceroy'. Serafin proposes that his show go ahead, but The Viceroy replies that it is his duty to arrest him. Serafin explains not only that he wishes to demonstrate his troupe's skills but that he is in love with a married woman. Recalling the power of romantic love in his younger days, the Viceroy finally agrees to sanction the performance and heads off to Pedro's house. Serafin bequeaths his props and professional secrets to Trillo and Bolo, and people 'white and colored, but mainly colored' drift in.

The Viceroy's Lieutenants wander over to Isabella's house whose occupants, the Viceroy among them, stroll over to the stage. Serafin says that this will be his last performance and that his trademark act will involve hypnosis, and calls for volunteers. 'Control cannot be exercised over anyone', he says. 'I have failed with the recalcitrant, with the confused, with the rebellious, with the evil ... in short Ladies and Gentlemen, to perform this experiment ideally, I need a pure person'. 'Manuela rises, already in a half trance' and Pedro tries to intervene, but is chastised by the Viceroy. 'This is not a divorce' but 'an experiment', says the Viceroy, and Serafin continues, using his revolving mirror as he does so. Pedro tries to intervene again, but the Viceroy chastises him for his 'bourgeois possessiveness', and Pedro leaves, claiming illness. Then Manuela reveals that Pedro is Estramudo and that she has proof in the form of a medallion that Pedro wears in the purse around his neck. A state of impasse prevails as Serafin seems unable to waken Manuela from her trance, and at this point the

Viceroy confirms that Pedro, who has now returned, is indeed pirate. Pedro pleads for mercy. But although he is taken away, the Viceroy says that he may be useful should war break out with the Berbers, that he may reprieved, and that legally Manuela is now a widow and is therefore free to marry someone else. But Manuela is still in a trance and is only awakened by Serafin. 'You are with me, Manuela ... forever and ever' he says, and Manuela replies that 'There are two kinds of lies – lies like Pedro's, intended to pervert the truth – and lies like yours, which widen the borders of experience, and open the windows of the imagination ... I shall follow you to the end'. Serafin walks toward Manuela's house, carrying Manuela in his arms as the crowd 'lifts its voice in song, a joyous epithalamium', and as the final curtain falls.

The Fulda and Berhrman versions of *The Pirate* are both set in the Caribbean in the nineteenth century. Both focus, often ironically or comically, on marriage, romance and fantasy, on money and riches (or the lack of them), and on pretence and masquerade, and both contain black characters, albeit in minor roles.[5] In comparing the two versions, Hess and Dabholkar point out that Manuela and Serafin are less obsessed with money in the Berhman version, and are more likeable insofar as they are drawn together by love rather the boredom and greed that motivates them in the Fulda version. In the Behrman version Pedro is a mayor and is thus more powerful, and although he is rich, he is both miserly and superstitious. And in the Berhman version Manuela is obsessed specifically with the pirate, not with romance books in general, and she and Serafin meet by chance rather than design.

The Film

With the key input of Goodrich and Hackett, and with additional input from Minnelli and Arthur Freed, the final version of the script prior to production was essentially a streamlined version of Behrman's play, with a considerable number of Behrman's lines intact. Cole Porter originally wrote seven songs for the film: 'Niña', 'Mack The Black', 'You Can Do No Wrong', 'Be A Clown', 'Love Of My Life', 'Manuela' and 'Voodoo'. But 'Manuela' was never recorded, 'Voodoo' was eventually dropped, and 'Love Of My Life' was initially designed to be sarcastic but was finally trimmed and presented as a straightforward love song.[6] Noting the relatively ubiquitous presence of black extras and the stunningly accomplished presence of The Nicholas Brothers when dancing in triangles with Kelly in to 'Be A Clown', *The Pirate* is, among other things, an attempt to incorporate black people along with white ones in a major Hollywood film (figures 1–5). Prompted by the presence of black characters in the plays, and limited though it is, this presence reflected Minnelli's anti-racist views, which were already evident in the all-black *Cabin in the Sky*, which Minnelli directed in 1943, and which were subsequently evident, albeit largely in musical numbers and crowd scenes, in *The Band Wagon* (1953) and *Bells Are Ringing* (1960).[7] *The Pirate*'s overall trajectory is one in which illusions are stripped away, in which costumes and pretence are both transformed, and in which the central couple find true love and happiness in the milieu of performance, where, paradoxically, they are best able to be themselves by transforming the world around them in accordance with their vision. In this way

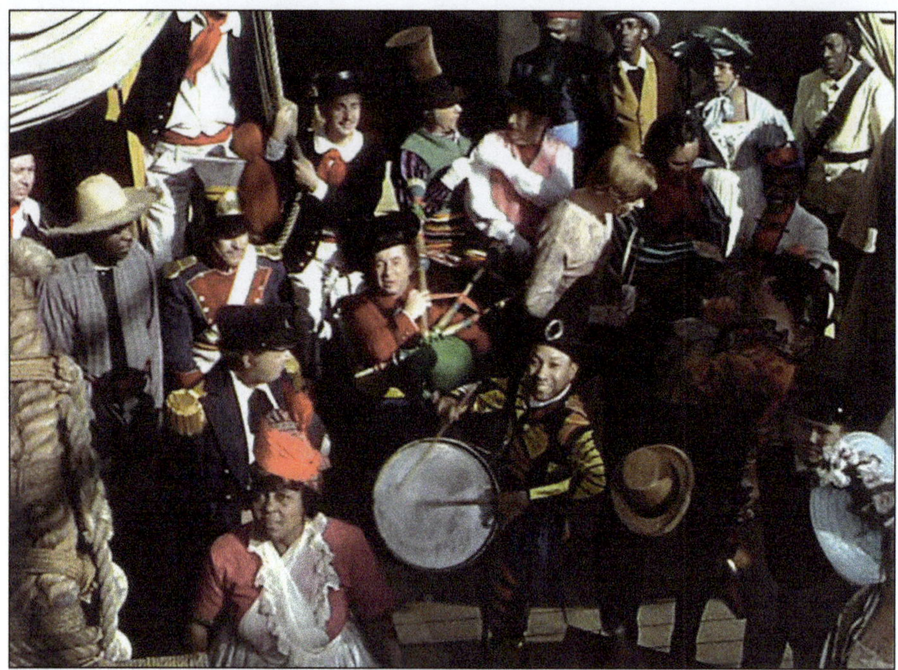

Figure 1

Figure 2

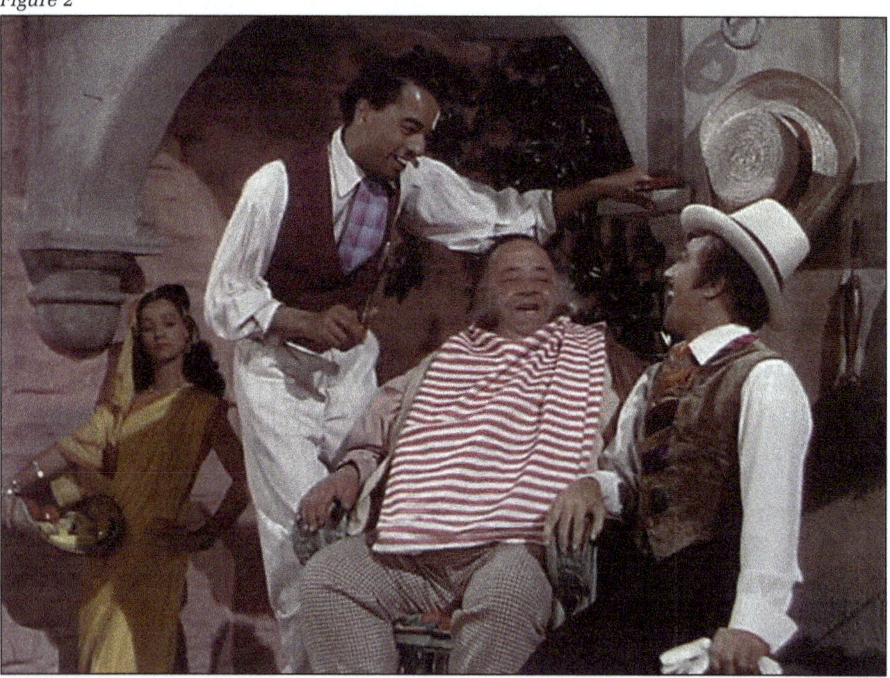

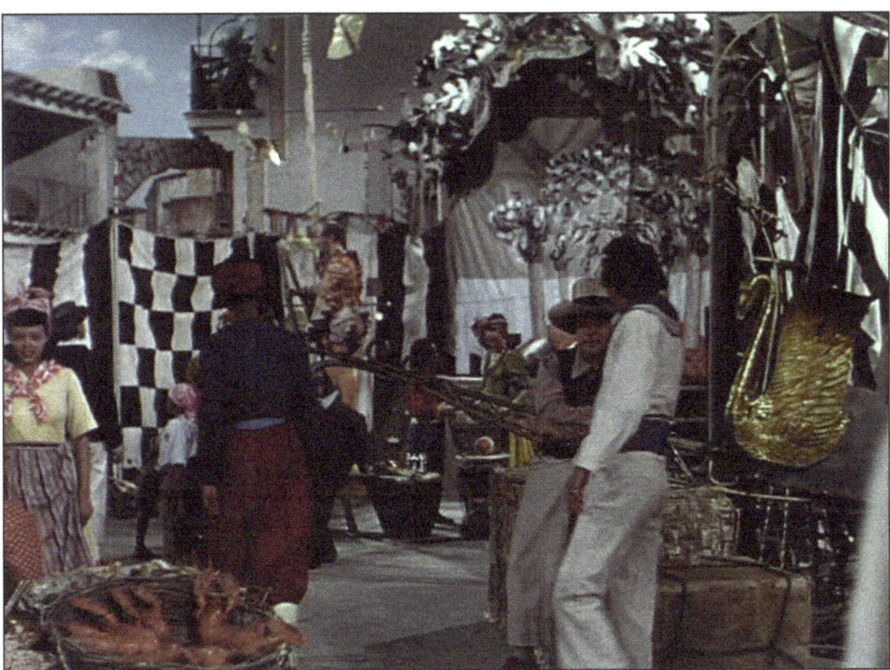

Figure 3

Figure 4

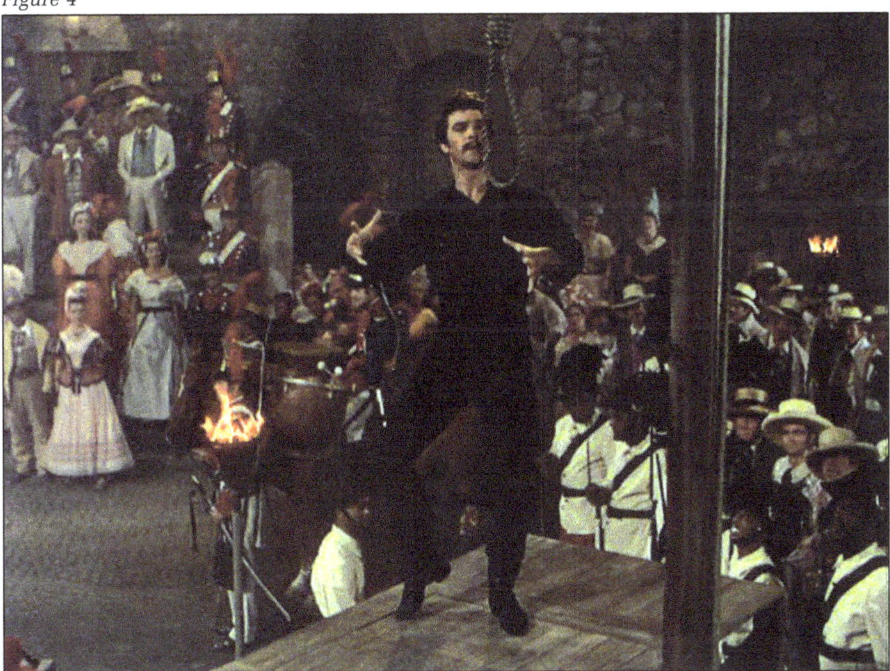

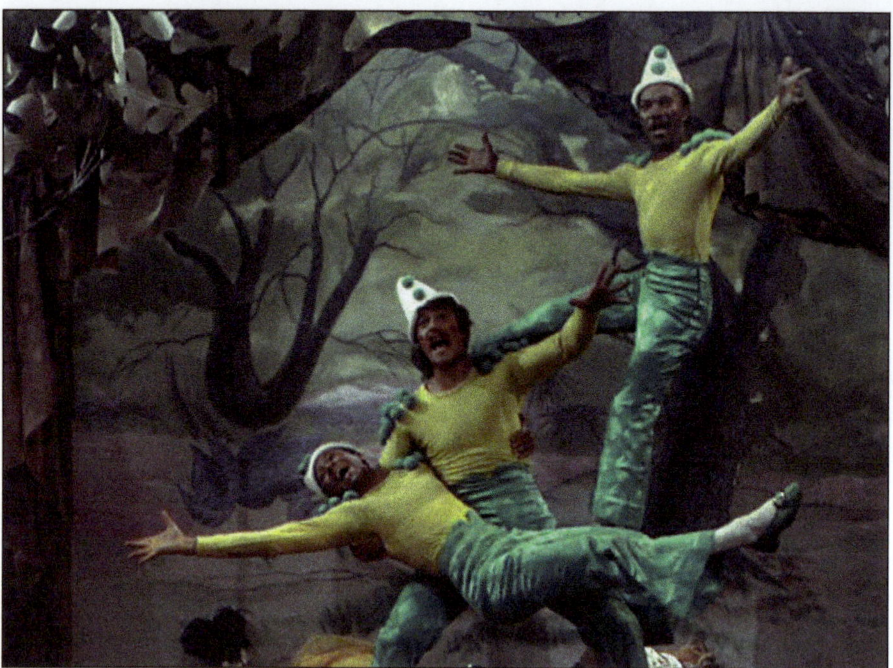

Figure 5

the film's preoccupations are consonant with Minnelli's other musicals and comedies, and here, along with the work of Fred Camper, Stephen Harvey and Joe McElhaney, Thomas Elsaesser's groundbreaking article on Minnelli's films is particularly pertinent.[8]

Elsaesser argues that Minnelli's 'conception of his art, indeed his "philosophy" is life, is formed by the conflict between the necessity of circumstance and the vital need to assert –not so much one's self, but rather one's conception of meaning, one's vision of things. It furnishes his "great theme": the artist's struggle to appropriate external reality as the elements of his own world, in a bid for absolute creative freedom. When I say artist, I hasten to add that this includes almost all of Minnelli's protagonists' insofar as 'they feel within them a world, an idea, a dream that seeks articulation and material embodiment'.[9] The protagonists' existence 'is justified by the incessant struggle in which they engage for total fulfilment, for total gratification of their aesthetic needs, their desire for beauty and harmony, their demand for an identity of their lives with the reality of their dreams'.[10] And what 'characterizes the Minnelli musical is the total and magic victory of the impulse, the vision, over any reality whatsoever. The characters in his musicals transform the world into a reflection of their selves, into a pure expression of their joys and sorrows, of the inner harmony or conflicting states of mind', and in this way the Minnelli musical 'transforms the movement of what one is tempted to call, for lack of a better word, the *soul* of the characters into shape, color, gesture, and rhythm. It is precisely when joy or sorrow,

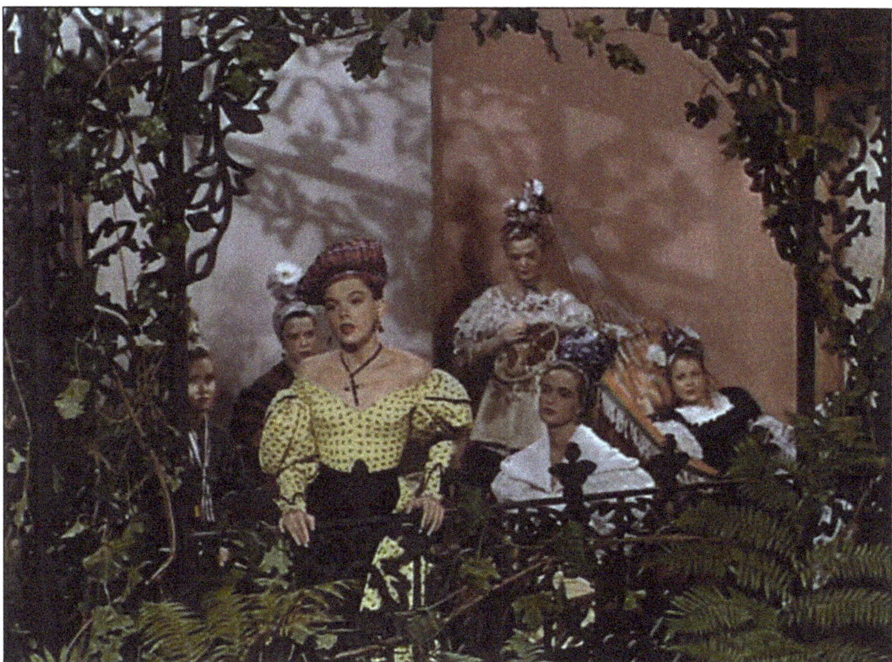

Figure 6

bewilderment or enthusiasm, that is, when emotional intensity becomes too strong to bear, that a Gene Kelly or Judy Garland has to dance or sing in order to give free play to the emotions that possess them.'[11] And in this way 'the Minnelli musical celebrates the fulfilment of desire and identity', giving rise to a five-part 'archetypal' structure: '(1) The moment of isolation (the individual vision as imprisonment), (2) the tentative communication (the vision materializes as decor), (3) the rupture (the decor as mere appearance and delusion), (4) the world as chaos, (5) the world as spectacle/the spectacle as world'.[12]

Marked by the nature, placement and purpose of Porter's songs, a modified version of this structure is clearly evident in *The Pirate*, which opens with Manuela (Judy Garland) sequestered in the house belonging to Aunt Inez (Gladys Cooper) (who tellingly wears black throughout) and Uncle Capucho (Lester Allen) (who tellingly utters not a single word). Manuela is reading the bloodthirsty description of Macoco in a book entitled *The Pirate*. She closes the book and puts it down. Then she intones the words 'Macoco where are you now?' as the camera crane-dollies out, enclosing a stationary Manuela with her more prosaic female friends behind the frame of an ornate trellis (figure 6). Following a shot of two of Manuela's friends, who say that Macoco must be dead, we cut to a different view of the terrace as Manuela continues to extol the virtues of the pirate, her eyes, voice and body ablaze with erotic energy as she paces back and forth. As the camera cranes out again, we see her hemmed in by her friends

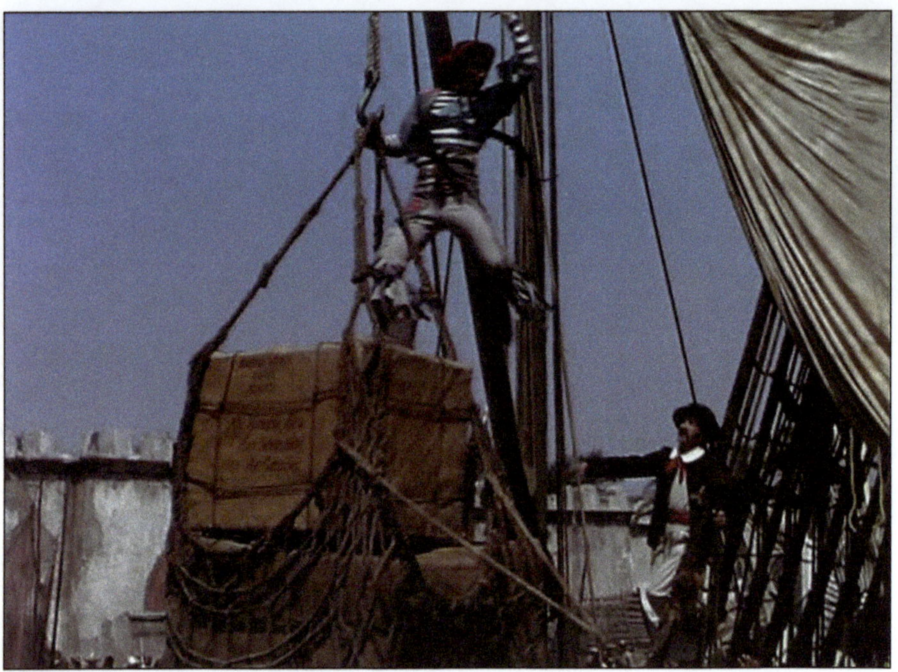

Figure 7

once more as she paces to and fro then turns her back to camera in order to look out into the distance. Inez and Capucho arrive and are only interested in Pedro's money, and when Pedro arrives he is something of a disappointment, with his portly middle-aged body and his desire to live a quiet life in Calvados far away from the high seas. Manuela's passionate interest in the world beyond Calvados is evident in the map of the Caribbean in the room nearby, and it is here that she begins to realise that marriage to Pedro may not be what she envisioned – that, as Stephen Harvey puts it, she will be 'perennially sequestered at dead center of a series of overdecorated still lives'[13] – so she persuades Inez to take her to Port Sebastian, ostensibly to pick up her wedding dress, but actually to witness the sights and sounds and colours of a large and vibrant sea port. It is here that the second phase of the Minnelli structure begins, and it here that the first two song-and-dance numbers can be both heard and seen.

The opening sequence in Port Sebastian focuses on Serafin, in reality an itinerant player, but the very image of the pirate that Manuela dreams of as he swoops effortlessly aloft along with Minnelli's camera on the crate bearing Manuela's trousseau 'from the Old World', as Stephen Harvey puts it (figure 7). In 'this one shot', Harvey continues, 'Minnelli establishes the free-spirited hero's supremacy over the seductive trappings which are the sum total of Don Pedro's appeal to Manuela', and from this point on, 'the unfettered Serafin bounds energetically through the artificial world of this movie, the camera sailing along beside him in animated synchrony'.[14]

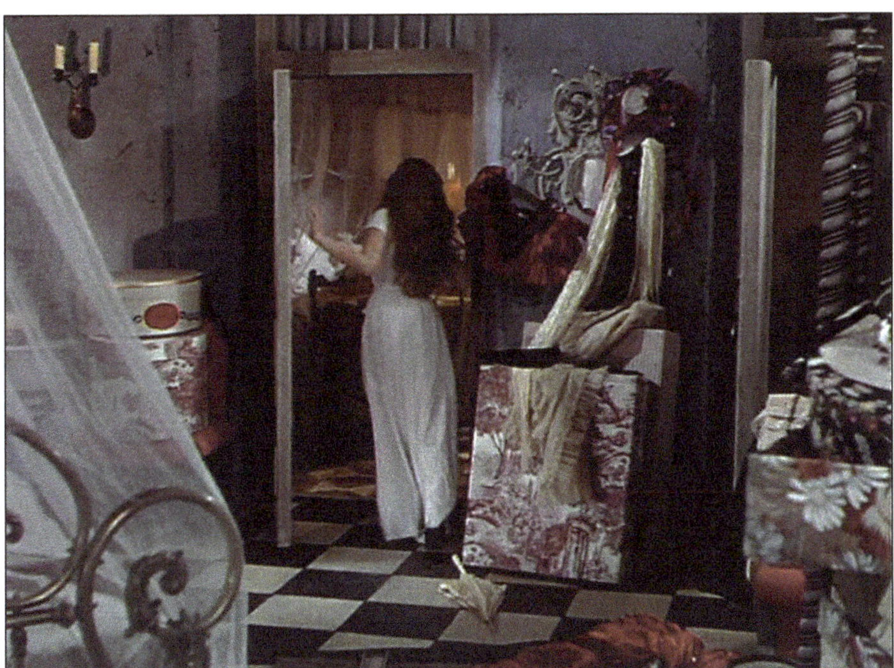

Figure 8

Having set the construction of his troupe's tent show in train, Serafin wanders off in search of female company and we move on to 'Niña', the film's first number. Extensive and rhumba-based, 'Niña' 'celebrates the hero's chronic restlessness, both erotic and athletic':

> Unfazed by gravity and untroubled by vertigo, he turns the town into his own set of monkey bars – snaking up and down balconies; suspended from a window while wrapped in a brief, passionate embrace; reclining casually atop a stone archway to serenade yet another damsel ... After shimmying down to earth, he bestows a kiss on a smouldering Carmencita ... As the brass of the MGM Orchestra switches to percussion and snake-charmer woodwinds, Serafin's mood shifts to flamenco. In a barber-pole-rigged gazebo he subdues a new group of dancing Niñas, who whirl their skirts and snatch his hat to fan themselves into further delirium ... [and then] creates circles within circles as Minnelli's camera vaults around the curvilinear set ... constantly redefining the space between the dancers and their immobile props .[15]

However, Serafin's promiscuity is brought to a stop when the number finishes and he spots Manuela, with whom he is instantly struck and whom he follows to a pathway overlooking the sea. Engrossed in romantic reverie as she looks out over the ocean, Manuela is interrupted by the presence of Serafin, whose circular movements are now focussed solely on her, and whom he seeks not only to marry, but to persuade her to come to his show later that evening. On discovering that Serafin is an actor, Manuela is initially dismissive. But having picked up her trousseau (a reminder of her impend-

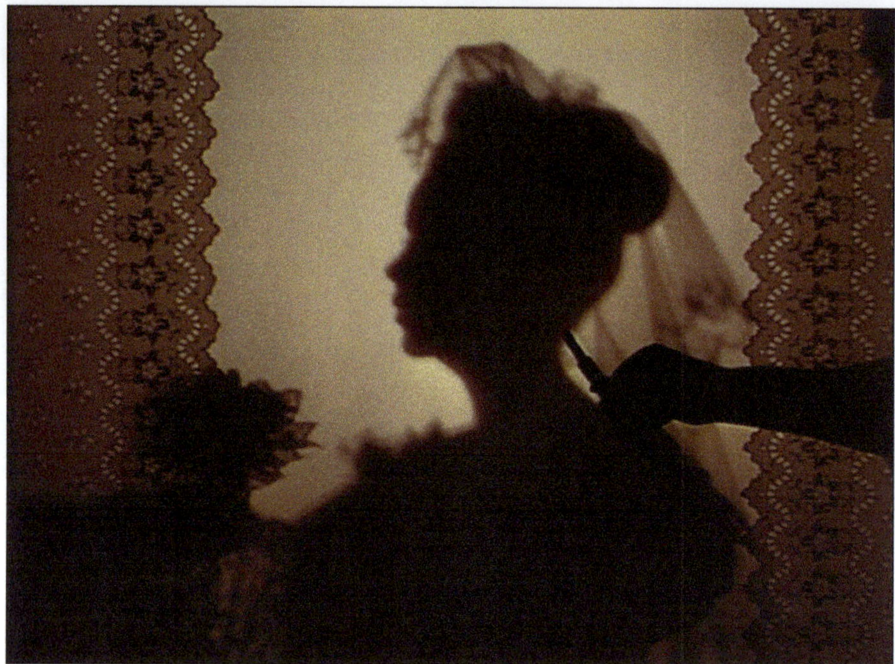

Figure 9

ing marriage to Pedro), she finds that she cannot sleep, opens the shutter of her window, and is tempted by the sights and sounds of the troupe to put on bangles and a fiery red skirt and head out to the show. Instantly hypnotised by Serafin's revolving mirror, Manuela's latent erotic energy is given full reign as she sings, moves and gestures to 'Mack the Black', prowling the stage with 'her hair flying free'.[16] Serafin wakes her with a kiss and she rushes back to her hotel, still unable to sleep but now in crisis as she sheds her red dress and bangles, closes the shutter on the window, and pauses amidst the chaotic clutter of wedding clothes and other items and purchases (figure 8). Chaotic clutter and inharmonious decor are often signs that all is not well in Minnelli's films, and this is the case here. But the destruction of over-decorated items of decor can lead to the stripping away of false illusions and fake identities, and this is what happens in the 'rupture' segment that follows.

Manuela begs Inez to take her home. 'Don Pedro was right', she says. 'Home is safe, and safe is protection. I want to go home'. Inez duly obliges her, and the next image we see is a shot of Manuela in her wedding dress in silhouette as an unseen artist traces her outline on her wedding day, his hands and those of another person emphasising Manuela's frozen stillness (figure 9), the very obverse of life and a distinct echo of her pictorial imprisonment in the opening sequence. However, as the silhouette artist dismantles the frame that encloses her, Manuela opens the shutters in the room, hears the sounds of Serafin and his troupe outside, and reacts by gazing in horror as she steps out onto the balcony, gesturing frantically with her hands as if to ward off their presence. Unable to enter through the door downstairs Serafin crosses to the balcony on a tightrope, eventually entering by opening the upstairs door as he attempts yet again to woo her and enlist her for his troupe. Pedro arrives with a whip, orders Inez and Capucho to leave, and threatens to teach Serafin a lesson. But Serafin recognises Pedro as Macoco, threatens to reveal his true identity, and pretends that he is Macoco in order to win Manuela over. Convinced that Serafin is Macoco, Manuela, who is still in her wedding dress, watches him in wide-eyed fascination from the balcony as 'The Pirate Ballet' (an orchestral dance-ballet version of 'Mack the Black') begins.

Choreographed by Kelly and Alton, 'The Pirate Ballet' serves to articulate Manuela's vision of Serafin, the hyper-masculine pirate based on Douglas Fairbanks' athletic persona in *The Black Pirate* (1926). As Bethe Genné points out, '*The Pirate*'s film and dance-drama blends ideas from both Minnelli and Kelly's previous films – the dream sequence in *Yolande* and Kelly's "balcony dance" in *Anchors Aweigh*. Like the former, it is set within the context of a dream that provides an insight into the thoughts and hidden desires of the dreamer and, like the latter, it serves as the hero's seduction and courtship dance'.[17] Influenced by 'the virtuoso male dancer roles from the nineteenth century *ballets d'action Raymonda*, *Le corsair*, and countless others' as well,[18] it begins in whimsical mode as an all-white donkey wanders into the square. Serafin is bearing a wooden sword and is still in the tight black trousers and the white shirt marked by a black-striped motif that he has worn in the Calvados sequence hitherto. But as a group of soldiers enter and engage him in stylised hand-to-hand combat the tone begins to change, and as Serafin conquers them all, it is Manuela's febrile imagination that seems to conjure up the visions that follow. Serafin is now dressed all in black, and is now the all-conquering version of the pirate that Manuela dreams of. Here, as Genné rightly puts it, 'it is *her* fantasy, her daydream, that we see enacted on the screen', burlesquing 'her adolescent vision of Macoco' as Serafin swings his cutlass, leaps and turns, cuts down his enemies, takes a young woman in his arms, scales 'masts seemingly hundreds of feet high', and plunges his hands into 'piles of jewels' amidst darkness, glowing red lights, and 'bright white smoke and orange flames'.[19]

This is the highlight of Manuela's and Serafin's masquerade. For shortly thereafter, as Manuela willingly agrees to sacrifice herself by marrying Serafin the pirate, she is informed by a member of Serafin's troupe that Serafin is in fact Serafin the actor, not the pirate Macoco. Manuela is furious, bombarding Serafin with insults, vases and other items of decor as she wrecks the room. As Serafin tries to defend himself, he is knocked cold by a large painting as it falls from the wall. But the consequent visual disorder is not a mark of destructive confusion (as it is in the hotel room earlier on), but a pretext to honest liberation as Manuela sings 'You Can Do No Wrong', cradles Serafin in her arms, compliments him on his acting, and kisses him as he begins to regain consciousness. However if the 'rupture' phase marks these shifts and changes in the relationship between Serafin and Manuela, the 'world as chaos' phase that follows is marked by threats to Serafin (and hence to Manuela and Serafin's new-found love) from Pedro, who has enlisted the help of the Viceroy (George Zucco), and

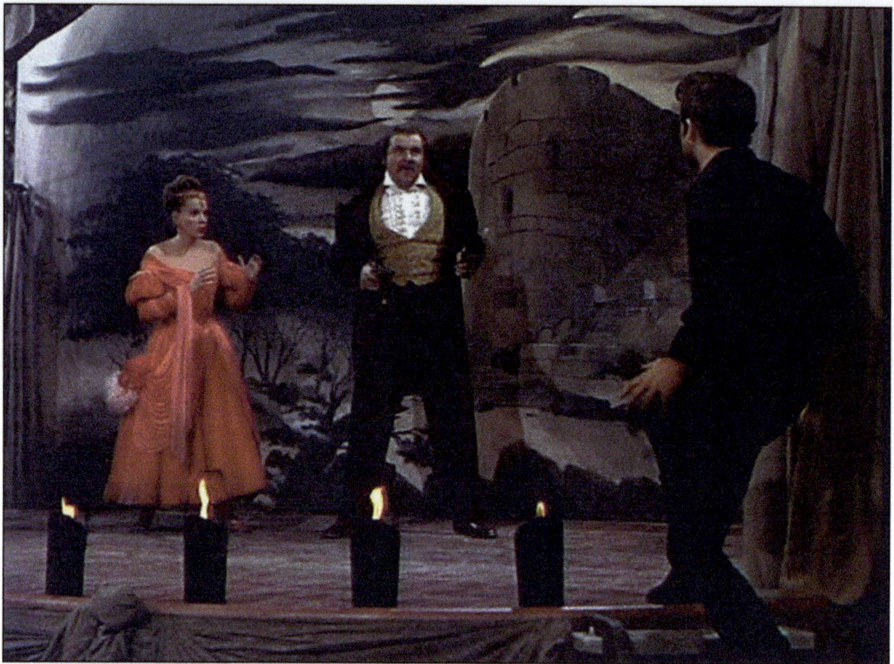

Figure 10

planted a chest full of precious jewels so as to ensure that Serafin will be identified as the real Macoco and hung.

In the square later on that evening, as drums roll and a noose dangles from a gibbet, the Viceroy shows Manuela the chest of jewels as further proof that Serafin is the guilty party. Manuela spots the fact that the bracelet she picks up is identical in design to that on her wedding ring and thus deduces that Pedro is Macoco. But there is no time to intervene, as at this point the Viceroy is as impatient to get on with the proceedings as Pedro. However, and much to Pedro's chagrin, Serafin succeeds in flattering the Viceroy, who says that he is particularly interested in mesmerism, and Serafin persuades him to give one final performance. As the performance begins we move toward the final phase in the Minnelli structure: 'the world as spectacle/the spectacle as world'. Serafin is now in his clown costume. He performs 'Be A Clown' and is joined by the Nicholas Brothers, as noted above, then dressed all in black, he announces that the next act will feature mesmerism. He begins to spin his mirror and Manuela responds and makes her way towards the stage. Inez breaks the mirror. But Manuela continues, pretending to be under Serafin's influence, and dedicates her life to Macoco, dismisses actors as 'piddling', and sings 'Love of My Life' to Serafin. Pedro can stand no more. Giving vent to his anger and frustration, he climbs on stage, pulls out his pistol, and declares that he is the real pirate in a classically melodramatic tableau (figure 10). Serafin is duly reprieved, and his troupe attack Pedro with custard pies and juggling balls, leading to Pedro's arrest and a final reprise of 'Be A Clown', which

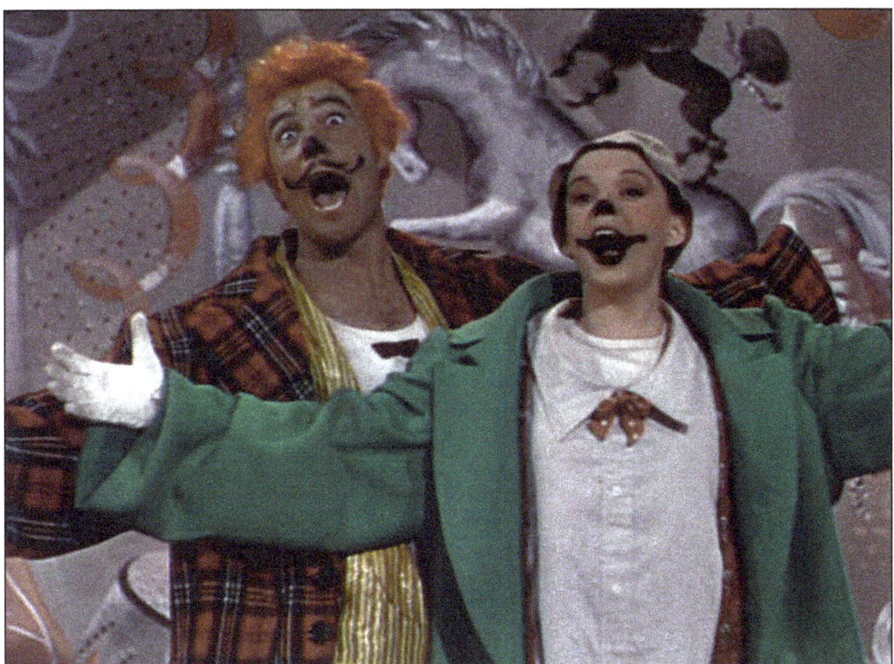

Figure 11

is performed by Manuela and Serafin together on stage, their other roles discarded and their gender identities almost indeterminate amidst the androgynous artifice of clown costumes and make-up (figure 11), and 'a riot of pratfalls, ear-wigglings, and gleefully klutzy dodges from an avalanche of juggler's pins cascading from all sides'.[20] In the end, it is 'teamwork, not passion, which is celebrated in *The Pirate*'s upbeat fadeout'.[21] And in the end, *The Pirate* identifies the couple's true selves in and through low-brow performance.

Notes

1. Hugh Fordin, *The Movies' Greatest Musicals Produced by Hollywood USA by the Freed Unit* (New York: Frederick Ungar Publishing Co., 1975), esp. pp. 203–213.

2. Earl J. Hess and Pratibha A. Dabholkar, *The Cinematic Voyage of* The Pirate*: Kelly, Garland, and Minnelli at Work* (Columbia, Missouri: University of Missouri Press, 2014). The history and nature of the plays, the scripts, and Breen's initial interventions are detailed in Hess and Dabholkat, *The Cinematic Voyage of* The Pirate, esp. pp. 1–49. Breen seemed solely concerned about 'the breakup of a marriage' and 'unacceptable statements concerning marriage and fidelity' in the scripts he saw. He also objected to the delivery of some of the lines in the song entitled 'Niña', but eventually passed them.

3. See the entry on Fulda in https://de.wikipdia.org/wiki/Ludwig_Fulda 30/10/2015, and 'A Tribute to Fulda' by S.N. Behrman in *The New York Times*, 7 February 1943, in http://snberhman.com/library/nytimes/43.2.7.htm 01/04/2015.

4. Berhman was a prolific playwright and screenwriter. He wrote or co-wrote 26 plays and musicals, 6 prose works, and 28 screenplays for films, among them *Liliom* (1930), *Lightning* (1930), *Daddy Long Legs* (1931), *Tess of the Storm Country* (1932), *Queen Christina* (1934), *A Tale of Two Cities* (1935), *The Cowboy and*

the Lady (1938), *Two-Faced Woman* (1941), *Quo Vadis* (1951), *Fanny* (1961) and *Stowaway in the Sky* (1962) in addition to the 1940 version of *Waterloo Bridge*. See Robert F. Gross, *S.N. Behrman: A Research and Production Sourcebook* (Greenwich, CT.: Greenwood Press, 1992) and Kenneth T. Reed, *S.N. Berhrman* (Boston: Twayne Publishers, 1975), who on page 26 argues that *The Pirate* was marked by references to and details from *The Tempest*, among them the Caribbean setting, the use of magic spells, the 'joyous epithalamium at the end', and the names of characters such as Calaban, Trinculo and Miranda. See also https://en.wikidepia.org/wiki/S._N._Berhman 01/11/2015.

5. According to Hess and Dabholkar, *The Cinematic Voyage of* The Pirate, p. 21, 'Tom Burley of the *New York Star-News* praised the mix of races seen on stage among the cast members' when reviewing the Behrman version. And in an interview conducted in 1978, Minnelli drew attention to the fact that the film version was 'set on a West Indian island; at the time it was a free port and Spanish and French and Creole were mixed together'. See Peter Lehman, Marilyn Campbell and Grant Munro, 'Two Weeks in Another Town – An Interview with Vincente Minnelli', *Wide Angle*, vol. 3 no. 1, 1979, p. 67. See also note 8 below.

6. Hess and Dabholkar, *The Cinematic Voyage of* The Pirate, pp. 66, 73–74. As Hess and Dabholkar point out, Roger Edens at MGM arranged the orchestrations and recordings. For more on Edens, see http://en.wikipedia.org/wiki /Roger_Edens 03/11/2015 and the entry on Edens in http://imdb.com/name/nm0249136/ 03/11/2015. Porter's songs, 'Niña' in particular, are marked by his ingenious trademark polysyllabic rhymes such as 'eurasthenia' and 'schizophenia', but with the possible exception of 'Be A Clown' are otherwise not regarded highly. According to Fordin, *The Movies' Greatest Musicals Produced in Hollywood USA by the Freed Unit*, p. 204, Porter was paid $100,000, and *The Pirate* was the third set of songs and musical numbers with a Central American theme. The others were *Panama Hattie* (1940) and *Mexican Hayride* (1944). For more details on Porter's songs and lyrics, see Philip Furia, *The Poets of Tin Pan Alley: A History of America's Lyricists* (Oxford and New York: Oxford University Press, 1990), pp. 153–80, and Furia and Laurie Patterson, *The Songs of Hollywood* (Oxford and New York: Oxford University Press, 2010), pp .147–149, which deals briefly with 'Be A Clown'. See also, http://en.wikipedia.org/wiki/Cole_Porter 01/11/2015.

7. Along with *Stormy Weather* (1943) and *Carmen Jones* (1952), *Cabin the Sky* was one of three all-black musicals produced on stage and adapted in Hollywood in the 1940s and early 1950s. The racial contexts from which they emerged and in which they were produced were complex, mixing Dixie-oriented tropes for the segregated Southern market alongside attempts to comply with the liberalism that marked official attempts to produce anti-racist films during the course of World War Two and its aftermath. The standard account of the latter can be found in Thomas Cripps, *Making Movies Black: The Hollywood Message Movie from World War II to the Civil Rights Era* (New York and Oxford: Oxford University Press, 1993), and an account of black plays and stage musicals in the 1940s can be found in Allen Woll, *Black Musical Theatre: From Coontown to Dream Girls* (Baton Rouge: Louisiana State University Press, 1989), pp. 193–228. A more nuanced account of Minnelli's version of *Cabin in the Sky* can be found in James Naremore, *The Films of Vincente Minnelli* (Cambridge and New York: Cambridge University Press, 1993), pp. 51–70, which notes on pp. 51 and 52, that '*Cabin* reminds us in the many ways in which the art of minorities has been coopted by show business, but at the same time it reveals a potentially affirmative or progressive tendency in Hollywood. Ultimately it enables us to understand the complicated and troubled relationship between ethnicity (or "difference") and modernity'. Meanwhile, it should also be noted that cinema managers in Memphis and a number of other Southern cities deleted the version of 'Be a Clown' that teamed the Nicholas Brothers with Kelly, though according to Hess and Dabholker, *The Cinematic Voyage of* The Pirate, p. 143, it 'remained in the release prints sent to the rest of the segregated South'. None of this means that 'there are no blacks on the Caribbean island in *The Pirate*', as Richard Dyer argues in 'Colour of Entertainment', in Bill Marshall and Robyn Stilwell, *Musicals: Hollywood and Beyond* (Exeter: Intellect Books, 2000), p. 27. Rather oddly, Dyer goes on to praise the film version *On the Town* (1949), seemingly unaware of the extent to which it was this adaptation that erased the multi-racial and multi-ethnic nature of the stage version. See Carol J.Oja, *Bernstein Meets Broadway: Collaborative Art in a Time of War* (Oxford and New York: Oxford University Press, 2014), esp. pp. 111–114.

8. Fred Camper, 'Depth Perception: Films by Vincente Minnelli' at http://chicagoreader.com/chicago/depth-perception/Content?oid=914205 01/11/2015 (originally written to accompany the 2004 Chicago retrospective of Minnelli's films), Stephen Harvey, *Directed by Vincente Minnelli* (New York: The Museum of Modern Art, Harper & Row Publishers, 1989), and Joe McElhaney, 'Vincente Minnelli' at http://sensesof-cinema.com/2004/great-direcors/minnelli/02/04/2015. Elsaesser's article, 'Vincente Minnelli', was in-

itially published in *Brighton Film Review*, no. 15, December 1969, pp. 11–13 and no. 18, March 1970, pp. 20–22, republished with a preface in Rick Altman (ed.), *Genre: The Musical* (London: Routledge & Kegan Paul, 1981), pp. 8–27, and republished again with new introductory material in Joe McElhaney (ed.), *Vincente Minnelli: The Art of Entertainment* (Detroit: Wayne State University Press, 2009), pp. 79–96, and this is the version I will cite. See also Minnelli's autobiography, *I Remember it Well* (which was written in conjunction with Hector Arce and first published by Doubleday in the US in 1974 and subsequently published by Angus Robertson in the UK in 1975). Minnelli's account of *The Pirate* can be found in Chapter 12, pp. 177–192, in the UK edition.

9. Elsaesser, 'Vincente Minnelli', pp. 83–84.
10. Elsaesser, 'Vincente Minnelli', p. 85.
11. Elsaesser, 'Vincente Minnelli', pp. 85–6.
12. Elsaesser, 'Vincente Minnelli', p. 92.
13. Harvey, *Directed by Vincente Minnelli*, p. 92.
14. Harvey, *Directed by Vincente Minnelli*, p. 92.
15. Harvey, *Directed by Vincente Minnelli*, p. 92.
16. Harvey, *Directed by Vincente Minnelli*, p. 92.
17. Beth Genné, 'Vincente Minnelli and the Dance Ballet', in McElhaney (ed.), *Vincente Minnelli*, p. 244–245.
18. Genné, 'Vincente Minnelli and the Dance Ballet', pp. 245.
19. Genné, 'Vincente Minnelli and the Dance Ballet', p. 245.
20. Harvey, *Directed by Vincente Minnelli*, p. 93.
21. Harvey, *Directed by Vincente Minnelli*, p. 93.

Chapter 10

I Remember Mama

The film version of *I Remember Mama* was produced by RKO and premiered at the Radio City Music Hall on 16 March 1948. Its inception, development and production was somewhat long and complex, beginning with the publication of a short story in the *Toronto Star Weekly* in 1941 and ending not just with the film, but with a subsequent spin-off television series. Along the way, the publication of a novel entitled *Mama's Bank Account* and the production of a play entitled *I Remember Mama* played key parts in what was clearly a minor but significant cultural phenomenon, a phenomenon best analysed in a book entitled *Visions of Belonging* by Judith E. Smith.[1] The short story was written by Kathryn Anderson McLean under the pen name of Kathryn Forbes, and its success gave rise to a second instalment, which was re-republished alongside the first in the February 1941 edition of *Reader's Digest*, and which eventually led to a book entitled *Mama's Bank Account*, which was initially published by Harcourt Brace in New York in 1943. Told on a loosely chronological basis by its author, who purports to be one of Mama's daughters, the book was a fictional account of various incidents and events in the lives of an immigrant Norwegian family in San Francisco in the 1920s. These events and incidents serve in large part to exemplify Mama's kindness and wisdom, and Mama's eponymous bank account, which turns out not to exist, serves as a trope for the family's security, ensuring that whatever crises arise, Mama will always find a way to solve her family's problems.

The novel was an instant success and a tie-in edition was published by Bantam alongside the film's release, and in the interim an equally successful stage-play adaptation premiered at the Shubert Theatre in New Haven on 28 September 1944 and went on to open at the Music Box Theatre in New York on 19 October. Eventually closing on 29 June 1946 after 713 performances, the play featured Mady Christians as Mama, Richard Bishop as Papa, Oscar Homolka as Uncle Chris, Marlon Brando as Nels (one of Mama's children) and Joan Tatzel as Katrin (the daughter who purports to write the novel). The play itself was a tie-in of sorts. For RKO part owned the rights to the novel, and it was RKO that commissioned Richard Rodgers and Oscar Hammerstein II to produce a stage-play version. This version was duly written and

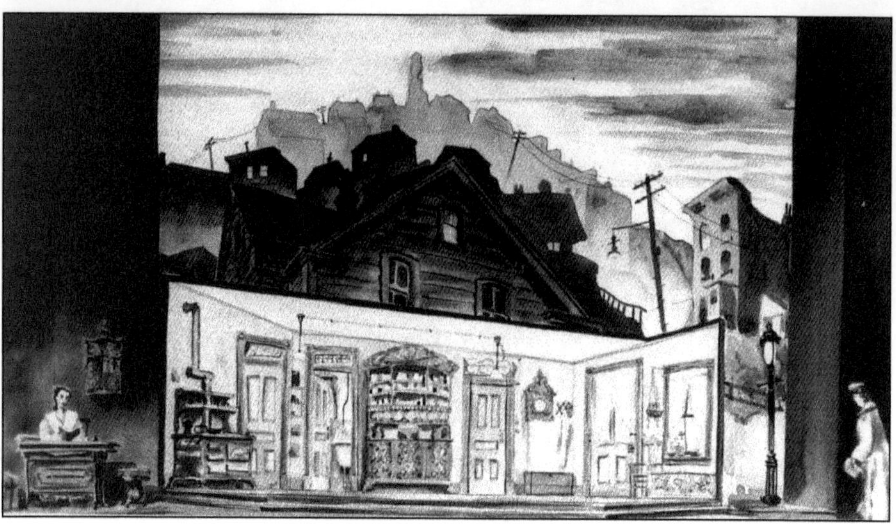

Figure 1

staged by John Van Druten, who was also responsible for re-titling the play,[2] and RKO ensured that its rights were retained by 'siphoning off a portion of the play's gross earnings until $150,000 was paid off', thus making 'a two-way profit' while 'building up an exploitation in the future film rights'.[3]

The Play

Marked by its unusual staging, structure and lighting, Van Druten's play comprised two separate acts, both of which were identically furnished. On 'each side of the stage, down front, are two small turntables, left and right, on which ... shorter front scenes are played against very simplified backgrounds. As each scene finishes the lights dim and the table revolves out, leaving an unobstructed view of the main stage. The main stage is raised by two steps, above which the traveler curtains open and close'. (Figure 1 is the sketch of the layout by stage designer George Jenkins, which is credited to The Billy Rose Theatre Collection).[4] Act One begins with Katrin in a spotlight. Now a young woman, she 'writes in silence for a few moments, then puts down her pen, takes up her manuscript, and begins to read aloud what she has written': 'For as long as I could remember, the house on Steiner Street had been home. Papa and Mama had both been born in Norway, but they came to San Francisco because Mama's sisters were all born here. All of us were born here. Nils, the older and the only boy – my sister Christine – and the littlest sister, Dagmar', who is inseparable from a tom cat whom she insists on calling Elizabeth. Katrin puts down her manuscript and looks out front. 'But first and foremost, I remember Mama', she says, and the lights dim. Then the lights come up on the main stage, revealing the interior of a kitchen, a view of the street outside, and 'a painted backdrop of the San Francisco hills, houses, and telegraph posts'. Katrin recalls 'that every Saturday night Mama would sit down by the kitchen table and count out the money Papa had brought home'. Then the light on Katrin dwindles further and we move on to the first conventionally-staged scene, which centres on whether there is enough money to meet the needs of the family and its members. Nils hopes to go to High School. But there appears to be insufficient money to pay for his fees, so the other family members volunteer to postpone their own financial needs, thus alleviating the necessity to go the bank, and thus underlining the family's solidarity.

Mama's sister Trina arrives wearing a hat and feather boa. A 'timid ... woman of about 40', Trina reveals that an undertaker named Torkelson has proposed to her and that the boa is a gift. However, she fears that her sisters, Jenny and Sigrid, will laugh at her, and that Uncle Chris, who is head of the extended family, will refuse permission for her to wed. Mama agrees to speak to Jenny and Sigrid. But she also insists that Torkelson must speak to Chris himself, and it is at this point that Jenny and Sigrid enter and ridicule Trina while taking the opportunity to point out that Mr Hyde (Mama and Papa's lodger) has as yet paid no rent. Mama praises Hyde's recitations of literary works and points out that Chris knows several embarrassing 'family stories' about Jenny and Sigrid, who become more amenable. But Jenny and Sigrid take the opportunity to ridicule the name of Dagmar's cat before they disappear into the wings stage left, leaving Hyde to read from *A Tale of Two Cities* in a hushed and crowded room.

The curtains close on the kitchen scene and Katrin reads from her diary once more. She notes that Mama calls Chris 'a black Norwegian, because of his dark hair and fierce moustache'. Then the spotlight goes up and we see Jenny and Trina in Jenny's kitchen. Jenny points out that Chris is prone to cursing, and although Trina points out that this may be because it hurts him to walk, Jenny goes on to complain that Chris wastes time and money on his orange groves and lives in sin with an unmarried woman. But when Sigrid arrives, we learn that Chris has paid for an operation on her young boy's knee, and may thus be more benevolent than he seems. The stage darkens and the turntable revolves out, and Katrin explains that Chris would 'descend on the city in his automobile and come roaring and stamping into our house' two or three times year, and as the light dims further, the 'sound of a very old and noisy Ford car changing gears' can be heard off left, 'grinding and screaming as it comes to a standstill'. Then Chris shouts 'Marta! Lars! Children – vere are you?', and the curtains part on Mama and Papa's kitchen once again. Chris gets the children to line up against the wall in order to see how much they have grown. He is pleased with their progress but concerned to hear that Doctor Johnson is upstairs with Mama and Dagmar and that Dagmar is in urgent need of an operation. The operation could be performed at the county hospital for free. But Mama insists on paying, and the doctor says that Dagmar can be treated at the clinic instead. Chris is adamant that everything should be done as quickly as possible, but Mama says that Chris must go to the hospital on his own because he frightens Dagmar, a fact that is backed up by the other children. Chris is dumbfounded: 'But that is very bad', he says. 'The aunts, yes, I like to frighten them ... That makes you laugh ... You cannot be frightened of me anymore'. Then the aunts arrive with Thorkelson, and Chris and his female partner drive off with Dagmar and Mama, leaving the aunts and Thorkelson to make their own way to the clinic.

Inside the clinic, Katrin, Christine, Nels and Mama are waiting, and Chris tells Sigrid that he has seen her son. Trina tells Chris that she wants to get married and Chris gives Trina his permission but refuses a dowry. Mama, meanwhile, is becoming more and more concerned about her daughter. Mama's sisters leave and Mama continues to fret. She notices a woman carrying a mop and pail then turns her attention to Doctor Johnson. Doctor Johnson tells her that the operation went well and that Dagmar is fine. However, he also tells her that patients cannot be visited by anyone for twenty-four hours, and although Mama decides to go home, she insists that 'I must see Dagmar today'. The stage darkens, the turntable revolves, and the curtain opens on an empty kitchen. Mama and Nels let themselves in, and Mama goes out to the pantry. Mama comes back wearing an apron and proceeds to scrub the floor. Then all of a sudden she declares 'I tink I tink of something', at which point the 'lights dim and the curtains close on the kitchen'. The lights come up slowly on the left-hand turntable, revealing Arne in a hospital bed with Uncle Chris sat beside him. Arne tells Chris that he is in pain, and Chris decides to teach him some swear words: 'When pain comes again. You say them. They help plenty. I know. I haf pain, too'. Comforted by Chris, Arne falls asleep. Then the light dims, the turntable table revolves, and the curtains part, revealing the hospital corridor as Mama and Katrin enter from the left. Noting that there has been a change of personnel at reception, Mama takes off her hat and coat and begins cleaning the floor. Chris arrives and Katrin tells him that Mama has gone to visit Dagmar, then Mama returns carrying a mop and pail 'and smiling triumphantly'. 'Dagmar is fine', she says, and as Mama and Katrin 'go off left' Act One comes to an end.

Act Two begins with Katrin reading at her desk, 'exactly as in Act One'. She gets up, puts on her hat and coat, and reaches centre stage as Mama comes through the curtains. Mama treats Katrin to a soda, and Katrin asks about Mama's life in the old country. Mama reveals that she had a daughter who died when only two, and says she that was attracted to San Francisco because it was like Norway, 'only better'. Mama and Katrin leave the drugstore and 'disappear behind the curtains', and the howls of a cat in pain are heard. Then the howls diminish, and 'as the curtains part on the kitchen scene once more, Mama, Papa and Dagmar are shown entering the house.' They are pleased to be home again, but the cat is ill and Dagmar is concerned. Mama and Papa persuade Dagmar to go to bed. But they are convinced that the cat is unlikely to last the night and administer chloroform to help alleviate her suffering. At this point Mr Hyde enters, says he has to go, and leaves his books and a cheque in an envelope. The cheque turns out to be worthless. But all family members are delighted about the books, and as the curtains close, Dagmar and her cat both show signs of recovery.

Katrin and Christine enter in their school clothes. Christine accuses Katrin of selfishness, caring only about her part in an upcoming school play and her forthcoming graduation while Papa is on strike and the family is short of money. Mama is planning to give Katrin her silver brooch for her graduation, but Katrin wants a dresser set and that is what she gets. Papa tells Katrin that Mama paid for the dresser set by selling her brooch, and Katrin realises the significance of the brooch and is truly distraught. At this point the 'lights fade and the curtains close' and we focus on Dorothy and Madeline, two of Katrin's school friends. Katrin rushes in with the dresser set, planning to return it to Dorothy's father, from whom it was purchased by Mama and Papa in the first place. Then we move on to Mama and Papa, who are now together in the kitchen. Papa is still on strike. But the dresser set has now been returned to Dorothy's father, who has agreed to give Katrin a job at his store, and when Katrin returns from the store, Mama pins the brooch on Katrin's dress and Papa gives Katrin her first cup of coffee. The curtains close and we move to the parlour in Trina's house. Trina is on the phone to Thorkill, who has now become more confident and who insists that the invitations to their wedding should be sent 'right away'. But before they can do so, Mama and her sisters are informed that if they want to see Chris again they should 'come without delay.'

Most of the family members decide to make the trip. Chris's partner invites the family through the curtains then the curtains part to reveal Chris propped up in bed. Chris knows that he is dying. He greets Mama and Arne with enthusiasm, but is rather impatient with Jenny, who is sent outside with Trina and Sigrid. Chris turns to Katrin and Mama, who agrees to pour him a whiskey. Chris tells Mama to sell the ranch and give the money to his partner, who is now identified as Jessie Brown, and who is also revealed to be Chris's wife. Chris asks Mama to bring Jessie in so that all three of them can sit together before he dies. They each take a sip of whisky as the lights dim and the curtains close. Then the spotlight goes up on the turntable right and we move on to the porch outside. Mama tells her sisters that Chris is dead and the sisters ask about a will. Mama tells them that whatever money Chris had left has been left to Jessie, and that Chris spent much of his life giving money to help cure and care for the lame. Jessie appears from between the curtains and invites the family members to pay their last respects. They all go in except for Mama and Jessie, who is grateful for Mama's warmth, respect, and friendship.

We move on briefly to Trina and Thorkelson, who now have a new-born baby boy. Thorkelson has changed. He is now more open in his love and respect for Trina, insisting that she has a waitress when he invites his in-laws over for a soirée. Then the turntable revolves once more, and the curtains part on Mama and Papa in their newly furbished kitchen. 'Dagmar, looking a little older, is seated on a chest' as Nels enters from the back of the stage carrying a newspaper, noting that there is a letter on the mat for Katrin as he does so. While Dagmar waits to see whether her Tom cat will produce any kittens, Katrin returns and is handed the letter by Mama. Katrin is disappointed: yet another of the stories she has written has been rejected. But Mama insists that she keep on trying, and plans in secret to visit one Florence Dana Moorhead, who describes herself 'a celebrated novelist and short story writer', and who is reportedly staying at the luxurious Fairmont hotel in San Francisco. Noting that Moorhead also describes herself as a gastronome, Mama heads off to the Fairmount and waits in the lobby. Moorhead walks by and Mama tells her about her daughter's stories. Moorhead is not really interested in the stories. But she is interested in one of Mama's Norwegian recipes, and Mama agrees to write down the recipe in return for reading a sample of Kristin's work. Moorhead and Mama disappear into the wings and Mama passes on Moorhead's advice that Kristin she should write about what she knows, not what she thinks she should write about. She also says that Moorhead thinks she has a gift, and has given her her agent's address. Katrin goes back to her desk. Then we flash forward as she mails a story called 'Mama and the Hospital', receives a cheque for five hundred dollars, and promises to buy a winter coat for Mama. Katrin reads out the story to her family, which begins with 'I remember Mama'.

In adapting the play from the novel, Van Druten sets the story further back in time to 1910. He also eliminates a number of secondary characters and locations, all but one of the various homes that Mama, her family and her extended family live in, and all but one of the family's numerous boarders, thus giving rise to a home that is much more central. He also expands on some of the incidents and characters (most notably those involving Chris), and either condenses or discards others (most notably those focussing on Katrin's school and schoolmates, and the chapter in which Nils visits the dysfunctional family of his would-be girlfriend). Judith E. Smith suggests that 'Van Druten's theatrical adaptation expanded the play's representations in the spirit of wartime concerns', offering 'images of nurture and safety rather than horror and uncertainty'; and she also suggests that through 'specific dramatic innovations, such as featuring the daughter as both narrator and dramatic actor' and 'imitating memory through a deliberate absence of plot', Van Druten created 'a prototype for looking back through ethnic nostalgia that could be adapted to a variety of postwar audiences' as well as wartime ones.[5] These observations are clearly pertinent, though it should be pointed that the novel was also published in wartime, that it consisted of a series of vignettes and was even more lacking in plot than Van Druten's play, and that it too could be accused of ethnic nostalgia. However Smith is right to point out that in 'Van Druten's adaptation, the aunts become negative "ethnic types"' and that in the novel the aunts readily pool their savings to help pay for an operation for Papa.[6]

The Film

Having profited from the extraordinary success of the play, RKO decided to resurrect its interest in a film version. Harriet Parsons maintained her commitment to the project as producer,[7] and it was Parsons who approached Irene Dunne to play the part of Mama as DeWitt Bodeen, who had already drafted two screenplay versions of the novel, went on to draft a screenplay version of the play. Dunne agreed to play the part of Mama,[8] and of the five directors she was offered, she chose George Stevens. Stevens had just returned from a devastated Europe and may well have seen the play in New York on his way back to Los Angeles. He agreed to act as executive producer and direct the film. But he was currently embroiled in the sale of Liberty Films, a company put

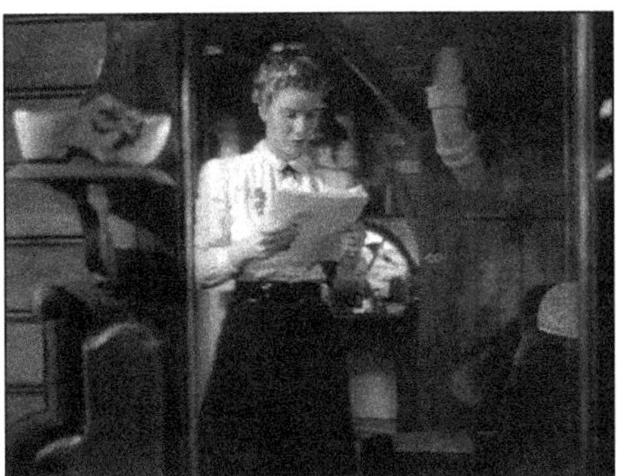
Figure 2

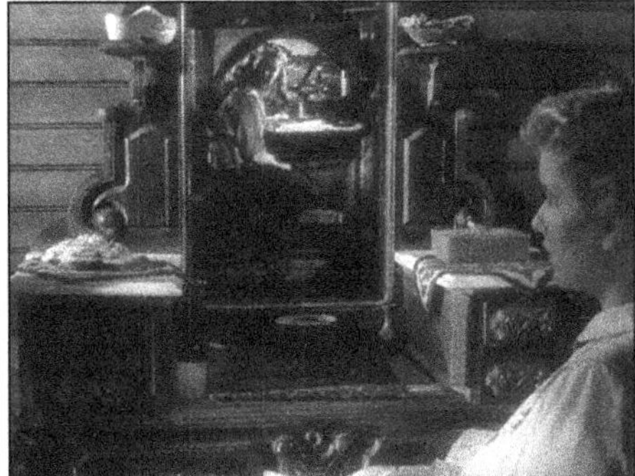
Figure 3

together by Stevens, Frank Capra and William Wyler. Liberty had been designed to produce independent films, but its only completed project was *It's a Wonderful Life* (1947) and the company was in debt. Liberty was eventually sold to Paramount on 14 April 1947, though by then Stevens had already been loaned to RKO for the period between 17 March 1947 to 16 March 1948, and RKO had agreed to pay Liberty '$6000 per week for twenty-six weeks beginning March 27 1947'.[9]

Aside from Oscar Homolka as Chris, none of the play's cast were cast for the film: Katrin was played by Barbara Bel Geddes, Papa by Patrick Dorn, Hyde by Cedric Hardwick, Thorkelson by Edgar Bergen, Doctor Johnson by Rudy Vallee, Jessie Brown by Barbara O'Neil, Nels, Christine and Dagmar by Steve Brown, Peggy McIntyre and June Hedin, and Trina, Jenny and Sigrid by Ellen Corby, Hope Landin and Edith Evanson respectively. With the input of Nicholas Musuraca (who won an Oscar for his camera work) and Albert S. D'Agostina and Carroll Clarke (who helped design the sets), production began on 26 May and ended in mid October. Scenes were shot in Telegraph Hill, Russian Hill, the Ferry Building and Liberty Street in San Francisco as well as at Agoura Ranch elsewhere in Southern California. But much of the film was shot on 'interior sets constructed within the house' rather than on separate stages,[10] and as we shall see, it was the use of the camera in and around the house as well as on location that gave it its distinctive visual style. As we shall also see, sound and the uses of sound (the province of sound recordists Richard Van Hessen and Terry Kellum) were distinctive too, and along with Roy Webb's musical score, these ingredients are evident in the film's first sequence.

Following the credits, which were superimposed on a series of line drawings, the film opens on a misty picture of San Francisco. A faint and distant female voice (a voice that appears to emanate from the past) can be heard on the soundtrack as the camera tilts downward to show the words she speaks being typed on a piece of a paper. The voice continues more loudly and clearly, remembering Mama and completing the typescript with the words, 'We do not have to go to the bank. The End'. We cut to a medium close-up of the speaker's back as she swivels to the side in her chair, places the paper on a pile, and sits up and stretches. Then she reaches out and picks up the

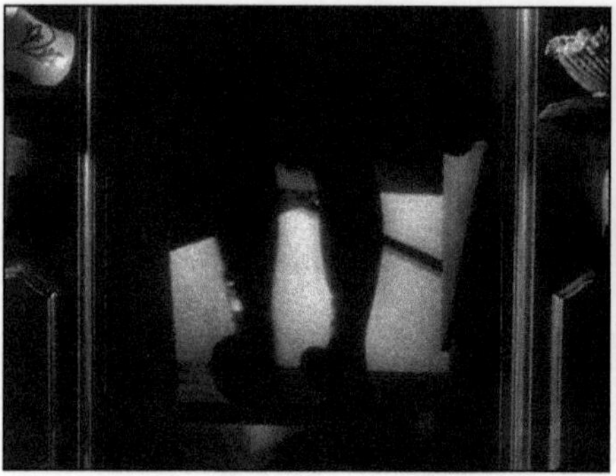
Figure 4

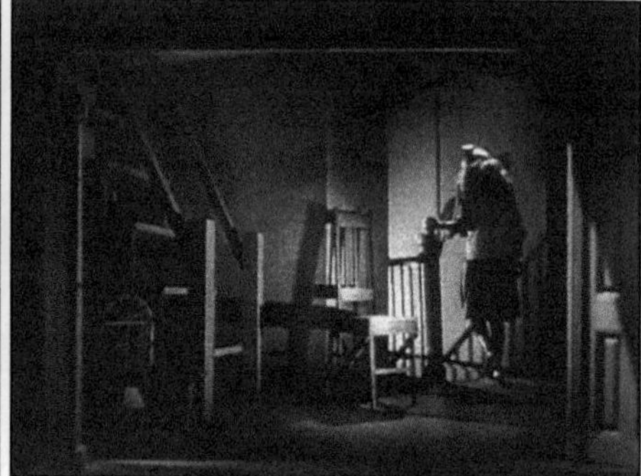
Figure 5

pile of paper, stands up as the camera moves up with her, and reads out the words at the end of manuscript: 'A novel by Katrin Hanson'. The speaker is Katrin, and as she smiles and looks up, we cut to her reflection in a full-length mirror as she walks forward and reads her manuscript out loud, makes corrections, and sits down (figure 2). Still framed in the mirror, though now in close-up sitting down, she explains that Mama and Papa were born in Norway, that Mama's sisters also live in San Francisco, and that Mama's children are called Nils, Christina and Dagmar. Now framed directly in her chair, Katrin recollects that 'first of all, I remember Mama', and goes on to recall the Saturday night ritual in the Hanson household. As she does so, we cut to a long shot of Katrin in her chair in the foreground looking at an image in the mirror of an empty chair and a typewriter, and as the camera slowly dollies in, and as Mama's distant voice calls her away from her desk and toward the kitchen below, we begin to see an emerging image of a younger Katrin at her desk in the mirror too (figure 3). Responding to Mama's calls, this younger Katrin blows out her candle, walks downstairs to the landing below, then down to the passage leading to the kitchen, where the rest of the family are already gathered to discuss the dispensation of its money for the forthcoming week.

This sequence is succinct, unique and remarkable, providing exposition and using a

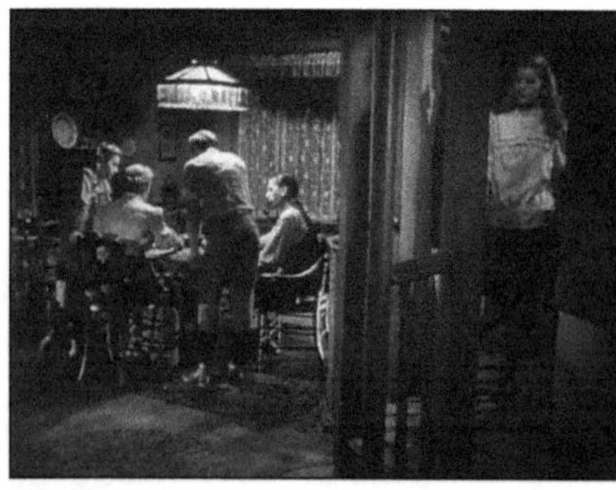
Figure 6

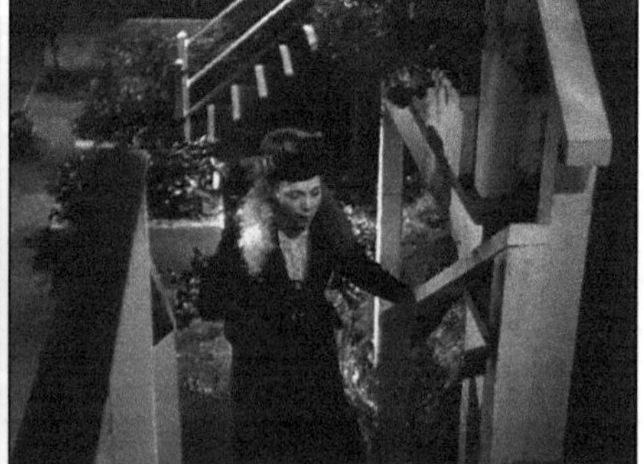
Figure 7

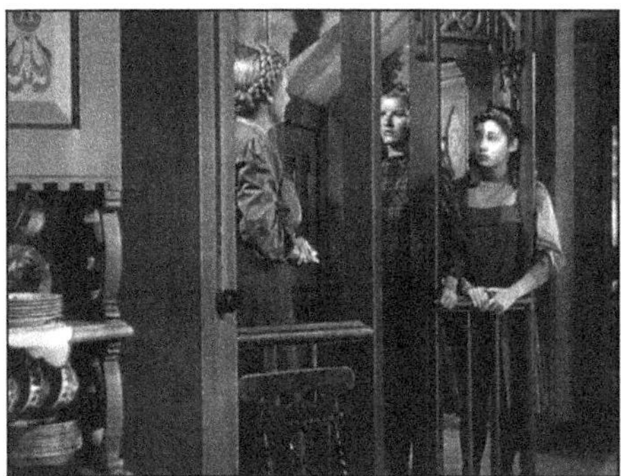
Figure 8

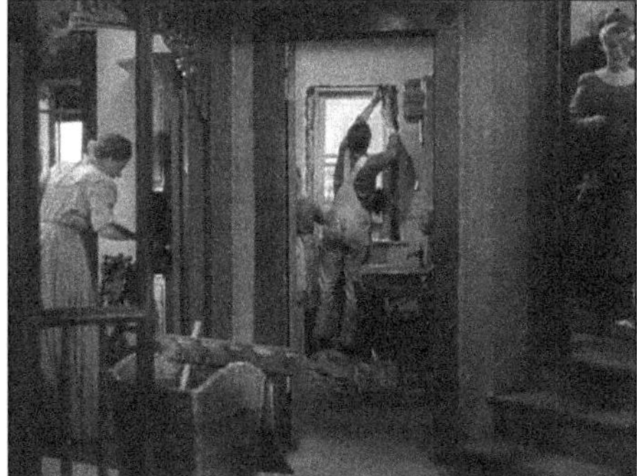
Figure 9

number of overt devices to do so. As David Bordwell has pointed out, the use of overt devices at the beginning of Hollywood films is by no means uncommon.[11] But here the use of these devices, both visual and aural, serves to generate an atmosphere of nostalgia that marks the film throughout. And here Katrin's descent into the kitchen in a single mobile take serves to establish another distinctive motif. What is striking about this take is not so much its continuous nature , but the way in which its movements and framings draw attention to the material nature of the decor and its constituents: the small wooden door and staircase down which Katrin walks; the wooden staircase, floor and wardrobe on the landing and the way in which Katrin is framed internally by a wooden structure as she walks across to a larger staircase; the wooden floor of the landing as the camera cranes down toward the ground floor; and the wooden features near the open interior space of the kitchen as Katrin stops for a moment prior to joining the rest of the family (figures 4–6). Thus in addition to the attic sequences and shots that pepper the film throughout and that function as allusive substitutes for the spotlight device in Van Druten's play, the attention paid to the features of the house and other interior locations is particularly distinctive.[12]

Being the site of numerous conversations, decisions and incidents, the house is itself clearly important. But it is not conventionally symbolic, and the attention paid it by

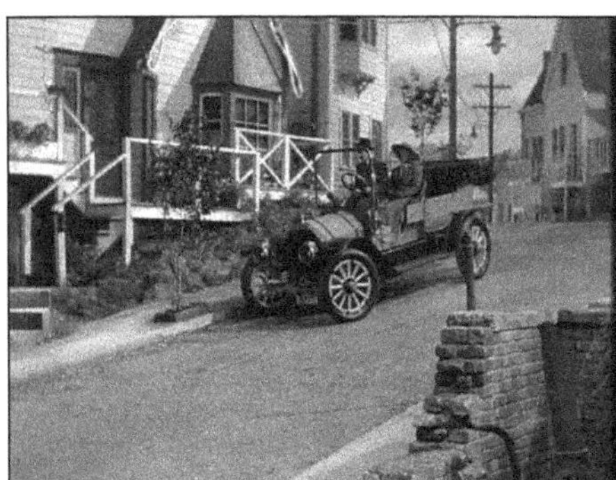
Figure 10

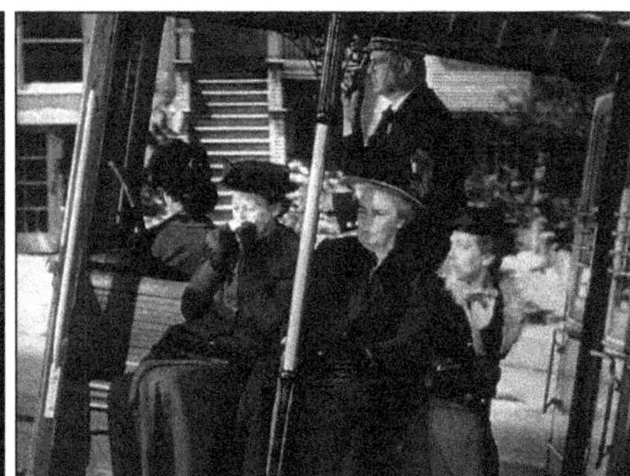
Figure 11

the camera serves largely to provide one of two stylistic threads that bind the film together, the first being the items of interior decor, and the second being the outdoor framings that underline the hilly nature of San Francisco. Following the scene in which Mama presides over the family's spending for the week, Trina's entrance briefly combines these threads as she climbs the steep wooden steps to Mama's porch (figure 7). But separate examples of each can be found in Trina's re-entry into the house following her discussion with Mama on the porch, and in the departure of Sigrid, Jenny and Arne (Tommy Ivo) running down the street to catch a tram. Subsequent examples of the former include the shots of Mama entering her house on the night of Dagmar's operation and the family cleaning and refurbishing the house later on (figures 8 and 9). And subsequent examples of the latter include the sequence showing the arrival of Chris and Jessie in their car (figure 10), a shot of Mama's sisters in a tram (figure 11), and a shot of Mama and Katrin walking up the street out shopping

Many of these outdoor scenes and moments are accompanied by the sounds of fog horns, horses, trams and wind, serving to underline the sonic landscape of San Francisco in the 1910s as they do so, and the sounds and noises associated with Chris in particular pick up these tropes and augment them. These sounds and noises, which are all identified in the novel and the play, include the splutters and bangs produced by Chris's car, the sound of Chris's car horn, and Chris's loud and booming voice. Thus when Chris dies in bed in his farmhouse, his death and its immediate aftermath are marked not only by silence, but also by the absence of Chris as a person and the numerous noises with which he has been associated. And when we cut to the porch outside, we are made aware not only of the silent respect that he merits, but of the noise produced by Arne – whom Chris has helped cure – as he sits in Chris's car sounding out its horn. In this way, as Mama reads out a list of all the children Chris has helped, Arne's ability to walk now is a further tribute to Chris's generosity. At the same time though, the framings used to articulate the death of Chris and its immediate aftermath are also used not only to extend the focus on the decor and its constituents by focusing on the bedroom and the porch, but to articulate the passage of time and its generations.

The earlier hospital scenes are also marked by the tropes of sound and silence. Chris's voice is a feature of the first of these scenes as he argues with Thorkelson about a dowry for Trina, then sings a song with Arne in order to help assuage Arne's pain . But the second scene, in which Mama finds a way to visit Dagmar by posing as a cleaner, is marked not just by silence, but also by occasional noises, and by Mama singing 'Sovnen', a Norwegian lullaby, to comfort Dagmar and the other children in her ward. To some extent this scene epitomises the ideal of selfless maternal love that Smith discusses in her analysis of the post-war response to the film, some of which focussed explicitly on white Norwegian motherhood even as it eschewed the themes of foreign ethnicity.[13] However, for a few moments at least, the film draws attention not just to Dagmar, nor just to other white children and babies, but to Chinese, Hispanic and black children and babies too as they finally respond and fall asleep to the sounds of Mama's lullaby (figures 12–13). As noted above, this sequence does not occur directly

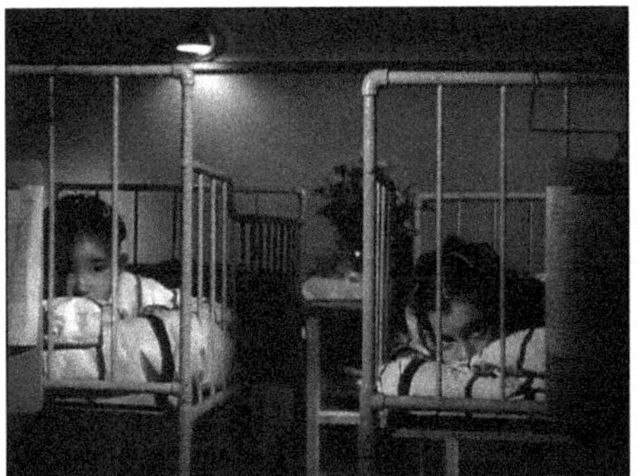

Figure 12

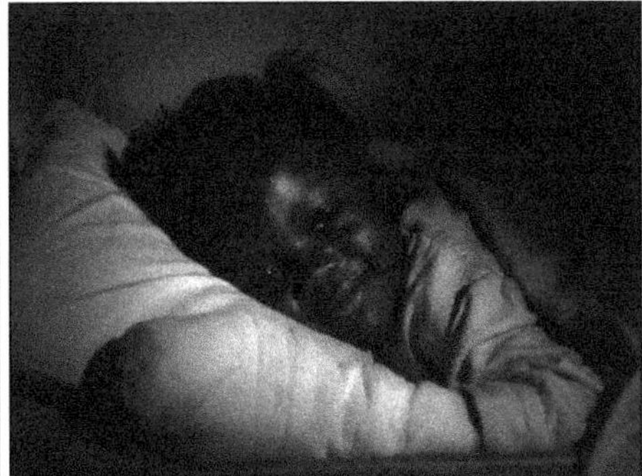

Figure 13

in the play, and is almost certainly the product of Stevens, whose anti-racist views were now well known within the industry. Though whether it served to articulate a more inclusive counterpoint to its otherwise all-white milieu is perhaps a matter of opinion.

Thomas Schatz relates *I Remember Mama* to a post-war cycle of domestic comedy-dramas such as *Easy to Wed* (1946), *Life with Father* and *The Egg and I* (both 1947), *Sitting Pretty* (1948), and *Mother Is a Freshman* and *Ma and Pa Kettle* (both 1949), all of which proved popular at the box-office.[14] *I Remember Mama* earned $3.06 million, but cost $3.068 million to make and never broke even. However its popularity was undimmed, and in addition to the *Lux Theatre* version aired on 30 August 1948, 'in 1949 a serial about the Hansen family called *Mama* ... became one of the first family situations comedies to air on television'.[15] This 'television *Mama* developed a large and devoted audience and remained in the same time slot (Friday nights, from 8.00 to 8.30) with the same sponsorship (General Foods, Maxwell House Coffee) on the same night network (CBS) from July 1949 to July 1956.'[16] But the television *Mama* was not the final spin off, for on 31 May 1979 producers Alexander H. Cohen and Hildy Parks opened a stage-musical version of *I Remember Mama* at the Majestic Theatre on Broadway.

Following difficulties in its tryouts in Philadelphia, which involved 40 different previews, this version ran for a total 108 performances, with a book by Thomas Meehan, lyrics by Martin Charnin and Raymond Jessel, music by Richard Rodgers, stage direction by Cy Feuer, set design by David Mitchell, and a cast that included Liv Ullmann as Mama, George Hearn as Papa, George S. Irving as Uncle Chris, Elizabeth Hubbard as Aunt Trina, and Carrie Horner as Christine (Katrin in the novel, play and film). The difficulties and problems that marked this musical version have been documented in detail by Geoffrey Block in his book on Richard Rodgers. They include the tryouts and changes of personnel, the fact that Ullmann could neither sing nor dance, and the fact Meehan 'developed the idea of creating a marital and family conflict at the end of the first act. In Meehan's scenario, Papa leaves his family without consultation to take a job in Norway, but Mama and the children refuse to join him there' and in this way the 'principal conflict is thus poverty and joblessness rather than character and personality'.[17] In the meantime, Chris is 'quick to help Dagmar get to the hospital for her appendicitis' as in the play, but in the musical 'Chris dies embittered, having squandered his wealth'.[18] Block also draws attention to the simplicity of Rodgers' melodies, most of which were 'written either for children or for an actress could not sing' and which were marked by 'narrow ranges', avoiding 'extremes of high and low'.[19] And according to Block, Clive Barnes was the only critic who praised it.[20]

Notes

1. Judith E. Smith, *Visions of Belonging: Family Stories, Popular Culture, and Postwar Democracy, 1940–1960* (New York: Columbia University Press, 2004), pp. 75–106.
2. John Van Druten was born in Britain in 1901 and died as a US citizen in 1957. The plays he wrote in Britain included *London Wall* (1931), *There's Always Juliet* (1931) and *Flowers of the Forest* (1934). He emigrated to the USA in the late 1930s, where he wrote *Leave Her to Heaven* (1940) and *The Voice of the Turtle* (1943). He became a US citizen in 1944 and went to write *Bell, Book and Candle* (1950) and the stage-play version of *I Am a Camera* (1951).
3. *Variety*, 22 November 1941, p. 1. See also, *Variety*, 19 April 1948, p. 2.
4. Jenkins' design can also be found alongside an article and a suite of stage photographs of *I Remember Mama* in *Life* magazine, vol. 17 no. 21, 20 November 1944, pp. 104–106, and 109.
5. Smith, *Visions of Belonging*, p. 85.
6. Smith, *Visions of Belonging*, p. 88.
7. According to the entry on *I Remember Mama* in the AFI Catalog, 'Parsons received an onscreen producing credit with director George Stevens because of her significant contributions to the final film.'
8. Other candidates for the role of Mama were Greta Garbo, who turned it down, and Marlene Dietrich, who was eventually considered unsuitable.
9. Marilyn Ann Moss, *Giant: George Stevens, a Life in Film* (Madison: University of Wisconsin Press, 2004), pp. 123–125. See also, Thomas Schatz, *Boom and Bust: American Cinema in the 1940s* (New York: Scribner, 1997), pp. 347–351.
10. Smith, *Visions of Belonging*, p. 96.
11. David Bordwell, 'Classical narration', in Bordwell, Staiger and Thompson, *The Classical Hollywood Cinema*, pp. 25–29.
12. Although Moss draws attention to the ways in which camera lingers on the features of the house and its layout in her chapter on *The Diary of Anne Frank* (1957) in *Giant*, pp. 256–257, she makes no mention of them in her chapter on *I Remember Mama*.
13. Smith, *Visions of Belonging*, pp. 90–93.
14. Schatz, *Boom and Bust*, p. 350.
15. Smith, *Visions of Belonging*, p. 98.
16. Smith, *Visions of Belonging*, p. 98.
17. Geoffrey Block, *Richard Rodgers* (New Haven and London: Yale University Press, 2003), p. 243.
18. Block, *Richard Rodgers*, p. 243.
19. Block, *Richard Rodgers*, p. 243.
20. Clive Barnes, 'Liv & Rodgers Will Make You Remember Mama', *New York Times*, 1 June 1979, reprinted in *New York Critics' Reviews*, vol. 40, pp. 229–230, and cited in Block, *Richard Rodgers*, p. 290, note 90.

Chapter 11

Dial M for Murder

Dial M for Murder was directed by Alfred Hitchcock and initially released in the US in 1954. Having been turned down by seven London theatre producers, it began life as a 90-minute television play by Frederick Knott, which was broadcast live on the BBC on 23 March 1952, which garnered rave reviews, and which was re-enacted live the following week as videotape recording was not yet available. Despite its success on television, Knott sold the film rights to Sir Alexander Korda for a mere £1000 and seems to have considered that the play would never be staged. But James P. Sherwood, a stage producer with a lease on the Westminster Theatre in London, had to cancel the production of another play and asked to produce *Dial M for Murder* instead. And 'after less than three weeks' rehearsal',[1] it opened to critical acclaim on 19 June 1952 under the direction of John Fernald, with Jane Baxter as Sheila Wendice, Alan MacNaughtan as Max Halliday, Emrys Jones as Tony Wendice, Olaf Pooley as Captain Lesgate (also known as C.A. Swann), and Andrew Cruickshank as Inspector Hubbard. At this point Maurice Evans, a well-known British actor who now lived and worked in the US, either saw the London production or 'read the play when he and Jones were at the same house party', and offered to star as Tony Wendice in a stage-play version on Broadway.[2] Having acquired the film rights, Korda 'had a clause barring future live productions until the movie came out'. But as Evans was about to start work on *The Story of Gilbert and Sullivan* (1953) he was able to persuade Korda to waive the proviso regarding a film release,[3] and having acquired the rights to present the play in the US, the New York version opened on 29 October 1952. This version was produced by Sherwood and directed by Reginald Denham. It ran for a total of 552 performances, first at the Plymouth Theatre then at the Booth Theatre, with Maurice Evans as Tony Wendice and Gusti Huber as Margot Wendice (the change of name should be noted and is discussed later on), and with Richard Derr as Max Halliday, Anthony Dawson as Captain Lesgate, and John Williams as Inspector Hubbard, and it was here, at the Booth, that it closed on 27 February 1954, a few months prior to the film's premiere at the Randolph Theatre in Philadelphia on 18 May.[4]

Born in Hankow, China, Knott was the son of missionaries, and his introduction to the theatre came through the Hankow Operatic Society and its performances of Gilbert and Sullivan. In 1926, his parents sent him to Oundle boarding school and on to Cambridge University, where he proved to be 'an exceptionally fine tennis player', playing for the Cambridge-Oxford tennis team against the Harvard-Yale team at Newport in 1937 prior to becoming an instructor in signals in the Artillery in World War Two.[5] 'In 1947 he joined the Rank Organisation as a trainee screenwriter and became a member of the Associate Branch of the (British) Screenwriters, of which he was elected chairman for 1950',[6] and the following year he adapted a story by James Hadley Chase for Hammer Film Productions. At this point, Hammer and Exclusive (Hammer's distribution wing) signed a mutual distribution agreement with Robert Lippert in the US, and Knott's adaptation was released in the early months of 1952 and entitled *Blonde Blackmail* and *Man Bait* in the US and *The Last Page* in Britain. But by then Knott had severed his links with Hammer and had completed the first draft of the stage-play version of *Dial M for Murder*, and the eventual success of *Dial M for Murder*, which 'was produced in over thirty countries and was translated into twenty-five languages',[7] led to three more plays and two more film adaptations. The first of these plays was *Mr Fox of Venice*, which premiered on the London stage on 15 April 1959, and which formed part of the basis of a film entitled *The Honey Pot* (1967); the second was *Write Me a Murder*, which was produced at the Belasco Theatre in New York and which ran for 196 performances from 24 October 1961 to 14 April 1962, but was never filmed; and the third was *Wait Until Dark*, which premiered at the Ethel Barrymore Theatre in New York in 1966, which ran for 373 performances at various New York venues, and which was filmed by Warner Bros-Seven Arts in 1967 with Audrey Hepburn as the lead. Like *Wait Until Dark*, *Dial M for Murder* focussed on an attempt to murder a young woman, and in this respect it echoed several previous Hitchcock films, among them *Shadow of a Doubt* (1943) and *Strangers on a Train* (1951).[8] And as we shall see, while the central female character in the play and film versions of *Dial M for Murder* is almost killed, she is also 'guilty' of having had an affair with another man, and along with her husband's plan to inherit her money, this is the ostensible motive for his plan to have her murdered.[9]

The Play

Before summarising the stage play, it is important to note some of the differences between the original British and US versions and their subsequent editions. Knott's play was originally copyrighted in 1952 as an unpublished work then published in acting editions in 1953 by Random House and in 1953 and 1954 by the Dramatists Play Service and Samuel French in the US, prior to the publication of a revised acting edition by Samuel French in Britain in 1955. In the London version of the play, the name of the heroine in peril is Sheila. But in the New York version her name is specified as Margot, and this is explained in a passage from Knott's obituary in *The Independent*: 'Evans ... praised Knott's ready acceptance to make minor changes to the play to accommodate American tastes and colloquialisms. The secret with which the villain blackmails an old school chum was changed from misappropriation of school funds to drug peddling, and since the M in the title refers to the villain's phone exchange, Maida Vale, which would mean nothing to American audiences, the heroine's name was changed to Margot'.[10] As we shall see, there was another change of name in the film version, which substitutes Mark for Max, but in the interim what follows is a summary of the US version.

The play consists of three acts, all of which are set in the living room of a ground-floor London apartment. Act One begins at 'about 6.20 p.m. on a Friday evening in September' and the second an hour later. As the curtain rises, Margot and Max are sat on the sofa. Margot hears a noise in the passage outside, goes out to investigate, then returns. 'For a moment I thought it was Tony', she says. Max is an American writer of murder mysteries for television and Margot's former lover. And Tony is Margot's husband and a former tennis player who has decided to become a salesman. Now that Tony has settled down, Margot's marriage appears to be back on track. But one of the love letters written during the course of Max and Margot's affair has been stolen, and Margot is now being blackmailed for money. Tony enters and is introduced to Max by Margot. Tony and Max are due to go to the theatre together, but Tony says that he has to write a report for his boss and suggests that Margot go with Max instead. While Margot is getting ready, Tony invites Max to a nearby stag party in a hotel the following evening. Tony informs Margot, and Max and Margot depart. Then Tony draws the curtains, looks thoughtfully at the telephone, and 'lifts the receiver and dials'. Calling himself Fisher, Tony asks for a Captain Lesgate, who confirms that he has a car for sale. Tony says that he would like to discuss the price of the car in person but has twisted his knee and is unable to go out. He invites Lesgate to Tony's Maida Vale flat instead, and as the first scene in Act One ends, Lesgate assents.

Act One Scene Two begins an hour later. Tony enters from the bedroom carrying a suit-case and 'surveys the room'. Then he places a pair of gloves on the arm of the sofa and crosses the room as the door-bell rings. Affecting a limp and walking with a cane, Tony opens the hall door and invites Lesgate in, takes off his overcoat and puts it on a coat rack, ushers him into living room, and invites him to sit on the sofa. 'Tony limps to the drink shelf' and Lesgate says that 'I can't help thinking I've seen you somewhere', and it emerges that they had been at Cambridge University together, and that Lesgate was really a fellow student called C.A. Swann. Lesgate says that he intends to drive a hard bargain for the car, and Tony takes down a picture of Lesgate at a reunion dinner and reminds him of the fact that nearly a hundred pounds of ticket money was stolen. Lesgate says that the money disappeared overnight and Tony says that the college porter was blamed despite the fact that the money was never found. Tony and Lesgate talk about tennis, and Tony discusses the fact that he married for money. Then Tony turns to the topic of his wife, to the fact she had an affair with another man, to the letters they exchanged with one another, and to the fact that Tony stole one of these letters from Margot's handbag, tried to blackmail her, and was 'actually planning to murder her' when he happened to attend a reunion dinner and recall Lesgate's more recent misdemeanours. These misdemeanours are numerous and sordid and include the death of a 'middle-aged woman found dead due to an overdose of cocaine', and in the light of these circumstances, Lesgate considers Tony's offer of a thousand pounds and agrees to undertake the murder of Margot, and Tony drops his limp.

Tony says that the murder must take place the following evening because he and Max will be at a party and his wife will be at home. He goes on to explain that Lesgate should 'enter the house by the street door' and that he will 'find a key to the flat under the stair carpet'. On entering the apartment, he should cross the room to the window and hide behind the curtains. 'At exactly twenty-three minutes to eleven I shall go to the telephone in the hotel to ring a friend', says Tony. 'I shall dial the wrong number – this number ... When the phone rings you'll see the light go on under the bedroom door'. When Margot opens the door 'the light will stream across the room, so don't move until she picks up the phone ... When you've finished – pick up the phone and give me a soft whistle. Then hang up'. Tony continues, directing Lesgate to tip the clothes in the suit case onto the floor as this will give the impression that this is not a premeditated murder but a burglary that went badly wrong, and to open the French window but leave by the front door, putting the key back under the stair carpet as he does so. Margot calls to confirm that the party is going well, and Lesgate checks the windows, lights and curtains. Tony ends the phone call with 'Bye sweet – enjoy yourself', then Lesgate pauses, picks up the bank notes and places them in his inside pocket, and Tony responds with a satisfied smile.

Act Two Scene One is set on Saturday evening. Margot and Max are looking at press cuttings, and Max and Tony are dressed for dinner. Tony says it is time to leave. He also says that he cannot find his latch key and Sheila leaves the room to look for it. Tony unlocks the French windows, Margot is unable to find Tony's key, and Tony asks to borrow hers. Margot says that she may want to go out and Tony 'suddenly goes sullen'. But Margot gives in and agrees to deal with the cuttings, placing the scissors on the desk as Max and Tony leave.

Act Two Scene Two takes place later that evening. Margot has finished with the cuttings and left them in the album on the desk. Her handbag is still on the table near the sofa as Lesgate enters, takes off his scarf, and knots it. He crosses to the French windows, and as the phone begins to ring, he hides behind the curtain. Margot enters from the bedroom and picks up the phone, and at this point Lesgate attempts to strangle her with his scarf. However Margot grabs the scissors on the desk and stabs him, then speaks into the phone: 'Tony, come back at once. A man attacked me ... Tried to strangle me ... No, I won't do anything ... please be quick'. When Tony enters, he 'stares at the body, then at Margot's handbag ... He takes the key out of the door, puts the key in his raincoat pocket and quietly closes the door'. He also looks at Lesgate's body, turns it over, and sees the scissors in his back. Margot enters and asks Tony why he phoned, and Tony says that he'll tell her later and phones the police. Margot enters the bedroom and Tony picks up Lesgate's scarf, puts it in his pocket and places a stocking on the stool near the sofa. Then he takes Max's letter to Margot from his wallet 'and is about to put it in Lesgate's pocket' as the curtain falls.

Act Two Scene Three takes place the following morning. Tony tells Margot that an inquest is likely to take place soon. He also tells her that he told the police that she did not call them because she assumed that Tony would ring them from the hotel. Margot is puzzled but agrees to corroborate Tony's story, and at this point Detective Inspector Hubbard arrives in the passage outside. Hubbard explores the flat while Tony confirms that he was at a nearby party, that he called Margot on the telephone at the very moment she was attacked, and that the subsequent phone call to the police took place at precisely three minutes to eleven. Margot asks Hubbard whether he knows who her assailant was, and Hubbard replies that he and his men have discovered where he lived, but that there 'seems to be some confusion as to his real name'. Hubbard shows Margot a pair of photos of her assailant, but Margot is unable to identify him because she never actually saw him. Tony says that he recognises her assailant from his school days, and as Hubbard lists the assailant's names, Tony recognises the name of Swann and tells Hubbard that he saw Swann at Victoria Station several months ago.

Margot recounts her antagonist's attack, Hubbard asks her whether the curtains were closed and the window locked, and Tony supports Margot's account that this was indeed the case. Hubbard is puzzled and announces that as 'a matter of fact we're quite certain he came in by the door'. Given that there were only two keys, and given that Margot had one and Tony the other, there seems to be no explanation for the lack of marks on the carpet that would have been produced by Lesgate had he entered from the garden. Tony has to provide an explanation, and in doing so he recalls that Margot may have lost her key when her bag was stolen. Hubbard turns to Margot, who remembers the theft and that all the money in her bag had gone, but says that there were no missing letters and that her key was still in the bag when it was returned. Hubbard is perplexed: it looks as though Sheila's assailant may have had something to do with the bag theft after all.

Max enters and confirms that he was with Tony the previous night. He also expresses surprise that Tony was on the phone to Margot when her assailant attacked her. Tony explains that he could not recall a friend's phone number and that he had phoned Margot to remind him what it was. Margot is as surprised as Max and Hubbard, and at this point Hubbard prepares to leave with Tony and Margot in order to take down their statements. As Tony heads for the hall door, Hubbard tells Max that he is aware that Max wrote a letter to Margot and that he himself found it on her assailant. Tony returns and exits through the French windows, leaving Hubbard to suggest to Max and Margot that they have been subject to blackmail and that they must tell him 'exactly what you know about this man and exactly what happened last night. If you try and conceal anything at all it may put you in a very serious position'. Tony re-enters from the garden and makes his presence felt when Hubbard suggests that there appear to be no witnesses. 'But I heard it all', says Tony. 'What I heard was perfectly consistent with what my wife told me'. Hubbard, however, is not convinced: 'You suggest that this man came to burgle your flat – but there's no evidence of that. There is evidence, however, that he was blackmailing you ... You suggest that he came in by the window – and we know came in [he points to the hall door] by that door'. Margot is troubled: 'That door was locked, and there are only two keys ... My husband has his with him and mine was in my handbag.' Hubbard replies that she could have let him in and caused the bruises on her throat herself. Tony responds by ringing his solicitor, and Margot is bewildered. 'Tony gives a brief glance around the room. He is now in complete control of the situation. He puts his hands in his pocket and follows Hubbard out'.

Act Three takes place in the flat a few months later. Tony is packing as the announcer on the radio reports that Margot Wendice has been found guilty of murder and that a reprieve has been turned down. The door bell rings and Max enters. Max is desperate, and as a writer of murder stories, he has a plan, a plan that means Tony would 'have to tell the police that you hired Swann to murder her'. There is a long pause. Then Max continues: 'Swann is dead. You can tell any story you like about him ... That you'd met him, and worked out the whole thing together. Now the blackmail. Swann was only suspected of blackmail for two reasons. Because my letter was found in his pocket and because you saw him the day Sheila's bag was stolen ... That the whole thing was an invention of yours to try and connect him with the letter.' Max's story contains much of the truth. But the irony mounts further when Max suggests that Tony confess to planning the murder, that he would only get a few years in prison, and that Margot's life could therefore be saved. At this point Max and Tony hear footsteps in the hallway and Hubbard arrives. Hubbard he says that there is no news about Margot, and that he is making enquiries in connection with a robbery. He also says that in circumstances such this the police are asked to keep an eye out for anyone spending large sums of money, and that it appears that Tony recently settled an account for just over sixty pounds in cash. Tony explainss. But Hubbard seems to be distracted and stops and picks up a latch key. Tony feels in his raincoat pocket and takes out his key, and Hubbard tries to put the other key in the door, finds that it doesn't fit, and says that it must be his: 'That's the trouble with keys', he says, 'they're all alike'.

Hubbard goes on to say that he knows that Tony recently spent a hundred pounds, and Tony replies that he 'won rather a large sum at dog racing'. Hubbard's questioning appears to have come to an end, but as he moves to the hall he asks whether Tony has 'a small fibre attaché case'. Tony is shaken. He claims that he left the case in a taxi. But Max says that he has seen it in the bedroom, leads Tony and Hubbard to it, prises it open, and reveals numerous bundles of bank notes. Hubbard turns to Tony, who explains that Max has been concocting a story involving Tony, blackmail, money, latch keys, and attempted murder. Max is frantic: Margot is due to hang and it appears that Hubbard is neither willing nor able to intervene. Max departs in anger and Tony turns to Hubbard, who tells Tony that Max's story would never be believed, and that Tony can pick up his wife's possessions from the police station. Hubbard secretly exchanges his raincoat with Tony's then exits by the hall door. Tony picks up his case, takes Hubbard's raincoat, and leaves. But following a pause, the sound of a key in the hall-door lock is followed by the sight of Hubbard, who re-enters, lifts the telephone receiver, and tells his men to 'Start the ball rolling'.

We are now nearing the play's denouement. Max returns and is startled by the presence of Hubbard, and at this point sounds of a street door opening and footsteps in the passage are followed by the sound of someone trying but failing to insert a key in the lock. There is a moment of silence, then the door-bell rings. 'The footsteps move away and the sound of the street door is heard'. 'You'd better prepare yourself for surprise', says Hubbard, and at this point Sheila enters by the French windows and asks where Tony is. Hubbard says that they are not sure where Tony is. He also appears to think that Margot should know why her key does not work. But this turns out to be a ruse that confirms Margot's innocence and Tony's guilt. Hubbard fills in the details of Tony's plans, and on hearing footsteps in the hall and further footsteps as the person leaves, Hubbard is informed by his men outside that this person is Tony. When Tony fails to open the street door yet again, this time using Margot's key, he realises that the key he took from Lesgate's body was Lesgate's, so he checks under the stairway carpet, retrieves the key he took from Margot's handbag, and unlocks the door. On finding Hubbard, Max and Margot waiting inside, Tony acknowledges that his scheme has failed and congratulates Hubbard on solving the case.

Billed as a melodrama (i.e. as a thriller), *Dial M for Murder* was a phenomenal success. In addition to layers of knowledge, ignorance and irony, intricate motifs (notably locked and unlocked doors and windows, and telephone calls, latch keys and the sounds they make), and instances of foregrounding help bind the play together, providing it with wit and humour as well as suspense. Along with a heroine in peril, these are the very qualities that Hitchcock prized, so it is no wonder that he was keen to direct the film version. Having had recent successes with Warner Bros., he turned to them again, and Warner Bros. proved keen not only to secure the rights, nor only to produce the film in colour, but to film it in 3-D and provide both 3-D prints and 'flat' ones.[11]

The Film

Hitchcock's film was shot in 36 days between 30 July and the second week of October 1953 at the Warner Bros. studios in California,[12] where Dimitri Tiomkin, who had earlier composed the music for *Shadow of a Doubt* (1943), *Strangers on a Train* (1951) and *I Confess* (1952), went on to write the score. Also billed as a melodrama in *Daily Variety*'s review,[13] the names of Max and Margot were changed to Mark and Margot, which not only produced a partially homophonic repetition consonant with their compatibility, but that also generated a repetition of the letter 'M' in the names of the Mark and Margot as well as in the title of the film. Much of the dialogue was transferred from the play verbatim. (Knott himself was credited as the writer of the screenplay).[14] And aside from minor adjustments to the layout of the apartment and the insertion of several exterior shots and mini sequences designed to 'open out' the film, and aside from minor verbal changes and deletions, the only significant addition is the courtroom scene in which Margot (Grace Kelly) is found guilty of murder and sentenced to death.

The first of the exterior sequences consists of a shot of a policeman outside the Wendice apartment followed by a reverse angle, which dollies in as the policeman exits right and as an apparently happy couple of a similar age to Tony and Margot walk by. On cutting to a close-up of the exterior door, we dissolve to a shot of Margot and Tony (Ray Milland) kissing one another somewhat perfunctorily at the breakfast table as they turn to read a newspaper (in Margot's case) and a letter (in the case of Tony). As Sheldon Hall points out, a similar shot of the policeman ends the film, and the equivalent of Act Two Scene Three begins with the self-same policeman 'shooing away spectators come to gawk at the place of the crime'.[15] The 'symmetry of these shots is matched by the first and last shots of the introductory montage' and by 'Tony's first and last acts (pouring himself a drink) in the action proper', and the montage itself comprises 'three short vignettes establishing the affair between Margot and Tony which has prompted Tony's murder plan'.[16] The first consists of shots of Tony and Margot at breakfast, which includes an insert item in Margot's newspaper announcing that mystery-writer Mark Halliday is among 'the passengers on board the Queen Mary arriving in Southampton today', and which is followed by 'Margot's furtive glance at Tony'.[17] The second consists of three shots separated by a pair of dissolves as we witness the Queen Mary sailing into the harbour, the Queen Mary docked, and Mark (Robert Cummings) stepping out on deck and into the foreground. And the third begins with a close up of Mark and Margot in a passionate embrace at the Wendice flat, which leads on to a lengthy conversation scene.

Elsewhere there is a 'brief, wordless sequence at the crime scene' when the police arrive; 'two short montage sequences and the elaboration, through cross-cutting with Tony at the stag night, of the murder attempt on Margot'; a brief exterior sequence showing Lesgate (Anthony Dawson) waiting for an opportunity to enter the flat on the night of the murder;[18] and a shot of the inner mechanisms of a telephone clicking into gear as Tony dials the flat from the stag-night venue.[19] Later on, there is a cut back to Tony when Margot speaks to him on the phone following the killing of Lesgate; a further two-shot sequence at the stag party (in which Tony explains that he has to leave but insists that Mark should stay); and, following a cut back to Margot, a shot of Tony in the back of a cab on his way to the flat. On arrival, we cut back and forth between Tony and a policeman on duty at the police station as the former informs the latter that there has been a killing, and at a point subsequent to Margot's trial, there are shots of a taxi arriving in the street, Tony in the back seat, Tony's point of view, his abortive attempt to open the street door, and another shot showing him in the back of a cab as it drives away. And finally, once Hubbard (John Williams) has cleared Margot of wrongdoing and honed in on Tony as the villain, a series of shots of Mark outside the flat waiting for Tony's return and subsequent comeuppance.[20]

Meanwhile, the use of colour in the courtroom sequence is particularly striking. Advertised as WarnerColor, the process used in the production of the film and its subsequent prints was a variant of Technicolor, which was adapted for 3-D filming by using 'three strip cameras with "selsyn" interlock motors that enabled them to photograph the dual strip image for dye transfer 3-D prints'.[21] This process added sharpness to the colour, and by 1954 'dye transfer prints derived from color negatives had a grain-free appearance', and these qualities were exemplified in *Dial M for Murder*, which was photographed by cinematographer Robert Burks (the cameraman on all bar one of Hitchcock's films from 1951 to 1966).[22] The courtroom sequence itself consists of three medium head-on close-ups, two of Margot, the other of a judge, who is handed the black cap worn when passing the death sentence. The initial close-up of Margot is a single shot. But as it proceeds, it comes to represent a condensed version of Margot's trial as a series of court officials and jurors voice the factors that lead to a guilty verdict, as Margot gazes at the camera in silence then turns her head to left and right as she responds mutely to their accusations, and as a set of modulated coloured lights intensify her predicament. Dressed in a suit and facing head on, Margot is at first shot in relatively even blue light against a featureless blue background (figure 1). But as the voices begin, the lights dim and the colours darken. Shadow appears, and a mix of orange and yellow light begins to play on Margot's face, and as the colours darken further, the left-hand side of her face is plunged further into shadow as the yellows on the right intensify. Then as a deep red pervades most of the image, Margot's sentence is finally read out. We hear a stentorian off-screen voice intoning the words 'guilty or not guilty?' and this is followed by the voice of the jury foreman, who delivers a guilty verdict. Then we cut to the judge, who is evenly and brightly lit, and who is wearing a bright red gown with a black shawl and an equally bright white trim. The black-clad arms of the court official enter the frame and place the cap on the judge's head. Then the judge pronounces Margot's death sentence, and we return to the close-up of Margot, who is now lit in a deep and garish red as she realises her fate (figure 2), and as the image darkens and fades to black.

Less obvious uses are made of colour elsewhere, but they are all equally telling. In the breakfast scene Margot is wearing a white dress and Tony a dark blue suit, thus echoing the colours worn by the passing couple, the man with dark hair and a dark blue suit like Tony, and the woman with blonde hair like Margot and a light grey coat similar to the colour of Margot's dress in the opening two-shot vignette (figures 3 and 4). On cutting to the last shot in the Queen Mary's arrival, Mark is wearing a light grey suit. But when we subsequently cut to Mark and Margot kissing passionately in the Wendice flat, Margot is no longer wearing a white dress but a revealing vibrant red one, and as the couple embrace again, we cut to a shot of their shadows on the door (figure 5). Elsewhere, Margot wears a white negligee in the murder scene and a grey-blue dress the following day (and, indeed, for most of the remaining scenes in which she features), and the other principal colour motif is the prominence of yellow light in the scene between Tony and Lesgate and the subsequent murder scene.[23]

These aspects of the film's style have rarely been noted, the use of colour being largely

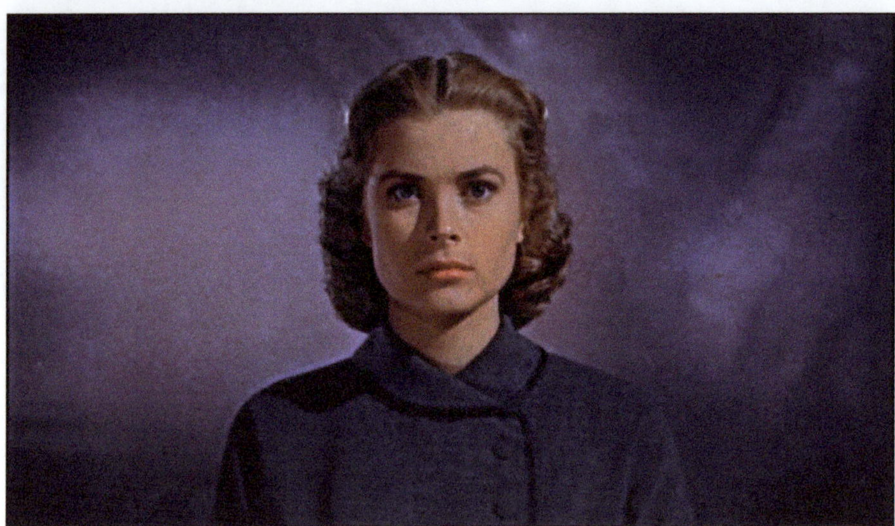

Figure 1

ignored in favour of a focus on 3-D. But the effects of 3-D are clearly important, serving as they do to articulate filmic space via camera shots and camera movements and the patterns of alignment, allegiance and 'identification' with which they intersect.[24] Here Hall provides an overall account, noting the relationship between the 3-D elements alongside other aspects of style and narration. He points out that 'the degree of character identification involved is partial, variable and intermittent', noting that the characters played by Grace Kelly, John Williams and Anthony Dawson 'are ...

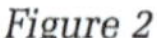

Figure 2

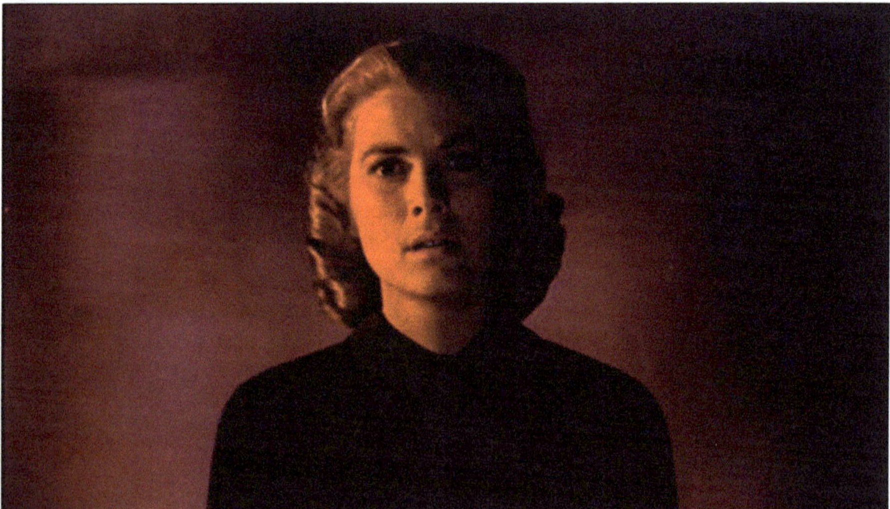

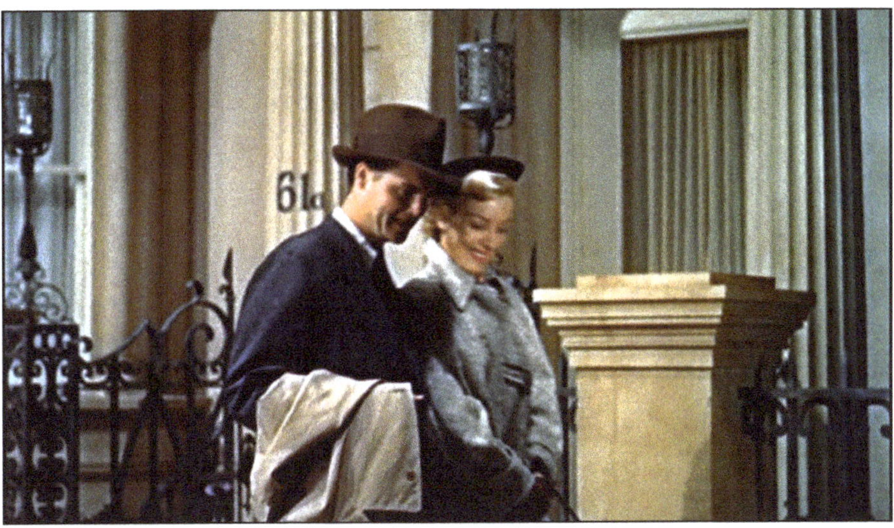

Figure 3

granted the audience's allegiance, in various degrees, at strategic moments'.[25] And in addition, and although we are largely aligned with Tony in the scene with Lesgate, we are also aligned with the latter at various points and moments, and both men are occasionally framed together. Whether we grant allegiance to either of them is perhaps a matter of debate. (There are moments in the film that encourage partial allegiance to Tony, notably in the shot in which he successfully retrieves Lesgate's key from the

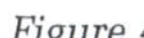

Figure 4

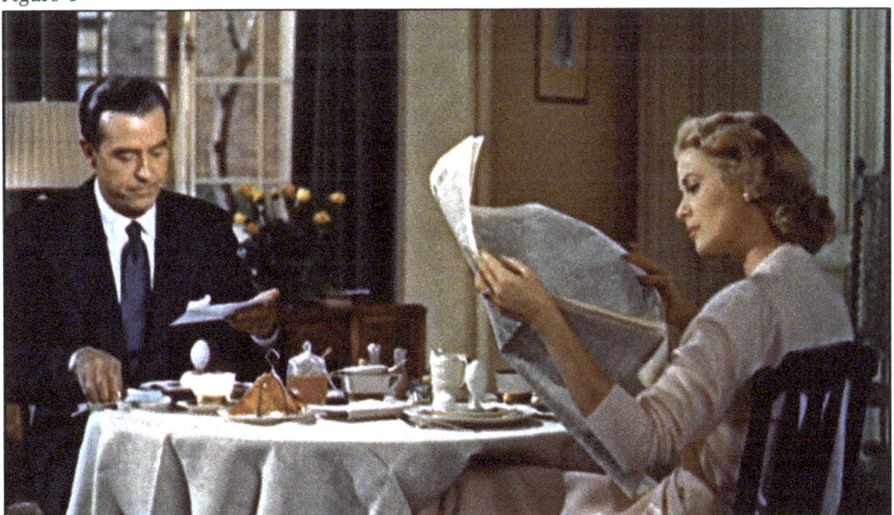

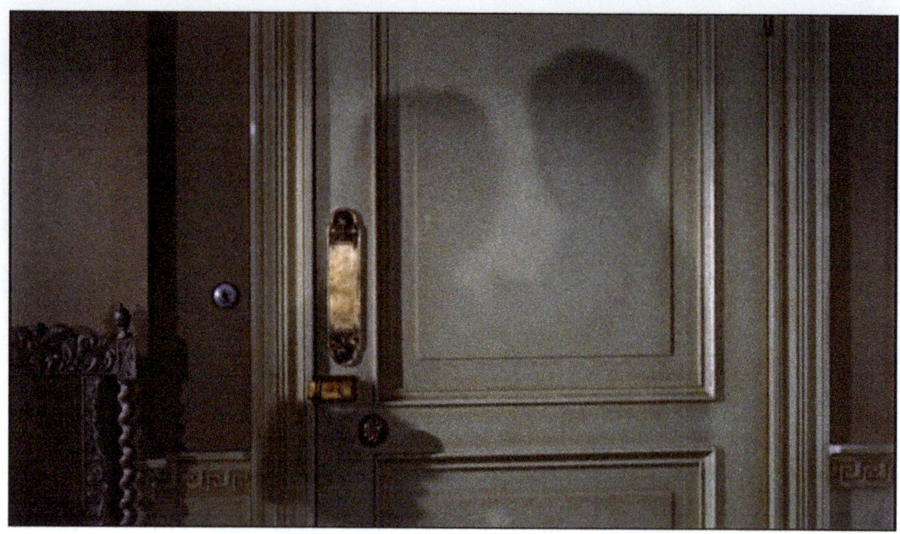

Figure 5

under the stair carpet). But we surely grant unalloyed allegiance to Margot and Hubbard whenever they appear.

Hall goes on to pinpoint several instances and aspects of 3-D, beginning with the conversation scene between Mark and Margot after Mark's disembarkation from the Queen Mary. As this scene proceeds, the protrusive effects generated by 3-D are usually anchored around items of decor, among them three jade-green lamps, each of which are placed on ledges or tables, a small vase of white and yellow flowers on a

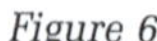

Figure 6

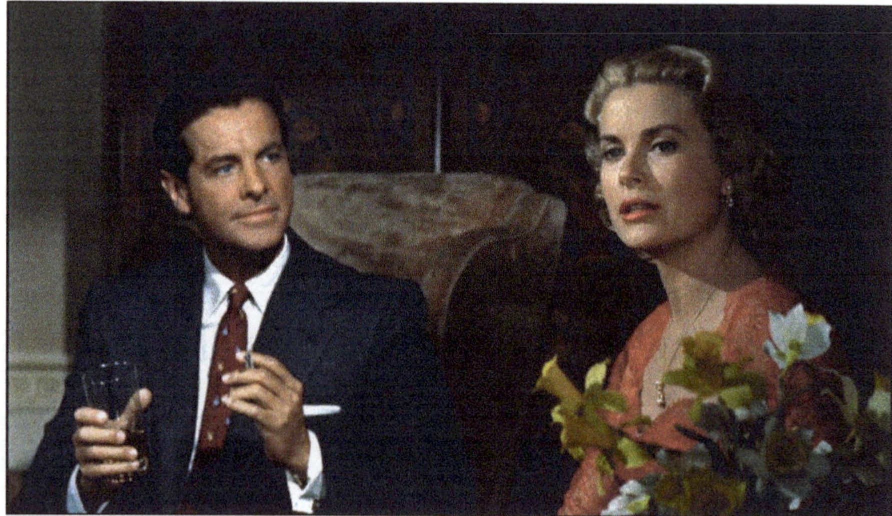

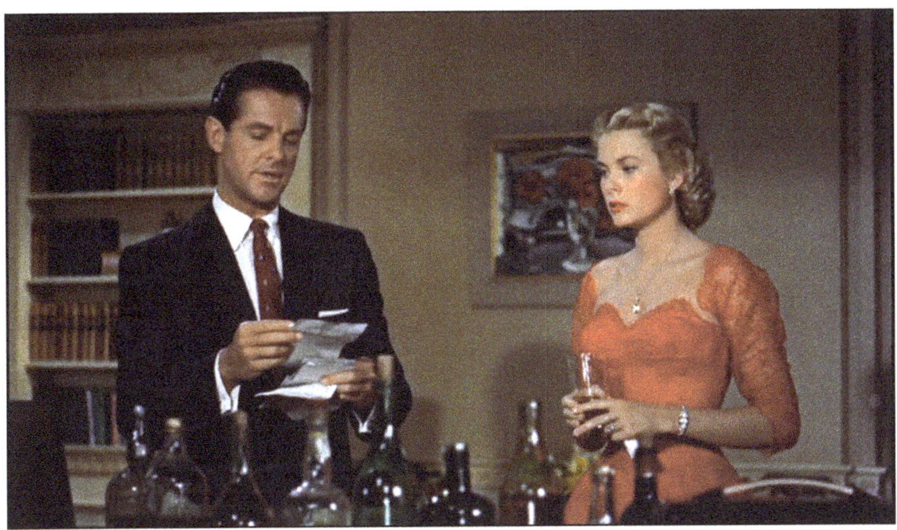

Figure 7

side-table next to Margot, and a prominent set of bottles arrayed across the screen in the foreground (figures 6 and 7). Some of these items are visible in the scene between Mark and Lesgate (the white and yellow flowers have disappeared and only one of the vases is prominent). But along with the addition of the telephone and a multi-coloured vase on the desk, most of these items are similar to those in the scene between Mark and Margot.[26] Perhaps the most striking shots, however, comprise a pair of panoramic shots filmed in high-angle, the first in moving long shot as Mark moves back and

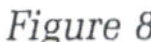

Figure 8

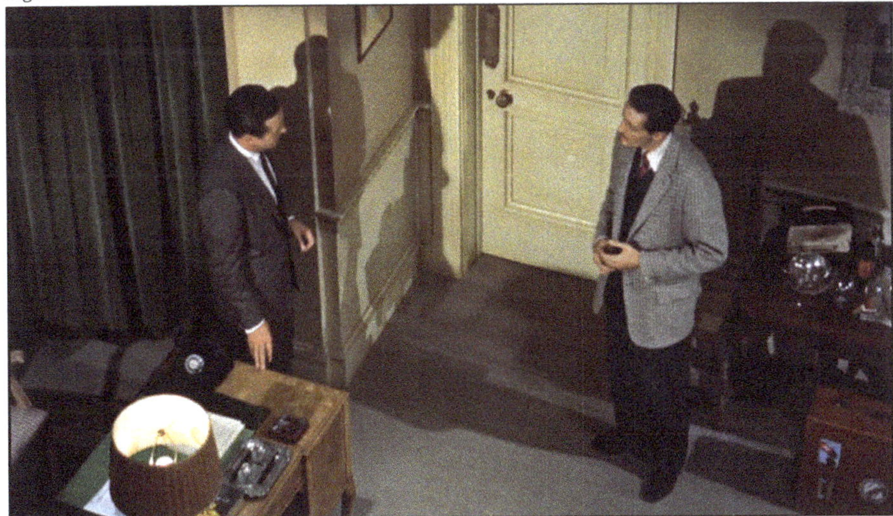

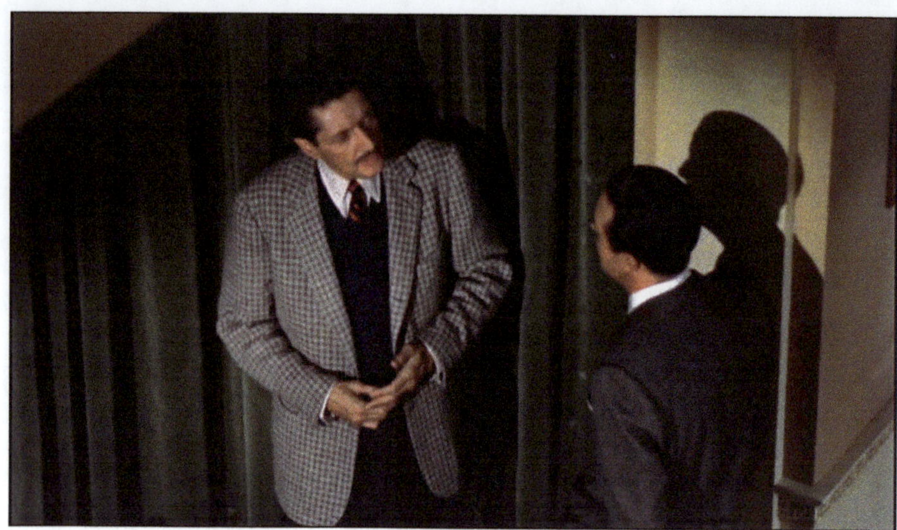

Figure 9

forth, demonstrating the whereabouts of various crucial items and the movements Lesgate must undertake (figure 8), the second a closer view tracking Mark and Lesgate as Mark continues his instructions to Lesgate (figure 9), both of which are occasionally interspersed by closer shots and edits. And as Hall points out, these high-position shots anticipate 'a later shot, just before the intermission, in which we are shown the aftermath of the crime as the police examine the flat for evidence'. Here the 'camera cranes down and cuts to a pair of close-ups, linked by a reaction shot of Tony placing

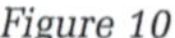

Figure 10

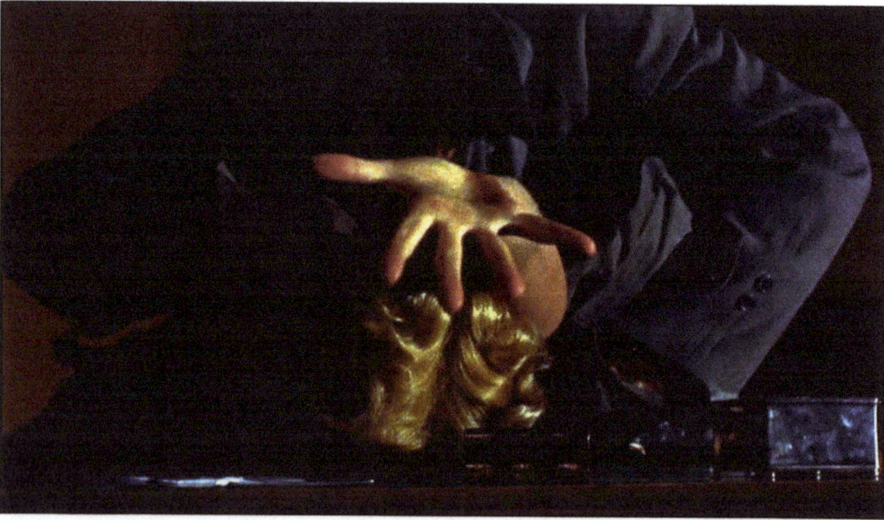

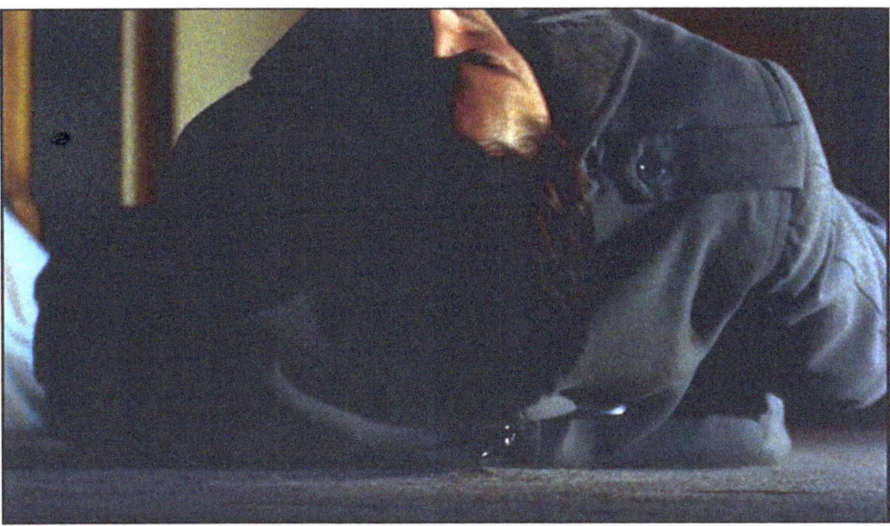

Figure 11

a tea tray on the writing desk by the window, nudging the blotter to reveal the spare stocking with which he hopes to incriminate Margot in Lesgate's death'.[27]

Later on, 3-D close-ups of keys play an important part in underlining the latchkey motif,[28] while the earlier scene of Margot's would-be murder includes gestures and bodies protruding into what Miriam Ross calls 'hyper-haptic' foreground space as Margot's arm reaches out and as Lesgate is stabbed by Margot's scissors and falls to the floor, thereby enhancing the sense of 3-D's tactility (figures 10 and 11).[29] The

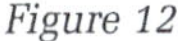

Figure 12

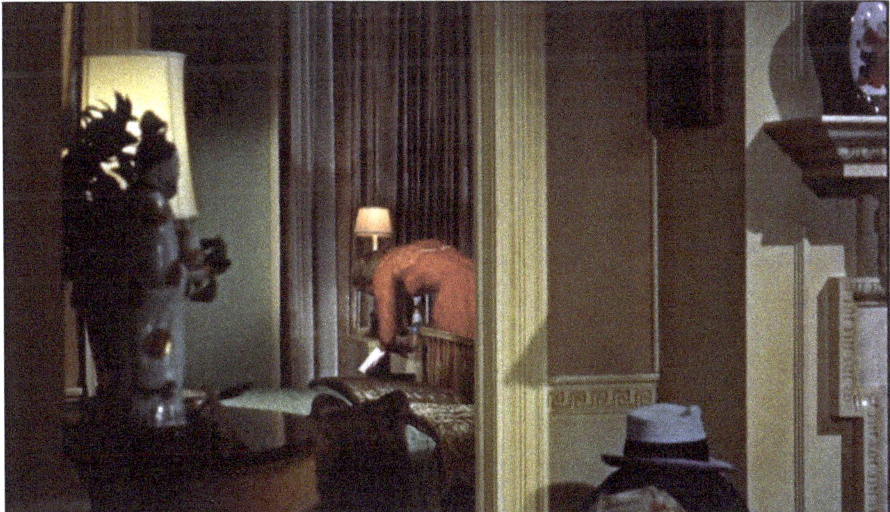

obverse of this is the shot of Margot in her bedroom in the early scene between Margot and Mark, which is taken from the living room, and which, as Ross points out, is framed by an open door that constitutes 'a portal towards an enclosed and secondary space that should be possible to enter were the audience only to lean a little closer' (figure 12),[30] thus enhancing the motifs of secrets and concealments. In all these cases, it is important to note that although the 3-D version was initially released in May (following nationwide pre-release screenings on 26 April), a 2-D version was released at the same time and appears to have performed equally well at the box office. At this point none of the major studios were engaged in making 3-D films,[31] and Warner Bros. had changed its distribution plans for Hitchcock's film: 'Originally ballied as a deepie and slated for national release in the 3-D version, Warners is now making the pic available in 2-D for the first time around. For previous 2-D pix, WB had always insisted on dimensional playdates in first-run situations. It has dropped this policy on "Dial". Picture opens Friday (28) at the Paramount, N.Y., as a 2-D picture.'[32] This is important to remember, as specialists in 3-D aesthetics (a growing topic in Film and Media Studies) tend to discuss *Dial M for Murder* as though it was never shown flat.

Given that the musical scores and use of sound in Hitchcock's films were nearly always distinctive, a paragraph on these elements is worth including here. Tiomkin's score is the fourth and last he wrote for Hitchcock. 'Martinis' is 'a silken variant on the title cue, "Dial M," a waltz that plays through the main title after the "Grandioso" opening fanfare' and that continues in the scenes in which Tony and Margot and Mark and Margot kiss.[33] Later on the dissonant 'Lesgate's Death' ends a cue 'that commences when Swann enters the apartment to murder Margot' and is repeated later on, sweeping aside 'the martini waltzes and divertissements' and making them seem 'part of a deceptively superficial overture'.[34] These ingredients are part of 'The Plan', a cue that rises to a crescendo when we cut to the telephone mechanism, and when we move on to the trial scene. But this cue is increasingly displaced by 'Hubbard' and 'The Key', which imply 'cerebral superiority and hidden depths', on the one hand, and Hubbard's 'uncontainable glee' on the other.[35] Meanwhile, the observations on sound by Elisabeth Weis are once again pertinent. Having pointed out that Hitchcock's films are frequently a marked by 'aural intrusion', which usually involves 'the use of offscreen noise to threaten an onscreen character', Weis goes on to argue that this technique is particularly marked in the single-set films, which 'depend greatly on the tension between inside and outside space'.[36] Thus in addition to the incoming phone-calls in *Dial M for Murder*, nearly all of which threaten Margot either directly or indirectly, we often hear the sound of footsteps, 'which alternatively bring rescuers or murderers.'[37]

Coda

According to the AFI Catalog, Anthony Dawson and John Williams reprised their roles in the Broadway and film versions on 25 April 1956 in an NBC-TV *Hallmark Hall of Fame* production of *Dial M for Murder* directed by George Schaeffer, and in which Rosemary Harris played Margot. Then in November 1967, Williams played the role of Hubbard again in an ABC-TV broadcast directed by John Moxey, which co-starred Laurence Harvey, Diane Cilento and Hugh O'Brien', and in 1981, 'Angie Dickinson and Christopher Plummer starred in television remake, directed by Boris Segal'. In the interim, an episode of *Alfred Hitchcock Presents* entitled 'Portrait of Jocelyn', which featured a character called Mark Halliday, was broadcast on 4 August 1956, and on 6 March 1959, an episode of *77 Sunset Strip* entitled 'The Fifth Chair' also drew on *Dial of M for Murder*. A Hindi-language spin-off version called *Aitbaar* was produced in 1985, and a Malayalam-language version was produced in 1989, but it was not until 1998 that Hollywood ventured an English-language re-make.[38] Now entitled *A Perfect Murder*, the re-make was directed by Andrew Davis from a screenplay by Patrick Smith Kelly, and as Hall points out:

> The new film retains certain plot elements (the confusion over the matching latchkeys, the murder timed to coincide with the phone call) while updating others (the call is now made from a cellphone, diverted to avoid its being traced) and altering some entirely. The characters' names have been changed, to Steven and Emily Taylor (Michael Douglas and Gwyneth Paltrow); husband and wife are both given high-profile jobs; the wife's lover and the hired assassin are conflated into a single character, now an artist with a criminal record (Viggo Mortensen), who in turn hires a second man to execute the killing; when he is killed ... the former blackmails the husband.
>
> Some of the changes seem to be motivated by 'political correctness': Emily performs most of the deduction herself, and is given two female confidantes ... ; the detective has become an Arab-American (David Suchet), who finds an instinctively sympathy with the multi-lingual Emily ... Perhaps the remake's most fundamental alteration is to move large parts of the action outside the central apartment ... [Either way] brutal physical confrontations replace psychological suspense, and the display of conspicuously lavish production values is offered as a substitute for the concentrated claustrophobia of Hitchcock's film.[39]

Notes

1. http://www.nytimes.com/2002/12/20/arts/frederick-knott-playwright-dies-at-86.html 28/09/2016.
2. http://www.nytimes.com/2002/12/20/arts/frederick-knott-playwiright-dies-at-86.html? r=0 28/09/2016. http://www.independent.co.uk/news/obituaries/frederick-knott-137362.html 29/09/2016.
3. http://www.independent.co.uk/news/obituries/frederick-knott-137362.html 29/09/20 16.
4. According to *Variety*, 5 November 1952, p. 56, the play's backers included Lee Shubert, Gilbert Miller, and Mrs. Boris Karloff, and according to *Variety* 12 November 1952, p. 2, 'the Broadway version was capitalized at $50,000, but involved a production cost of only about $35,000'. According to Bordman, *American Theatre: A Chronicle of Comedy and Drama, 1930–1969*, p. 309, 'William Hawkins in the *World Telegraph and Sun* reported [that] "Evans dominates the performance ... He is thoroughly unpleasant, yet retains a superficial charm that reasonably takes in his associates. Whenever the ice gets thin for him it is quite remarkable how he is able to show his apprehension to the audience without tipping off the people of the story'. The same might be said of Ray Milland's performance in Hitchcock's version, though the reprise of John Williams' performance as Chief Inspector Hubbard in the film is a tour-de-force too. According to the *Independent* obituary, p. 4, 'Evans also praised Knott's ready acceptance to make minor changes to the play to accommodate American tastes and colloquialisms. The secret with which the villain blackmails an old school chum was changed from misappropriation of school funds to drug peddling, and since the M in the title refers to the villain's phone exchange, Maida Vale, which would mean nothing to

American audiences, the heroine's name was changed to Margot'. For more on the heroine's name, see below.

5. http://www.independent.co.uk/news/obituaries/frederick-knott-147362.html 29/09/2016; *Dial M for Murder*, un-paginated programme brochure for the 1952 Plymouth Theatre production.

6. 'Knott, Frederick M. P.', in Chris Steinbrunner and Otto Penzler (Editors-in-Chief), *Encyclopedia of Mystery and Detection* (New York, St. Louis, San Francisco: McGraw-Hill Book Company, 1978), p. 235.

7. 'Knott, Frederick M.P.', p. 236.

8. Later examples included *Psycho* (1960) and *Frenzy* (1972). There are, of course, other ways of grouping Hitchcock's films and other ways of thinking about Hitchcock's female characters. Aside from the divisions between British and US films, silent and sound films, black-and-white and colour films, films adapted from plays and films adapted from novels and short stories, Thomas L. Leitch, in *Find the Director and Other Hitchcock Games* (Athens G.A.: University of Georgia Press, 1991), pp. 136–137, identifies a group of films that emphasise 'the pathos of homelessness', such as *Rebecca* (1940), *Shadow of a Doubt* (1943) and *Notorious* (1946), and a group of films that explore 'the motif of homes as traps', as in *Rope* (1948) and *Dial M for Murder*, and Elisabeth Weis identifies a group of 'single set films' such as *Lifeboat* (1944), *Rope*, *Dial M for Murder* and *Rear Window* in *The Silent Scream: Alfred Hitchcock's Sound Track* (Rutherford, Madison and Teaneck: Fairleigh Dickinson Press, 1982), pp. 125–135. In addition, Sheldon Hall notes a number of similarities between *Dial M for Murder* and *Strangers on a Train* (1951), both of which 'concern a tennis player with an inconvenient wife, whose murder is to be executed by a disinterested third party', in '*Dial M for Murder*', *Film History*, vol. 16 no. 3 (2004), p. 244, and Tania Modleski provides a distinctive view of Hitchcock's female characters in *The Women Who Knew Too Much: Hitchcock and Feminist Theory* (London and New York: Routledge, 1988 and 2015).

9. Leitch argues that both the play and the film are exercises in 'in turning the screws on its heroine, who is so resoundingly innocent that the film marks the greatest possible contrast between the scheming villain and his innocent victim', and that 'Margot's affair with Mark is glossed over as an episode in the past; even when her guilt motivates her actions, as when she refuses to go to Tony about the letter from Mark that he has stolen from her, she is represented as a passive figure in Tony's game, since he has stolen the letter himself in order to encourage her to reveal the affair with him ... Later, when Margot is on trial, Hitchcock emphasizes her passivity still further'. He also argues that, as in *Strangers on a Train* and *I Confess* (1952), 'Hitchcock establishes from the beginning an equivocal attitude toward acts of betrayal by organizing each story around the betrayal of a pair of sympathetic lovers whose relationship itself constitutes a betrayal of marriage. Each film presents as part of its background a romantic triangle in which the audience's sympathies are enlisted against the institutional bonds of marriage and on the side of the lovers'. See Leitch, *Find the Director*, pp. 162–163 and p. 152, respectively.

10. http://www.independent.co.uk/news/obituaries/frederick-knott-147362.html 29/09/2016.

11. *Daily Variety*, 7 May 1953, p. 7.

12. *Daily Variety*, 19 October 1953, p. 5.

13. *Daily Variety*, 27 April 1954, p. 3.

14. According to Hall, '*Dial M for Murder*', p. 244, 'three successive screenplay drafts were produced: the first credited to Hitchcock alone, the second to Hitchcock and Knott, and the last (as per the on-screen credit) solely to Knott. However ... even this draft, dated 30 July 1953, differs significantly from the completed film'.

15. Hall, '*Dial M for Murder*', p. 247.

16. Hall, '*Dial M for Murder*', p. 247.

17. Hall, *Dial M for Murder*, p. 247.

18. The play tends to refer to 'Lesgate' rather than 'Swann', but the film uses both.

19. Hall, '*Dial M for Murder*', p. 246.

20. In addition to these instances, there are number of points in the film at which we are shown characters in and around the flat that would be difficult or impossible to see in the theatre, wherever members of the audience were sat. For instance, there is a high-angle shot of Margot outside the French windows as she awaits Tony's return after the death of Lesgate, and a shot of Tony planting the stockings outside the self-same windows prior to the arrival of Hubbard and his men. Margot's moment outside occurs in the

play as well, but the stage directions suggest that she moves off stage entirely. Elsewhere, the framing of closed, open, and opening doors is a minor but notable motif in the film, but is impossible to replicate on stage given the layout of the flat itself, which precludes any views of the street door, and which relies on sounds instead.

21. Richard W. Hines, *Technicolor Movies: The History of Dye Transfer Printing* (Jefferson, N.C.: McFarland, 1993), p. 72.

22. Hines, *Technicolor Movies*, p. 73.

23. Steven Jacobs, 'Color and Containment: Domestic Spaces and Restrained Palettes in Hitchcock's First Color Films', in Simon Brown, Sarah Street, and Liz Watkins (eds.), *Color and the Moving Image: History, Theory, Aesthetics, Archive* (New York and London: Routledge, 2013), p. 185.

24. As coined by Murray Smith in his book *Engaging Characters: Fiction, Emotion, and Cinema* (Oxford: Oxford University Press, 1995), 'alignment' is the term used to identify the extent to which characters are focussed on, and 'allegiance' the extent to which and the ways in which characters and their actions generate sympathy, antipathy, or a mixture of the two.

25. Hall, '*Dial M for Murder*', p. 244.

26. It is shortly after Lesgate's arrival that we spot Hitchcock in a black and white photograph on the wall showing him seated at a table with Tony, Lesgate and others at a re-union banquet. Both Tony and Swann (whose real name is revealed here) refer to the banquet as taking place in a Cambridge college.

27. Hall, '*Dial M for Murder*', p. 249.

28. Hall, '*Dial M for Murder*', p. 252.

29. Miriam Ross, *3D Cinema: Optical Illusions and Tactile Experiences* (Houndmills: Palgrave Macmillan, 2015), p. 30.

30. Ross, *3D Cinema*, p. 32.

31. *Variety*, 10 February 1954, p. 11.

32. *Variety*, 26 May 1954, p. 1. The screening of *Dial M for Murder* at the Paramount was preceded by a premier screening at the Randolph Theatre in Philadelphia (Grace Kelly's home town), and according to the AFI Catalog a print of the 3-D version was shown on18 and 19 May, but 'switched to exhibiting only a flat (2-D) that evening, and for all subsequent showings'. And on 29 May, p. 13, the *New York Times* reported that the 2-D version was the version premiered in New York, and that prints of the 2-D version were shown extensively in the US. Research on 2-D and 3-D versions in other countries is scant. But Hall reports that at least one venue screened a print of the 3-D version in the UK in 1954, that a 3-D restoration was unveiled at the Tiffany Theatre in Los Angeles in 1979, and that a copy was screened a number of times at the National Film Theatre in London. Following the release of the Blu-ray version in 2012, a newly restored 3-D print was premiered at the TCM Classic Film Festival in Hollywood in 2013.

33. Jack Sullivan, *Hitchcock's Music* (New Haven and London: Yale University Press, 2006), p. 165.

34. Sullivan, *Hitchcock's Music*, p. 166.

35. Sullivan, *Hitchcock's Music*, pp. 166, 167.

36. Weis, *The Silent Scream*, p. 125.

37. Weis, *The Silent Scream*, p. 130.

38. See http://wikipedia.org/wiki/Dial_M_for_Murder 21/09/2016.

39. Hall, '*Dial M for Murder*', pp. 253–254.

Chapter 12

Attack

Having recently completed production of *The Big Knife* and *Autumn Leaves* (both 1955), Robert Aldrich was keen to acquire the rights to a property that would deal with aspects and events of World War Two from a critical standpoint, but having discovered that the film rights to novels such as *The Naked Dead* and *The Young Lions* had already been acquired by major studios, Aldrich purchased the rights to a play entitled *Fragile Fox* instead. *Fragile Fox* was written by Norman Brooks and set in what became a front-line combat zone at the beginning of the Battle of the Bulge in 1944. The play eventually opened at the Belasco Theatre in New York and ran for a total of 55 performances from 12 October to 27 November 1954. But Aldrich may have come across it earlier, in 1951, when Clifford Odets, an established playwright whom Aldrich knew well, recommended an early manuscript version to the actor John Garfield.[1] Garfield was intrigued by a character named Sidney Joseph and interested in playing his part. But Garfield died shortly thereafter, and it was not until 1954 that the play was finalised. By then Colonel Shehan's surname had been changed to Bartlett and Lieutenant Joseph's to Costa, and under the direction of Herbert Swope Jr., its cast comprised Dane Clark as Costa, Don Taylor as Lieutenant Harry Woodruff, Andrew Duggan as Captain Erskine Cooney, James Gregory as Lieutenant Colonel Bartlett, Lionel Wilson as Corporal Jackson, Clem Fowler as Private Bernstein, Crahan Denton as Sergeant Tolliver, Addison Powell as Captain Gerstad, Richard Carlyle as Private Herman Ricks, William Hellinger as Private Jacob Abramowitz, Robert McQueeney as Private Sneider, and Eugene Smith and Leonard Bell as the Tall German Soldier and the Short German Soldier, respectively.[2]

Although at least one review was enthusiastic,[3] the play's run was short and has not been revived. Its published script is currently out of print and is only available in libraries or in typed and photocopied form via Amazon.com. But in addition to its specificities, of which more below, it is worth noting that *Fragile Fox* was one of a number of twentieth-century war plays written or produced in the USA. As early as 1914, Beulah Marie Dix wrote an allegorical anti-war play entitled *Across the Border*, which played in repertory alongside a number of other short plays at The Princess

Theatre in New York from 17 October 1914 to 2 January 1915. Similar anti-war sentiments and allegorical tropes can be found in *Moloch*, Dix's first full-length war play, which ends with the destruction of a peace treaty when the victorious combatants fall out, and which ran at the New Amsterdam Theatre in New York from 20 September to October 1915. Other 1910s war plays included *The Iron Cross* and *Lilac Time* (both of which opened in 1917, the former at the Comedy Theatre and the latter at the Republic). *The Iron Cross* was written by Elmer Reizenstein (later known as Elmer Rice) and *Lilac Time* by Jane Cowl and Jane Murfin. In the former 'a soldier finds that his wife has been seduced and had a child by an invader' but 'eventually resigns himself to circumstances',[4] and in the latter, a French villager falls in love with an English soldier. Early on in *Lilac Time*'s run, the soldier is killed in battle. But when the US entered the war in Europe, there were reports that the ending was altered and that the English soldier was only wounded.[5]

Although the production of World War One films such as *The Big Parade* (1925) and *Wings* (1928) gave rise to a trend in the US in the 1920s and 1930s, the only stage-play adaptations were *What Price Glory* (1927), *Lilac Time* (1928), and *Journey's End* (1930), an Anglo-US production. Toward the end of the period, the rise of fascism and the potential imminence of another world war prompted the production of plays such as *Abe Lincoln in Illinois*, *Our Town* and *Waltz in Goose Step* (all 1938), *The American Way* and *The Time of Your Life* (both 1939), *There Shall Be No Night* and *Flight to the West* (both 1940), and *Candle in the Wind* and *Watch on the Rhine* (1941). Film versions of *Abe Lincoln in Illinois* and *Our Town* were produced in 1940, and by the end of December 1941 the USA was at war with the Axis powers.[6] The period between 1942 and 1945 was marked by the production of numerous war and war-related films, and the official ending of the war in Europe and the Far East on VE and VJ day respectively led to the playing out of a number of such films, among them *Back to Bataan*, *The Story of G.I. Joe* and *They Were Expendable* (all 1945) and *A Walk in the Sun* (1946).

The next few years witnessed the disappearance of war films, and with the exception of *Fighter Squadron* (1948), it was not until 1949 and 1950 that a new cycle of combat-oriented war films was inaugurated with *Command Decision*, *Home of the Brave*, *Task Force*, *Battleground* and *Sands of Iwo Jima* (all 1949) and *Twelve O'Clock High*, *American Guerilla in the Philippines* and *Breakthrough* (all 1950).[7] Of these, the only stage-play adaptations were *Command Decision* and *Home of the Brave*, the former based on the play by William Wister Haines, which ran for 409 performances at the Fulton Theatre in New York between 1 October 1947 and 18 September 1948, and the latter on the play by Arthur Laurents, which ran for 69 performances at the Belasco Theatre in New York between 27 December 1945 and 23 February 1946. In addition to *Attack*, the only other war films based on stage plays in the 1950s were *What Price Glory* (1952), an updated adaptation of the Anderson-Stallings play, and *Eight Iron Men* (1953), which was based on *A Sound of Hunting*, a 1945 play by Harry Brown which ran for 23 performances at the Lyceum Theatre in New York.

The Play

Fragile Fox comprises three acts, the first and second of which are subdivided into two scenes, and the version I draw on here is the one that uses the surname of Joseph rather than Costa, and that uses the surname of Shehan rather than Bartlett. Act One Scene One is set in Fox Company headquarters in the city hall of a Belgian village called Plainvieux. As the curtain rises Captain Cooney is talking to Corporal Jackson, who is trying to work and listen to Cooney at the same time. Cooney helps himself to a drink and berates the army's lack of business skills. He also boasts that he never went to West Point, underlines his pride in the small-town Georgia background he shares with Lieutenant Colonel Shehan, recalls that people used to say that 'Erskine Cooney's gonna own this State and Clyde Shehan'll be Governor', and notes that Jackson is due leave in Paris and advises him to make money by selling cigarettes on the black market. Cooney is planning a card game, and Lieutenant Woodruff enters and joins him. Cooney goes off to fetch the cards and another bottle, and Lieutenant Joseph enters. Woodruff assumes that Joseph will participate, but Joseph refuses to play cards with Cooney, and Woodruff tells Joseph to be careful: 'You want what happened at Aachen to happen again?' he says. 'If we're gonna handle Cooney we need the Colonel on our side'.

Joseph leaves, Cooney re-enters with another bottle of whiskey and a deck of cards, Shehan enters, and Woodruff goes off to find Joseph. Shehan expresses his admiration for Woodruff, Cooney endorses his father's view that Shehan will one day become State Governor and asks Shehan whether his Company Commander citation has come through yet, but Shehan says that Cooney will have to wait on account of the incident at Aachen and that he'll 'slip the citation through later'. Joseph and Woodruff re-enter, and Shehan says that the war will soon be over and that 'we can all go home with a record to be proud of'. But Joseph turns the conversation to Aachen again, and Woodruff recalls that Cooney provided insufficient support. Cooney says that Ingersoll disobeyed orders. But Joseph says that Ingersoll 'was a damn good Sergeant', and leaves in anger. Shehan tells Cooney to cool off outside and asks Woodruff to tell him what really happened, and Woodruff says that Ingersoll's squad up was cut off, that Cooney 'didn't do a damn thing' to help, and that Cooney 'no longer enjoys the confidence of the men or officers of this company'. Shehan listens. But he says that 'we're out of the shooting war now', that 'anything of this nature would be very difficult to prove', and that 'it's best to just forget it'. Woodruff says that 'It's not just the past, Colonel. The man's lost his judgment, he ... can't make decisions ... he's drinking like hell', but Shehan replies that 'you got nothing to worry about ... There's not one chance in a hundred that we'll see combat again', and offers Woodruff a drink. 'What'll we drink to?' says Shehan, Woodruff lists the names of those killed Aachen, and Shehan departs, leaving Woodruff to deal himself a hand of poker as Jackson knocks and enters. Jackson asks Woodruff for advice regarding a young woman he met in Paris, and when Woodruff he realises that Jackson is a virgin he is sensitive and understanding. Woodruff helps Bernstein to draft a letter to Ingersoll's folks, and says that his men will no longer be required to engage in any more combat. But Joseph reminds Woodruff of the fourteen dead men at Aachen and says that if anything like it happens again he'd 'put a slug in Cooney's gut', and at this point Tolliver enters and tells Woodruff 'to have your company on the road in twenty minutes ... They say there's hell of a breakthrough'. Woodruff tells Jackson to find Cooney, picks up the phone, says that Fragile Fox is ready, and mutters 'Yes sir, Fragile Goddam Fox, sir' as the curtain falls.

Act One Scene Two takes place in 'a war-battered room' near the front. Woodruff is bending over a map on a table and Gersted, the battalion surgeon, walks in unnoticed, speaks to Woodruff amidst the chaos, and asks where Cooney is. Woodruff replies that Cooney is out on reconnaissance and expresses concern as to Cooney's state of mind. But Gerstadt says that if he had to send 'everybody back with a screw loose ... those sick bastards on the other side'll win the war, and they're sicker than we are – so I can't do it'.[8] Ricks enters with a request for more ammunition, and although Woodruff reckons that most of this ammunition is wasted, he agrees to do so. Then Shehan and Cooney enter and study the map on the table, and Shehan calls Woodruff over to explain the plan for dealing with the town of La Nelle. Shehan reckons that the town might contain German troops and orders his men to use Fox Company to flush them out if necessary. Woodruff agrees that 'hitting the town from both sides might do it', and although Cooney concurs, he also suggests that a platoon be sent to determine the level of resistance. Woodruff is hesitant, but Cooney is confident: 'You get into real trouble and we'll be right behind you', he says. Costa tells Cooney that 'We can take that farmhouse, but I'd hate to get stuck in it', but Cooney says that he will back him up and offers him a swig from his bottle. Joseph declines the drink and tells Cooney that if he has to 'lose another man because of you, you'll never see the States again'. Cooney begins to waver. But the operation has now begun, Woodruff and Jackson rush out, and Cooney is left alone, rocking back and forth as gunfire can be heard in the distance. Then when Woodruff returns and puts the plan in motion, Cooney hesitates, and 'The two men stand facing each other at an impasse' as the curtain falls.

Act Two Scene One is set in a house in La Nelle. Cast-off German and American equipment litter the floor, and what once might have been a sitting room is now a wreck with gaping holes in the walls. A 'battle is in evidence by offstage gunfire, and two German soldiers carrying carbines come down a stairway to the left', then run to the cellar door and exit. Joseph rushes in and Ricks and Bernstein follow. As they check out the house, Tolliver and Snowden enter with an unnamed mortally-wounded soldier. Bernstein throws a grenade down the steps in order to ensure that enemy soldiers are not in hiding, and the wounded soldier expires. The remaining soldiers check out who is dead and who is still alive, and Tolliver tells Joseph that 'it's just plain crazy ... sendin' one platoon in here'. Joseph says that as long as they stay in the house they should be OK, and although Bernstein says that the Germans 'will be after us ... come dark', Joseph reiterates his point, and suggests that the men cook something to eat. Joseph radios headquarters and says that La Nelle is 'occupied by at least a reinforced platoon, maybe a company. They caught us out in the open and chopped us up ... Only five of us got here. Is the rest of the company coming in? ... No, I didn't think they would be. Okay, we'll wait here till dark and make a break'.

The men realise the gravity of the situation, Joseph points out to Ricks that for the Germans he is 'the enemy', and Ricks replies that 'I'm an American, for Christ sake, they're the enemy'. Tolliver and Joseph discuss whether or not the Germans have tanks, and as they do so, a bullet from sniper 'smacks into the wall'. The men rig up a dummy in order to pinpoint the sniper's whereabouts and Tolliver shoots him dead. Ricks and Tolliver spot what is either a truck or a tank in the distance, Joseph turns to the body of a dead US soldier named Abramowitz, and for 'once in his life' Joseph is frightened. At this point sounds from the cellar below betray the presence of the two German soldiers, who come in with their hands up quarrelling. The US soldiers part the Germans, and Joseph tries to get as much information from them as he can. The smaller German begs Joseph not to shoot him as he has three children, and Joseph learns that there a lot of German tanks in the vicinity and kills the larger German. Joseph requests more artillery cover, leads his men out of the house behind the remaining German, tells Woodruff to inform Cooney that he's coming back, and lurches out the door as the curtain falls.

Act Two Scene Two takes place five minutes later in the same setting as Act One Scene One. 'Cooney is lying on a cot' and Woodruff enters and tells him that Joseph has pulled out but is coming back. Cooney says that he has a fever and that like any other soldier he has simply misjudged the enemy's strength, Woodruff exits, and Jackson enters and expresses concern for Cooney's state of mind. Then Jackson leaves and Tolliver enters with the remaining German prisoner. Cooney asks Tolliver where Joseph is, and Tolliver says that Joseph never showed, and that several German tanks are present in the town. Cooney attacks the German prisoner and offers a drink to Tolliver. But Tolliver declines, Cooney takes another drink, and Woodruff brings in Sneider, a German-speaking US soldier, in order to interrogate the prisoner. The prisoner says that the tank unit is full of 'SS sonsofbitches' and that he hopes the Americans 'blow the hell out of 'em'. He also says that the Germans have at least ten tanks in hiding, and as Woodruff lays out a plan to deal with them, Cooney reaches for his bottle again as the sound of heavy shells can be heard outside. The men grab grenades and bazookas, and as Woodruff exits, Cooney stares at the map, 'puts his hands to his ears' and 'crouches'.

Woodruff re-enters and asks Cooney what he wants him to do, Cooney says that the only thing to do is fall back, and an angry Shehan enters. Shehan asks Cooney why he isn't up ahead at La Nelle, demands that Cooney halt the Germans, and turns to Woodruff, who understands the plan and leaves. Shehan tells Cooney 'that they'll be no favours': 'you hold this cross road and you've got a chance, fall back and I'll show you what hell really is'. Woodruff re-enters and says 'They're coming in. Straight down the road' and Shehan exits. Cooney begins to fall into a state mental disintegration. Then Joseph bursts in, Cooney says that he'd rather be dead than alive, and as Joseph approaches, Cooney tries to shoot him. Woodruff stands between the two men, then

Jackson runs in, Joseph, Jackson and Woodruff gather their weapons, and as Jackson and Joseph leave, Woodruff watches Cooney on his knees in prayer as 'the curtain slowly falls'.

Act Three takes place in the same setting two hours later. Bernstein has a broken leg, and Ricks and Snowden carry him in and hand him over to Gerstad. Bernstein is pleased that he will be sent back home, and Snowden says that the Germans have been stopped thanks to the efforts of Joseph and Woodruff. Gerstad leaves and Tolliver enters and tells Snowden to find the German, who can help to carry Bernstein out. Snowden is unable to find the German, Bernstein and Tolliver pick Bernstein up, and Woodruff says that the others can go ahead as they move toward the door. But at this point Cooney enters, blocks their exit, and says that 'We're going to hold'. The SS enter at the top of the stairs, Woodruff insists on quiet, Cooney says that they should surrender, Woodruff replies that 'We aren't giving up and neither are you', and at this point the figure of Joseph 'appears at the top of the stairs'. Joseph comes down the stairs, 'his field jack smeared with blood'. 'He stands for a moment adjusting himself to the darkness' then turns and spots Cooney. He lurches toward Cooney, tommy gun in hand, and collapses on the floor. Tolliver carries Joseph out. But when Tolliver returns he says that Joseph is dead.

Cooney heads for the stairs, Woodruff grabs him, and when Cooney responds by saying that he is in charge, he is finally shot and killed by Woodruff. Tolliver and Bernstein each fire a shot into Cooney's corpse, and Tolliver says that they are all equally responsible for Cooney's death. Then the 'distant sound of firing suddenly increases and seems to break out directly about the cellar', and at this point Shehan enters, steps over Cooney's body, and says that Cooney died 'like a real soldier'. Shehan tells Tolliver and the others to 'get back to the company' and 'send a graves detail', and the men begin to carry Costa's body away and philosophise about what has happened. Shehan says that Cooney's father would be proud of his son and that he intends to draw up a citation. But Woodruff says that Cooney 'had it coming' and Shehan threatens an investigation. Woodruff responds by saying that 'I killed him' and demands to be arrested. But Shehan tells Woodruff that 'it's all a card game' and leaves, and Sneider and Private McLiam enter with a stretcher for Cooney's body. Woodruff reiterates his demand to be arrested, but the other men say that Cooney 'needed killin''. 'Woodruff watches them exit. He slowly sits on the bottom stair, and suddenly he is weeping. His sobs are convulsive and uncontrolled as the curtain falls'.

The Film

According to the entry on *Attack* in the AFI Catalog, the film's working title was *Fragile Fox* and was changed to *Attack* on 31 July 1956. James Poe, who had written the script for *The Big Knife* the previous year, also wrote the script for *Attack*. It is likely that Aldrich worked closely with Poe, but as far as I know the processes of adaptation, scripting and production have not been recorded. According to the Catalog, the 'battle scenes were shot on the Universal Studios and RKO-Pathé backlots and at Albertson Ranch in Agoura, CA', and a *New York Times* article 'dated 19 Feb 1956 reported that the production cost approximately $850,000'. However, although the script was approved by the Production Code Administration, 'information in the Department of Defence Film Collection at Georgetown University Library indicates that the Army and Department of Defense (DOD) refused cooperation during the film's production', and as a result Aldrich was forced 'to purchase or rent military equipment'.[9] In a letter dated 13 January 1956, The Department of the Army, Office of the Chief of Information stated that 'the negative evaluation of *Attack* was because "it is a very distasteful story and derogatory of Army leadership during combat including weak leadership, cowardice, and finally, the murder of the Company Commander"', of which more below. Aldrich protested, and 'US Congressman Melvin Price of Illinois, a member of House Armed Services Committee, charged the DOD with censorship for its failure to assist *Attack*', and when members of the State Department saw the film at the Venice Film Festival, they reported 'that they found nothing objectionable'.

Following 'a private screening for Pentagon officials in September 1956, the DOD maintained its stance against the picture', but on 14 September the American Veterans Committee opposed the DOD's decision, and the 'matter was taken up by the Senate Committee on the Judiciary, Subcommittee on Constitutional Rights'. The 'subcommittee Chief Counsel and Staff Director Charles H. Slayman, Jr. wrote to the DOD on 18 September 1956 inquiring as to the constitutionality' of the DOD's ruling. The outcome of their investigation is not known. But although a November memo 'indicated that *Attack* was denied exhibition at Army bases in Germany', a news item in *The Hollywood Reporter* dated 19 Sep 1956, p. 1, reported that 'Army and Air Force officials have given their seal of approval', and on 2 October, *Daily Variety* reported that 'Army and Air Force officials have given their seal of approval' too. The film was premiered in New York and Los Angeles on 19 September and 26 September respectively, and by then it had won the Pasinetti Award for the Best Foreign Film at the Venice Film Festival. During the course of its circulation some advertisements and posters added an exclamation mark to the film's title, but there were no such marks on 35mm prints or subsequent video and DVD copies. Frank DeVol's unusually discordant and fragmentary score is rarely mentioned in discussions of the film. But the score is important, so I will draw attention to at least some its cues as and when I can.[10]

The film is structured around four scenes of combat, all of which hinge on the decisions and behaviour of Captain Cooney (Eddie Albert). The first scene opens prior to the title and the credits in the midst of a battle. A close up of a nondescript piece of open ground is accompanied by the whistle of a falling shell and a discordant blare of trumpets (a cue entitled 'Europe'). And as the camera moves briefly from left to right amidst the smoke and the hole caused by the shell blast, three barely visible GIs rush in and dive into the hole, and a title informs us that it is 'Europe 1944'. As the smoke begins to clear we cut to a reverse angle of the GIs in the shell hole, onto a shot of enemy machine gun fire from a well-protected pill box, then on to a reverse angle

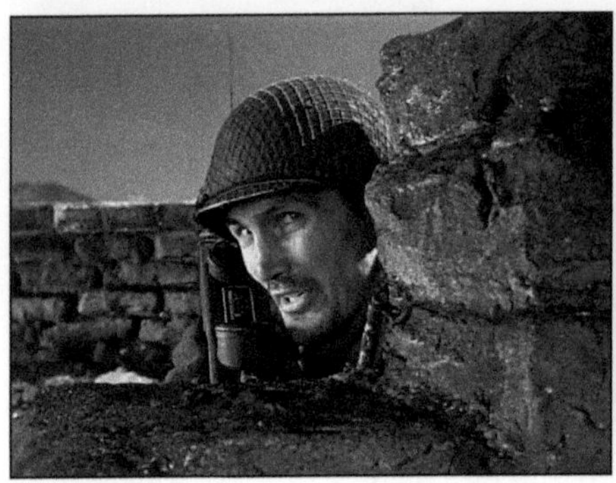

Figure 1

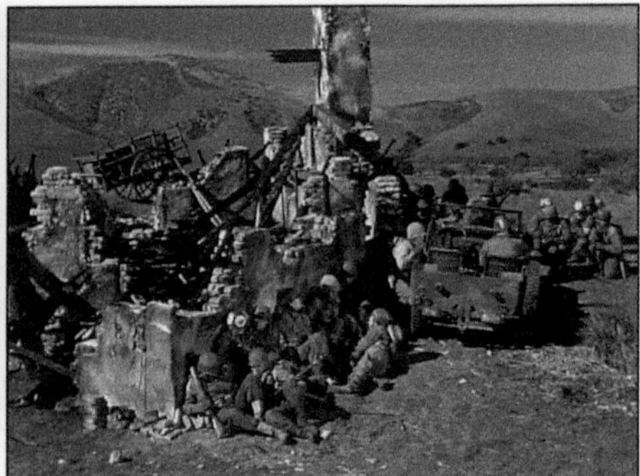

Figure 2

of three more GIs. One of these GI's is Lieutenant Costa (Jack Palance), who radios Cooney for assistance from behind one of the badly damaged and barely protective walls that litter the otherwise danger-laden open landscape (figure 1). Then we cut to Cooney, who is barely visible in long shot from behind on the right hand side of the frame alongside a number of other soldiers (figure 2), and back to Costa, who requests Cooney's permission for Sergeant Ingersol (Strother Martin) and his men to take out the pill box, but only if sufficient cover is provided.[11] Still framed from behind but closer in, Cooney waves his hand in assent (figure 3). But as the operation continues he puts down his walkie-talkie and fails to provide back up, and despite a further call from Costa, no cover or assistance is provided, and Ingersol and his men are decimated. The last remaining GI in Ingersol's squad is killed, and as his helmet rolls down the hill, the title and credits begin to appear in typewriter style over further shots of the terrain, then over a montage of various off-duty activities behind the lines, which are accompanied initially by a blast of jazz music ('Foxhole Jump') from an outdoor loudspeaker. Like the opening sequence, the credit sequence contains a number of tightly-framed or densely-staged shots, and when the credits are over we cut to a group of GIs waiting in line for food, then on to an extreme long shot of Cooney calling for Corporal Jackson (John Sheppod) outside his headquarters in the distance, far away

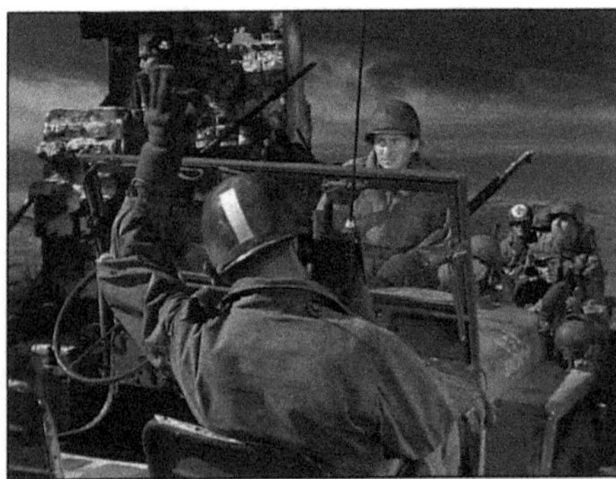

Figure 3

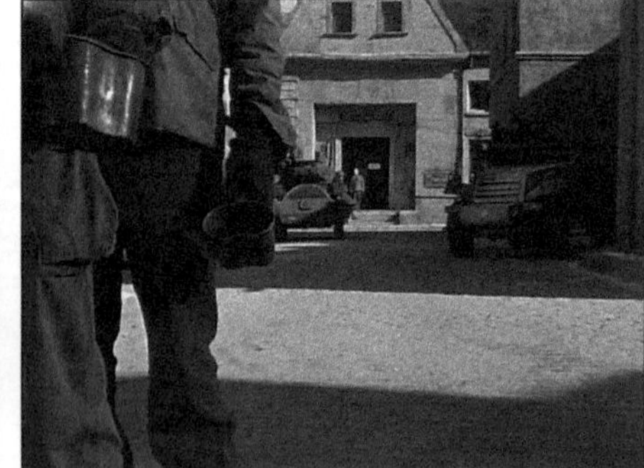

Figure 4

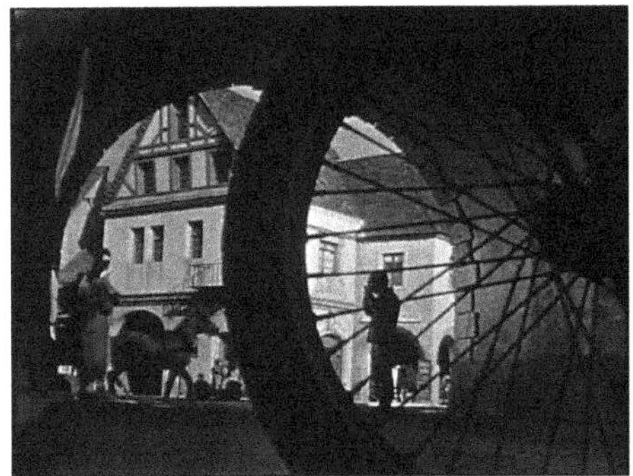
Figure 5

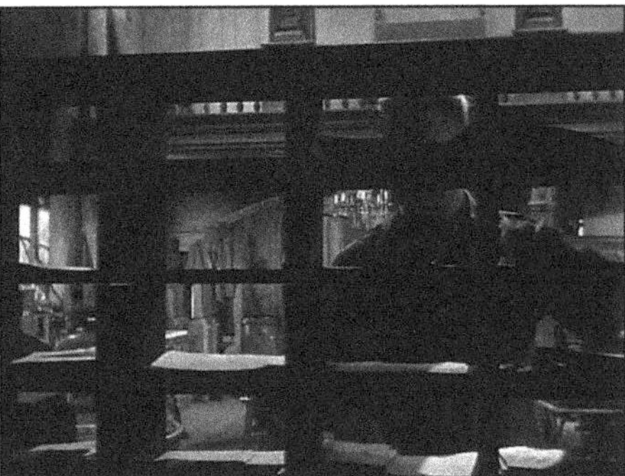
Figure 6

from most of the ordinary men (figure 4). One of the shots in the credit sequence frames a soldier taking a photograph of a couple through the spokes of a wheel (figure 5), and in this way it inaugurates Aldrich's penchant for foreground mise-en-scene as well as for his penchant for high-angle shots and canted angles.

These ingredients are all evident in the film's equivalent to the play's first scene, which Aldrich divides into five scenes and two locations separated by minor temporal elisions. The first, third and fifth scenes are set in Fox Company headquarters (figures 6–7), and the second and fourth in a nearby forge, a new location in which Woodruff (William Smithers) finds Costa and persuades him to join the card game prior to the sudden breakout of German forces (figure 8).[12] News of the breakout leads to conversations among the GIs outside, and among them are Woodruff and Costa, who says of Cooney that 'I got it figured. Just let him goof once more'. Tolliver (Buddy Ebsen) tells Costa to have his men on the road in twenty minutes, and as the men rush and gather in the streets, they are accompanied by the discordant blare of a trumpet on the soundtrack ('City Square'). Drawing on aspects of Act One Scene Two in the play, we cut to company headquarters. Bartlett (Lee Marvin) is framed alongside Cooney and Woodruff, and outlines plans to deal with situation and leaves. As Bartlett gets into his jeep and is driven away on the left, a medic is prominent on

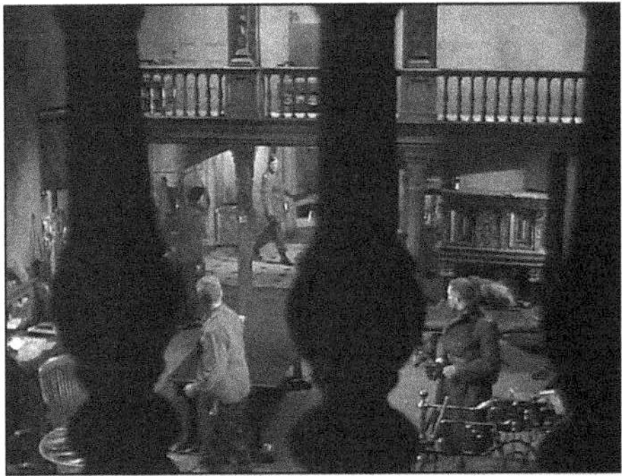
Figure 7

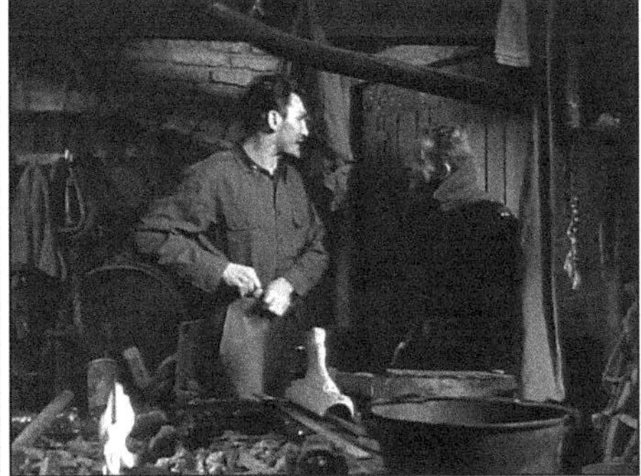
Figure 8

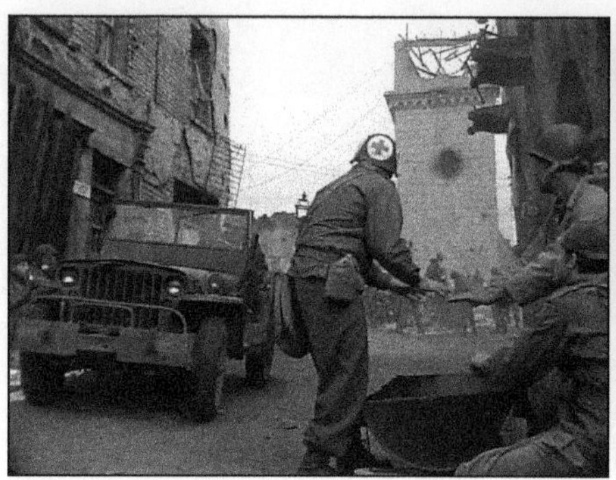

Figure 9

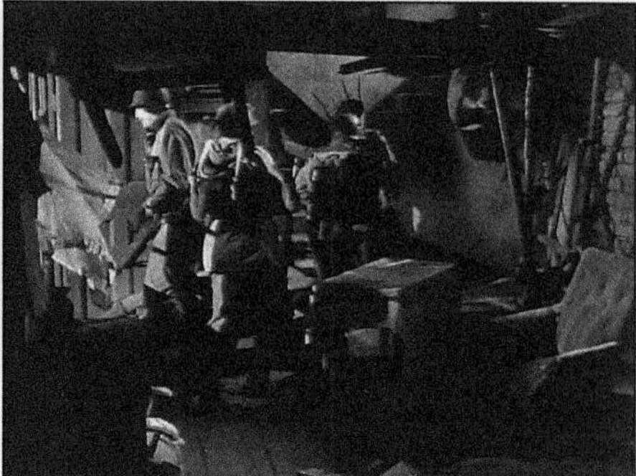

Figure 10

the right, and in this way the possible stakes and consequences are underlined (figure 9). Cooney takes charge and says that this is a 'strictly Fragile Fox operation'. But at this point Costa enters and says 'If I ever lose another man on account of you, just one, you'll never see the States the again'. Cooney responds with 'That's court-martial talk'. But Costa responds in turn with 'You play the gutless wonder just once and I'll get you, Cooney. I'll shove this grenade down your throat and pull the pin' and a discordant piano chord ('Threatsville') underlines the issues at stake.

Cooney promises support for the ensuing operation. But Costa is well aware of Cooney's promises and ensures the presence of medics as he organises his men in waves and intervals so as to minimise casualties as they head off across open ground toward the distant town of La Nelle. La Nelle is heavily protected by German troops, and as the GIs and medics find themselves in range they are hit by fire from tanks, machine-guns and snipers. The German troops move back and vanish. But a large number of Costa's men have been killed, and the few that remain only just make it to a nearby farmhouse. The farmhouse interior is marked by jagged edges and splinters, and these are augmented by shadows and chiaroscuro lighting effects and the fluttering of curtains (figures 10–11). In addition to Costa and Tolliver, the remaining GIs are Bernstein (Robert Strauss), Snowden (Richard Jaeckel), and the very young Ricks (Jimmy Goodwin). The narrative content and dialogue draw on Act Two in the play. But some of the dialogue has been cut, and although we witness the reappearance of the two German soldiers from cellar, the Tall German (a senior officer played by Peter Van Eyck) is shot and killed by German soldiers outside the farmhouse, not by Costa inside the farmhouse as in the play. During the latter part of this scene Costa radios for help. But as we cut back to Cooney in conversation with Woodruff, it is clear that help is not forthcoming, and when artillery bombardments from both the US and German sides begin, Costa decides to lead his men (and the remaining German prisoner) back across open ground. Tolliver, Bernstein and Snowden make it. But although Costa gives his helmet to Ricks for protection, Ricks is killed, and Costa's anguish is palpable.

Back at headquarters, in the equivalent scene to Act Two Scene Two, Cooney is

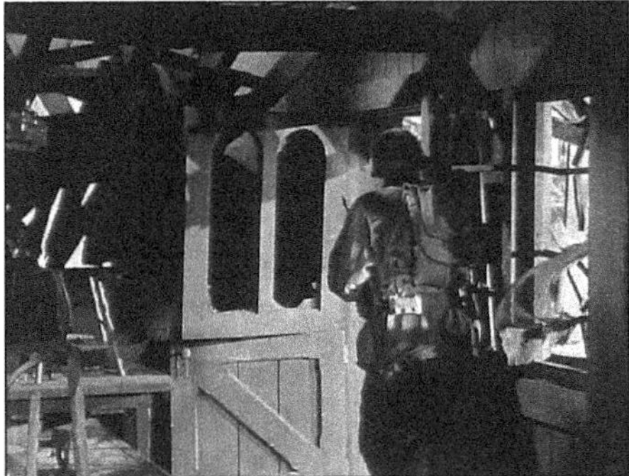

Figure 11

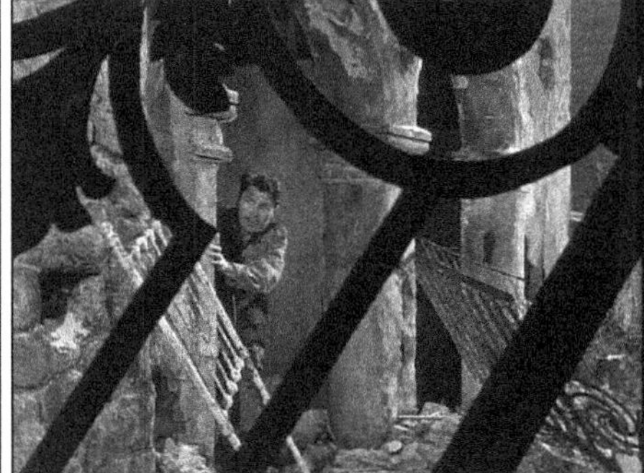

Figure 12

beginning to disintegrate under fire from advancing German panzers and the general pressure of events. He punches the German prisoner in the stomach and takes a swig from one of his whiskey bottles, and as the prisoner is led away by Tolliver, Cooney declares that 'There's only one thing to do – fall back'. But at this point a furious Bartlett enters, berates Cooney's lack of action, underlines his contempt for Cooney and his second-rate Southern pretensions, socks him on the jaw, and leaves. Cooney exhibits signs of regression as he clutches a slipper and a bottle of whiskey to the accompaniment of a cue entitled 'London Bridge'(a particularly childlike version of a well-known children's chant), and Woodruff promises to 'take care of everything'. Costa enters looking for Cooney, but as German tanks approach outside, Costa grabs a bazooka and heads out into the street, and Jackson and Woodruff follow.

Amidst what is now the fourth and final scene of combat, we cut to Bernstein and Tolliver, who are framed beneath an image of Christ in a partially bombed out house, and who crawl towards its cellar steps in order to find more safety. But as we cut outside then back again, a German tank fires one of its shells and the falling masonry breaks Bernstein's leg. We cut to the battle outside again, and Costa is framed by foreground ironwork (figure 12). Costa uses his bazooka to disable a German tank and a grenade to kill its driver, and having advised Tolliver to join his men in the cellar, he prepares to attack another tank. But this time his bazooka does not work, and as his left arm is crushed by the tank he screams in pain. A sound bridge takes us back to the cellar, where Bernstein is also screaming in pain. Tolliver and Snowden remind Bernstein that he will be shipped home, and Woodruff enters, says that the Germans are 'breaking through', and leaves. We cut back to Costa, who is still alive, and on to Cooney, who is outside nearby and at least partially deranged. 'Come out, you cowards!' he says. 'We're holding for Clyde! We're holding the town! Come on, fight! ... You're yellow, yellow, yellow!' Then we cut to Costa again, and on to Cooney, who he enters down the cellar steps, brandishes his machine-gun, and yells 'Nobody's running out! We're holding! We'll hold at the church and courthouse'. Woodruff re-enters and German soldiers approach the house outside. The German soldiers turn away and leave, but as Cooney changes tack and demands surrender, Costa enters and

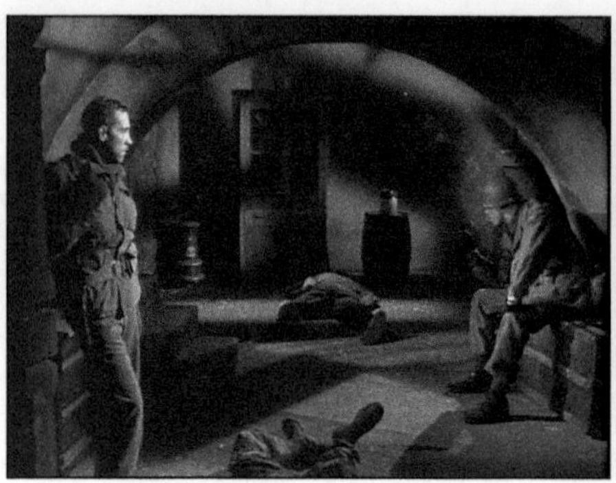
Figure 13

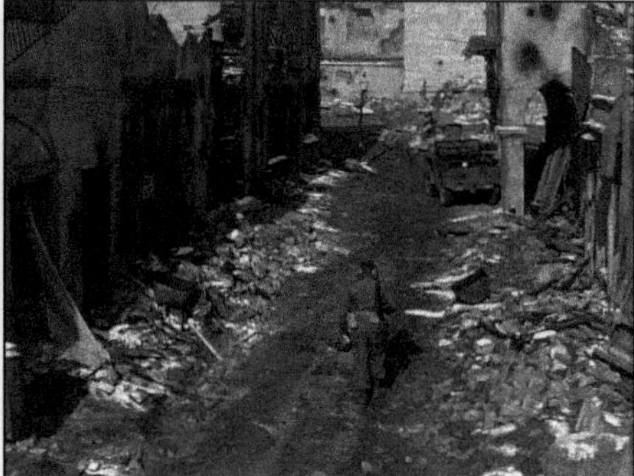
Figure 14

shuffles in agonising pain toward him. Costa prays for sufficient time to kill Cooney, but collapses into Tolliver's arms and dies on the floor before he can do so ('Costa Dies'), thus exemplifying the extent to which Aldrich's protagonists 'find their own integrity in doing what they do the way they do it, even if it causes their own deaths'.[13] Underlined by a reprise of 'London Bridge', Cooney says that 'I think we'll just carry on as planned'. But Woodruff raises his rifle and shoots him dead, then turns to Tolliver and says that 'if we ever get out of here, place me under arrest'. We cut to an ensemble tableau shot as the soldiers present take in what has happened and discuss the situation. Then they each fire a single bullet into Cooney's body, concur that they have done the right thing, and further concur that Cooney 'caught a storm of lead' from enemy troops at the top of the stairs.

The killing of Cooney by his own men is a major event and constitutes an instance of what is now known as 'fragging', a term that emerged during the course of the the Vietnam War, but a practice that marked earlier wars as well, and its presence in the play and the film adaptation draw attention to issues that as far as I know had never been dealt with before.[14] Either way these issues mark the remainder of this scene and the coda that follows, as Snowden reports that the Germans have left and that Bartlett is 'on his way over'. Bartlett duly arrives, and Marvin conveys Bartlett's understanding as to what has really happened in a single glance. Bartlett walks over to Cooney's body, and a long shot tableau lays the situation out in cross formation, with Bartlett seated right and Woodruff standing left, and with Cooney's body in the centre in the background and Costa's in the centre foreground (figure 13). What follows is lengthy conversation between Bartlett and Woodruff, during the course of which the dead bodies are removed, and during the course of which Bartlett says that Cooney will be honoured and Woodruff offered command of Fragile Fox. The conversation continues into the street as the bodies of Costa and Cooney are taken out and transported, and on telling Woodruff that 'Life can be very pleasant ... Even in war', Bartlett leaves. Woodruff heads off through the decimated town in a crane shot (figure 14), walks past the bodies of Cooney and Costa again, and enters Fragile Fox headquarters. He radios General Parsons, and when Parsons comes on the line and identifies himself,

Woodruff ends the film with the words 'This is Lieutenant Harold Woodruff' – all of which replace the more indeterminate and tear-filled ending that marks the play.[15]

Notes

1. Larry Swindell, *Body and Soul: The Life of John Garfield* (New York: Morrow, 1975), p.126.
2. Daniel Blum, *Theatre World, Season 1954–1955* (New York: Greenberg, 1955), p. 23. Among the suite of photographs of the production and its players is an actor who is identified as George Gilbreath. Gilbreath is not listed as cast member. But as George Gilbreth, he is identified as a minor 1950s television actor in the Internet Movie Database (IMBd), and it is possible that he replaced a regular member of the cast when the photographs were taken.
3. See John Chapman, '"Fragile Fox" Is War Play on Fragile Side', *Chicago Daily Tribune*, 14 October 1954, Part 2, p.8, who wrote that the play was 'a first class melodrama and should make a dandy movie. In fact, it plays like a movie on the stage, offering excitement, vigorous characterizations, and a slightly mystifying but very noble finale'.
4. Bordman, *American Theatre: A Chronicle of Comedy and Drama, 1914–1930*, p. 59.
5. Bordman, *American Theatre: A Chronicle of Comedy and Drama, 1914–1930*, p. 58.
6. For more details and background, see Wertheim, *Staging the War*, esp. pp. 2–53, and for more on war and combat films and their contexts and sources, see note 76 in the general introduction to this book.
7. Jeanine Basinger, *The World War II Combat Film: Anatomy of a Genre* (Middletown, C.T.: Wesleyan University Press, 2003 edition), pp. 120–154, 277–281.
8. It should be noted that Gerstadt does not figure in the film version, probably because his pronouncements are redundant or too explicit.
9. In an interview with Aldrich in Arthur Knight, 'Aldrich Against the Army', *The Saturday Review*, 1 September 1956, p. 25, the Army's policy of non-cooperation not only meant that Aldrich 'couldn't borrow troops and tanks for my picture', but that he 'couldn't even get a look at Signal Corps combat footage' and 'had to buy a tank for $1,000 and rent another from 20th Century-Fox'.
10. The title cues for the music in DeVol's score are listed in Box 75 of The Frank De Vol Collection.
11. For reasons that remain unclear, Ingersoll is spelt with two 'l's in the play, but only one in the film.
12. These scenes underline Costa's delicate physical skills as well his physical power as he first mends a horse's harness with a needle then operates the forge. His ease with and respect for ordinary men is also evident in the ways in which he talks to Woodruff and Monsieur Bouisse, the French forge owner (Louis Mercier). In *Whatever Happened to Robert Aldrich? His Life and His Films* (New York: Limelight Editions, 1995), p. 120, Alain Silver and James Ursini argue that Costa works the forge to relieve his fury at Cooney's behaviour; and in *Body and Soul: The Cinematic Vision of Robert Aldrich* (Lanham, M.D., Toronto, Oxford: The Scarecrow Press, 2004), p. 244, Tony Williams argues that Costa is an ambivalent figure: he 'appears as a man of the people and potential messiah', and like 'the original Messiah, he is artisan. But he is also a warrior'; and in 'Robert Aldrich (1953 to 1961)', Richard Combs (ed.), *Robert Aldrich* (London: BFI, 1978), p. 16, Combs points out that two scenes are here 'explicitly paralleled: Costa (the name signalling immigrant origins) is working the forge in a French smithy, talking to the owner about his own experience as a railroad worker; Cooney is meanwhile preparing for his regular card game with Colonel Bartlett ... his immediate superior, whose protection can be counted on because Bartlett is counting on Cooney's well-placed family to help fulfil his political ambitions after the war'. Williams also draws attention to Costa's use of Biblical language, and to the way in which he appears to rise from the dead like a messiah, praying to 'go to hell' in exchange for killing Cooney even as he dies before doing so and is thus redeemed. See Williams, *Body and Soul*, p. 245.
13. Paul Sauvage, 'Aldrich Interview', *Movie*, Winter 1976–1977, p. 55, cited in Alain Silver, 'Robert Aldrich', *Senses of Cinema*, no. 20 (2002).
14. See http://en.wikipedia.org/wiki/Fragging22/08/2016.
15. As Williams points out in *Body and Soul*, p. 246, this ending may have been forced on Aldrich by the Production Code Administration, though the entry in the AFI Catalog makes no reference to it, and Aldrich may have recognised that the ending of the play would have had to be altered. As it is, the behaviour

and principles of Cooney and Bartlett are contrasted with those of Woodruff, Costa and other low-rank officers and men, and the fact that Parsons is a general could have been used to pinpoint the difficulties that Woodruff would have faced in court. According to Edwin T. Arnold and Eugene Miller, *The Films and Career of Robert Aldrich* (Knoxville: University of Tennessee Press, 1986), p. 75, as paraphrased by Williams in *Body and Soul*, p. 265, 'Aldrich disliked the conventional ending of *Attack!* (sic) stating that he would have preferred Woodruff to have accepted Bartlett's proposal. When Truffaut disagreed, Aldrich said that he believed that a compromise ending could have occurred when Woodruff stood before the corpses of Costa and Clooney. The audience could then assume that Woodruff would make the phone call later'.

Bibliography

Plays

Abbott, George and Ann Preston Bridger, *Coquette* (1927)
Ade, George and Viña Delmar, *As Young as You Feel* (1931)
Aladár, László, *Becsuletes Megtalalo* (*The Honest Finder*) (1931)
Anderson, Maxwell, *Candle in the Wind* (1941)
The Eve of St. Mark (1942)
Armont, Paul and Léopold Marchant, *Le Tailleur au Château* (*The Tailor in the Castle*) (1924)
Atkins, Zöe, *The Greeks Had a Word for It* (1930)
Morning Glory (1939)
Balderson, John L., *Dracula* (1927)
Ballard, John F., *Young America* (1932)
Barker, John Nelson, *The Indian Princess, or La Belle Sauvage* (1808)
Barrie, J.M. *Peter Pan* (1904)
Behrman, S.N., *The Pirate* (1942)
Belasco, David, *The Girl of the Golden West* (1905)
Belasco, David and Franklyn Fyles, *The Girl I Left Behind Me* (1893)
Besier, Rudolph and May Edington, *Secrets* (1924)
Biró, Lajos and Melchior Lengyel, *The Czarina* (1913)
Bisson, Alexandre, *La Femme X* (*Madame X*) (1908)
Boker, George Henry, *Francesca da Rimini* (1853)
Bolton, Guy and Winchell Smith, *Wages for Wives* (1925)
Brewer, Jr., George Emerson and Bertram Bloch, *Dark Victory* (1934)
Brooks, Norman, *Fragile Fox* (1954)
Brown, Harry, *A Sound of Hunting* (1945)
Bus-Feketé, László, *Szuletesnap* (*Birthday*) (1934)
Carpenter, Edward Childs, *Tongues of Men* (1913)
Chase, Mary, *Bernadine* (1952)
Cohan, George M., *Get-Rich-Quick Wallington* (1922)
Colton, John and Clemence Randolph, *Rain* (1922)
Coppée, François, *Le Luthier de Crémone* (*The Violin Maker of Cremona*) (1876)
Coward, Noel, *Design for Living* (1933)
Cowl, Jane and Jane Murfin, *Lilac Time* (1917)

Smilin' Through (1938)
Craven, Frank, *The First Year* (1926)
Crothers, Rachel, *When Ladies Meet* (1932)
Susan and God (1937)
Curtis, George Washington Parke Curtis, *The Indian Prophesy* (1827)
Dane, Oscar, *Dr Jekyll and Mr Hyde* (1906)
Davis, Owen, *Lazybones* (1925)
Deane, Hamilton, *Dracula* (1924)
Dix, Beulah Marie, *Across the Border* (1914)
Moloch (1915)
Dix, Beulah Marie and Evelyn Greenleaf Sutherland, *The Road to Yesterday* (1906)
Dixon, Thomas, *The Birth of a Nation* (1905)
Dumanoir, Philippe François Pinel and Adolphe Philippe Dennery, *Don Cézar de Bazan* (1844)
Dumas, Alexandre, *Le Comte de Monte-Cristo* (*The Count of Monte Cristo*) (stage play version) (1850)
Dunning, Philip and George Abbott, *Broadway* (1926)
Eunson, Dale and Katherine Albert, *Loco* (1946)
Fallon, Thomas, *The Last Warning* (1926)
Fechter, Charles, *The Count of Monte Cristo* (1868)
Ferber, Edna and George S. Kaufman, *Bravo* (1949)
Dinner at Eight (1932)
The Land is Bright (1941)
The Royal Family (1927)
Stage Door (1936)
Fitch, Clyde, *The Cowboy and the Lady* (1899)
Fletcher, Lucille, *Sorry, Wrong Number* (1948)
Franken, Rose, *Claudia* (1941)
Fulda, Ludwig, *Der Seeräauber* (1911)
The Pirate (trans. 1917)
Garrett, H.P., *Waltz in Goose Step* (1938)
Gates, Eleanor, *The Poor Little Rich Girl* (1913)
We Are Seven (1913)
Gilda, Jeannette L, *Quo Vadis* (1900)
Goetz, Ruth and Augustus, *The Heiress* (1947)
Gordon, Ruth, *Years Ago* (1946)
Haines, William Wister, *Command Decision* (1947)
Harris, Jed, Philip Dunning and George Abbott, *Broadway* (1927)
Hart, Frances Noyes, *The Last Warning* (1929)
Hart, Moss, *Winged Victory* (1943)
Hastings, Charlotte, *Bonaventura* (1951)
Hecht, Ben and Charles MacArthur, *The Front Page* (1928)
Twentieth Century (1932)
Hellman, Lillian, *The Little Foxes* (1939)
Watch on the Rhine (1941)
Hitchens, Robert and Cosmo Gordon Lennox, *Vanity Fair* (1911)

Hobart, George V., *The Yankee Girl* (1910)
Hoff, Marsh Harwood, *Street Angel* (1928)
Hopwood, Avery, *The Gold Diggers* (1919)
Hopwood, Avery and Mary Roberts Rinehart, *The Bat* (1930)
Ibsen, Henrik, *A Doll's House* (*Et dukkehjem*) (1879)
Jerome, Helen, *Pride and Prejudice* (1935)
Joudry, Patricia, *The Restless Years* (1955)
Kaufman, George S., and Marc Connelly, *Beggar on Horseback* (1924)
Dulcy (1921)
Kaufman, George S. and Moss Hart, *The American Way* (1939)
The Man Who Came to Dinner (1939)
Once in a Lifetime (1930)
You Can't Take It With You (1936)
Kenwood, Allan, *Cry Havoc* (1943)
Kingsley, Sidney, *Dead End* (1935)
Knott, Frederick, *Dial M for Murder* (1952)
Mr Fox in Venice (1959)
Wait Until Dark (1966)
Write Me a Murder (1961)
Kramer, Theadore, *The Fatal Wedding* (1901)
Laurents, Arthur, *Home of the Brave* (1947)
László, Nikolaus, *Illatszertár* (also known as *Parfumerie*) (1936)
Lengyel, Menhért, *Angyel* (1932)
Levi, Maurice and Edgar Smith, *The Squawman's Girl of the Golden West* (1906)
Lindsay, Howard, *She Loves Me Not* (1933)
Luce, Clare Booth, *Kiss the Boys Goodbye* (1939)
The Women (1936)
Mailhac, Henri and Ludovic Halévy, *Réveillon* (1872)
Mannes, Marya, *Café* (1930)
Marble, Scott, *The Great Train Robbery* (1896)
Marcin, Max and Edward Hammond, *Badges* (1924)
Marlow, Brian, *Bad Girl* (1931)
Maugham, W. Somerset, *The Circle* (1925)
McCloskey, James J., *Davy Crockett* (1872)
McCullers, Carson, *The Member of the Wedding* (1950)
McNally, John J., *The Widow Jones* (1895)
Meilhac, Henri, *L'attaché d'ambassade* (*The Embassy Attaché*) (1861)
Meyer-Förster, Wilhelm, *Alt Heidelberg* (*Old Heidelberg*) (1901)
Molnár, Ferenc, *Olympia* (1928)
Liliom (1930)
McCloskey, James J., *Across the Continent* (1870)
Moreau, Eugène, Paul Siraudin and Alfred Delacour, *Courrier de Lyons, Le* (1850)
Müller, Hans (pseud. Hans Lothar), *Die blaue Küste* (*The Blue Coast*) (1914)
Murdock, Frank, *Davy Crockett* (1872)
Murray, Alfred, *Till We Meet Again* (1944)
Neumann, Alfred, *Der Patriot* (1927)

Nichols, Anne, *Abie's Irish Rose* (1922)
Nicholson, Kenyon, *The Barker* (1917)
Nicholson, Kenyon and Charles Robinson, *Sailor, Beware* (1933)
O'Neil, Eugene, *Anna Christie* (1921)
Paulding, James Kirke, *The Lion of the West* (1831)
Pellico, Silvio, *Francesca da Rimini* (1818)
Pertwee, Roland and Harold Dearden, *Interference* (1927)
Pollock, Channing, *The Pit* (1904)
Raphaelson, Samson, *The Jazz Singer* (1925)
Reade, Charles, *The Courier of Lyons* (1854)
Drink (1897)
Reizenstein, Elmer (Elmer Rice), *The Iron Cross* (1917)
Rice, Edward E., *The Prisoner of Zenda* (1895)
Rice, Elmer, *Street Scene* (1929)
Flight to the West (1940)
Rostand, Maurice, *L'Homme que j'ai tue* (c.1925)
Royle, Edwin Milton, *The Squaw Man* (1905)
Sardou, Victorian and Émile de Najac, *Divorçons* (*Let's Get a Divorce*) (1880)
Sardou, Victorien and Émile Moreau, *Dante* (1903)
Madame Sans-Gêne (1893)
Saroyan, William, *The Time of Your Life* (1939)
Scarborough, George, *The Lure* (1913)
Schmidt [Goldschmidt], Lothar, *Nur ein Traum* (*Only a Dream*) (1909)
Sheriff, R.C., *Journey's End* (GB 1928; US 1929)
Sherwood, Robert E., *Abe Lincoln in Illinois* (1937)
There Shall Be No Light (1940)
Waterloo Bridge (1930)
Siraudin, Paul and Louis-Mathurin Moreau, *Le Courier de Lyon* (*The Courier of Lyon*) (1850)
Solomon, Louis and Harold Solomon, *SNAFU* (1944)
Sommer, Edith, *A Roomful of Roses* (1955)
Stallings, Laurence, *What Price Glory?* (1926)
Stange, Hugh S. and John Golden, *After Tomorrow* (1932)
Stange, Stanislaus, *Quo Vadis* (1900)
Steinbeck, John, *Of Mice and Men* (1937) (stage play version)
Stevenson, Janet and Phillip Stevenson, *Counter-Attack* (1943)
Stoddard, Lorimer, *Tess of the D'Urbervilles* (1897)
Strong, Austin, *Seventh Heaven* (1922)
Sullivan, Thomas Russell, *Dr Jeckyll and Mr Hyde* (1887)
Szekely, Hans and R.A. Stemmle, *Desire* (1936)
Tearle, Edmund, *From Cross to Crown* (1897)
Tennyson, F. Jesse and Harold Marsh, *The Pelican* (1926)
Thomas, Augustus, *Arizona* (1899)
In Mizzoura (1893)
Uncle Tom's Cabin, adapted for the stage by George Aiken in 1852 and by numerous others throughout the latter half of the nineteenth and the first half of the twentieth century.
Van Druten, John, *Bell, Book and Candle* (1950)

Flowers of the Forest (1934)
I Am a Camera (1951)
I Remember Mama (1944)
London Wall (1931)
There's Always Juliet (1931)
Veiller, Bayard, *The Trial of Mary Duggan* (1928)
Walter, Eugene, *The Easiest Way* (1909)
West, Mae, *Diamond Lil* (1928)
White, Jessie Graham, *Snow White and the Seven Dwarfs* (1912)
Wilde, Oscar, *Lady Windermere's Fan* (1892)
Wilder, Thornton, *Our Town* (1938)
Winter, Keith, *The Shining Hour* (1934)
Wister, Owen and Kirke La Shelle, *The Virginian* (1904)
Woods, Walter, *Billy The Kid* (1906)
Wray, John Griffith, J.C. Nugent and Elaine S. Carrington, *Nightstick* (1927)
Xanrof, Léon (pseud. Léon Fourneu) and Jules Chancel, *Le Prince Consort* (c.1919)
Young, Rida Johnson, *Glorious Betsy* (1908)

Extravaganzas, Operas, Operettas, Musicals and Musical Comedies

Berlin, Irving, *This Is the Army* (1943)
Berlin, Irving and George S. Kaufman, *The Cocoanuts* (1925)
Berlin, Irving and Moss Hart, *As Thousands Cheer* (1933)
Face the Music (1932)
Bolton, Guy and Fred Thompson, *Tip-Toes* (1925)
Rio Rita (1927)
Davis, Owen, Lorenz Hart and Richard Rogers, *Spring is Here* (1929)
Donnelly, Dorothy and Sigmund Romberg, *The Student Prince* (1924)
Frank, Yasha, *Pinocchio* (1938)
Gershwin, George and Ira, and Guy Bolton and P.G. Wodehouse, *Oh, Kay!* (1926)
Gershwin, George and Sigmund Romberg, Guy Bolton and William Anthony McGuire, and P. G Wodehouse and Ira Gershwin, *Rosalie* (1928)
Gershwin, George and Ira, and George S. Kaufman and Morrie Ryskind, *Of Thee I Sing* (1931)
Giordano, Umberto, *Madame Sans-Gêne* (1915)
Jacobson, Leopold and Felix Doerman (pseud. Felix Biedermann), *Ein Walzertraum (A Waltz Dream)* (1907)
Kaufman, George S and Morrie Ryskind, and Bert Kalmar and Harry Ruby, *Animal Crackers* (1928)
Puccini, Giacomo and Guelfo Civinini and Carlo Zangarini, *La fanciulla del West* (*The Girl of the Golden West*) (1910)
Romberg, Sigmund, Oscar Hammerstein II, Otto Harbach and Frank Mandel, *The Desert Song* (1926)
Schanzer, Rudolph and Ernst Welisch, *Die Frau im Hermelin* (*That Lady in Ermine*) (1919)
Stein, Leo, Victor Léon, and Franz Lehár, *Die Lustige Witwe* (*The Merry Widow*) (1905)
Tarkington, Booth and Evelyn Greenfleaf Sutherland, *Monsieur Beaucaire* (1901)

Radio Play

Fletcher, Lucille, *Sorry, Wrong Number* (1943)

Unproduced Plays and Musicals

Anderson, Maxwell and Rouben Mamoulian, *The Devil's Hornpipe*

Burnett, Murray and Joan Alison, *Everybody Comes to Rick's*

Clarke, Alan R and Bradbury Foote, *The High Wall*

Leary, Helen and Nolan Leary, *Make Way for Tomorrow*

Rice, Elmer, *Landscapes with Figures*

The Sidewalks of New York

Royle, Edwin Milton, one-act version of *The Squaw Man*

Székely, Hans and Robert Adolph Stemmle, *Die schönen Tage von Aranjuez*

Books

Abel, Richard, *The Red Rooster Scare: Making Cinema American, 1900-1919* (Berkeley and Los Angeles: University of California Press, 1999).

Americanizing the Movies and 'Movie-Mad' Audiences, 1910-1914 (Berkeley and Los Angeles: University of California Press, 2006).

Abel, Richard (ed.), *Encyclopedia of Early Cinema* (New York and Oxford: Routledge, 2005).

Abel, Richard and Rick Altman (eds.), *The Sounds of Early Cinema* (Bloomington: Indiana University Press, 2001).

Adamson, Joe, *Groucho, Harpo, Chico and sometimes Zeppo* (London: W.H. Allen & Co. Ltd., 1973).

Afron, Charles, *Cinema and Sentiment* (Chicago: University of Chicago Press, 1982).

Allan, Robin, *Walt Disney and Europe: European Influences on the Animated Feature Films of Walt Disney* (London: John Libbey & Company Ltd., 1999).

Allen, Robert C., *Vaudeville and Film: A Study in Media Interaction* (New York: Arno Press, 1983).

Alonso, Harriet Hyman, *Robert E. Sherwood: The Playwright in Peace and War* (Amherst and Boston: University Press of Massachusetts Press, 2007).

Altman, Rick, *Silent Film Sound* (New York: Columbia University Press, 2001).

Anderson, Gillian B., *Music for Silent Films, 1894-1929: A Guide* (Washington, D.C.: Library of Congress, 1988).

Arnold, Edwin T. and Eugene Miller, *The Films and Career of Robert Aldrich* (Knoxville: University of Tennessee Press, 1986).

Bacher, Lutz, *Max Ophuls in the Hollywood Studios* (New Brunswick, N.J.: Rutgers University Press, 1996).

Balio, Tino, *United Artists: The Company Built by the Stars* (Madison: University of Wisconsin Press, 1976).

Balio (ed.), *The American Film Industry* (Madison: University of Wisconsin Press, 1985).

Balio, *United Artists: The Company That Changed the Film Industry* (Madison: University of Wisconsin Press, 1987).

Balio (ed.), *Hollywood in the Age of Television* (Boston: Unwin Hyman, 1990).

Balio, *Grand Design: Hollywood as a Modern Business Enterprise, 1930-1939* (New York: Scribner's, 1993).

Bandy, Mary Lea (ed.), *The Dawn of Sound* (New York: Museum of Modern Art, 1989).

Barlow, Judith E. (ed.), *Plays by American Women, 1900-1930* (New York and London: Applause Theatre Book Publishers, 1981).

Barrios, Richard, *A Song in the Dark: The Birth of the Musical Film* (New York and Oxford: Oxford University Press, 1985).

Baskin, Ellen and Mandy Hicken, *Enser's Filmed Books and Plays, 1928-1991* (Aldershot, Brookfield USA, Singapore, Sydney: Ashgate, 1993 edn.).

Basinger, Jeanine, *A Woman's View: How Hollywood Spoke to Women, 1930 to 1960* (London: Chatto and Windus, 1993).

The World War II Combat Film: Anatomy of a Genre (Middletown, CT: Wesleyan University Press, 2003 ed.).

Beauchamp, Cari, *Without Lying Down: Frances Marion and the Powerful Women of Early Hollywood* (New York: Scribner, 1997).

Belton, John, *The Hollywood Professionals, Volume 3: Howard Hawks, Frank Borzage, Edgar G. Ulmer* (London: The Tantivy Press and New York: A.S. Barnes & Co. 1974).

Widescreen Cinema (Cambridge, M.A.: Harvard University Press, 1992).

Berg, A. Scott, *Goldwyn: A Biography* (London: Pan Books, 1999 ed.).

Berg, Charles Merrell, *An Investigation of the Motives and Realization of Music to Accompany the American Silent Film, 1896-1927* (New York and Oxford: Oxford University Press, 2010).

Berry, Sarah, *Screen Style: Fashion and Femininity in the 1930s* (Minneapolis and London: University of Minneapolis, 1997).

Birchard, Robert S., *Cecil B. DeMille's Hollywood* (Lexington: University Press of Kentucky, 2004).

Blake, Michael, *Code of Honor: The Making of Three Great American Westerns* (Lanham, New York, Oxford: Taylor Trade Publishing, 2003).

Block, Geoffrey, *Richard Rodgers* (New Haven and London: Yale University Press, 2003).

Bluestone, George, *Novels into Films* (Baltimore and London: The Johns Hopkins University Press, 1957).

Bordman , Gerald, *American Musical Theatre: A Chronicle* (Oxford and New York: Oxford University Press, Expanded Edition, 1986).

American Theatre: A Chronicle of Comedy and Drama, 1869-1914 (Oxford and New York: Oxford University Press, 1994).

American Theatre: A Chronicle of Comedy and Drama, 1913-1930 (Oxford and New York: Oxford University Press, 1995).

American Theatre: A Chronicle of Comedy and Drama, 1930-1969 (New York and Oxford: Oxford University Press, 1996).

Bordwell, David, *Poetics of Cinema* (New York: Routledge, 2008).

Bordwell, David, Janet Staiger and Kristin Thompson, *The Classical Hollywood Cinema: Film Style & Mode of Production to 1960* (London, Melbourne and Henley: Routledge & Kegan Paul, 1985).

Bowers, David, *Nickelodeon Theatres and Their Music* (New York: Vestal Press, 1986).

Bowser, Eileen, *The Transformation of Cinema, 1907-1915* (New York: Scribner's, 1990).

Blum, Daniel, *Theatre World, Season 1954-1955* (New York: Greenberg, 1955).

Brewster, Ben and Lea Jacobs, *Theatre to Cinema: Stage Pictorialism and the Early Feature Film* (Oxford and New York: Oxford University Press, 1997).

Brown, Royal S., *Overtones and Undertones: Reading Film Music* (Berkeley, Los Angeles, London: University of California Press, 1994).

Buhler, James, David Nuemeyer, Rob Deemer, *Hearing the Movies: Music and Sound in Film History* (New York and Oxford: Oxford University Press, 2010).

Burt, George, *The Art of Film Music* (Boston: Northeastern University Press, 1994).

Cabarga, Leslie, *The Fleischer Story* (New York: Da Capo Press, 1988 ed.).

Cameron, Evan William (ed.), *Sound and the Cinema: The Coming of Sound to American Films* (New York: Redgrave Publishing Company, 1980).

Carringer, Robert L. (ed.), *The Jazz Singer* (Madison: University of Wisconsin Press, 1979).

Cherchi Usai, Paulo and Lorenzo Codelli (eds.), *Sulla via di Hollywood, 1911-1929* (Pordenone: Le Giornato del Cinema Muto, 1988).

Coniam, Matthew, *The Annotated Marx Brothers: A Filmgoer's Guide to In-Jokes, Obscure References and Sly Details* (Jefferson, N.C.: McFarland & Company, 2015).

Cooke, Mervyn, *A History of Film Music* (Cambridge: Cambridge University Press, 2008).

Cooke (ed.), *The Hollywood Film Music Reader* (Oxford: Oxford University Press, 2010).

Cooper, Mark Garrett, *Universal Women: Filmmaking and Institutional Change in Early Hollywood* (Urbana: University of Illinois Press, 2010).

Cosssar, Harper, *Letterboxed: The Evolution of Widescreen Cinema* (Lexington, Kentucky: University Press of Kentucky, 2011).

Crafton, Donald, *The Talkies: American Cinema's Transition to Sound, 1926-1931* (New York: Scribner's, 1997).

Cripps, Thomas, *Making Movies Black: The Hollywood Message Movie from World War II to the Civil Rights Era* (New York and Oxford: Oxford University Press, 1993).

Curtis, James, *James Whale: A New World of Gods and Monsters* (Boston and London: Faber and Faber, 1998).

Darby, William and Jack Du Bois, *American Film Music: Major Composers, Techniques, Trends, 1915-1990* (Jefferson, N.C. and London: McFarland & Company, Inc., Publishers, 1990).

DeMille, Cecil, *The Autobiography of Cecil B. DeMille* (Englewood Cliffs, New Jersey: Prentice-Hall, 1959).

De Mille, William C., *Hollywood Saga* (New York: E.P. Dutton, 1939).

Doherty, Thomas, *Projections of War: Hollywood, American Culture, and World War II* (New York: Columbia University Press, 1993).

Dowd, Nancy and David Shepard, *King Vidor* (Metuchen, N.J. and London: Director's Guild of America and the Scarecrow Press, 1988).

Duckett, Victoria, *Seeing Sarah Bernhardt: Performance and Silent Film* (Urbana, Chicago, and Springfield: University of Illinois Press, 2015).

Dumont, Hervé, *Frank Borzage*. Trans. Jonathan Kaplinsky (Jefferson, N.C. and London: McFarland & Company, Inc, 2006).

Enticknap, Leo, *Moving Image Technology: From Zoetrope to Digital* (London: Wallflower Press, 2005).

Eyman, Scott, *Mary Pickford* (London: Robson Books, 1992).

Ernst Lubitsch: Laughter in Paradise, A Biography (New York: Simon & Schuster, 1993).

The Speed of Sound: Hollywood and the Talkie Revolution, 1926-1930 (Baltimore and London: Johns Hopkins University Press, 1999).

Empire of Dreams: The Epic Life of Cecil B. DeMille (New York: Simon & Shuster, 2010).

Irving Thalberg: Boy Wonder to Producer Prince (Berkeley: University of California Press, 2010).

Faversham, Julie Opp, *The Squaw Man* (New York: Grosset & Dunlap, 1906).

Fell, John L.(ed.) *Film Before Griffith* (Berkeley, Los Angeles and London: University of California Press, 1983).

Finler, Joel, *Stroheim* (London: Studio Vista, 1967).

Fordin, Hugh, *The Movies' Greatest Musicals Produced by Hollywood USA by the Freed Unit* (New York: Frederick Ungar Publishing Co., 1975).

Frankel, Glenn, *The Searchers: The Making of an American Legend* (New York: Bloomsbury USA, 2013).

Frohman, Daniel, *David Frohman Presents: An Autobiography* (New York: Claude Kendall and Willoughby Sharp, Inc., 1935).

Furia, Philip, *Irving Berlin: A Life in Song* (New York: Schirmer Books, 1988).

The Poets of Tin Pan Alley: A History of America's Lyricists (Oxford and New York: Oxford University Press, 1990).

Furia, Philip, and Laurie Patterson, *The Songs of Hollywood* (Oxford and New York: Oxford University Press, 2010).

Gabler, Neal, *Walt Disney: The Triumph of the American Imagination* (New York: Vintage Books, 2006).

Gallafent, Edward, *Astaire and Rogers* (New York: Columbia University Press, 2000).

Geraghty, Christine, *Now a Major Motion Picture: Film Adaptation of Literature and Drama* (Lanham: Rowman & Littlefield Publishers, Inc., 2008).

Gilbert, Julie, *Ferber: Edna Ferber and Her Circle* (New York and London: Applause Books, 1999 ed.).

Glancy, Mark, *When Hollywood Loved Britain: The Hollywood 'British Film', 1939-45* (Manchester: Manchester University Press, 1999).

Golden, John and Viola Brothers Shore, *Stage-Struck John Golden* (New York: Samuel French, 1930).

Goldstein, Malcolm, *George S. Kaufman: His Life, His Theater* (London and New York: Oxford University Press, 1979).

Gomery, Douglas, *The Coming of Sound: A History* (New York: Routledge, 2005 ed.).

Gross, Robert F., *S.N. Behrman: A Research and Production Sourcebook* (Greenwich, C.T.: Greenwood Press, 1992).

Grun, Bernard, *Gold and Silver: The Life and Times of Franz Lehar* (New York: David McKay Company, Inc., 1970).

Haines, Richard W., *Technicolor Movies: The History of Dye Transfer Printing* (Jefferson, N.C. and London: MacFarland Company, Inc., 1993).

Hall, Roger A., *Performing the American Frontier, 1870-1906* (Cambridge: Cambridge University Press, 2003).

Hall, Sheldon and Steve Neale, *Epics, Spectacles, and Blockbusters: A Hollywood History* (Detroit: Wayne State University Press, 2010).

Halls, W.D., *Maurice Maeterlinck: A Study of His Life and Thought* (Oxford: Clarendon Press, 1960).

Hampton, Benjamin B., *History of the American Film Industry from its Beginnings to 1931* (Toronto and London: Dover Edition, 1970).

Harmetz, Aljean, *The Making of Casablanca: Bergman, Bogart, and World War II* (New York: Hyperion, 2002, ed.).

Harvey, Stephen, *Directed by Vincente Minnelli* (New York: Harper & Row, 1989).

Hatch, Kristen, *Shirley Temple and the Performance of Girlhood* (New Brunswick N.J. and London: Rutgers University Press, 2015).

Henry, Nora, *Ethics and Social Criticism in the Hollywood Films of Erich von Stroheim, Ernst Lubitsch, and Billy Wilder* (Westport, C.T.: Praeger Publications, 2001).

Hess, Earl J. and Pratibha A. Dabholkar, *The Cinematic Voyage of* The Pirate*: Kelly, Garland, and Minnelli at Work* (Columbia, Missouri: University of Missouri Press, 2014).

Higham, Charles, *Hollywood Cameramen* (Thames and Hudson: London, 1970).

Higgins, Scott, *Matinee Melodrama: Playing with Formula in the Sound Serial* (New Brunswick N.J. and London: Rutgers University Press, 2016).

Hilmes, Michele, *Hollywood and Broadcasting: From Radio to Cable* (Urbana and Chicago: University of Illinois Press, 1990).

Hines, Richard W., *Technicolor Movies: The History of Dye Transfer Printing* (Jefferson N.C.: McFarland, 1993).

Hischak, Thomas S., *American Plays and Musicals on Screen: 650 Stage Productions and Their Film and Television Adaptations* (Jefferson, N.C.: McFarland and Company, 2005).

Holston, Kim, *Movie Roadshows: A History and Filmography of Reserved-Seat Limited Showings* (Jefferson, N.C. and London: McFarland & Company, 2013).

Hubbert, Julie (ed.), *Celluloid Symphonies: Texts and Contexts in Film Music History* (Berkeley, Los Angeles, London: University of California Press, 2011).

Irwin, Will, *The House That Shadows Built* (Garden City, New York: Doubleday, Doran & Company, Inc., 1928).

Jacobs, Lea, *The Wages of Sin: Censorship and the Fallen Woman Film, 1928-1942* (Madison: University of Wisconsin Press, 1991).

Film Rhythm after Sound: Technology, Music and Performance (Oakland, Cal.: University of California Press, 2015).

Jewell, Richard B., *RKO Radio Pictures: A Titan is Born* (Berkeley, Los Angeles, London: University of California Press, 2012).

Johnson, Katie N., *Sisters in Sin: Brothel Drama in America, 1900-1920* (Cambridge: Cambridge University Press, 2006).

Jones, Eugene H., *Native Americans as Shown on Stage, 1753-1916* (Lanham, M.D.: Scarecrow Press, 1990).

Kalinak, Kathryn, *Settling the Score: Music and the Classical Hollywood Film* (Madison: University of Wisconsin Press, 1992).

How the West Was Sung: Music in the Westerns of John Ford (Berkeley, Los Angeles, London: University of California Press, 2007).

Kalinak (ed.), *Sound: Dialogue, Music, and Effects* (New Brunswick, N.J.: Rutgers University Press, 2015).

Kasson, John F., *The Little Girl Who Fought The Great Depression: Shirley Temple and 1930s Hollywood* (New York and London: W.W. Norton & Company, 2014).

Keating, Patrick, *Hollywood Lighting from the Silent Era to Film Noir* (New York: Columbia University Press, 2010).

Keil, Charlie, *Early American Cinema in Transition: Story, Style and Filmmaking, 1907-1913* (Madison, Wisconsin: University of Wisconsin Press, 2001).

Keil, Charlie and Shelley Stamp (eds.), *American Cinema's Transitional Era: Audiences, Institutions, Practices* (Berkeley, Los Angeles, London: University of California Press, 2004).

Kendall, Elizabeth *The Runaway Bride: Hollywood Romantic Comedy in the 1930s* (New York and London: Anchor Books, 1990).

Kincaid, James R., *Erotic Innocence: The Culture of Child Molesting* (Durham, N.C.: Duke University Press, 1998).

King, Rob, *The Film Factory: The Keystone Film Company and the Emergence of Mass Culture* (Berkley, Los Angeles, London: University of California Press, 2008).

Klinger, Barbara, *Melodrama and Meaning: History, Culture, and the Films of Douglas Sirk* (Bloomington: Indiana Press, 1994).

Knapp, Bettina, *Maurice Maeterlinck* (Boston: Twayne Publishers, 1975).

Konrad, Linn Bratteteig, *Modern Drama as a Crisis: The Case of Maurice Maeterlinck and the Making of Modern Theatre* (New York: Peter Lang Publishing., Inc. 1986).

Koppes, Clayton R. and Gregory D. Black, *Hollywood Goes to War: How Politics, Profits, and Propaganda Shaped World War II Movies* (London: The Free Press, 1987).

Koszarski, Richard, *An Evening's Entertainment: The Age of the Silent Feature Picture, 1915-1928* (New York: Scribner's, 1990).

Fort Lee: The Film Town (Rome: John Libbey-CIC Publishing, 2004).

Von: The Life and Times of Erich Von Stroheim (New York: Limelight Editions, 2001 edn.).

Lahue, Kalton, *Dreams for Sale: The Rise and Fall of the Triangle Film Corporation* (Cranbury, N.J.: Barnes, 1971).

Lamster, Frederick, *Souls Made Great Through Love and Adversity: The Film Work of Frank Borzage* (Metuchen, N.J.: Scarecrow Press, 1981).

Lastra, James, *Sound Technology and the American Cinema: Perception, Representation, Modernity* (New York: Columbia University Press, 2000).

Leff, Leonard J., *Hitchcock and Selznick: The Rich and Strange Collaboration of Alfred Hitchcock and David O. Selznick in Hollywood* (Berkeley, Los Angeles, London: University of California Press, 1999 ed.).

Leitch,Thomas L, *Find the Director and Other Hitchcock Games* (Athena, G.A.: University of Georgia Press, 1991).

Leiter, Samuel L, *The Encyclopedia of the New York Stage, 1920-1930* (Westport, Conn.: Greenwood Press, 1985), vol. 2, N-Z.

LeRoy, Mervyn, *Mervyn LeRoy: Take One* (London and New York: W.H. Allen, 1974).

Lev, Peter, *The Fifties: Transforming the Screen, 1950-1959* (New York: Scribner's, 2003).

Levy, Emanuel, *George Cukor, Master of Elegance: Hollywood's Legendary Director and His Stars* (New York: William Morrow and Company, Inc., 1994).

Louvish, Simon, *Cecil B. DeMille and the Golden Calf* (London: Faber and Faber, 2007).

Monkey Business: The Lives and Legends of the Marx Brothers (London: Faber and Faber, 1999).

Macqueen-Pope, W. and D.L. Murray, *Fortune's Favourite: The Life and Times of Franz Lehár* (London: Hutchinson, 1953).

Madsen, Axel, *William Wyler: The Authorized Biography* (New York: Thomas Y. Crowell, 1973).

Magee, Jeffrey, *Irving Berlin's American Musical Theater* (Oxford and New York: Oxford University Press, 2012).

Mahar, Karen Ward, *Women Filmmakers in Early Hollywood* (Baltimore: The Johns Hopkins Press, 2006).

Mann, Denise, *Hollywood Independents: The Postwar Talent Takeover* (Minneapolis and London: University of Minnesota Press, 2008).

Mantle, Burns and Garrison P. Sherwood (eds.), *The Best Plays of 1899-1909 and the Year Book of Drama in America* (New York: Dodd, Mead and Company, 1944 edn.).

Marks, Martin M., *Music and the Silent Film: Contexts and Case Studies, 1895-1924* (New York: Oxford University Press, 1997).

Mayer, David, *Stagestruck Filmmaker: D.W. Griffith and the American Theatre* (Iowa City: Iowa University Press, 2009).

Mayer (ed.), *Playing Out the Empire: Ben-Hur and Other Toga Plays and Films, 1883-1908. A Critical Anthology* (Oxford: Clarendon Press, 1994).

Mayer, Stephen, *Epic Sound: Music in the Postwar Hollywood Biblical Films* (Bloomington and Indianapolis: Indiana University Press, 2015).

McBride, Joseph, *Searching for John Ford: A Life* (New York: St. Martin's Press, 2001).

McCarthy, Todd, *Howard Hawks: The Grey Fox of Hollywood* (New York: Grove Press, 1997).

McElhaney, Joe (ed.), *Vincente Minnelli: The Art of Entertainment* (Detriot: Wayne State University Press, 2009).

McGuiness, Patrick, *Maurice Maeterlinck and the Making of Modern Theatre* (Oxford and New York: Oxford University Press, 2000).

McLaughlin, Robert, *Broadway and Hollywood* (New York: Arno Press, 1974).

Melnick, Ross, *American Showman: Samuel 'Roxy' Rothafel and the Birth of the Entertainment Industry* (New York: Columbia University Press, 2012).

Meyer, William R., *The Making of the Great Westerns* (New Rochelle, N.J.: Arlington House Publishers, 1979).

Miller, Gabriel, *William Wyler: The Life and Films of Hollywood's Most Celebrated Director* (Lexington, Kentucky: University of Kentucky Press, 2011).

Milne, Peter, *Motion Picture Directing* (New York: Falk, 1922).

Minnelli, Vincente (with Hector Arce), *I Remember it Well* (New York, Garden City: Doubleday and Company, 1974, and London: Angus and Robertson, 1975).

Mitchell, Glenn, *The Marx Brothers Encyclopedia* (London: B.T. Batsford, 1996).

Modleski, Tania, *The Women Who Knew Too Much: Hitchcock and Feminist Theory* (London and New York: Routledge, 1988 and 2015 eds.).

Mordden, Ethan, *Rodgers & Hammerstein* (New York: Harry N.Abrams, Inc., 1992).

Moss, Marilyn Ann, *Giant: George Stevens, a Life in Film* (Madison: University of Wisconsin Press, 2004).

Raoul Walsh: The True Adventures of Hollywood's Legendary Director (Lexington, Kentucky: University Press of Kentucky, 2011).

Murphy, Brenda (ed.), *The Cambridge Companion to American Women Playwrights* (Cambridge and New York: Cambridge University Press, 1999).

Musser, Charles, *The Emergence of Cinema: The American Screen to 1907* (New York: Scribner's, 1990).

Before the Nickelodeon: Edwin S. Porter and the Edison Manufacturing Company (Berkeley, Los Angeles, Oxford: University of California Press, 1991).

Naremore, James, *The Films of Vincente Minnelli* (Cambridge, New York, and Victoria: Cambridge University Press, 1993).

Neale, Steve (ed.), *The Classical Hollywood Reader* (London and New York: Routledge, 2012).

Oja, Carol J., *Bernstein Meets Broadway: Collaborative Art in a Time of War* (Oxford and New York: Oxford University Press, 2014).

Palmer, Frederick, *Photoplay Plot Encyclopedia: An Analysis of the Use in Photoplays of the Thirty-Six Dramatic Situations and Their Subdivisions* (Los Angeles: Palmer Photoplay Corp., 1922 edn.).

Palmieri, Anthony F.R., *Elmer Rice: A Playwright's Vision of America* (Rutherford, Madison, Teaneck: Fairleigh Dickinson University Press, and London and Toronto: Associated University Presses, 1980).

Paul, William, *Ernst Lubitsch's American Comedy* (New York: University of Columbia Press, 1983).

Pickford, Mary, *Sunshine and Shadow* (London, Melbourne, Toronto: William Heinemann Ltd., 1956).

Pollack, Rhoda-Gale, *George S. Kaufman* (Boston: Tawyne Publishers, 1988).

Polti, George, *The Thirty-Six Dramatic Situations* (Ridgewood, N.J.: The Editor Company, 1917 ed.).

Prendergast, Roy M., *Film Music: A Neglected Art* (New York and London: W.W. Norton, 1992).

Price, Steven, *A History of the Screenplay* (London: Palgrave Macmillan, 2013).

Rathgeb, Donald L., *The Making of Rebel Without a Cause* (Jefferson, N.C.: McFarland & Company, 2004).

Reed, Kenneth T., *S.N. Berhman* (Boston: Twayne Publishers, 1975).

Rice, Elmer, *Minority Report: An Autobiography* (London, Melbourne, Toronto: William Heinemann, 1963).

Ross, Miriam, *3D Cinema: Optical Illusions and Tactile Experiences* (Houndmills: Palgrave Macmillan, 2015).

Ryskind, Morrie with John H.M. Roberts, *I Shot an Elephant in My Pajamas: The Morrie Ryskind Story* (Lafayette: Huntington House Publishers, 1994).

Salt, Barry, *Film Style & Technology: History & Analysis* (London: Starword Press, 2009).

Sanjek, Russell, updated by David Sanjek, *Pennies from Heaven: The American Popular Music in the Twentieth Century* (New York: Da Capo, 1996 ed.).

Schatz, Thomas, *Boom and Bust: American Cinema in the 1940s* (New York: Scribner's, 1997).

Shafer, Yvonne, *American Women Playwrights* (New York: Peter Lang Publishing, Inc., 1995).

Sikov, Ed, *On Sunset Boulevard: The Life and Times of Billy Wilder* (New York: Hyperion Press, 1998).

Silver, Alain and James Ursini, *Whatever Happened to Robert Aldrich? His Life and Films* (New York: Limelight Editions, 1995).

Simmon, Scott, *The Invention of the Western Film: A Cultural History of the Genre's First Half-Century* (Cambridge and New York: Cambridge University Press, 2003).

Slide, Anthony, *Silent Topics: Essays on Undocumented Areas of Silent Film* (Lanham M.D.: Scarecrow Press, 2005).

Slowik, Michael, *After the Silents: Hollywood Film Music in the Early Sound Era, 1926-1934* (New York: Columbia University Press, 2014).

Smith, Andrew Brodie, *Shooting Cowboys and Indians: Silent Western Films, American Culture, and the Birth of Hollywood* (Boulder: University Press of Colorado, 2003).

Smith, Judith E., *Visions of Belonging: Family Stories, Popular Culture, and Postwar Democracy, 1940-1960* (New York: Columbia University Press, 2004).

Smith, Murray, *Engaging Characters: Fiction, Emotion, and Cinema* (Oxford: Oxford University Press, 1995).

Solomon, Aubrey, *Twentieth Century-Fox: A Corporate and Financial History* (Lanham, M.D. and London: The Scarecrow Press, 2002).

Spoto, Donald, *The Dark Side of Genius: The Life of Alfred Hitchcock* (New York: Da Capo Press, 1999 ed.).

Staggs, Sam, *When Blanche Met Brando: The Scandalous Story of A Streetcar Named Desire* (New York: St. Martin's Press, 2006).

Born to be Hurt: The Untold Story of Imitation of Life (New York: St. Martin's Press, 2009).

Stubblebine, Donald J., *Cinema Sheet Music: A Comprehensive Listing of Published Film Music from The Squaw Man (1914) to Batman (1989)* (Jefferson, N.C.: McFarland & Company, 1991).

Styan, J.L., *Modern Drama in Theory and Practice: Symbolism, Surrealism, and the Absurd* (Cambridge: Cambridge University Press, 1981).

Sullivan, Jack, *Hitchcock's Music* (New Haven and London: Yale University Press, 2006).

Swindell, Larry, *Body and Soul: The Life of John Garfield* (New York: Morrow, 1975).

Taves, Brian, *Thomas Ince: Hollywood's Independent Pioneer* (Lexington: University Press of Kentucky, 2012).

Robert Florey, The French Expressionist (Duncan, O.K.: BearManor Media, 2014).

Tibbetts, John C., *The American Theatrical Film: Stages in Development* (Bowling Green, Ohio: Bowling Green University Popular Press, 1985).

Tibbetts, John C. and James M. Walsh, *The Encyclopedia of Stage Plays into Film* (New York: Facts on File, Inc., 2001).

Turk, Edward Baron, *Hollywood Diva: A Biography of Jeanette MacDonald* (Berkeley: University of California Press, 1998).

Uricchio, William and Roberta E. Pearson, *Reframing Culture: The Case of the Vitagraph Quality Films* (Princeton, N.J.: Princeton University Press, 1993).

Vasey, Ruth, *The World According to Hollywood, 1918-1939* (Exeter: Exeter University Press, 1997).

Vidor, King, *A Tree Is A Tree* (London, New York, Toronto: Longmans, Green and Co., 1954).

On Film Making (London and New York: W.H. Allen, 1973).

Waldman, Harry, *Maurice Tourneur: The Life and Films* (Jefferson, N.C. and London: MacFarland & Company, Inc., 2001).

Walkerdine, Valerie, *Daddy's Girl: Young Girls and Popular Culture* (Cambridge, M.A.: Harvard University Press, 1997).

Waller, Gregory A. (ed.), *Moviegoing in America: A Sourcebook of Film Exhibition* (Oxford: Blackwell Publishers, 2002).

Wattenberg, Richard, *Early Twentieth-Century Frontier Dramas on Broadway: Situating the Western Experience in Performing Arts* (New York: Palgrave Macmillan, 2011).

Weales, Gerald, *Canned Goods as Caviar: American Film Comedy of the 1930s* (Chicago: Chicago University Press, 1985).

Weirzbecki, James, *A History of Film Music* (New York and London: Routledge, 2009).

Weis, Elisabeth, *The Silent Scream: Alfred Hitchcock's Sound Track* (Rutherford, Madison and Teaneck: Fairleigh Dickinson Press, 1982).

Wertheim, Albert, *Staging the War: American Drama and World War II* (Bloomington & Indianapolis: Indiana University Press, 2004).

White, Jerry, *Zeppelin Nights: London in the First World War* (London: The Bodley Head, 2014).

Whitfield, Eileen, *Pickford: The Woman Who Made Hollywood* (Lexington: University Press of Kentucky, 2007).

Williams, Tony, *Body and Soul: The Cinematic Vision of Robert Aldrich* (Lanham, M.D., Toronto, Oxford: The Scarecrow Press, 2004).

Wilson, Garff, *Three Hundred Years of American Drama and Theatre: From Ye Bare and Ye Cubb to Chorus Line* (Englewood Cliffs, N.J.: Prentice-Hall, Inc., 1982 ed.).

Winokur, Mark, *American Laughter: Immigration, Ethnicity, and 1930s Hollywood Film Comedy* (Houndmills: Macmillan Press, 1996).

Woll, Allen, *Black Musical Theatre: From Coontown to Dream Girls* (Baton Rouge: Louisiana State University Press, 1989).

Zukor, Adolph, *The Public is Never Wrong: The Autobiography of Adolph Zukor* (New York: G.P. Putnam's Sons, 1953).

Articles and Chapters

Abel, Richard, 'The "Imagined Community" of the Western', in Keil and Stamp (eds.), *American Cinema's Transitional Era,* pp. 131-170.

Altman, Rick, 'Deep Focus Sound: *Citizen Kane* and the Radio Aesthetic', *Quarterly Review of Film & Video*, vol. 15 no. 3 (1994), pp. 1-33.

Anderson, Christopher, 'Television and Hollywood in the 1940s', in Schatz, *Boom and Bust,* pp. 422-444.

Anderson, Robert, 'The Role of the Western Film Genre in Industry Competition, 1907-1911', *Journal of the University Film Association*, vol. 31 no. 2, 1979, pp. 19-26.

Azlant, Edward, 'Screenwriting for Early Silent Film: Forgotten Pioneers, 1897-1911', *Film History*, vol. 9 no. 3 (1997), pp. 228-256.

Bank, Rosemary Katherine, 'Staging the "Native": Making History in American Theatre Culture, 1828-1838', *Theatre Journal*, vol. 45 no. 4 (1993), pp. 461-486.

Barlow, Judith E., 'Introduction' to *Plays by American Women*, pp. ix-xxxiii.

Block, Geoffrey, 'The melody (and the words) linger on: American musical comedies of the 1920s and 1930s', in William A. Everett and Paul R. Laird (eds.), *The Cambridge Companion to the Musical* (Cambridge: Cambridge University Press, 2008 ed.), pp. 103-123.

Bordwell, David, 'Classical narration', in Bordwell, Staiger and Thompson, *The Classical Hollywood Cinema*, pp. 24-41.

'Deep-focus photography in the 1940s and 1950s', in Bordwell, Staiger and Thompson, *The Classical Hollywood Cinema*, pp. 341-352.

'The introduction of sound', in Bordwell, Staiger and Thompson, *The Classical Hollywood Cinema*, pp. 298-308.

'Shot and scene', in Bordwell, Staiger and Thompson, *The Classical Hollywood Cinema*, pp.60-67.

'Technicolor', in Bordwell, Staiger and Thompson, *The Classical Hollywood Cinema*, pp. 353-357.

'Time in the classical film', in Bordwell, Staiger and Thompson, *The Classical Hollywood Cinema*, pp. 42-49.

Brewster, Ben, '*Alias Jimmy Valentine* and Situational Dramaturgy', *Film History*, vol. 9 no. 4 (1997), pp. 388-409.

'The Circle: Lubitsch and the Theatrical Farce Tradition', *Film History*, vol. 13 no. 4 (2001), pp. 372-389.

'multiple-reel /feature films: USA', in Abel (ed.), *Encyclopedia of Early Cinema*, pp. 605-608.

'Periodization of Early Cinema', in Keil and Stamp (eds.), *American Cinema's Transitional Era*, pp. 66-75.

'staging in depth', in Abel (ed.), *Encyclopedia of Early Cinema*, pp. 605-608.

Cagle, Chris, 'Classical Hollywood 1928-1946', in Patrick Keating (ed.), *Cinematography* (New Brunswick, N.J.: Rutgers University Press, 2014), pp. 34-59.

Cassady Jr., Ralph, 'Monopoly in Motion Picture Production and Distribution: 1908-1915', *Southern California Law Review*, vol. 32 no. 4, 1959, pp, 325-390.

Cludary, Josh, 'Dear Friend: *The Shop Around the Corner* and *In the Good Old Summer Time*', *Movie* 5 (2014), pp. 1-15.

Combs, Richard, 'Robert Aldrich (1953 to 1961)', in Combs (ed.), *Robert Aldrich* (London: BFI, 1978), pp. 3-21.

Crafton, Donald, 'The View from Termite Terrace: Caricature and Parody in Warner Bros. Animation', *Film History*, vol. 5 no. 2. (1993), pp. 204-230.

Dickey, Jerry, 'The expressionist moment: Sophie Treadwell', in Murphy (ed.), *The Cambridge Companion to American Women Playwrights*, pp. 66-81.

Dyer, Richard, 'Colour of Entertainment', in Bill Marshall and Robyn Stilwell, *Musicals: Hollywood and Beyond* (Exeter: Intellect Books, 2000), pp. 23-30.

Film History, vol. 16 no. 3 (2004), 3-D edition.

Fischer, Lucy, '1929: Movies, Crashes and Finales', in Lucy Fischer and Angela Dalle Vacche (eds.), *American Cinema of the 1920s: Themes and Variations* (New Brunswick, N.J.: Rutgers University Press, 2009), pp.234-256.

Forrest, Jennifer, 'Sadie Thompson Redux: Postwar Reintegration of the Wartime

Wayward Woman', in Jennifer Forrest and Leonard K. Koos, *Dead Ringers: The Remake in Theory and Practice* (New York: State University of New York Press, 2002).

Frick, John, 'A Changing Theatre: New York and Beyond', in Don B. Wilmeth and Christopher Bigsby (eds.), *The Cambridge History of American Theatre, Volume Two: 1890-1945* (Cambridge and New York: Cambridge University Press, 1999), pp. 222-223.

Genné, Beth, 'Vincente Minnelli and the Dance Ballet', in McElhaney (ed.), *Vincente Minnelli*, pp. 229-251.

Gerould Daniel, 'The Art of Symbolist Drama, A Re-Assessment', in Gerould (ed.), *Symbolist Drama* (New York: Performing Art Journal Publications, 1985), pp. 7-33.

Gevinson, Alan, 'The Birth of the Feature', in Cherchi Usai and Codelli (eds.), *Sulla via di Hollywood, 1911-1929*, pp.132-155.

Greene, Janet, 'The Road to Reno: *The Awful Truth* and the Comedy of Marriage', *Film History*, vol. 13 no. 4 (2001), pp. 337-358.

Hall, Sheldon, *'Dial M for Murder'*, *Film History*, vol. 16 no. 3 (2004), pp. 243-255.

Hanson, Helen, 'Sound Affects: Post-production Sound, Soundscapes and Sound Design in Hollywood's Studio Era', *Music, Sound, and the Moving Image*, vol. 1 no. 1 (2007), pp. 27-49.

Hanson, Helen and Steve Neale, 'Commanding the Sounds of the Universe: Classical Hollywood Sound in the 1930s and Early 1940s', in Neale (ed.), *The Classical Hollywood Reader*, pp. 249-261.

Higgins, Scott, 'Suspenseful Situations: Melodramatic Narrative and the Contemporary Action Film', *Cinema Journal*, vol. 47 no. 2 (2008), pp. 74-96.

Higgins, Steven, 'American Éclair, 1911-1915', *Griffithiana*, nos. 44/45, 1992, pp. 89-129.

Horak, Jan-Christopher, 'Maurice Tourneur and the Rise of the Studio System', in *Sulla via di Hollywood, 1911-1920*, pp. 296-317.

Hovet, Ted Jr., 'The Case of Kalem's *Ben-Hur* (1907) and the Transformation of Cinema', *Quarterly Review of Film and Video*, vol. 18 no. 3 (2001), pp. 283-294.

Jacobs, Lea, 'The Paramount Case: The Role of the Distributor', *Journal of the University Film and Video Association*, vol. 35 no. 1 (1983), pp. 44-49.

'Keeping Up with Hawks', *Style*, vol. 32 no. 3 (1998), pp. 403-426.

'The Seduction Plot: Comic and Dramatic Variants', *Film History*, vol. 13 no. 4 (2001), pp. 424-442.

'Innovation of Re-Recording in the Hollywood Studios', *Film History*, vol. 24 no. 3 (2012), pp. 5-34.

Jacobs, Steven, 'Color and Containment: Domestic Spaces and Restrained Palettes in Hitchcock's First Color Films', in Simon Brown, Sarah Street, and Liz Watkins (eds.), *Color and the Moving Image: History, Theory, Aesthetics, Archive* (New York and London: Routledge, 2013), pp. 179-188.

Jewell, Richard, 'Hollywood and Radio: Competition and Partnership in the 1930s', *Historical Journal of Film, Radio and Television*, vol. 4 no. 2 (1984), pp. 125-141.

Kalinak, Kathryn, 'Classical Hollywood, 1928-58', in Kalinak (ed.), *Sound: Dialogue, Music and Effects*, pp. 37-45.

Kaufman, George S., 'The Cocoanuts', in Kaufman, *By George: A Kaufman Collection* (London: Angus and Robertson, 1980 ed.), pp. 202-258.

King, Rob, '"Made for the Masses with an Appeal to the Classes": The Triangle Film Corporation and the Failure of Highbrow Film Culture', *Cinema Journal*, vol. 44 no. 2 (2005), pp. 3-33.

Kirkham, Pat, 'Loving Men: Frank Borzage, Charles Farrell and the Reconstruction of

Masculinity in 1920s Hollywood Cinema', in Kirkham and Janet Thumim (eds.), *Me Jane: Masculinity, Movies and Women* (London: Lawrence & Wishart, 1995), pp. 94-112.

Krasner, Orly Leah, 'Birth pangs, growing pains and sibling rivalry: musical theatre in New York, 1900-1920', in Everett and Laird (eds.), *The Cambridge Companion to the Musical*, pp. 54-71.

Krutnick, Frank, '"Barbed Wire and Forget-Me-Not': The Radio Adventures of *Laura*', *Journal of Adaptation in Film & Performance*, vol. 5 no. 3 (2012), pp. 297-314.

'"Be moviedome's guest in your own easy chair!" Hollywood, Radio and the Movie Adaptation Series', *Historical Journal of Film, Radio and Television*, vol. 33 no. 1 (2013), pp. 25-54.

Lehman, Peter, Marilyn Campbell, and Grant Munro, 'Two Weeks in Another Town – An Interview with Vincente Minnelli', *Wide Angle*, vol. 3 no. 1, 1979.pp. 64-71.

Makowsky, Veronica, 'Susan Glaspell and modernism', in *The Cambridge Companion to American Women Playwrights*, pp. 49-65.

Maltby, Richard, 'The Production Code and the Hays Office', in Balio, *Grand Design*, pp. 37-72.

'"To Prevent the Prevalent Type of Book": Censorship and Adaptation in Hollywood, 1924-1934', *American Quarterly*, vol. 44 no. 4 (1992), pp. 554-583.

'The Production Code and the Mythologies of "Pre-Code" Hollywood', in Neale (ed.), *The Classical Hollywood Reader*, pp. 23-249.

Maras, Steven, 'In Search of "Screenplay": Terminological Traces in the Library of Congress Catalog of Copyright Entries, Cumulative Series, 1912-20', *Film History*, vol. 21 no. 4 (2009), pp. 346-358.

Mayer, David, 'A Select Filmography of Toga Films', in Mayer (ed.), *Playing Out the Empire*, pp. 315-321.

'Theatrical Sources', in the entry on *The Birth of a Nation* (1915), in Paulo Cherchi Usai (ed.), *The Griffith Project*, vol. 8, *Films Produced in 1914-15* (London: BFI Publishing, 2004), pp. 81—87.

Merritt, Russell, 'Nickelodeon Theaters, 1905-1914: Building an Audience for the Movies', in Tino Balio (ed.), *The American Film Industry* (Madison: University of Wisconsin Press, 1985 ed.). pp. 83-102.

Murphy, Brenda, 'Feminism in the marketplace: the career of Rachel Crothers', in Brenda Murphy (ed.), *The Cambridge Companion to American Women Playwrights*, pp. 82-97.

Musser, Charles, 'Divorce, DeMille and the Comedy of Remarriage', in Kristina Brunovska Karnick and Henry Jenkins (eds.), *Classical Hollywood Comedy* (New York: Routledge, 1995), pp. 283-313.

Loughney, Patrick, 'Selected Examples of Early Scenario/Screenplays in the Library of Congress', *Film History*, vol. 9 no. 3 (1997), pp. 290-299.

Neale, Steve, 'Revisiting *Waterloo Bridge*: Censorship, Representation, Adaptation and the Persisting Myth of "Pre-Code" Hollywood', *Film Studies*, no. 12 (Spring 2015), pp. 71-81.

Osterwell, Ara, 'Reconstructing Shirley: Pedopophilia and Interracial Romance in Hollywood's Age of Innocence', *Camera Obscura*, no. 73, 2009), pp. 1-39.

Paul, William, 'The Aesthetics of Emergence', *Film History*, vol. 5 no. 3 (1993), pp. 321-355.

Pearson, Roberta E., 'biblical films', in Abel (ed.), *Encyclopedia of Early Cinema*, pp. 68-71.

'The Menace of the Movies: Cinema's Challenge to the Theater in the Transitional Period', in Keil and Stamp (eds.), *American Cinema's Transitional Era*, pp. 315-331.

Platte, Nathan, 'Postwar Hollywood, 1947-1967', in Kalinak (ed.), *Sound*, pp. 59-82.

Quinn, Michael, 'Distribution, the Transient Audience and the Transition to the Feature Film', *Cinema Journal*, vol. 40 no. 2 (2001), pp. 25-56.

'Paramount and Early Feature Distribution, 1914-1921', *Film History*, vol. 11 no. 1 (1999), pp. 98-133.

'USA: Distribution', in Abel (ed.), pp. 659-661.

Rosen, Philip, 'Difference and Displacement in *Seventh Heaven*', *Screen*, vol. 18 no. 2 (1977), pp. 89-104.

Sargent, Eapes Winthrop, Jeanie MacPherson and Lloyd Lonergan, 'A Screenwriting Sampler from the *Moving Picture World*', *Film History*, vol. 9 no. 5 (1997), pp. 269-276.

Schlotterbeck, Jesse, 'Killing noir?: The Adaptation of Robert Siodmak's *The Killers* to Radio', *Journal of Adaptation in Film and Performance*, vol. 3 no. 1 (2010), pp. 59-70.

Schroeder, Patricia R., 'Realism and feminism in the Progressive Era', in Murphy (ed.), *The Cambridge Companion to American Women Playwrights*, pp. 31-46.

Schwartz, Nancy, 'Lubitsch's Widow: The Meaning of the Waltz', *Film Comment*, March-April, 1975, pp. 13-17.

Shafer, Yvonne, 'Whose Realism? Rachel Crothers's Power Struggle in the American Theatre', in William W. Demestes (ed.), *Realism in the American Dramatic Tradition* (Tuscaloosa and London: University of Alabama Press, 1996), pp. 37-52.

Solomon, Jon, 'The Kalem *Ben-Hur* (1907', in Michelakis and Wyke (eds.), *The Ancient World in Silent Cinema* (Cambridge and New York: Cambridge University Press, 2013), pp. 189-204.

Solomon, Matthew, 'Adapting "Radio's Perfect Script" : "Sorry, Wrong Number" and *Sorry, Wrong Number*', *Quarterly Review of Film & Video*, vol. 16 no. 1 (1995), pp. 23-40.

Spring, Katherine, 'Pop Go the Warner Bros., et.al.: Marketing Film Songs during the Coming of Sound', *Cinema Journal*, vol. 48 no. 1 (2008), pp. 68-89.

Staiger, Janet, 'Mass-Produced Photoplays: Economic and Signifying Practices in the First Years of Hollywood', *Wide Angle*, vol. 4 no. 3 (1980), pp.14-23.

'Individualism versus Collectivism: The Shift to Independent Production', *Screen*, vol. 24 no. 4-5 (1983), pp. 68-79.

'Blueprints for Feature Films: Hollywood's Continuity Scripts', in Balio (ed.), *The American Film Industry*, pp. 173-192.

'The "cameraman" system of production (1896-1907)', in Bordwell, Staiger and Thompson, *The Classical Hollywood Cinema*, pp. 116-117.

'The "central producer" system: centralized management after 1914', in Bordwell, Staiger and Thompson, *The Classical Hollywood Cinema*, pp. 128-141.

'The director system: management in the first years', in Bordwell, Staiger and Thompson, *The Classical Hollywood Cinema*, pp. 113-127.

'The formulation of the classical narrative', in Bordwell, Staiger and Thompson, *The Classical Hollywood Cinema*, pp. 174-193.

'The package-unit system: unit management after 1955', in Bordwell, Staiger and Thompson, *The Classical Hollywood Cinema*, pp. 330-337.

'The producer-unit system: management by specialization after 1931', in Bordwell, Staiger and Thompson, *The Classical Hollywood Cinema*, pp. 320-329.

Steinbrunner, Chris and Otto Penzler (Editors-in-Chief), 'Knott, Frederick M.P.', in *Encyclopedia of Mystery and Detection* (New York, St. Louis, San Francisco: McGraw-Hill Book Company, 1978), pp. 235-236.

Stichele, Caroline Vander , 'Silent Saviours: representation of Jesus' Passion in early cinema', in Michelakis and Wyke (eds.), *The Ancient World in Silent Cinema*, (Cambridge and New York, Cambridge University Press, 2013), pp. 169-188.

Thompson, Kristin, 'The formulation of the classical narrative', in Bordwell, Staiger and Thompson, *The Classical Hollywood Cinema*, pp. 174-193.

'The Limits of Experimentation of Hollywood', in Jan-Christopher Horak (ed.), *Lovers of*

Cinema: The First American Avant-Garde (Madison, Wisconsin: University of Wisconsin Press, 1995), pp. 67-93.

Toles, George, 'Eloquent Objects, Mesmerizing Commodities in William Wyler's *The Heiress*', *Film International*, vol. 4 no. 5 (2006), pp. 48-67.

'Acting Ordinary in *The Shop Around the Corner*', *Movie* 1 (2010), pp. 1-15.

Turconi, David, 'From Stage to Screen: Notes for a five-year history of Famous Players Film Company, Jesse L. Lasky Feature Film Company, and Triangle Film Corporation between 1912-1917', in Cherchi Usai and Codelli (eds.), *Sulla via di Hollywood, 1911-1920*, pp. 16-131.

Verma, Neil, 'Hollywood Shocker: Lucille Fletcher's "Psychological" Sound Effects and Wartime Radio Drama', *Journal of American Studies*, vol. 44 no. 1 (2010), pp. 137-153.

Vermilion, Billy Budd, 'The Remarriage Plot in the 1910s', *Film History*, vo. 13 no. 4 (2001), pp. 359—371.

Walkerdine, Valerie, 'Reconstructing Shirley: Pedophilia and Interracial Romance in Hollywood's Age of Innocence', *Camera Obscura*, no. 73 (2009), pp. 1-39.

Wasko, Janet, 'Hollywood and Television in the 1950s: The Roots of Diversification', in Peter Lev, *The Fifties*, pp. 127-132.

Wertheimer, John, 'Mutual Film Reviewed: The Movies, Censorship, and Free Speech in Progressive America', *The American Journal of Legal History*, vol. 37 no. 2 (1993), pp. 158-189.

Whitmore, Mariana, 'Reinventing the Western Score: Jerome Moross and *The Big Country*', in Kalinak (ed.), *Music in the Western: Notes on the Frontier* (New York and London: Routledge, 2012), pp. 51-76.

Whitney, Simon N., 'Antitrust Policies and the Motion Picture Industry', in Gorham Kindem (ed.), *The American Movie Industry* (Carbondale and Edwardsville: Southern Illinois University Press, 1982), pp. 161-204.

Wierzbicki, James, 'The Silent Screen', in Kathryn Kalinak, *Sound: Dialogue, Music, and Effects* (New Brunswick, New Jersey: Rutgers University Press, 2015), pp. 15-36.

Wolf, Charles, 'Vitaphone Shorts and *The Jazz Singer*', *Wide Angle*, vol. 12 no. 3 (1990), pp. 58-78.

Online Entries, Journals and Newspaper Reports

Gänzl, Karl, '*Die Lustige Wittwe, Operetta in 3 Acts*', http://operetta-research-center.org/die-lustige-witwe-operetta-3-acts/30/12/2014

Kenrick, John, '*The Merry Widow* 101: History of a Hit', *Musicals 101 com: The Cyber Encyclopedia of Musical Theatre, Film & Television*: http://www.musicals101.com/widowwhist.html/30/12/2014

http://en.wikipedia.org/wiki/The_Merry_Widow/01/01/2015

http://en.wikipedia.org/wiki/John_Golden/15/10/2015

McElhaney, Joe, 'Frank Borzage', *Senses of Cinema*, no. 25 (2003) (online).

The New York Times report on the premiere of *The Blue Bird* (1918) can be found at http://www.nytimes.com/movie/review?res=9807E1DA1E3FE433A25752C0A9629C94 96D6CF/29/07/2016

http://en.wikipedia.org/wiki/Joseph_Santley 24/11/2015

http://en.wikipedia.org/wiki/Street_Scene (opera) 31/2/2015

http://en.wikipedia.org/wiki/Street_Scene (play) 23/11/2016

http://georgeskaufman.com/play_catalog/15-play-catalog/library-of-america-collection 12/04/2016

http://de.wikipedia.org/wiki/Ludwig_Fulda 30/10/2015

http://snberhman.com/library/nytimes/43.2.7.htm 01/04/2015

http://en.wikipedia.org/wiki/S_N_Behrman 01/11/2015

http://en.wikipedia.org/wiki/Roger_Edens 03/11/2015

http://imdb.com/name/nm0249136/03/11/2015

http://en.wikipedia.org/wiki/Cole_Porter 01/11/2015

Camper, Fred, 'Depth Perception: Films by Vincente Minnelli' at http://chicago/depth-perception/Content?oid=914205 01/11/2015

McElhaney, Joe, 'Vincente Minnelli', Senses of Cinema, no. 31 (2004) (online)

http://www.independent.co.uk/news/obituaries/frederick-137362.html 29/09/2016

http://www.nytimes.com/2002/12/20/arts/frederick-knott-playwright-dies-at-86.html 28/09/2016

Silver, Alain, 'Robert Aldrich', *Senses of Cinema*, no. 20 (2002) (online)

Blog

Whelehan, Imelda, What Is Adaptation Studies? https://blogs.utas/edu/au/adapt/2012/04/18/what-is-adaptation-studies/10/02/2016

Other Sources

The AFI Catalog of Feature Films

Chicago Daily Tribune

The Film Daily

Daily Variety

Life

Motion Picture Classic

Motion Picture News

Moving Picture World

New York Times

Variety

Unpublished Phd. Dissertations

Anderson, Robert, 'The Motion Picture Patents Company', Phd. Dissertation, University of Wisconsin-Madison, 1983.

Bank, Rosemary Katherine, 'Rhetorical, Dramatic, Theatrical, and Social Contexts of Selected American Frontier Plays, 1891 to 1906', Phd. Dissertation, University of Iowa,1972.

Cole, Carol L., 'The Search for Power: Drama by American Women, 1909-1929', Phd. Dissertation, University of Purdue, 1991.

Hyde, Stuart Wallace, 'The Representation of the West in American Drama from 1849 to 1917', Phd. Dissertation, Stanford, 1954.

Liepa, Torey, 'Figures of Silent Speech: Silent Film Dialogue in the American Vernacular', Phd. Dissertation, New York University, 2008.

Quinn, Michael, 'Early Feature Distribution and the Development of the Motion Picture Industry: Famous Players and Paramount: 1912-1921', PhD. Dissertation, University of Madison-Wisconsin, 1998.

Index

I

J

K

L